A Century of Revolution

Social Movements, Protest, and Contention

Series Editor: Bert Klandermans, Free University, Amsterdam
Associate Editors: Sidney G. Tarrow, Cornell University
                            Verta A. Taylor, Ohio State University
                            Mark Traugott, University of California, Santa Cruz

A Century of Revolution

Social Movements in Iran

John Foran, editor

Social Movements, Protest, and Contention
Volume 2

University of Minnesota Press

Minneapolis

Published by the University of Minnesota Press
111 Third Avenue South, Suite 290, Minneapolis, MN 55401-2520
Printed in the United States of America on acid-free paper

Library of Congress Cataloging-in-Publication Data

A Century of revolution : social movements in Iran / John Foran,
    editor.
        p.   cm. — (Social movements, protest, and contention : v. 2)
    Includes bibliographical references and index.
    ISBN 0–8166–2487–9 (HC : acid-free paper). — ISBN 0–8166–2488–7
(PB : acid-free paper)
    1. Social movements—Iran—History—20th century. 2. Social
change—Iran—History—20th century. 3. Iran—Politics and
government—20th century. 4. Revolutions—Iran—History—20th
century. I. Foran, John. II. Series.
HN670.2.A8C45 1994
306'.0955—dc 20
                                                                94–14028

Contents

Acknowledgments

This is a collective product, and I would first of all like to thank my collaborators on it—Mansoor Moaddel, Janet Afary, Michael Zirinsky, Amir Hassanpour, Sussan Siavoshi, Misagh Parsa, and Val Moghadam. I have learned much from each of you, and I appreciate your enthusiasm, encouragement, and *patience* in bringing this project to the public!

Second, thanks are owed to several people at the University of Minnesota Press—Janaki Bakhle, who first took the volume seriously as a book; her assistant, Robert Mosimann; and Lisa Freeman, for seeing the project through. I am indebted to Ruth Frankenberg for suggesting that I approach the Press, and to Kum-Kum Bhavnani, my best friend, for bringing the volume to Ruth's attention. Bert Klandermans and Sidney Tarrow, editors of the Press's series Social Movements, Protest, and Contention, gave helpful advice and encouragement, and insisted on my writing the concluding chapter, for all of which I am (in the end) quite grateful. Finally, three anonymous readers gave feedback on the whole manuscript from which we have benefited in many ways, large and small. Other scholars read one or more chapters in draft form: Farideh Farhi, Homa Katouzian, Mark Gasiorowski, Nikki Keddie, Ervand Abrahamian, and Reza Afshari—all helped us clarify our arguments at an early point in the process (and, to be sure, none of them is responsible for advice stubbornly resisted in some cases!).

Two journals gave permission for the use of some material from essays originally published by them in earlier forms: my thanks to Plenum Publishers and *Sociological Forum* for permission to publish a revised version of Mansoor Moaddel's "Shi'i Political Discourse and Class Mobilization in the Tobacco Movement of 1890–92," which appeared in *Sociological Forum,* volume 7, number 3 (September 1992), pages 447–68; and to Cambridge University Press, which allowed Michael Zirinsky to use parts of his article, "Imperial Power and Dictatorship: Britain and the Rise of Reza Shah, 1921–1926," from *International Journal of Middle East Studies,* volume 24, number 4 (November 1992), pages 639–64.

Thanks also to Princeton University Press for permission to use a map of Iran from Ervand Abrahamian's *Iran between Two Revolutions* (1982).

This volume is affectionately dedicated to two great friends and companions, Kum-Kum Bhavnani and the late Little Man.

John Foran
Santa Barbara, California

A Note on Names and Dates

Discounting the discredited imperial calendar, there are three systems of dates in use in Iran: Western style, Islamic lunar style, and the Iranian calendar. This last runs from March 21 to March 20, and the year 1 is equal to 621 A.D. Thus, some dates, especially in the bibliography, are given in the form "1372/1993," for example. The reader will occasionally encounter a date such as 1978/79 to indicate the year from March 21, 1978, to March 20, 1979. We have not used Islamic lunar years, but some months, such as Ramazan and Muharram, may be reported, with the Western equivalent attached, as there is no regular correspondence between the two sets of months from one year to the next.

Transliteration of Middle Eastern names and words is always difficult. For Persian words we have basically followed the system used by the *International Journal for Middle East Studies,* without the diacritical marks. This means that the only vowels used (with very few exceptions) are *a, i,* and *u.* As a result, the well-known name Khomeini is here rendered Khumaini. The exception is Amir Hassanpour's chapter, which also uses the Hawar system of transcription for the Kurdish language. This should pose little problem for the Middle East specialists among our readers; for all others, it is an occasion to learn something about the current scholarly convention.

Iran and its neighbors. From Ervand Abrahamian, *Iran between Two Revolutions*.
Reprinted with permission.

Introduction:
On the Study of Social Movements in Iran

John Foran

The dramatic events of 1978 and 1979 in Iran and their stormy aftermath sent shock waves rippling through the United States and the international policy-making and scholarly communities that continue to this day, in addition to touching, directly or indirectly, the lives of millions of people worldwide. Before late 1978 Iran did not occupy a large place in the public mind, mass media, or academic division of labor. The country was, to be sure, an object of considerable interest to multinational oil companies, arms manufacturers, and those in high U.S. policy circles, but extensive economic and geostrategic relations were kept largely from public view, helped by the near-unanimous opinion that Iran was a highly stable ally with nothing in its foreseeable future that would be cause for alarm. There was also a small but dedicated cohort of Iran scholars in the United States, England, France, Germany, and elsewhere producing work, notably in history, of high quality and considerable interest, but for an audience limited to those aware of the complexity and significance of Iran's domestic politics and its place in the larger world-system.

All of this would change in a few extraordinary months filled with street demonstrations, religious protests, bloody massacres, a determined general strike, and finally the flight of the most powerful monarch in the world. Just as U.S. foreign policy would never be quite the same in the region or the world, so the scholarly and journalistic communities began to devote enormously greater resources and attention to the "discovery" of social change in Iran. My own story is part of this process—as a beginning graduate student in the fall of 1978 with a growing interest in critical social theory, I found first an empirical referent in issues of Third World social change generally, and then, by the summer of 1980, the continuing drama of revolution in Iran, coupled with the chance to know a community of progressive Iranians in the United States, prompted me to change my master's thesis project from the depressing rise and fall of the Allende regime in Chile to a study of what I took to be a more hopeful revolution in the making. In a sense I was already too late, but as I realized that the roots of the revolution went far back into Iran's history, I embarked on what has become a continuing preoccupation with the long and rich story of social movements in Iran.

As I continued to become a student of Middle Eastern and Latin American social change, and the historical sociology of revolutions, I also began to realize that few countries in world history can claim such a revolutionary heritage over so long a period as Iran. France from the seventeenth to nineteenth centuries, China from 1850 to 1949 (or should it be 1989?), Mexico from 1750 to 1940, Bolivia with more than 2,000 local rebellions between 1861 and 1952 come to mind as instances of multiple sustained rebellions with occasional national-level consequences. In the past one hundred years, Iran stands out even in this company with no less than five major potentially revolutionary movements (in 1905–11, 1918–21, 1945–46, 1951–53, and 1977–79) in addition to the nationwide agitations of 1891, the coup and overthrow of the Qajar dynasty between 1921 and 1925, and the turmoil and religious uprising of 1960–63. These events, which form the subject of this volume, call for in-depth historical investigation and systematic theoretical and comparative reflection.

The social scientific and historical fields of social movements are no less conflictual than the stormy history of Iran. Paradigms abound, proliferating and passing in the night with dizzying and alarming regularity. In sociology, the generational clash between functionalist puzzlement in the face of persistent change and neo-Marxian celebration of its pervasiveness are now both challenged by the abrupt end of the Cold War (if not of history itself) and the post-Gulf War agenda for a new world order. Postmodernist, feminist, and ethnic studies approaches call all fixed positions into question and demand more attention to the interplay of race, class, and gender. The controversy stirred by Edward Said's identification and critique of Orientalism as a mechanical and hegemonic application of Western categories to non-Western societies can be similarly leveled at alternative, critical, and radical approaches to some degree.

For anyone still interested in understanding societies other than their own there is no way around these problems. They exist, they filter into our work, they must be balanced against the imperative to tell the best story one can. Many of the contributors to this volume confront these dilemmas existentially as Iran-born academics teaching and working in the United States. Writing as a historian with a sociological imagination or as a social scientist with a deep concern for history, each has been charged with accounting for a critical moment in Iranian social history, both on its own terms and in some larger theoretical or comparative context. Some are working with new materials to uncover neglected dimensions of what have been thought to be well-known events. Others are trying new theoretical optics, not just for a fresh angle on the events, but to use the rich complexity of Iranian social movements to refine the theories and concepts themselves. All seek to blend history and theory in one way or another.

No theoretical uniformity can be placed on the essays that follow. Cultural analysis, feminism, resource mobilization theory, diplomatic history, ethnic and nationalist perspectives, Weberian political sociology, neo- and post-Marxism—all find critical proponents and echoes here. As editor, I do see some common threads emerging from this diversity of approaches, and some lessons of Iranian social history for wider theoretical debates. One recurring theme must be the heterogeneous social bases of movements for change in Iran. Populist alliances and cross-class coalitions permeate the events chronicled in these pages. This seems to be the product of the complexities inherent in Iranian social structure, with its urban and rural, settled and tribal dimensions, its ethnic and religious cleavages, its gender constraints and opportunities. At various moments, grievances with diverse origins have been articulated in discourses of opposition that reflect this complexity—nationalisms, Islam (in various guises), and socialist and radical strands of protest have fueled these movements in varying combinations.

This raises the knotty question of the *causes* of social movements in Iran. Here, too, these chapters collectively suggest findings with wide theoretical import. Efforts to posit single causes, to privilege economics, politics, or culture over all others, have been rejected by our authors, who take as their brief the specification of the interplay among these dimensions of change. Surely this is a way forward with broad implications for social theory. Moreover, both internal and external logics of change have been uncovered, typically interacting in ways that are separable only analytically (and hence artificially). We argue neither that "the West caused everything" nor that Third World societies are completely responsible for the plight in which so many find themselves today. From the first stirrings of protest against an English monopoly of Persian tobacco in 1890 to the latest revelations about secret dealings between Iran and the United States, foreigners have played some role in all national-level instances of social change in Iran, as has another key actor that has lately attracted much attention in the social sciences—the state. Iran has been governed by two dynasties and an Islamic republic in the century covered here, affording rich material to give substance to such conceptual abstractions as the "potential autonomy of the state." The history of social movements in Iran, then, can be read as a series of courageous popular struggles involving remarkable coalitions of lower- and middle-class elements, different ethnic groups, women and men, arrayed against powerful vested interests, foreign and domestic. That this long history must be told in the genre of tragedy underscores the stakes involved and the consequences of defeat for the Iranian people. That this history is so long and persistent, and that each defeat has brought some gains, is the only hope offered by this study. "The history of all the dead generations" need not weigh *only* "like a nightmare on the brains of the living," in Marx's famous aphorism. It may point the way to further struggles with better prospects for change.

In the first chapter of this volume, Mansoor Moaddel reinterprets the role played by the ulama in the tobacco rebellion of 1891–92 through the prism of debates in the sociology of social change and social movements. Engaging a central theoretical controversy over the nature of discourse and ideology and how these shape class conflict, he locates the sources of the movement in the very real material grievances of Iran's tobacco merchants, noting that their complaints were voiced in a religious discourse with incipient strands of nationalism and secular radicalism emerging alongside the rituals and language of Shi'a Islamic culture in Iran. The ulama were not uniformly mobilized as a cohesive class across the principal urban sites of protest, whereas the affected merchants were. Just as individual ulama had varying material and ideological interests motivating their support of or resistance to the monarchy and the British, so the merchants used religious symbolism and their organizational assets to address definite economic concerns. Islam *facilitated* rather than caused the movement, and the economic and cultural dimensions of the struggle were inextricably and complexly linked to one another.

In chapter 2, Janet Afary draws attention to previously underanalyzed aspects of the constitutional movement of 1905 to 1911, in particular to the roles played by peasants and ethnic communities, and to socialist ideals in the struggle. Combined with her other pioneering work on the roles played by peasants and women, this strongly suggests that this movement, known in Persian as the *Mashrutiyat,* had the potential to be a truly *social* revolution, that it was in some sense decisively class (and gender) based, and that only by making genuinely radical demands for more than could actually be obtained did it make some of the striking gains it actually registered. The intensity and ultimate exhaustion of these sharp internal struggles provided a crucial opening for the outside intervention of 1911 that sealed its defeat. Afary's contribution provides an important counterpoint to Moaddel's reflections on the relationships between class and ideology in social movements, by making crucial connections among the largely neglected activities of the most radical secular groups in the period, their political cultural frameworks, and the outcome of the movement. This work, and her forthcoming book on the subject, promises to bring the socialist current in the Constitutional Revolution into the clear light of day, where it will be found closer to the political center of gravity than has hitherto been recognized.

In his contribution to this volume, Michael Zirinsky assesses two of the key unresolved historical issues in the fateful rise to power of Reza Khan in the early 1920s. First, meticulous archival research into the available British documents allows him to trace definitively the contours of the actual extent of support that British officers and diplomats provided in the events of late 1920 and early 1921 that facilitated Reza's February coup. The conclusion he reaches here is that although this aid was not the result of a unified London-based strategy, the actions of British officials on the spot probably determined the success of the coup. Second, Zirinsky explores the context of Reza's subsequent accession to the throne in the period from 1921 to 1926, with due emphasis placed on Reza's ability to defeat serious domestic challenges from the northern Jangali rebels and other local movements, to garner further Western support as the strongman needed to safeguard Western interests in the country, and to maneuver astutely in the maze of political parties and key social groups constituting the Iranian polity. Zirinsky's two contributions judiciously resolve some rancorous polemics that have dominated the literature on the rise of Reza Khan and the establishment of the Pahlavi dynasty.

Amir Hassanpour tackles in chapter 4 the knotty and controversial subject of the postwar nationalist social movements in Kurdistan and Azarbaijan, offering a thorough, trenchant overview of the politicized historiography on this period. He acknowledges the historically contingent and external factors that World War II and Soviet occupation afforded the Kurds and Azarbaijanis, but insists on the salience of the *internal* determinants of these movements as *national* movements. Hassanpour's linguistic and ethnographic analyses trace the deep cultural and historical roots of the identities of the Azeri and Kurdish peoples. Similarly, Hassanpour assesses the achievements of the two movements and their differential degrees of radicalism attributed to their dissimilar economic structures and social bases. He views the outcome in terms of the intersection of international, national, and local balances of forces, with emphasis on Soviet pressures on the leadership in Azarbaijan and the limited possibilities for further resistance in Kurdistan. He thus sketches a dialectic of resistance and ultimate defeat owing to the failure of larger forces to support or facilitate the very real and deep grassroots movements.

The nature of nationalist protest is dissected in chapter 5 by Sussan Siavoshi, who finds that Musaddiq's oil nationalization movement had much in common with other Third World liberation movements of the 1950s and 1960s, but that Musaddiq himself was, in addition, a committed democrat. The United States, trapped in the prism of the Cold War, was unable to make any fine-grained distinctions among such movements. Siavoshi argues that the coup would not have occurred without U.S. organization, but establishes that it could not have succeeded without the prior fragmentation of the alliance over the pressing domestic, economic, and cultural issues of the day. Siavoshi therefore traces the ideological and personal conflicts within the constituent parties of the National Front to the diverging political and economic horizons of the leaderships and social bases of each. The complex role played by the Tudeh Party in this equation is assessed from the perspectives of the party, the Front, and the United States. The resulting analysis lays bare the political logic of the movement's defeat.

In chapter 6, Misagh Parsa ably illustrates the power of resource mobilization theory to shed light on the seriously under-studied events of 1960–63. The fiscal crisis of the newly institutionalized Pahlavi state toward the end of the 1950s intersected with powerful external pressures from the world economy and the Kennedy administration to force the shah to accelerate the structural transformation of Iranian society. Parsa then locates the June 1963 uprising in its larger context of secular, trade union, student, and bazaar protests attendant at the start of structural reforms undertaken by the Pahlavi state. The failure of "the" movement then becomes evident in terms of the distinct nature of this series of separate movements, and their relative capacities faced with the various strategies employed by the state. The several key actors were effectively isolated from one another, and a combination of cooperation and repression allowed the state to emerge stronger than ever, with fateful consequences leading to a social revolution some fifteen years later.

In chapter 7, I take up the vast literature on the causes of the 1977–79 revolution in light of current trends in the sociology of revolution, and try to use each to inform the other. In the process, I offer a synthetic multicausal approach to Iran's recent revolution and a potential model for other Third World social revolutions—Mexico (1910–20), Cuba (1953–59), and Nicaragua (1978–79) among them. The revolution is studied at the intersection of the mixed results of the shah's model of capitalist industrialization in a dependent and authoritarian context, the diverse political cultural responses to this experience articulated by secular and religious opponents, and the fortuitous opportunity afforded by an economic downturn and perceived pressures for reform emanating from the United States in the late 1970s. The 1977–79 events should be viewed as the latest instance of Iran's populist alliance, in which a multiclass urban coalition came temporarily together and used creative tactics to topple the monarchy. The aftermath has been at best ambiguously more successful than previous efforts in the twentieth century, as the coalition abruptly disintegrated in ways recalling other instances of social change in Iran.

In the penultimate chapter, Val Moghadam examines this outcome in more detail. She uses elements of neo-Marxism, feminism, and discourse analysis to cast Iran's postrevolutionary transitional experience in the context of Third World populist movements, which she thereby enriches. The effective use of such populist symbolic elements as anti-imperialism and social justice by Khumaini and then the Islamic Republican Party immobilized many potential opponents among the left and liberal groups that had contributed to the seizure of power. Combined with the skillful control of key institutions and ultimate coercive force, the party successively isolated its rivals and consolidated its grasp on civil society. This nexus of power and discourse enabled the regime to weather the horrific war with Iraq, but the 1989 death of Khumaini and the subsequent end of the Cold War have brought long-deferred underlying issues of the proper developmental model, gender relations, and distributional equity back to the fore. Moghadam's chapter represents a significant step in linking social change in Iran to larger trends such as populism, and in establishing how struggles over politics, economics, and gender can be mutually constitutive in a concrete case.

In my concluding chapter I reflect on the broad comparative, theoretical, and historical issues posed by the study of Iran's century of revolution. Theoretically, I locate this project with respect to the very different literatures on social movements and on revolution, arguing that Iran's pattern of persistent rebellions has much to say to social theorists interested in the specific gravity of social movements in the Third World, which possess certain distinctive characteristics marking them off from social conflict elsewhere. In addition, the comparative-historical study of Iran's social movements with each other and with revolutions elsewhere in the Third World can yield insights about the circumstances under which revolutions occur and the factors that shape their chances of success. Finally, I close the volume with some thoughts on where Iran may be heading as its (first?) century of revolution draws to an end.

What ties these chapters together is the effort on the part of a younger generation of Iran scholars to contribute to the historiography of Iran and larger debates on social movements by offering carefully researched historical accounts informed by both well-established and emerging approaches to social change. Each has been asked to review the state of debates on the movement in question, and each has elaborated a distinctive position vis-à-vis the literature. Taken as a whole, this book thus offers the beginnings of new ways of thinking about social movements in Iranian history, challenging in important respects a certain amount of received wisdom and in other ways confirming past work on the basis of new data. I hope that readers will benefit from these soundings and carry the discussion forward.

Chapter 1

Shi'i Political Discourse and Class Mobilization in the Tobacco Movement of 1890–92

Mansoor Moaddel

The tobacco protest movement of 1890–92 is one of the most celebrated events of nineteenth-century Iran. In this movement, religion played a significant role in mobilizing the people against a concession granted by the Qajar shah to a British company. Because religion was so crucial to the success of the movement and the religious tactic used by the opposition so effective, the event provided a historical precedent and justification for subsequent intervention of the Shi'i establishment in politics. It has generated considerable debate among historians and area specialists as to the causes of the significance of Shi'i religion in Iran's political affairs.

In this chapter, I first critically evaluate the existing explanations of the political role of religion in Iran, offering an alternative explanation, one that focuses on the role of social classes in the historical trajectory that culminated in the tobacco movement of 1890–92. I then extend the lessons of the empirical case of the tobacco movement to the relationship between ideology and class capacity.

Explaining Shi'i Politics in the Nineteenth Century

The existing literature offers three dominant interpretations of the role of Shi'i Islam in the politics of nineteenth-century Iran. The first is constructed in terms of the specificity of the political theory of early Shi'ism. The second interpretation considers the institutional autonomy of the Shi'i ulama within the context of the weakness of the Qajar state. The third considers the de facto separation, yet mutual reinforcement, of political and Shi'i hierocratic domination in the Qajar polity.

In the first interpretation, the ideology of Shi'ism is presumed to have an independent role, directly dictating the political actions of the ulama — the learned religious scholars and organized men of religion. For example, Hamid Algar, following Montgomery Watt, derives the oppositional role of Shi'ism from its political theory and primordial political values. Given that Shiʻi Muslims believe in the Imamate, a succession of charismatic figures who are believed to be the dispensers of true guidance after the death of Prophet Muhammad, and that the twelfth Imam is in hiding or occultation, no worldly legitimate authority has been left on earth. Thus, "insofar as any attitude to the state and existing authority can be deduced from the teaching of the Imams, it is one that combines a denial of legitimacy with a quietistic patience and abstention from action."[1] Similarly, Roger Savory claims that "there is no theological basis in Twelver Shiʻi states for an accommodation between the *mujtahids* ... and any form of polity."[2] Shiʻi political theory is, then, presumed to be the principal factor governing ulama political behavior under varying historical conditions, and their participation in protest movements, including the tobacco movement, a manifestation of their belief in the illegitimacy of any worldly authority.

Nikki Keddie questions the centrality of early Shiʻi political theory in explaining ulama politics. Instead, she relates the new doctrinal development among the Shiʻi ulama in the late eighteenth century—the rise of the Usuli school and the decline of the Akhbari—to the growth in ulama power. The Usuli, who demanded that all believers pick a *mujtahid* (a high-ranking cleric) to follow and abide by his judgments, "gave the living mujtahids a power beyond anything claimed by the Sunni ulama, and gave to their rulings a sanction beyond anything merely decreed by the state."[3] Whereas the Usuli doctrine provided an important organizational ideology justifying ulama intervention in politics, the weakness of the Qajar state provided a favorable political condition for the growth and consolidation of Shiʻi institutional autonomy.

These interpretations face two problems. First, they assume that the ulama are politically a homogeneous category. As will be seen, the ulama were not unified vis-à-vis the tobacco concession. Second, they fail to address the question of how and why Shiʻism shaped the political action of certain social classes in society. Neither the specificity of the political theory of early Shiʻism nor the ulama's conscious effort to protect their traditional social status adequately explains how a significant number of people decided to participate in protest movements behind the banner of Islam, for it is evidently true that without devout followers any attempt on the part of the ulama to oppose the state was doomed at the very outset. The ulama demanding that they should be followed is one thing; the laity actually following their lead is quite another.

A third interpretation is advanced by Said Amir Arjomand, who follows Weber in using the concept of hierocracy to describe the social organization of the Shiʻi religion. He argues that the Safavid period (1501–1722) marks the transition of the Shiʻi ulama from a privileged sodality to a hierocracy. The Safavid rulers enjoyed a caesaropapist admixture of political and religious authority. From the overthrow of the Safavids in 1722 until the advent of Aqa Muhammad Khan Qajar in

1796, the Shi'i hierocracy suffered severe blows. With the consolidation of the Qajar political order, the hierocracy gained power and influence. Indeed, these two forms of political and hierocratic domination began to reinforce each other, representing "the twin functions of imamate—supreme political and religious leadership of the community." The functional differentiation of the doctrine of imamate into the rulers and the ulama was further reinforced "by the financial autonomy of the hierocracy, and by its appropriation of extensive judiciary functions that were independent of state control."[4]

Arjomand's elaborate conceptual scheme, however, provides little guidance for analyzing the role of religion in the tobacco movement. Indeed, at one point he seems to imply that his theory of ulama institutional consolidation has little bearing on the actual political behavior of the ulama:

> The clearly defined and sharply stratified hierarchy of deference was incapable of generating action, or of controlling the individual members and disciplining them as a unified organization and in consistent pursuit of doctrinal and institutional interests.... As an organization, the hierocracy was poorly isolated from its sociopolitical environment and was therefore permeable by environmental forces. The forces of its political environment, extraneous factors emanating from the interests of the state or of social groups, could easily impinge upon the action of the hierocracy or prevent such action from being initiated.[5]

Although Arjomand does not seem to contemplate the implications of these statements for his explanatory model, his emphasis on "extraneous factors" is consistent with the argument advanced here.

A common problem with the existing explanations of Shi'i politics in Iran is the tendency to conflate Shi'ism and the ulama into one category. For Algar, the ulama are the carriers of Shi'i religion, and their behavior is dictated by the teachings of Shi'a Islam. For Keddie and Arjomand, it seems that the ulama are coterminous with Shi'ism, and the dynamic of Shi'a Islam, as a world religion, is reduced to the dynamic of ulama action. In this chapter, I treat Shi'ism and the ulama as two analytically distinct categories. The ulama are a group of learned religious scholars and jurists who have interests in maintaining religious uniformity and protecting their culturally advantageous position and social privilege. Yet, pressured by conflicting interests of the state and social classes, such as the merchants and their allies in the craft guilds, they have seldom displayed a unified front for political action. Diverse political factions have developed in their midst, having different ties with the state and social classes. Shi'ism, on the other hand, is the ideology neither of the ulama nor of a particular social class such as the merchants. Shi'a Islam constitutes a discourse that, in this case, provides a language for addressing the issue of the tobacco concession. Shi'a Islam shaped the political action of the merchants and enhanced their capacity to act in their mobilization efforts against the state and the British.

The Tobacco Movement in the Scholarly Works

Interpretations of the causes of the rise of the anti-British tobacco movement found in the existing scholarly works revolve around British-Russian rivalry in Iran, the intrigues between rival Iranian politicians, the ulama's alleged traditional role of opposing the state and foreign intervention, and the resistance of the tobacco merchants. Investigators have mentioned all these factors in their works. Nevertheless, each has emphasized one or more of these factors as the central causes of the movement. An early description of the movement appeared in E. G. Brown's 1910 work *The Persian Revolution of 1905–1909*.[6] Much later, in the 1960s, Ann Lambton offered a more systematic analysis of the event in her article "The Tobacco Régie: Prelude to Revolution."[7] This was followed shortly by a more comprehensive book-length study by Nikki Keddie, *Religion and Rebellion in Iran*.[8] Another analysis of this event was presented by Hamid Algar in *Religion and State in Modern Iran*.[9] Finally, Faridun Adamiyyat and Homa Natiq have offered the most recent full-length interpretations of the tobacco movement.[10]

For Lambton, crucial to the rise of the movement were Russian hostility to the concession, intrigues between rival politicians, the merchants' misunderstanding of the intention of the officials of the tobacco corporation, and the rise of a middle class, of which the ulama were the most vocal members, who wanted to be informed of and consulted on steps taken by the government. Therefore, for her, diplomatic failure seems to have been the central cause of the public rebellion against the concession. If there had been no Russian opposition, no political intrigue, and no misunderstanding among the merchants, and if the ulama had been adequately consulted, the movement would have not occurred. In Keddie's interpretation, on the other hand, the rivalry between the British and the Russians, and then the role of the ulama, figures prominently. To be sure, on several occasions Keddie mentions the merchants' opposition to the rebellion, but she treats their role as secondary. Algar, on the other hand, emphasizes the domestic factor. For him, the movement is another instance of the ulama's traditional role in opposing the state and resisting foreign encroachment.

Adamiyyat and Natiq question the independent role of the ulama in the movement, emphasizing instead the centrality of the role of the merchants. They argue that the merchants were the leaders of the movement in virtually all the cities, whereas on various occasions the ulama were actively involved in defending the state and the tobacco concession. Although I am highly indebted to these authors, in this study I discuss the role of the merchants as a class in a more systematic manner. I also analyze the role of the ulama as a function of the nature of their relationship to the Qajar state and the merchants.

The Merchant Class

The rise in nineteenth-century Iran of a merchant class with sufficient resources to be able to resist the state was greatly facilitated by a host of economic, political, and cultural factors. Owing to geographic location and active petty commodity production, commerce was already well developed. In 1800, Iran's main trade partners were Afghanistan and the principalities of Central Asia, Turkey, and India. Trade with India consisted mainly of native products on both sides, the East India Company's export of British goods to Iran being very small. John Malcolm put the total trade for Iran at 2.5 million pounds sterling; this figure is the sum of imports, exports, and reexports, and, according to Malcolm, the last item accounted for over half the total.[11]

The consolidation of state power under the newly established Qajar dynasty at the turn of the nineteenth century no doubt contributed to Iran's commercial expansion. The rule of the first two Qajar shahs (1796–1834) was one of rapid recovery from the devastations of the previous century, which was followed by some improvement in the economic condition of the peasants and the country as a whole.[12] Trade increased with extraordinary rapidity during the early part of the reign of Fath 'Ali Shah—the second Qajar shah—because of both greater security and the greater attention paid by the government of India to commerce in the Persian Gulf. Whereas around 1784 annual imports of Indian chintz through Bushire averaged sixty to seventy bales, by 1811 they had risen to five hundred to six hundred bales. There was also rapid growth in Persian Gulf trade between the 1780s and the 1820s and perhaps a doubling again by 1860. Russian trade with Iran, expressed in gold rubles, about doubled between the early 1830s and mid-1860s. Altogether, it seems unlikely that total trade around 1860 could have been much below 5 million pounds sterling.[13] In southern Iran, largely because of the influence of trade between Iran and India that was carried on through the Persian Gulf port of Bushire, the agricultural economy changed from one designed overwhelmingly to meet the needs of local consumption to one that, to a large degree, was geared to meeting the demands of expanding foreign markets.[14] In short, in real terms, trade rose about threefold between 1800 and 1850 and quadrupled again by 1914, a total rise of about twelvefold during the whole period under review.[15]

Iranian merchants were actively involved in this economic endeavor. These included wholesale merchants engaged in relatively large-scale domestic and international trade. Because of their economic and political resources, a few merchants dictated economic life in each city.[16] The merchants also played an important part in financing the activities of the government, and the payment of the revenue quota due from a provincial governor sometimes had to be guaranteed by a merchant before the governor-designate set out for his post.[17] It was not, however, their economic position that was the sole factor in the constitution of

the merchants as a class. The merchants occupied a high position in the distribution of social honor. They "were considered to be more respectable than any
other social class."[18] It is also reported that the merchants were among the better-
educated section of the Iranian population. For instance, in northern Iran more
than half, and sometimes up to 90 percent, of the merchants could read and
write.[19] As Willem Floor concludes, "It is, therefore, no wonder that they were
considered notables of the city in which they lived. Every small-scale trader or
even a prosperous *sarraf* (banker) wanted to become a *tajir* [merchant] as soon
as possible, for 'it was the best occupation there is.' "[20]

The merchants' prestige was also rooted in Islamic culture. Islam displays favorable attitudes toward commerce and commercial activities. More than a century
ago, Torrey noted that the "Koran manifests everywhere a lively interest in matters of trade."[21] He argues that the theology of the Koran is expressed in the language of trade: "Words elsewhere used to express some familiar commercial idea,
[are] here transferred to the relations between God and man." Torrey observes
that these commercial terms—he lists "reckoning," "weights," "measures," "payments," "loss," "gain," "fraud," "buying," "selling," "profits," "wages," "loans,"
and "security"—occur some 370 times in the Koran, and thus "impart a certain
commercial tone to the whole."[22] Besides the Koran's favorable attitude toward
merchants, one may find considerable eulogistic formulations about the merchants in the sayings of the Prophet and other religious texts. It is reported that
the Prophet said, "The merchant who is sincere and trustworthy will (at the
Judgment Day) be among the prophets, the just and the martyrs," or "The trustworthy merchant will sit in the shade of God's throne at the Day of Judgment,"
or "Merchants are the messengers of this world and God's faithful trustees on
Earth." According to holy tradition, trade is a superior way of earning one's livelihood: "If thou profit by doing what is permitted, thy deed is djihad."[23] The taste
for business that was characteristic of the Prophet and of the holy caliphs, his
first successors, was reported with tenderness. Umar is alleged to have said:
"Death can come upon me nowhere more pleasantly than where I am engaged in
business in the market, buying and selling on behalf of my family.... If God let
the dwellers in Paradise engage in trade," the Prophet is claimed to have said,
"they would trade in fabrics and in spices." Or, again: "If there were trading in
Paradise, I should choose to trade in fabrics, for Abu Bakr the Sincere was a
trader in fabrics."[24] It is recorded, says an eighteenth-century commentator on
Ghazali, that Ibrahim an-Nakha'i, a pious authority of the first century A.H., was
asked which he preferred: an honest merchant or a man who has given up all
forms of work so as to devote himself wholly to the service of God. He is said to
have replied, "The honest merchant is dearer to me, for he is in the position of
one waging a holy war."[25] Finally, Lambton observes that "Jahiz in an essay in
praise of trade and censure of the service of sultans ... maintains that mer-

chants were held in high estimation and that people of discrimination consider them to be the most pious members of the community and their life to be the most secure; they were in their houses like kings on their thrones, the people seeking them out to satisfy their needs."[26]

Other classes tied to trade and closely allied with the merchants were craftsmen and retail traders. They were among the most stable and populous classes in nineteenth-century Iran. The division of labor among the craftsmen was extensive, and considerable differentiation existed in the type of commodities they produced.[27] Craftsmen and retail traders were organized into guilds by type of occupation. A guild consisted of "a group of townspeople engaged in the same occupation, who elect their own chief and officers, who pay guild taxes, this group having fiscal and administrative functions."[28] Lambton believes that the craft guilds existed well before the nineteenth century, and were "highly organized," having "clearly defined associations in the cities."[29] Furthermore, she observes that "most of the craft gilds had their own bazaars, which fact no doubt strengthened their sense of corporate life. Throughout the Middle Ages craft gilds played an important part in the life of the cities."[30]

Foreign Economic Infiltration and the Merchants' Weakness

Beginning in about the second quarter of the nineteenth century, the merchants and craft guilds began to face strong competition from European concerns. Foreign companies gradually took over a greater part of Iranian commerce. Notwithstanding the economic recovery and commercial boost associated with the consolidation of the Qajar political order, Iran's primitive accumulation relative to the emerging international order was too little and too late. Iran had neither the economic resources nor the political power to meet challenges from Europe and Imperial Russia successfully. For one thing, Iranian merchants were no match for these foreign interests. They "lacked the organizational and administrative capabilities as well as the capital necessary to finance and run their affairs on the same scale as the European merchants did."[31] For another, the situation was exacerbated by the very different manners in which European government and the Iranian government treated their domestic interests. Equipped with unprecedented modern military technology, the European governments were largely the gendarme of their native economic interests. In contrast, the Qajar state—sandwiched in military competitions between the British and the Russian empires and weakened by its repeated defeats in the Perso-Russian wars of 1813 and 1828—not only left the merchants unprotected, but also began granting concessions to foreign concerns.

As a result, the merchants and the guilds began to engage in protest activities against the state and international capital. "The first sign that European influence had penetrated and was resented by the Iranian mercantile community was about 1830, when 'the quality of English and Masulipatam chintzes alarmed the manufacturers so much that they petitioned the King to put a stop to the importation.'"[32] When in 1837 the trading house of Ralli opened a branch in Tabriz, the first of many protests against European merchants occurred. This was followed by a ban on the consumption of tea, which was issued in Tabriz and Tehran against the Russian Georgians, "who have the principal traffic in that article, whereas native merchants have none."[33] Three years later, the British consul reported that the "Persian merchants had asked the government to prohibit imports of European manufactures 'on the ground principally of the ruin Persian manufacturers are reduced to by the constant and immense importation of foreign goods.' This attempt was, however, unsuccessful, and the combination formed by the merchants for that purpose was dissolved."[34] Similar, and equally fruitless, attempts were made by "traders and manufacturers of Cashan ... and other manufacturers and traders."[35] According to K. E. Abbott, the British consul in 1844, "a memorial was presented to His Majesty the Shah by the traders and manufacturers of Cashan praying for protection to their commerce which they represented as suffering in consequence of the introduction of European merchandise into their country."[36] Again, in 1849, he reported that "the manufacturers have however rapidly declined for some time past in consequence of the trade with Europe which has gradually extended into every part of the kingdom to the detriment or ruin of many branches of native industry."[37] In 1864 there was another unsuccessful protest against European trade.[38]

The 1828 Treaty of Turkmanchai fixed customs at 5 percent on foreign trade, giving foreigners an economic advantage because Iranian merchants had to pay higher taxes. The British consul in Iran in 1851 reported that "the position ... of the Persian Merchant compared to that of the European may be understood by the following statements; The European importing a load of Sugar of the value of 10 Tomans—pays his 5 per Cent once for all and may re-export it to Tehran. The Persian pays for the load ... 14 per Cent and if he re-exports to Tehran is charged Rohdarlik [a road tax] at Meeana, Zenjaun, Kazveen and Tehran."[39] Similar differential taxes were applied on the manufactures. The same report then concludes that "unless these duties are not [sic] considerably reduced the natives must abandon Commercial pursuits, and the Trade will then be reduced in amount, and remain entirely in the hands of Europeans."[40]

Finally, the concessions granted by the monarch to foreign companies further intensified economic pressure on the merchants. These included the scandalous Reuter concession of 1872, which granted a British citizen the right to farm the customs; set up a state bank; build railroads, telegraph lines, and factories; and exploit virtually all the mineral wealth of Iran. This was eventually withdrawn because of local and Russian opposition, but the sale of concessions continued. Inflation and other economic crises also forced Nasir al-Din Shah to sell high offices: "As one modern historian has commented, hardly a day passed in the court without a sale of something to someone for some price."[41]

Gradually, the merchants lost their hold on the domestic markets, and by the end of the nineteenth century they were dominated by foreign companies. In the north the Russian merchants had about half of the foreign trade in hand, and in the south the British merchants handled "the bulk of the transactions."[42] Not only was Iranian trade seriously hurt by the Western impact, but Iranian industry was also virtually ruined.[43] In his report, a tax collector in Isfahan noted the deteriorating conditions of the weavers' guilds:

> In the past, high-quality textiles were manufactured in Isfahan since everyone—from the highest to the lowest—wore local products. But in the last few years, the people of Iran have given up their body and soul to buy the colorful and cheap products of Europe. In doing so, they incurred greater losses than they imagined: local weavers, in trying to imitate imported fabrics, have lowered their quality; Russians have stopped buying Iranian textiles; and many occupations have suffered great losses. At least one-tenth of the guilds in this city were weavers; not even one-fifth have survived. About one-twentieth of the needy widows of Isfahan raised their children on the income they derived from spinning for the weavers; they have now lost their source of livelihood. Likewise, other important guilds, such as dyers, carders, and bleachers have suffered. Other occupations have also been affected: for example, farmers can no longer sell their cotton for high prices.[44]

In the course of the nineteenth century, many merchants bought land and, along with some traditional landlords, began to meet Western demand by using their lands increasingly for export crops such as cotton and opium, which made them vulnerable to the economic fluctuations in the world market.[45] The fall in agricultural prices on the international markets, which started in 1871 and continued to the end of the century, brought insecurity to many Iranian exporters. The price per bushel of wheat, for example, declined from $1.50 in 1871 to $.23 in 1894; the volume of wheat exported from Bushire increased almost eight times, but the real value failed to rise significantly. Finally, the introduction of European capital and the capitulations granted to European business created outside the bazaars a comprador bourgeoisie.[46] The government's failure to support domestic commerce and industry, coupled with interference by the Russian and British governments on behalf of their mercantile interests in Iran's internal affairs, weakened the Iranian merchants to the extent that they

> became for the greater part dependent on the European firms, not as equal partners, but as agents (*dallal va dastkar*) and hired hands (*muzdur*), whose best asset was their personal honesty.... The Iranian merchant who at the beginning of the 19th century had the reputation of a liberal, freethinking man among a bigoted nation, became a scoundrel in the eyes of the Europeans, whom one could not trust, and whose favorite pastime was to outdo and deceive foreign merchants.[47]

Economic pressures from a common enemy on both the merchants and the craft guilds provided them with a common political platform. The alignment between these two classes was the decisive factor underpinning the tobacco movement of 1890–92.

Shi'i Discourse and Class Capacity

Despite their numerical growth and economic power, the merchants and craft guilds were unable to change their status vis-à-vis the Europeans. Their repeated attempts to boycott foreign goods or to petition the monarch to implement some sort of protective measures failed. Their traditional organizations, the merchant and craft guilds, did not by themselves produce an effective vehicle for their mobilization against foreign domination. In 1301 H.Q. (1882/83), the Society of the Representatives of the Merchants (Majlis-i Vukala-yi Tujjar) was established with legal and political status in Tehran and then branched out into virtually all the provinces. Its central purposes were to protect domestic commerce and industry and to end foreign economic domination.[48] In his letter to the shah, an active merchant representative in Tehran, Hajj Muhammad Hasan Amin al-Zarb, pointed out that all the affairs of the country were based on commerce. A strong commerce was a foundation for self-sufficiency—the establishment of factories, the discovery and exploitation of mines, and the production and distribution of commodities all over the country. Yet, despite several attempts and initiatives by the government, no significant progress had been made, because the people who were in charge were incompetent and corrupt, wasted the government's resources, and usurped the people's property.[49] The society, however, was liquidated by the government and the merchants were deprived of an important organizational resource.

The society was dissolved not because of its defense of the merchants and commerce, but because it was a modern institution apparently incompatible with monarchical absolutism and the institution of the ulama. On occasion, the ulama expressed their opposition to the society because it was against paying taxes to the clerical establishment.[50] Nevertheless, when the merchants invoked religious principles against the tobacco concession, it was not so easy for the state to repress their protest. Given that Muslim interests were in conflict with those of non-Muslims, Islamic discourse became an effective language for addressing the problem of Western domination and a generally callous state. By invoking religious principles, the merchants not only overcame the anticipated charges that they were acting out of self-interest, but also transformed their conflict with the British in the direction of a confrontation between Muslims and infidels, thereby very effectively mobilizing the people against economic intervention.

The movement was a rebellion against a concession granted by the shah in

1890 to Major G. F. Talbot, a British citizen, for the monopoly of buying, selling, and manufacturing all the tobacco in the interior or exterior of the Kingdom of Iran for fifty years in return for an annual rent of 15,000 pounds sterling, and a quarter of the annual profits after the payment of all expenses and a 5 percent dividend on the capital.[51] The concession was particularly damaging to the merchants and retail traders whose income depended on this profitable tobacco trade. Tobacco was one of the country's major exports, and had the concession come into force, it would have affected the livelihood of a significant section of the population in Iran.[52] Between March 20, 1890, when the concession was signed, and late January 1892, when it was cancelled by the shah, there were intense conflicts between the British and the shah, on one hand, and the merchant-led resistance movement and the ulama, on the other.

The merchants of Tehran were the first group to rise in protest against the concession. Before it was publicly announced, they wrote a protest letter to the shah. An underground leaflet criticizing state policies was also distributed in the city; it stated that "tobacco belongs to Iranians, the buyers and consumers are Iranians, why should then tobacco trade be monopolized by foreigners?"[53] Haj Muhammad Rahim Isfahani, a merchant from Tabriz, rejected the concession on political and economic grounds. He argued that it was not even beneficial to the government and demanded its cancellation. Reproaching the government, he charged that "this government does not care about the people.... It acts as it wishes and is accountable to no one." He then asked Amin al-Zarb, an influential merchant in Tehran, to take steps against the concession. Thus the merchants and small businessmen acted independently, well before some of the ulama rose against the concession.[54]

Following Tehran, the merchants of Fars stood up against the concession. Tobacco trade in Fars was under the control of sixty well-known and influential merchants, who began sending telegrams against the concession to the prime minister and the shah. At the same time, they attempted to gain the support of the ulama.[55] According to a Shirazi merchant, the people asked the ulama to protest by refusing to go to the mosques or to hold classes. Kennedy, the British chargé d'affaires at Tehran, reported that "the Mollas were refusing to enter the Masjid, and were preventing the people from answering the 'Azan' or call for prayer, and that they had expressed their intention of continuing this line of conduct until Mr. Binns, the local Manager of the Tobacco Régie, had been expelled from Shiraz."[56] As a result of the people's persuasion, a leading mulla, Sayyid 'Ali Akbar Fal-Asiri, began to criticize the government and the concession. The government quickly arrested the sayyid and deported him to Karbala. This move backfired, however, and produced considerable unrest in the city. The bazaar was shut down and the people began convening at the Shah-i Chiragh. In response, the government troops resorted to violence, wounding and killing several people.[57] In a dramatic act of protest, a merchant in Fars burned up all his inventory of tobacco, and then told the British company that he had sold it to God.[58]

Among the first religious principles the merchants invoked against the concession was the one that pertains to the consent of the buyer and seller. The merchants argued that this Islamic principle was violated because the concession required that all tobacco growers sell their product to a British monopoly. The merchants also began sending complaints and petitions to the eminent Mirza Hasan Shirazi, the sole *marja'-i taqlid* (highest religious authority of the time) in Karbala. Consequently, after three and a half months, Shirazi sent a telegram to the shah that stated:

> Permitting the foreigners to interfere in the internal affairs of the country, their intermingling and closeness with the Muslim people, and the act of the banking, tobacco and railroad concessions and so forth are contrary to the Koran and Godly principles, weaken the independence of the state and the order of the country, and cause the condition of the people to deteriorate.[59]

Karbala'i, however, notes that the protest of the leading *mujtahid* did not resolve the issue, and the company's agents began working everywhere.

As a result of the government repression, the movement in Shiraz subsided temporarily. However, it reemerged with greater strength and on a larger scale in Azarbaijan. Unlike Fars, Azarbaijan was not a tobacco-growing region. Foreign trade of tobacco, however, was under the control of the merchants. This explains why here also it was the merchants and retail traders who organized the movement.[60] According to the British Consul:

> I AM informed from the most reliable sources that it is not true that the Mollahs have been preaching in the mosques against the Régie. In the bazaar and in private houses it is the all-engrossing subject of conversation, but no amount of inquiry elicited the information that the matter has been referred to in the mosques.[61]

An anonymous placard posted in Tabriz in reply to a notice issued by the British company warned the ulama, the Europeans, and the Armenian merchants about the consequence of supporting the concession:

> Ulemas [*sic*] of the town! Law is the law of religion and not the laws of the Europeans!

> Woe to those Ulemas who will not co-operate with the nation! Woe to those who will not spend their lives and property! Anyone of the Ulemas who will not agree with the people will lose his life. Woe to anyone who may sell one muskal of Tobacco to the Europeans! Woe to the Europeans who may wish to enforce these customs of the Infidels. We will kill the Europeans first, and then plunder their property. Woe to the Armenians, who will be killed, and will lose their property and their families! Woe to those who will keep quiet!

We write this in answer to the Notice.

Curses on the father of anyone who may destroy this Notice![62]

In the meantime, "Haj Mirza Yousof Aqa Mujtahid preached very strongly against the Régie, saying among other things, that the Kaffirs [infidels] had come here to interfere in the tobacco business, and any Mussulman who joined them was also a Kaffir and deserving of death."[63] To quell the movement in Azarbaijan, the shah requested the assistance of Haj Mirza Javad, the influential *mujtahid* of Tabriz. In reply, the *mujtahid* indicated that "the entire population of Azerbaijan are dissatisfied with him on account of the Régie, and that if it is maintained by the Shah he cannot answer for the order of the district, and fears riots."[64] And when the shah's envoy, Amin-i Huzur, informed the chief *mujtahid* that the concession must proceed and that he was expected to use his influence with the people to this end, the *mujtahid* responded that "the people would never consent, and he could not tell them this."[65] Evidently, the *mujtahid* was acting more as a liaison between the shah and the people than as a leader of the movement. Consequently, the government and the concessionaire agreed that the company should temporarily suspend its activities in the province. Later, Ornstein, the company's director, came up with the suggestion that its affairs in Azarbaijan be given to another company solely consisting of Iranian merchants for one year.[66] These tactics helped calm the excited situation in Tabriz.

Now it was Isfahan's turn to rebel. There the idea of boycotting the consumption of tobacco was contemplated and executed for the first time. As elsewhere, the tobacco movement in Isfahan began with the merchants' initiatives. In early September, the merchants sent a protest letter to Zill al-Sultan, an Anglophile and the governor of Isfahan. The governor responded by threatening to punish or even execute the protesters if they continued to interfere in government affairs. His threat was ineffective, however, and the rebellion began in mid-November 1891, with the cooperation of two leading ulama, Aqa Najafi and his brother Shaikh Muhammad 'Ali. Aqa Najafi was a major landowner and an influential *mujtahid,* whose power and influence matched the governor's. Shaikh Muhammad 'Ali was an able preacher.[67] The cooperation between the ulama and the merchants in Isfahan was far stronger than in other places. Karbala'i reports:

> After extensive discussions, the ulama of Isfahan realized that the best way to resolve the issue was to forbid all Muslims to consume tobacco, hence totally halting the tobacco trade. Evidently, if there was no buyer for the commodity, there would be no seller either. Moreover, the government could not intervene under the pretext of maintaining order because this tactic would cause no disorder and chaos in the affairs of the country.[68]

The ulama then began criticizing the government's policies of granting concessions to foreigners. Aqa Najafi "preached that, according to the Koran, all tobacco is unclean; all servants of Europeans are unclean; they must not be allowed in baths, coffee-houses, or to purchase in bazaars, or be tolerated as friends."[69] The British council named Haj Ahmad Bunakdar, an Isfahani merchant, as the person responsible for mobilizing the ulama against the concession.[70] The shah, on the other hand, blamed Aqa Muhammad, Isfahan's *Malik al-Tujjar* (leading merchant representative) as Amin al-Zarb's accomplice.[71] In either case, the merchants were the central force behind the anticoncession movement.

The tobacco boycott in Isfahan was not effective enough to cause a change in the shah's decision, nor did the idea gain much acceptance elsewhere. Karbala'i vaguely indicates that the ulama of Tehran believed that boycotting tobacco was "the elimination of an evil by a worse evil."[72] The movement gradually subsided, particularly after the shah sent a message to the ulama requesting their cooperation in controlling the movement. One or two of the ulama even lifted the boycott on tobacco.

In Mashhad, tobacco merchants and traders organized opposition to the concession, but were unable to attract the cooperation and support of the ulama. Only a few of the ulama—such as Va'iz Sabzivari, Mirza Abdurrahman, and Sayyid Muhammad Kalati—and a group of *tullab* (students of religion) joined the movement. The tobacco company, on the other hand, was successful in gaining the support of Khurasan governor Fath 'Ali Khan Sahibdivan and the leading ulama. Kennedy reported that "the Governor-General and the principal Ulemas [*sic*] are endeavoring to the best of their ability to allay the excitement which still continues at Meshed [Mashhad]."[73] Among these ulama were Mirza Ahmad Razavi, Haj Shaikh Muhammad Taqi, Sayyid Habibullah, and Shaykh Muhammad Rahim, who sent this telegram to the shah:

> These tobacco sellers and some ruffians who know nothing about the affairs of the state and the nation, and do not understand all aspects of the issue, have behaved ignorantly, causing the disappointment of His Majesty, the protector of Islam.... While praying for the shah's well-being, we began calming down the people; thanks to God ... and to the intelligence and competence of Sahibdivan, the people were calmed down and dispersed. In every respect, we consider obeying the orders of the Islam protector Shahanshah our necessary duty.[74]

Haj Abulqasim Malik al-Tujjar, Amin al-Zarb's brother, reported that despite the persistence and persuasion of the people, the ulama did not support the anticoncession movement; one of the ulama who supported the movement was even punished by the *mujtahid* Mirza Ahmad. Given ulama complicity with the government and the company, the movement in Mashhad was relatively quickly defeated without the government having to resort to violence. In Kirman, while the merchants and traders closed their shops, the ulama remained silent on the issue.[75] As a result of these rebellions and the flood of petitions and protest letters he was receiving, the shah began to contemplate canceling the concession. The company and the British government naturally resisted this idea. The British embassy, however, began to realize that the tobacco monopoly was not going to work, and its forced imposition did not seem to be in Britain's best interest in Iran. The Russians were also active against the concession, although their role in the tobacco movement was by no means central. Given this background, another wave of protests was necessary to break the balance of forces in favor of the resistance movement. The idea of a tobacco boycott had already been tested with some success in Isfahan, although the ulama of Tehran believed that the act was tantamount to "the elimination of an evil with a worse evil." Nevertheless, by late November 1891, talk of a boycott became popular in Tehran. Then it was rumored that a *fatva* (religious decree) regarding the boycott of tobacco had been issued by the eminent Shirazi and sent to Isfahan. In early December 1891, it was announced that the *fatva* had arrived, and that the original was in the possession of Ayatullah Ashtiyani, a leading *mujtahid* of Tehran.[76] The *fatva* read: "In the name of God, the Merciful and the Forgiving. As of now, the consumption of tobacco in any form is tantamount to war against the Imam of the Age."[77] The *fatva* was quickly copied and distributed throughout the country. The tobacco movement hence culminated in a nationwide tobacco boycott. The *fatva,* however, was not real; it was fabricated by a group of merchants that included Haj Kazim Malik al-Tujjar, with the cooperation of Mirza Hasan Ashtiyani.[78] When news of the boycott reached Shirazi, he was prudent enough not to deny its authenticity. The nationwide boycott, followed by huge demonstrations at the shah's palace that left dozens of people dead and wounded, eventually forced the shah to repudiate the concession by the end of January 1892.

The connection between class interests and religious opposition is therefore a matter of historical fact. The merchants, small traders, and craftsmen protested foreign economic infiltration by first attempting to boycott foreign goods or petitioning the king for the protection of their trade for many years preceding the tobacco concession. The tobacco movement was indeed a culmination of these protest activities. The merchants played a leading role in virtually all the major cities, effectively utilized religious idioms and metaphors against the shah and the British company, and persuaded the ulama to participate in the movement. The forged *fatva* further signifies the leading role of the merchants and the secondary role of the ulama in the movement. In contrast, the ulama's position on the concession was inconsistent. They were torn between supporting the shah and supporting the merchants. The available evidence seems to suggest that variations in ulama positions vis-à-vis the concession were related to variations in their sources of support. In Isfahan, the leading ulama became actively involved in the movement because they were connected to the landed interests whose tobacco income had been affected by the concession. Keddie also concedes that ulama hostility to the concession partly "reflected their ties to merchant families and merchant guilds and their interest in tobacco grown on their private or *vaqf* [religiously endowed] land."[79] In Mashhad, however, the ulama supported the concession because they were financially tied to the shah. The administration of the property of the Shrine of Imam Reza in Mashhad was under the shah's control, and the ulama were benefiting considerably from its *vaqf* properties.[80] Similarly, in Tehran, those among the ulama who refused to participate in the tobacco movement had close connections with the shah and Amin al-Sultan. For example, Ayatullah Bihbihani, a leading *mujtahid* in Tehran, was bribed by the British and actively worked against the movement.

This does not mean that the ulama did not occupy a crucial ideological position in Iranian society. Certainly, the very fact that the public observed the alleged authoritative dictum of Ayatullah Shirazi attests to the ulama's extensive political power and social influence, and indicates the limits of the power of the merchants and craft guilds outside Shi'i discourse. But what is important to realize is that the *fatva* itself was the product of the social dialectics of the protest movement, and not a manifestation of the political theory of early Shi'ism or the ulama's leading role as defenders of the national interest. At any rate, once religious principles were successfully invoked against foreign interests and the state in the tobacco movement, a significant historical precedent was set for the politics of religious opposition in subsequent periods. In this process, the connection between material interests and the forged *fatva* was later overlooked in many historical and political commentaries. Also overlooked was the fact that a significant portion of the ulama failed to participate in the movement. In its stead, the idea that the Shi'i ulama were fundamentally against the state and tyranny was decontextualized from the very material conditions that caused its growth. Pro-ulama propagandists then began perpetuating the myth that the ulama had saved Iran's resources from being plundered by imperialism.

Conclusion

The foregoing analysis has shown that there was a systematic connection between class interests and the political role of Shi'ism in nineteenth-century Iran. As we have seen, the struggle of the merchants, retail traders, and craftsmen against the state and international capital *preceded* the emergence of religious opposition to the state. There was a historical *correlation* between the increasing hostility of the merchants and the craft guilds toward the state and the emergence of religious opposition. These classes utilized Islamic principles, metaphors, and idioms in their mobilization efforts against the state and foreign interests. Such a correlation is not spurious simply because other factors that have been cited as the cause of religious involvement in politics (i.e., the political theory of early Shi'ism and ulama institutional autonomy) fail to provide an adequate explanation for ulama political behavior in the movement.

The case of the tobacco rebellion also has important theoretical implications for the connection between ideology and class mobilization. Although the historical narrative shows that the merchants used Shi'i discourse to defend their interests, closer scrutiny of the history of the merchants' struggle against foreign capital points to a more complex relationship between ideology and class capacity. In this particular case, class capacity was highly conditioned by the ideological context within which the struggle was taking place. The numerical weight and the economic resources of the merchants and craft guilds were not sufficient to combat foreign economic intervention, nor did their organizations, such as the guilds or the newly constituted Society of the Representatives of the Merchants, provide an effective vehicle for the defense of their interests. The merchants were successful when their action was constituted in terms of a Shi'i oppositional discourse. Far from being an instrument of the merchants, Shi'i discourse transcended their particularistic interests and transformed the merchant-British conflict into a confrontation between Muslims and infidels. The merchants' capacity to act was shaped by and through Shi'i discourse.

In more general theoretical terms, then, contrary to some views, ideology is not simply a set of ideas internalized by social actors or connected to interests. Rather, ideology is a discourse, a language for addressing the problems faced by social actors in a particular historical juncture. Such discourse is not simply a back-and-forth argument between opposing forces based on rational calculation of interests. Diverse sets of ideas can articulate the same interests. Discourse is shaped within the dynamics of ideological debate itself, as each side of a conflict structures the kind of argument its opponents are likely to advance against it, and vice versa. The efficacy of a discourse in rallying people to action is often contingent upon the degree to which it transcends social differences in a communitarian direction. Because discourse tends to form within the dynamic of presentation and rebuttal of ideological arguments, it adds a dimension to social processes that cannot be predicted by the dynamics of class and political interests but rather is caused by the constraints and limits of the discourse itself.

The role of ideology in affecting the course of historical events may vary in different situations. Further research in this direction should start with an account of broad environmental conditions such as the relationship between the state and various social classes, within the international context. Next, because ideology is conceptualized as a discourse, the rise of the ideology of a protest movement should be analyzed within the context of the interaction between both sides of the conflict. Adequate consideration should also be given to the ideology of the target of the protest movement because it provides a clue for predicting the probable form of the ideology of the protest movement. The degree of congruity between the ideology of the protest movement and its general cultural context is also consequential for the outcome. A strict organizational analysis and evaluation of the kinds of resources available to a social movement may not be adequate to allow us to understand why some movements fail and others succeed. The prevailing cultural environment structures the legitimacy of the claims advanced by a protest movement. Finally, consideration should be given to the basic themes, ritual performances, and symbolic structure of the ideology of protest movements.[81]

Notes

Work on this chapter was partially supported by fellowships from the National Endowment for the Humanities and Eastern Michigan University, and a grant from the National Science Foundation. Comments by anonymous reviewers for University of Minnesota Press and the assistance of Robert Abrams are gratefully acknowledged.

1. Hamid Algar, *Religion and State in Modern Iran, 1785–1906: The Role of the Ulama in the Qajar Period* (Berkeley: University of California Press, 1969), 2. See also Montgomery Watt, "Shi'ism under the Umayyads," *Journal of the Royal Asiatic Society*, pts. 3–4 (1960): 155–72.

2. Roger M. Savory, "The Problem of Sovereignty in the Ithna Ashari ('Twelver') Shi'i State," *Middle East Review* (1979): 10.

3. Nikki R. Keddie, "The Roots of the Ulama's Power in Modern Iran," in *Scholars, Saints, and Sufis: Muslim Religious Institutions since 1500* (Los Angeles: University of California Press, 1972), 223; see also 214.

4. Said Amir Arjomand, *The Shadow of God and the Hidden Imam* (Chicago: University of Chicago Press, 1984), 255, 230, 14.

5. Ibid., 246.

6. Edward G. Browne, *The Persian Revolution of 1905–1909* (Cambridge: Cambridge University Press, 1910), 31–58.

7. Ann K. S. Lambton, "The Tobacco Régie: Prelude to Revolution," *Studia Islamica* 22 (1965): 119–57.

8. Nikki R. Keddie, *Religion and Rebellion in Iran: The Tobacco Protest of 1891–1892* (London: Frank Cass, 1966).

9. Algar, *Religion and State*, 205–21.

10. Faridun Adamiyyat, *Idi'uluzhi-yi Nahzat-i Mashrutiyat-i Iran* (The ideology of the constitutional movement in Iran) (Tehran: Intisharat-i Payam, 1355/1976); Faridun Adamiyyat, *Shurish bar Imtiaznameh-i Rizhi* (The struggle against the tobacco concession) (Tehran: Intisharat-i Payam, 1360/1981); Faridun Adamiyyat and Homa Natiq, *Afkar-i Ijtima'i va Siyasi va Iqtisadi dar Asar-i Muntashir-Nashudeh-i Dauran-i Qajar* (Sociopolitical and economic thought in unpublished documents of the Qajar period) (Tehran: Agah, 1356/1977).

11. Charles Issawi, ed., *The Economic History of Iran, 1800–1914* (Chicago: University of Chicago Press, 1971), 71, 130.

12. Ibid., 17; Ann K. S. Lambton, *Landlord and Peasant in Persia: A Study of Land Tenure and Land Revenue Administration* (London: Oxford University Press, 1953), 134.

13. Issawi, *The Economic History of Iran*, 130–31.

14. Roger T. Olson, "Persian Gulf Trade and the Agricultural Economy of Southern Iran in the Nineteenth Century," in *Modern Iran: The Dialectics of Continuity and Change*, ed. Michael E. Bonine and Nikki R. Keddie (Albany: State University of New York Press, 1981), 173–89.

15. Issawi, *The Economic History of Iran*, 132; John Foran, "The Concept of Dependent

Development as a Key to the Political Economy of Qajar Iran (1800–1925)," *Iranian Studies* 22, nos. 2–3 (1989): 15–23.

16. Willem M. Floor, "The Merchants (*tujjār*) in Qājār Iran," *Zeitschrift der Deutschen Morgenländischen Gesellschaft* 126, no. 1 (1976): 107.

17. Ann K. S. Lambton, *Theory and Practice in Medieval Persian Government* (London: Variorum Reprints, 1980), 130 n. 1.

18. Floor, "The Merchants," 102.

19. Issawi, *The Economic History of Iran*, 24.

20. Floor, "The Merchants," 102.

21. Charles C. Torrey, *The Commercial-Theological Terms in the Koran* (Leyden, Netherlands: E. J. Brill, 1892), 2.

22. Ibid., 3, 4, 8.

23. Cited in Maxime Rodinson, *Islam and Capitalism* (London: Penguin, 1974), 16.

24. Quoted in ibid., 17.

25. Quoted in ibid., 11.

26. Lambton, *Theory and Practice*, 22.

27. Ehsan Tabari, *Furupashi-yi Nizam-i Sunnati va Zayish-i Sarmayedari dar Iran* (Disintegration of the traditional socioeconomic system and the rise and development of capitalism in Iran) (Stockholm: Tudeh, 1975), 29.

28. Willem M. Floor, "The Guilds in Iran: An Overview from the Earliest Beginnings till 1972," *Zeitschrift der Deutschen Morgenländischen Gesellschaft* 125, no. 1 (1975): 100.

29. Lambton, *Theory and Practice*, 19.

30. Ibid., 20.

31. Floor, "The Merchants," 124–25.

32. Ibid., 129, quoting J. B. Fraser, *Travels and Adventures in the Persian Provinces on the Banks of the Caspian Sea* (London: n.p., 1826), 368.

33. Issawi, *The Economic History of Iran*, 76.

34. Ibid., quoting a report of the English consul Bonham, 1844.

35. Ibid.

36. Cited in ibid., 258.

37. Ibid., 259.

38. Ibid., 103–4.

39. Ibid., 80–81.

40. Ibid., 81.

41. Ervand Abrahamian, *Iran between Two Revolutions* (Princeton, N.J.: Princeton University Press, 1982), 56–57, citing Reza Sheikholeslami, "The Sale of Offices in Qajar Iran, 1858–1896," *Iranian Studies* 4 (Spring-Summer 1971): 104–18.

42. Floor, "The Merchants," 176; see also Lord George Curzon, *Persia and the Persian Question*, vol. 1 (London: Longman, Green, 1892), 573; Issawi, *The Economic History of Iran*, 71–72.

43. Floor, "The Merchants," 130; Issawi, *The Economic History of Iran*, 259.

44. Cited in Abrahamian, *Iran between Two Revolutions*, 59.

45. Nikki R. Keddie, *Roots of Revolution: An Interpretive History of Modern Iran* (New Haven, Conn.: Yale University Press, 1981), 28.

46. Abrahamian, *Iran between Two Revolutions*, 60.

47. Floor, "The Merchants," 133.

48. Adamiyyat and Natiq, *Afkar-i Ijtima'i*, 299–371.

49. Cited in ibid., 304–5.

50. Ibid., 302, 370.

51. "Sir F. Lascelles to the Marquis of Salisbury," in "Correspondence respecting the

Persian Tobacco Concession," Great Britain, *Sessional Papers* 79 (1892): 210–11. Hereafter cited as *Sessional Papers.*

52. Adamiyyat, *Shurish,* 13.

53. Cited in ibid., 15; translation mine. All translations from non-English works in this chapter are my own.

54. Adamiyyat, *Idi'uluzhi,* 36–39.

55. Ibid., 19; Shaykh Hasan Karbala'i, *Qarardad-i Rizhi-yi 1890 M.* (The Régie contract of 1890) (Tehran: Mubarizan, 1361/1982), 31.

56. "Mr. R. J. Kennedy to the Marquis of Salisbury," in *Sessional Papers* (June 2, 1891).

57. Adamiyyat, *Shurish,* 20–21.

58. Karbala'i, *Qarardad,* 46.

59. Cited in ibid., 40; see also 45.

60. Adamiyyat, *Shurish,* 31–32.

61. "Acting Consul-General Paton to Mr. R. J. Kennedy," in *Sessional Papers* (May 6, 1891).

62. Quoted in "Mr. R. J. Kennedy to the Marquis of Salisbury," in *Sessional Papers* (July 27, 1891).

63. "Acting Consul-General Paton to Mr. R. J. Kennedy," in *Sessional Papers* (August 15, 1891).

64. Ibid.

65. "Acting Consul-General Paton to Mr. R. J. Kennedy," in *Sessional Papers* (September 10, 1891).

66. Adamiyyat, *Shurish,* 45; "Mr. R. J. Kennedy to the Marquis of Salisbury," in *Sessional Papers* (September 9, 1891).

67. Adamiyyat, *Shurish,* 49–53.

68. Karbala'i, *Qarardad,* 45.

69. "Consul Preece to Sir F. Lascelles," in *Sessional Papers* (November 20, 1891).

70. Ibid.

71. Adamiyyat, *Shurish,* 55.

72. Karbala'i, *Qarardad,* 56.

73. "Mr. R. J. Kennedy to the Marquis of Salisbury," in *Sessional Papers* (October 6, 1891).

74. Quoted in Adamiyyat, *Shurish,* 62.

75. Ibid., 64–66.

76. Karbala'i, *Qarardad,* 67–68.

77. Cited in ibid., 68–69.

78. Adamiyyat, *Shurish,* 75.

79. Keddie, *Religion and Rebellion,* 65.

80. Adamiyyat, *Shurish,* 65.

81. For a more extended discussion of these propositions, see Mansoor Moaddel, "Ideology as Episodic Discourse: The Case of the Iranian Revolution," *American Sociological Review* 57 (June 1992): 353–79. See also my recent book *Class, Politics, and Ideology in the Iranian Revolution* (New York: Columbia University Press, 1993).

Chapter 2

Social Democracy and the Iranian Constitutional Revolution of 1906–11

Janet Afary

The Russian revolution of 1905 was followed by a series of revolutions in Iran (1906), Turkey (1908), Mexico (1910), and China (1911) that marked a new stage in the history of the developing world and brought several competing ideologies—nationalism, democracy, religion, and socialism—into open confrontation. The Iranian Constitutional Revolution is remembered most for its establishment of a parliament and a democratic constitution in the country for the first time. Less known are the roles of various social democratic tendencies that were active in Iran in this period. These groups, which became politically important organizations in their own right, are of crucial importance in an understanding of the course and development of the revolution. Moreover, the social and cultural aspects of the revolution, in which the social democrats played an active part, were not marginal and insignificant but rather at the very heart of the revolution, helping to define both the scope and the limitations of the movement.

The Constitutional Revolution was made possible through an initial hybrid coalition of forces, which included liberal reformers, members of the ulama, merchants, shopkeepers, students, trade guildspeople, workers, and radical members of secret societies who promoted the formation of an assembly of delegates and a constitution. This coalition was first formed during the tobacco protests of 1891–92, partially overcoming a long history of hostility and animosity between the religious/secular reformers and the orthodox members of the ulama.

Greater interaction with the capitalist world economy, and resentment over the increasing domination of Iran by the European powers in the second half of the nineteenth century, was a major contributor to the creation of this alliance, as well as to the revolutionary upheavals that followed in Iran in the beginning of the twentieth century. From the 1880s onward, Iran's trade with Europe increased substantially in response to the improved transportation system, new telegraph lines to Europe, the introduction of steamboats in the Caspian Sea and the Persian Gulf, and especially the opening of the Suez Canal. The European demand for cotton, rice, fruit, silk, and opium had a significant impact on domestic agriculture, leading to a stress on cash crops at the expense of subsistence farming and manufactured products. Meanwhile, a variety of treaties signed with European countries, beginning with the 1813 Gulistan and 1828 Turkamanchay treaties with Russia, prohibited the establishment of protective measures that could have saved local industries in Iran. Ann Lambton, Charles Issawi, Nikki Keddie, and Willem Floor have argued that the transition from subsistence agriculture to the growing of cash crops, and the accompanying sale of *khalisah* crown lands to private landlords, a process that accelerated in the last decade of the nineteenth century, led to much material deterioration in the lives of the majority of the small merchants, artisans, and the peasants.[1] More recently, John Foran, following the Latin American dependency school, has argued that the process of development in Iran was a dependent development. It brought a degree of modernization to the country and even benefited some sectors of society in the short period, but in the long run, it was a type of development that served the interests of the foreign merchants rather than the native community and left the general population much worse off. Using Immanuel Wallerstein's world-system analysis, Foran argues that Iran, by the latter part of the nineteenth century, had moved from being a "non-European core" economy in the Safavid period to being part of the "periphery" of the world capitalist market.[2]

There were also important ideological components that cemented what Nikki Keddie has called the "religious-radical alliance" that ultimately brought forth the Constitutional Revolution.[3] The tendency in contemporary studies of this revolution has been to move away from some earlier interpretations that emphasized the leadership of the ulama and attributed their role to a strong sense of justice embedded in Shi'ite doctrines. Instead, new emphasis has been placed on the diversity of the coalition that made the revolution possible. Gad Gilbar has argued that it was the merchants, together with the members of the trade guilds, who initially supported the ulama and later held a *bast* (sit-in) at the British embassy. It was they who fought for and gained a constitution and a parliament along European lines.[4] Vanessa Martin emphasizes some of the economic factors that underlined the political alliances of the ulama in the revolutionary period. Shaikh Fazlullah Nuri, who soon sided with the opposition, handled the court's litigation, whereas Sayyid Abdullah Bihbahani and Sayyid Muhammad Tabataba'i had closer ties to the merchants and the guilds of Tehran.[5] Said Amir Arjomand has argued that the two ranking clerics, Bihbahani and Tabataba'i, hung back as the movement gradually came to call for a multiclass parliament and a secular constitution.[6] Three monographs published in the past two decades have shed new light on the organization of social democrats in Iran. Faridun Adamiyyat describes the involvement of social democrats with the Majlis (national assembly) and the peasant rebellions of the Caspian region and introduces the later writings of Muhammad Amin Rasulzadeh, an important theoretician of the Democrat

Party (1909–11). Mansureh Ittihadiyah Nizam Mafi uses private family archives to present new material on the role of political parties in this period. Nizam Mafi examines the contribution of the National Revolutionary Committee and the Democrat Party, whose leading members were social democrats. Mangol Bayat, using Russian sources, turns to the origins of the Iranian social democrats in the Russian Caucasus and describes their influence in the first constitutional period.[7]

Although some progressive members of the ulama joined the opposition because of their interest in liberalism and constitutionalism, many nonclerical groups joined for a variety of other reasons. First, the fiscal policies and foreign concessions of Nasir al-Din Shah (1848–96) and Muzaffar al-Din Shah (1896–1907) adversely affected the fortunes of the merchants, shopkeepers, and members of the trade guilds, as well as some of the ulama. This was especially true of the customs reforms of the years 1900–1905, enacted by the Belgian customs official Joseph Naus, which brought increased revenue to the royal court and favored the Russian merchants. Iranian merchants and their supporters, including some members of the ulama, now joined the nationalist alliance with the specific aim of ending foreign concessions.

Second, some of the orthodox members of the ulama who joined the movement in its very late stages, such as the conservative Shaikh Fazlullah Nuri, resented the popularity of modernist ideas and envisioned a "constitutional order" in which the rulings of the ulama and Shi'ite Islam were codified and elevated above those of both the government and the reformers. This conflict between *mashruteh* (constitutionalism) and *mashrua'eh* (rule according to the Shari'a) would arise soon after the formation of the parliament and the ratification of the constitution on December 30, 1906, and would haunt the revolutionary movement to the end.

Third, some members of the government, the landed elites, and some clerics, such as the supporters of former premier Amin al-Sultan, joined the coalition because they were motivated by the centuries-old politics of intrigue endemic among factions that were temporarily out of favor, and not out of reformist or revolutionary motives.

Fourth, and perhaps most important of all, the radical intellectuals and members of the secret societies encouraged the recruitment of both disgruntled orthodox members of the ulama and alienated politicians, seeing this as the only way to create a national coalition with broad mass appeal. This policy, as Nikki Keddie has argued, had been advocated since the 1890s by Malkum Khan and Jamal al-Din Afghani Asadabadi. Both Edward G. Browne, author of the classic *The Persian Revolution of 1905–1909,* and Keddie have pointed out that most of the "religious" reformers who became active supporters of the Constitutional Revolution and called for the creation of a broad national front with the conservative ulama and politicians were in fact freethinkers and in some cases Azali Babis. The latter was true of Malik al-Mutikallimin, the leading orator of the

Constitutional Revolution, and Mirza Jahangir Khan Shirazi, the founder of the radical satirical paper *Sur-i Israfil* (1907–8), both of whom were executed after the June 1908 coup against the parliament in Tehran.[8] In a more recent study, Mangol Bayat goes further and persuasively argues that there was a large network of religious dissidents, including many Azali Babi activists, who were involved throughout the revolutionary years. They pushed for the adoption of modern secular law and helped lead the calls for religious pluralism in the new order.[9]

But in order to understand the rapid radicalization of the movement in Iran after 1906, we have to take into account the bearers of yet another ideology, social democracy, and their political and social organizations. Social democratic societies began to have an important impact on the movement once the initial battle for a constitution and a parliament was won. Between 1906 and 1911, three major social democratic tendencies emerged in the country with the help of alliances with Azari and Armenian intellectuals.[10] These included (1) the Firqah-yi Ijtima'iyyun Amiyyun (Organization of Iranian Social Democrats), which maintained its headquarters in Baku, Russia, whereas many branches, known as the Anjumans of the Mujahidin, were formed inside Iran after August 1906; (2) the Tabriz Social Democrats, mainly Armenians, who aligned themselves with the revolutionaries in Tabriz and helped lead the resistance against the army of Muhammad 'Ali Shah in 1908–9; and (3) the Democrat Party, formed during the second constitutional period of 1909–11, which had a social democratic program. The Democrat Party maintained a minority representation in the second parliament and joined the government in a coalition with the Bakhtiari tribal leaders in the summer of 1910.

The fact that the contribution of social democrats and religious dissidents has been so little acknowledged has had important political ramifications as well. In the 1960s and 1970s, radical intellectuals, including Jalal al-Ahmad and 'Ali Shari'ati, reiterated the commonly accepted claim that the alliance of two classes, "merchants" and members of the "ulama," brought about the Constitutional Revolution. They seemed to suggest a similar scenario in the struggle to overthrow the government of Muhammad Reza Shah and claimed an inherently progressive role for members of the ulama and Islamic theology in general. It was certainly true that many of the constitutionalists had important religious credentials, with several *mujtahids* among them, and that there were also many merchants in leading roles in the revolution. Radical intellectuals of the 1960s and 1970s failed to note, however, that many of these same people were in fact religious dissidents or social democrats who did not always make their ideological affiliations public. While the role of ranking clerics such as Tabataba'i and Bihbahani, as well as the ulama of Najaf, was certainly important in the struggle against the two Qajar shahs, the progressive agenda of the revolution during the years 1907–11 was put forth mainly by the social democrats. A number of factors, including a response to the crisis of modernization, fueled the revolution of 1978–79. But the earlier revisionist historiography of the Constitutional Revolution that was articulated during the two decades before the revolution, an account that downplayed the secular and leftist elements of the revolution, took on concrete importance in 1978. It helped set the ideological context for the uncritical attitudes of liberals and radicals toward the ulama during the revolution of 1978, one that pushed Khumaini to the forefront of the revolutionary movement.

The Organization of Iranian Social Democrats and the *Anjumans* of the Mujahidin

After more than a year of strikes and sit-ins, which culminated in the July 1906 *bast* at the British embassy in Tehran, Muzaffar al-Din Shah agreed to sign the royal proclamation of August 5, 1906, in which he granted the right to a constitution and parliament known as the Majlis. The Electoral Laws of September 9, 1906, gave limited representation to members of the Qajar tribe, the ulama and theological students, the urban notables, landowners and smallholders, merchants, and representatives of the trade guilds. Despite property limitations on both the voting and election of merchants, smallholders, and members of trade guilds, the inclusion of guild members in the parliament was a major achievement at the time. It was a result of the active participation of the guilds of Tehran in the *bast* at the British embassy. Half of the sixty-four delegates from Tehran were members of the guilds, and, together with the delegates from Azarbaijan, they became some of the most consistent supporters of the new order during the first constitutional period of 1906–8. A secular constitution, modeled after those of France and Belgium, was ratified on December 30, 1906, just before the king died and a hostile Muhammad ʿAli Shah took over the throne.

Meanwhile, a new and direct expression of democracy continued to grow in the streets—the grassroots *anjumans* (councils) that sprang up throughout the country after the August 1906 strikes. In the immediate prerevolutionary period of 1905 a few secret *anjumans* had been formed whose radical members called for the creation of an assembly and advocated alliances with disgruntled politicians and influential members of the ulama.[11] In contrast, the revolutionary *anjumans,* formed after August 1906, were open, active, and mass organizations that became organs of direct democracy. The Electoral Laws of September 1906 called for the formation of *anjumans* in local towns, as councils that would supervise the elections. But the *anjumans,* beginning with the Tabriz Anjuman, chose to remain in session after the elections, and soon became alternative organs of direct grassroots political participation, despite the protests of Crown Prince Muhammad ʿAli Mirza and other anticonstitutionalists.

One of the few achievements of the October 7, 1907, supplements to the constitution was to legalize these provincial *anjumans.* The provincial and departmental *anjumans* (in smaller provinces) supervised tax collection and monitored the activities of the local governors. Hundreds of popular *anjumans* were also formed throughout the country in the late fall of 1906. The provincial and departmental *anjumans* maintained dual power with the parliament and the government, with the Tabriz Anjuman becoming the strongest and most vocal of such councils. The popular *anjumans* represented various social, political, trade, and class interests. Members of these *anjumans* — in which intellectuals, craftsmen, merchants, workers, and low-level clerics played prominent roles — began to both support and challenge the parliament on many fronts. The Tabriz Anjuman almost immediately confronted the major political institutions in the country, including the royal court, and established itself as an alternative government. Tabriz established the first independent newspaper, the *Anjuman,* reduced bread prices, fixed prices of other basic commodities, and began a secular system of education.[12]

The more liberal and left-wing councils, including the Tabriz Anjuman, had been influenced by the ideas of social democracy from the Russian Caucasus. Social democratic societies, many known as the Anjumans of the Mujahidin, were formed throughout the country. Members of these *anjumans* were mostly workers, craftsmen, and young activists from merchant families. The headquarters of the Anjumans of the Mujahidin (literally meaning "warriors of the jihad, or holy war") was the Organization of Iranian Social Democrats in Baku, which was composed primarily of Iranian immigrant workers and merchants. During the first years of the twentieth century there were several hundred thousand Iranian workers who, because of vast unemployment in Iran and greater economic opportunities in southern Russia, spent years there, often working in the Baku oil fields and their related industries.[13] Many of these workers were radicalized by the experience of the 1905 Russian revolution and the activities of the Azari social democratic organization Himmat, which was formed in 1904. The Organization of Iranian Social Democrats, which was founded in 1905, kept close ties with both the Himmat Party and the Baku and Tiflis committees of the Russian Social Democratic Workers Party (RSDWP). After the August 1906 revolution in Iran, the Organization of Iranian Social Democrats formed revolutionary cells of the Mujahidin inside Iran by sending some of its members to Iran. The Anjumans of the Mujahidin were especially active in the northern areas of Iran, such as Azarbaijan, the Caspian region, Tehran, and Mashhad. They involved themselves in the political affairs of the country, tilting the movement further to the left.

The Mujahidin, whose center in Tabriz was known as the Secret Center (Markaz-i Ghaybi), were in close collaboration with the Tabriz Anjuman. Among the more daring actions of the Tabriz Anjuman was the exile of two conservative clerics, the Imam Jum'ah (Leader of the Friday Prayer) and Haj Mirza Hasan Mujtahid, a leading local cleric and owner of several villages. In the spring of

1907, when peasants from a village near Tabriz known as Qarachaman (Black Grass) entered a dispute with the village owner, Haj Mirza Hasan Mujtahid sided with the landowner and sanctioned the governor's order to send two hundred armed men to the village to put down the rebellion. When the peasants took their grievances to the Tabriz Anjuman, some members of the *anjuman,* such as the radical low-ranking cleric Shaikh Salim, sided with the peasants. Haj Mirza Hasan Mujtahid and the conservative local landowners decided to force the radical members of the Tabriz Anjuman to leave town. But the radical Mujahidin turned the tables. With the support of 3,000 members of the Mujahidin, the conservative *mujtahid* and his supporters in the Tabriz Anjuman were expelled from town. The Tabriz Anjuman was reorganized, with the position of the left-wing members becoming more secure, and the Mujahidin developing a much closer relation to the Tabriz Anjuman. The Majlis in Tehran was outraged by the actions of the Tabriz Anjuman, and the ulama in Tabriz began to boycott the meetings of the Tabriz Anjuman. Both, however, found that the Tabriz Anjuman ignored repeated calls for the return of the exiled clerics.[14]

In Tehran, as in Tabriz, the Mujahidin were active in confrontations with the conservative ulama who opposed the secular constitution and the progressive measures that the Majlis adopted. The anticonstitutionalist Shaikh Fazlullah Nuri opposed the free press of the constitutional era, including journals such as *Sur-i Israfil* (1907–8), which advocated fundamental social and cultural changes in society. Dihkhuda, the radical satirical poet and editor of *Sur-i Israfil,* mocked religious superstitions, belief in predestination, and patriarchal traditions that degraded women and children. This important cultural movement, initiated by the newspapers of this period, was intensified by the participation of a number of urban women. Some activist women formed their own *anjumans* and schools, and called upon the Majlis to recognize and support these institutions.[15]

The Tabriz Anjuman and the Mujahidin would play an important role when new supplements to the constitution were proposed. The supplements, which were originally formulated by the Tabriz Anjuman and the prominent left-wing delegate from Azarbaijan, Sayyid Hasan Taqizadeh, were essentially a bill of rights, guaranteeing freedom of the press and of organization, and calling for equal treatment of all citizens regardless of religious affiliation. They were meant to solidify the gains that were made during the course of the revolution. But the conservative opposition, headed by Shaikh Fazlullah Nuri and backed by Muhammad 'Ali Shah, had a different set of supplements in mind. Shaikh Fazlullah proposed a Council of Ulama with veto power over the deliberations of the Majlis, and demanded that this council be given the authority to determine the compatibility of any law submitted to the Majlis with the laws of the Shari'a. The Tabriz Anjuman and the Mujahidin were infuriated by this idea of a Council of Ulama proposed as Article 2 of the supplements to the constitution. A stream of angry letters from Tabriz attacked the conservative ulama and criticized the delegates in the Majlis for not confronting Shaikh Fazlullah Nuri and his followers more vigorously. In late May 1907, one telegram to the Majlis read:

> We want a constitution that would determine the limits of a constitutional monarchy and the rights of people. Otherwise, the Shari'a of Muhammad is protected and in place and everyone knows their religious duties. We loudly proclaim that unless you sign and give to the nation the constitution which was written by the learned representatives and others and has been completed, we will lose patience, and will say what should not be said.[16]

A general strike continued in Tabriz in May and June 1907 and spread throughout the province of Azarbaijan, including many small towns and villages. The strike was embraced by tribal groups and minorities, including the Armenians, who were strong supporters of the Tabriz Anjuman. Despite these protests, the Majlis gave in to the pressures by Shaikh Fazlullah Nuri and the royal court and ratified Article 2. Residents of Tabriz were outraged. Rumors began to spread that Tabriz might take independent action and create a republic of its own.[17]

The Mujahidin and the Tabriz Anjuman continued to call for major social and economic reforms and began to oppose the conservative chief minister, Amin al-Sultan. On August 31, 1907, the Anglo-Russian Agreement was signed, in which Iran was effectively partitioned into spheres of influence by the two powers. On the same day, Amin al-Sultan was shot as he left the parliament. The two events were not directly connected, even though Amin al-Sultan had been the architect of two unpopular Russian loans in 1900 and 1902, much of which had been wasted on Muzaffar al-Din Shah's extravagant trips to Europe, and in August 1907 Amin al-Sultan had been very close to gaining a majority in the Majlis to ratify the proposal for yet another unpopular Russian loan.[18] The assassination of Amin al-Sultan was carried out by a young merchant known as 'Abbas Aqa, a member of the Mujahidin, who belonged to the small secret circle of Fada'is ("devotees" within the organization, or those willing to sacrifice themselves for the cause). The Mujahidin had opposed the new chief minister ever since he set foot in Iran in the spring of 1907. They had criticized the Majlis delegates for supporting Amin al-Sultan, and called for new elections to that assembly.[19] The assassination of Amin al-Sultan strengthened the radical and liberal factions in the Majlis and dried up a major source of support for Shaikh Fazlullah Nuri and other opponents of the Majlis.

The formation of *anjumans* in small towns and villages had been opposed by the Majlis, and specific directives were issued calling for the closing of these *anjumans*. At the same time, in northern provinces of the Caspian region and Azarbaijan, rent strikes continued among villagers, and a variety of peasants' and craftsmen's *anjumans* were formed. In the spring of 1907, cocoon growers of the city of Rasht, the center of Iran's silk trade, organized a rent strike and expelled both landlords and overseers from their villages. In the year that followed, a series of peasants' and craftsmen's *anjumans* known as the 'Abbasi Anjumans were established, with fourteen branches in the provinces of Gilan. In Tavalash, by the Caspian Sea, villagers gained autonomous control of the area for several years. They expelled the governor and local landowner, and in the summer of 1908 successfully resisted a military expedition financed by Sardar Afkham, the Gilan governor, and Muhammad 'Ali Shah.[20]

As a result, ministers complained to the Majlis in 1907 that they no longer had control over their land, as villagers had taken over and expelled their overseers or joined the organizations of the Mujahidin, calling themselves Fada'is.[21] Meanwhile, the Majlis came under increasing pressure from radical intellectuals, members of the Mujahidin, and some peasants to abolish the *tuyul* land allotment.[22] Many people believed that the solution to both the problem of peasant poverty and the budget deficit was extensive land reform. But the tax and land reforms the parliament adopted in the early spring of 1907 were aimed at balancing the deficit-ridden budget and improving the treasury rather than ameliorating the situation of the peasants. No provisions for distribution or sale of land to the peasants or steps to lessen government taxes were taken by the First Majlis.

The grievances of peasants and workers *were* addressed by the Anjumans of the Mujahidin in a program they adopted in the fall of 1907. By this time, according to British intelligence accounts reported in the Persian daily *Habl al-Matin*, the number of Mujahidin had grown to more than 86,000, and secret networks of the Anjumans of the Mujahidin had been formed in Tehran, Tabriz, Ardabil, Khuy, Mashhad, Isfahan, Qazvin, Rasht, Anzali, and other cities.[23]

The first party congress of the Mujahidin was held in early September 1907 in the northern city of Mashhad in the province of Khurasan. What social democracy, or *Ijtima'iyyun 'Amiyyun,* meant as an ideology to the organization of the Mujahidin can perhaps best be seen through the proceedings of this congress. Whereas the program of the Mujahidin called for active support of liberalism and constitutionalism in Iran, it also enumerated a number of socialist principles that addressed workers' and peasants' rights. The Mujahidin's declared support for the Majlis and the constitution was based on the condition that the elected deputies uphold justice and "introduce equalities." They also recognized themselves as an indispensable part of the constitutional regime. The preservation of constitutionalism in Iran, the program declared, depended on an active populace, one that joined the Anjumans of the Mujahidin, through which the events in the Majlis were closely monitored. The Mujahidin shared a commitment to social revolution with their mentors, the Russian Social Democrats, but at the same time they were equally committed to selective acts of political terror.

The program of the Mujahidin drew justification for political activism from Qur'anic precepts and declared the very aims of the Anjumans of the Mujahidin as sacred. The degree of religiosity among the Mujahidin varied, however, with those who came from the Caucasus generally known to be less religious than those recruited inside Iran.

In calling for universal (male) suffrage "without regard for position, nationality, poverty, or wealth," the Mujahidin challenged the limited franchise of the Majlis. The most radical articles of the program were a six-point bill of rights, provisions for land distribution, and a call for limitations on the working day. Individual freedom and freedom of speech, publication, and association, as well as the right to strike, were explicitly defined. The right to strike, it was emphasized, belonged to workers regardless of the issues involved, be they "private, general, or political." The Mujahidin also demanded an eight-hour day, a first in Iran's history. Finally, provisions for land distribution were discussed. Crown lands and villages belonging to the royal family were to be expropriated without compensation, and those belonging to private landowners (exceeding the land needed for the maintenance of the owners) were to be bought through a national bank and distributed among the peasants and agricultural workers.[24]

In February 1908, the Organization of Iranian Social Democrats and the Mujahidin were implicated in an assassination attempt against the shah. On December 15, 1907, Muhammad 'Ali Shah and Shaikh Fazlullah had tried to carry out a coup against the Majlis. A large number of anticonstitutionalists, including both clerics and low-level employees of the court, had surrounded the Majlis, but the attempted coup quickly failed as members of the *anjumans* came out to support the Majlis. A thousand members of the Mujahidin in Tabriz stated that they were ready to come to Tehran. The Tabriz Anjuman arrested Iqbal Lashgar, the ranking military officer in Azarbaijan. Other Azarbaijani officers and soldiers in the service of the shah were warned that if they fought against the Majlis, the province of Azarbaijan would declare its independence and the Mujahidin would take their revenge upon the relatives of the Azari military men in Tehran.[25]

The coup in Tehran failed, in part as a result of the activities of the Tabriz Anjuman and the Mujahidin. Then, on February 28, 1908, Muhammad 'Ali Shah was nearly assassinated as he left his palace for the first time in months. The *anjuman* of Azarbaijan in Tehran was once again accused. Haydar Khan Amu Ughlu, an active member of the Organization of Iranian Social Democrats, was briefly arrested but soon released because of popular pressure.[26]

The Tabriz Social Democrats

The high point of the activity of the Mujahidin came during the civil war in Tabriz. When the parliament in Tehran was closed by a coup in June 1908, it was the city of Tabriz that led the resistance. The story of the ten-month siege of Tabriz, which ended with Russian military intervention on April 29, 1909, is one of the most moving chapters in twentieth-century Iranian history. Despite the ongoing war, the Tabriz Anjuman, which had replaced the Majlis as the center of constitutionalism in Iran, gained both national and international recognition for keeping the revolutionary spirit alive. This was made possible through the support of the Mujahidin, who continued to resist at a time when many leading constitutionalist figures had either left the country or gone into hiding. Sattar Khan, an illiterate horse dealer in his forties who had been recruited as a rank-and-file member of the Mujahidin with the responsibility of protecting the Tabriz Anjuman, emerged as the uncontested revolutionary leader of this period, fighting against both the Azarbaijani anticonstitutionalist clerics and the army of the central government.

Prominent members of the European Social Democrats such as Karl Kautsky, George Plekhanov, and V. I. Lenin, were asked by Iranian intellectuals in exile to support the struggling movement in Iran. Because of the role of the Russian Cossack Brigade in carrying out the June 1908 coup, the RSDWP considered the defense of the resistance movement inside Iran to be part of its struggle against the tsarist government.

The most crucial and direct support, however, came from revolutionaries from the Russian Caucasus, among them more than five hundred Armenians, Georgians, and Azari socialists. Together with the aid of volunteers known as Caucasian revolutionaries, many of whom were in fact Iranian immigrants returning home, the Tabriz activists organized an army of workers, artisans, peasants, theological students, and some tribesmen, as well as women fighters. These forces were also known as the Mujahidin, as the term had come to encompass all revolutionaries who fought on the side of the constitutional cause. Once the resistance movement in Tabriz gained the upper hand, democracy returned to the streets, the Tabriz Anjuman was reorganized, schools were reopened, hospitals were organized, and public bakeries were established for the poor.

The leadership of the resistance in Tabriz was held by a committee composed of Sattar Khan, his colleague the stone mason Baqir Khan, other members of the Tabriz Anjuman, and radical social democrats and Armenian Dashnaks who had joined the Tabriz constitutionalists both from within Iran and from the Russian Caucasus. The Tiflis and the Baku branches of the RSDWP sent volunteer fighters to Tabriz, including Azari, Georgian, and Armenian revolutionaries. The Georgians set up a laboratory for explosives, which gave the revolutionary side a decisive technological advantage in the war.[27] Armenian members of both the Dashnak Party and the Hnchack Social Democratic Party were also active in the resistance movement in Azarbaijan and Gilan. Two members of the Dashnak Party—Stepan Zoranian, known as Rustam, and Yephrem Khan—would play important parts in the leadership of the movement. The revolutionaries in Gilan would later move toward Tehran under the leadership of Yephrem Khan and reinstitute the constitutional government.[28]

In 1909, the Russian social democrat and Bolshevik G. K. Orjonikidze, an active supporter of the Himmat and the Organization of Iranian Social Democrats, came to Rasht as head of a detachment of Caucasian Bolsheviks and secretly helped organize a political club that distributed Marxist literature.[29] In addition, Mikhail Pavlovitch, the influential Russian social democrat who lived in Paris at the time, was in close contact with the Iranian émigré society. As one of the best-informed European socialists in matters related to Iran, Pavlovitch often contributed articles on the Iranian situation to journals he collaborated with, among them *Social Demokrat, Golos Social Demokrata, Neue Zeit,* and *Revue du Monde Musulman.*[30]

The tsarist government was outraged by the support that the resistance movement in Iran received from Russian and Caucasian revolutionaries. *Novoye Vremya,* organ of the deeply conservative Russian Black Hundred, openly called upon the tsarist government to intervene militarily in Azarbaijan:

> Whether Russia can endlessly tolerate these outrages, which are ruining our lucrative trade on the Persian frontier ... it should be borne in mind that all Eastern Transcaucasia and Aderbaijan [Azarbaijan] are an ethnological whole.... Tatar semi-intellectuals in Transcaucasia, forgetting that they are Russian subjects, have displayed warm sympathy for the disturbances in Tabriz and are sending volunteers to that city.
> ... *What is much more important for us* is that Aderbaijan, which borders on Russia, should be pacified. Deplorable though it may be, circumstances might compel Russia, despite her strong desire not to interfere, to take this task upon herself.[31]

The social democrats of Tabriz soon formed their own political organization and began to debate the future course of development of Iran according to social democratic principles.

Ever since 1905, a group of Armenian social democrats had existed in Tabriz. During the civil war their ranks were bolstered by some of the Caucasian social democrats who had joined the resistance and who now also participated in the political activities and debates of this group. In mid-July 1908 Arshavir Chalangarian, an Iranian-Armenian member of the group, wrote a letter to Kautsky, informing him of an impending conference that was to take up the organization's political and theoretical perspectives on the revolutionary movement in Iran. Chalangarian wrote that there were two political tendencies in the group and asked Kautsky to take a position on the analyses presented by the two wings.[32] Everyone seemed to have agreed, he wrote, that the process of capitalist development was a necessary prerequisite of the creation of a class of industrial workers and, eventually, a socialist revolution in Iran. However, members of the group differed in their assessment of the Constitutional Revolution as a means of achieving this end. The main question thus became the following: Should the young Iranian social democrats be active in the democratic movement, or should they also agitate for social democracy in the midst of the Constitutional Revolution?

Kautsky replied that the Iranian social democrats must participate actively in the democratic movement *alongside* bourgeois and petty bourgeois democrats, even though the ultimate aim of the struggle for the socialists was a class struggle. The Iranian Marxists were asked to wait for the "triumph of democracy," when new avenues would open to them, including "new struggles that were virtually impossible to wage under the previous despotic rule." Kautsky referred to Marx's participation in the 1848 revolution alongside the democratic movement, as an example of a situation in which there was "no chance of establishing a strong proletarian party in Germany."[33]

Moreover, although acknowledging the great hardship for the masses of the peasants in Iran who were taxed heavily and were thus "unable to buy industrial goods," Kautsky extended his own questionable views of the European peasantry, which were challenged by several leading social democrats of the time, such as Rosa Luxemburg, to the mostly tenant Iranian peasantry.[34] He thus wrote off the "small peasants," putting them alongside the "petty bourgeoisie" as elements that brought "reactionary tendencies" to the democratic movement, and insisted that the peasants needed to be confronted by the social democrats.

Kautsky's letter to the Tabriz Social Democrats resulted in certain modifications to their program, for example, the dropping of a reference to the progressive nature of foreign investments. However, in a subsequent conference the left wing of the Tabriz group challenged Kautsky's notion of stages of the revolutionary movement in Iran and his emphasis on first bringing forth the "triumph of democracy" before they would begin to struggle openly as social democrats.

On October 16, 1908, after the initial victory of the Tabriz Mujahidin over the royalist army of 'Ain al-Daula, the conference of the Tabriz Social Democrats, with thirty participants, took place. The secretary of the meeting was Vasu Khachaturian, an Armenian from the Russian Caucasus, who on August 28, 1908, had brought a group of social democrats from the Baku branch of the RSDWP with him to Tabriz. Khachaturian was also active with the Azarbaijani workers and was instrumental in establishing the fledgling trade union movement in Tabriz.

The two different political tendencies in the conference presented their proposals at this meeting. A majority view, which was to the left of Kautsky's proposal, was presented by Arshavir Chalangarian and Vasu Khachaturian and was ratified by twenty-eight votes. The minority view, presented by Sedrak and Pilusian, received only two votes. It is almost certain that this Pilusian was Vram Pilusian, who later became a close colleague of Sayyid Hasan Taqizadeh, the prominent left-wing delegate of the Majlis and leader of the influential Democrat Party during the second constitutional period. Pilusian, who would also play an active part in the organization of the Democrat Party, corresponded with Taqizadeh over the organizational details of the party in early 1909.[35]

The majority proposal argued that Iran had entered the stage of manufacturing and industrial production, as seen in the introduction of the steam engine, tobacco companies, cotton cleaning plants, and other innovations. The nation had thus developed a small class of industrial workers alongside its larger class of small artisans. Therefore, the foundation for socialist agitation already existed in the nation. If social democrats abandoned the industrial workers, there was a possibility that the workers would become a weapon in the hands of the bourgeoisie for its domination. On the other hand, the examples of the European revolutions of 1789, 1830, and 1848, as well as that of Iran, had demonstrated that the most revolutionary sectors of society were the propertyless elements. Therefore, the role of social democrats, in addition to their general struggle in the Constitutional Revolution, was "to fight for the social and economic progress of the revolutionary masses and the propertyless masses," all the more so because the very low wage levels of Iranian workers prevented the introduction of full-scale industrial development in the nation. The responsibility of social democrats was to mobilize the small strata of industrial workers and "to give them class consciousness for the socialist struggle." Socialists could not proceed as bourgeois democrats, because they had a different worldview, and their concept of democracy differed from the "mere democracy" of the bourgeoisie; moreover, "a socialist who maintained his class analysis of the [role of the] proletariat could succeed much further in the bourgeois revolution." The Tabriz Social Democrats voted to organize a "permanent social democratic group" to agitate among workers and intellectuals for a class struggle in Iran.[36]

According to the minority proposal, Iran had only recently entered the capitalist stage. There were no modern industrial workers and thus no foundation for social democratic work. Even if there were such industrial workers, the objective and subjective conditions were not yet ripe for such organizing. Under such circumstances, agitation among workers for socialism was not only useless, but would deprive the democratic movement of its most radical elements and throw them into the arms of "reaction" by creating disunity in the democratic struggle. The success of the bourgeois revolution was essential, and it was the responsibility of social democrats to "abandon momentarily purely social democratic work," to enter the democratic movement to "cleanse it of reactionary tendencies," to cooperate in its ranks, and to struggle as the most radical elements within it. These activists foresaw the emergence of a class struggle only after the successful democratic revolution was won. This, they argued, did not mean that individuals would abandon their social democratic ideology, "their conception of the world and its principles," because the position adopted by the group was "a matter of politics and wise tactics and not a matter of principles."[37]

Vasu Khachaturian and Arshavir Chalangarian, on behalf of the majority, and Tigran Darvish, an Iranian-Armenian representative of the minority from Geneva, each sent copies of the minutes of the meeting to Plekhanov and asked for his opinion. Khachaturian asked Plekhanov to share his letter with both the Bolshevik and Menshevik wings of the RSDWP, and Chalangarian asked that Azaris from the Baku branch of the RSDWP join them in their task of spreading the ideas of social democracy among the population in Tabriz.

Of particular interest are the letters by Chalangarian and Khachaturian, who expressed their disagreements with the course of action prescribed by Kautsky.[38] They informed Plekhanov of the close relationship of the group with the residents and workers of Tabriz, pointing to a rally of the social democrats in early December 1908 that had drawn a crowd of 10,000, including Sattar Khan himself, and noted that social democrats were consulted on all matters by the Tabriz Anjuman and leaders of the Mujahidin.

Khachaturian argued that some Azarbaijani workers had shown interest in both the political and economic aspects of social democracy. The Tabriz Social Democrats, who until then had pursued mostly political objectives, now also turned their attention to economic and trade union activities, and Khachaturian argued that the formation of a workers' trade union would facilitate the creation of political organizations among the workers: A powerful trade union movement could confront a hostile but largely unorganized "bourgeoisie," thus helping to maintain the achievements of the revolutionary period.

Khachaturian challenged Kautsky's suggestions that if "the economic situation of the country has not yet created a modern industrial proletariat, the socialists must unite themselves with the democratic movement in the revolutionary struggle." The breakup of the old system and its replacement with capitalism had already begun in the country, he wrote, and "the process of proletarianization of workers proceeds with great speed among the artisans." It was true that Iran's economy had not yet created a class of modern industrial workers in the European sense, but there were many other laborers in Iran "who do not own their means of production and sell their labor power or knowledge to the owners." What then were the social democrats to do? Should they *not* agitate among the workers, *not* organize them, *not* struggle for higher wages, and, if so, how would they then force the capitalists and managers to adopt a more modern system of production? The exceedingly low wages of Iranian workers meant that even in the face of world competition, capitalists felt no need to import modern machinery. The fight for higher wages, Khachaturian argued, meant the introduction of a more sophisticated stage of capitalism in Iran, which in turn brought about a more advanced industrial worker. And yet disagreements over this issue among Tabriz Social Democrats had resulted in several members leaving the majority and establishing their own tendency.[39]

Given the very small number of industrial workers in Iran in this period, it is surprising that the relationship of the Tabriz Social Democrats to the large peasant population and the continuing peasant protests in the north were not addressed in the congress. Perhaps this was because of Kautsky's letter, which had discouraged any discussion of the peasantry and alliances with them, calling them "petit-bourgeois" elements that had to be confronted. Both wings of the tendency were well aware of continuing peasant protests in Azarbaijan and Gilan. Tigran Darvish, who sided with the minority "Democrat" wing of the group, in his February 1909 article "Die Persische Revolution," published in the authoritative German socialist journal *Neue Zeit,* traced landlord-peasant relations in prerevolutionary Iran and pointed out that vast peasant movements were continuing in the country: "In the recent period, general principles of freedom, equal rights, and land questions have become issues of primary concern. Villagers, especially in Azarbaijan, the province where Tabriz is located, rise up every day and begin peasant revolts."[40] Arshavir Chalangarian, who represented the majority left wing of the Tabriz Social Democrats, wrote in *Neue Zeit* in May 1909: "In Iran we do not see a land crisis as powerful as that of Russia. However, will the peasants who have refused to pay taxes and have appropriated the land and property of big landowners be content with political reforms alone? The near future will teach us the answer to this question."[41]

In contrast to the Mujahidin, who had shown great interest in issues related to the peasantry, the question of the relation of the Tabriz Social Democrats to the peasant revolts was prematurely abandoned by these young intellectuals. The issue of organizing workers and peasants was taken up briefly in 1911, especially by Tigran Darvish, who had earlier been a member of the minority "Democrat" wing of the group. Once Darvish arrived in Tehran and joined the editorial board of the organ of the Democrat Party, *Iran-i Nau,* however, he quickly began to criticize the inaction of the majority of the Democrat members and helped create workers trade unions in Tehran. As we shall see, these efforts were minimal and in no significant way altered the course of action of the Democrat Party, which had been quickly dragged into the quagmire of party politics and maneuvers for coalition building with the Bakhtiari tribal leaders, leaving behind its social and economic reform programs.

The Democrat Party

In July 1909, the Mujahidin fighters of Gilan, whose ranks were bolstered by Caucasian revolutionaries, together with Bakhtiari tribesmen from the south, marched toward the capital and reestablished the constitutional government. Muhammad 'Ali Shah was expelled from the country and replaced by his twelve-year-old son Ahmad, and the Second Majlis was formed. The prominent left-wing delegate from Azarbaijan, Sayyid Hasan Taqizadeh, then helped form the influential Democrat Party, a coalition of liberals and social democrats, which gained a minority representation of between twenty and thirty delegates in the Second Majlis, out of 111 delegates. The Democrats opened branches of the party in the provinces and gained many recruits among the youth. Several members of the Organization of Iranian Social Democrats in Baku joined the Democrat Party, among them the Azari intellectual Rasulzadeh, who, soon after his arrival from the Russian Caucasus, became editor of *Iran-i Nau,* later the organ of the party. Haydar Khan Amu Ughlu now headed the executive section of the party. He gathered a number of the radical Mujahidin under his command, and was in charge of carrying out acts of political terror.[42] The Democrats were not affiliated with the Organization of Iranian Social Democrats in Baku; rather, there was close collaboration between leaders of the Democrat Party, especially Taqizadeh, with the minority wing of the Tabriz Social Democrats, Armenian intellectuals such as Vram Pilusian, and Tigran Darvish.[43] Throughout their existence, the Democrats kept their ties to the Armenian social democrats secret. Together they proposed a new program of reform for the country that emphasized economic growth and secularization of politics.

To some extent the differences between the two wings of the Tabriz Social Democrats represented the divisions that had emerged within the radical wing of the constitutional movement as a whole. It included the social democratic leadership, which now aligned itself with the liberal as well as influential politicians in the establishment, and the rank-and-file Mujahidin and the grassroots *anjumans,* who had made victory possible but now grew more estranged from the leadership.

The Democrats saw their task as one of accelerating the development of Iran from an "outmoded feudalist order" to a new and more advanced capitalist one. The party program reflected the desire for a capitalist state and called for a number of social reform programs for the workers and craftsmen, as well as peasants. Economic development and social reform were vehicles that paved the way for the emergence of a socialist order in the distant future. The new economic order in Iran was to be based on the three principles of "centralism, parliamentarianism, and democracy."[44] The country needed a strong central government that would end the regional control of the powerful khans and tribal leaders and that would initiate a program of industrialization, enabling Iran to challenge foreign economic penetration.

In adopting some provisions from the earlier 1907 program of the Mujahidin, the Democrats included a broad range of civil rights in their program, such as freedom of expression, publication, and association; equality before the law for all Iranians, regardless of race, ethnicity, or religion; and the right to strike. Free compulsory education for all, including women, was also stipulated. In a challenge to the 1907 supplements to the constitution that had given extraordinary powers to a Council of Ulama, Article 5 of the Democrats' program called for the separation of politics from religion. This strong emphasis on secularization of politics, which was a break with the old program of the Mujahidin, resulted in many innuendos against the Democrats, who were labeled "atheists" and "non-Muslims" by the opposition.

The program of the Democrat Party called for nationalization of rivers, forests, and pastures, and supported direct rather than indirect taxation. It required a minimum age of fourteen for workers and called for the abolition of forced labor. It also proposed to limit the working day to ten hours and the working week to six days, and suggested the installation of safe machinery and equipment in workshops and factories. Finally, a good portion of the program, seven articles, was devoted to the regulation of relations between landlords and peasants, attesting to the strong belief of the party that "feudal" relations of production had to give way to new capitalist ones.

But the program of the Democrat Party remained largely on paper. Even when it seemed they could have, the Democrats never pushed for its implementation. This was the case during the summer and fall of 1910, when the Democrats joined the Bakhtiari tribal leaders in a coalition government. During this period, a number of factors increased the public's sense of resentment and alienation toward the Second Majlis and the Democrats. A much-despised salt tax, which benefited no one but the tax collectors, became a key factor adding fuel to this sense of indignation.

Sattar Khan, Baqir Khan, and the Mujahidin in their service, as well as many of the Mujahidin from Gilan who had helped reinstitute the constitutional order in Tehran, were shunned by the Democrats and their Bakhtiari allies. Disillusioned by the Democrats and the Bakhtiaris, Sattar Khan and some of the Mujahidin were now courted by the conservative Moderate Party. Together with the help of Sayyid Abdullah Bihbahani and the Najaf ulama, this group accused Taqizadeh of conduct that was "in conflict with the Muslim characteristics of the nation and the holy Shari'a laws," and barred him from the Majlis on July 2, 1910.[45]

Two weeks later, on July 15, 1910, Sayyid Abdullah Bihbahani was assassinated by several members of the Mujahidin who were under the command of Haydar Khan Amu Ughlu, member of the Democrat Party. Bihbahani had been an early supporter of the constitutional revolution—some have suggested more because of factional and personal conflicts with the government of 'Ain al-Daula than because of any strong commitment to the constitutional cause. His death resulted in much public anger. On August 1, the Moderates retaliated against the Democrats and assassinated two close associates of the Democrat Party, including 'Ali Muhammad Tarbiyat, Taqizadeh's nephew, who had been designated head of the Mujahidin in Tehran.[46] At the same time, the Democrats were implicated in the assassination of Bihbahani, and Taqizadeh was forced to leave for Istanbul on August 9, 1910.[47]

On August 7, 1910, encouraged by the Russian and British governments, the Bakhtiari-Democrat cabinet retaliated and forcibly disarmed those members of the Mujahidin who had held sanctuary under the command of Sattar Khan. Among the military officers on the government side were the Dashnak Armenian leader Yephrem Khan, who was now chief of police of Tehran, and the social democrat

Haydar Khan Amu Ughlu.[48] The public became disillusioned and resentful as it watched the former revolutionary leaders killing one another. Meanwhile, neither the Democrats and the Bakhtiaris nor the more conservative Moderates who had now aligned themselves with the former revolutionary leaders of Tabriz and Gilan proposed any steps to improve the deteriorating economic and political situation. After several years of close collaboration between the Muslims and the Armenians in the constitutional movement, new anti-Armenian hostilities broke out as chief of police Yephrem Khan was criticized, especially as the shooting had left Sattar Khan, the popular hero of the Tabriz resistance, disabled.[49]

The showdown between the Mujahidin of Sattar Khan and supporters of the Democrat Party in 1910 signaled the beginning of the end of the constitutional movement, which was now bereft of much of its mass support. This facilitated the political maneuvers of both the Russian and British governments, which ever since the 1907 Anglo-Russian Agreement had tried to curb the powers of the Majlis. With the appointment of the new regent, Nasir al-Mulk, and the subsequent ascendency of the conservatives in the Majlis in the winter of 1911, several leading Azari social democrats were expelled from the country. The British ultimatum, demanding the institution of its military forces in the south of Iran, and the Russo-German Potsdam meeting in the fall of 1910 increased the involvement of the two powers in Iran. The arrival of the American financial adviser Morgan Shuster in May 1911 briefly helped to revive the Democrat Party, but the Tsarist government, which resented the financial reforms and appointments instituted by Shuster, gave an ultimatum to the Majlis calling for Shuster's expulsion. This was done with the support of the British government. The Russian government followed this ultimatum by moving its military forces further into Azarbaijan and Gilan. Russian forces waited in Qazvin, just outside Tehran, as the cabinet continued to pressure the Majlis into accepting the ultimatum. However, until the very end nearly all the Democrats refused to accept the ultimatum, whereby Iran would become a de facto colony of the two powers and the Majlis would surrender its independence. Finally, Regent Nasir al-Mulk and the cabinet closed down the Majlis on December 24, 1911, bringing the constitutional era to an end.

Conclusion

The Iranian Constitutional Revolution of 1906–11 brought forth a new type of grassroots democracy not only among the middle-class male city dwellers, but also among craftsmen, workers, and peasants, as well as some urban women's circles. New ideas of social democracy came to influence many of these *anjumans,* as well as the courses of action of new political institutions, such as the Majlis. With the help of Armenian and Azari radicals, three social democratic tendencies were formed in Iran during the years 1906–11. The Organization of Iranian

Social Democrats in Baku opened branches of that organization in Iran known as the Anjumans of the Mujahidin after the 1906 royal proclamation. The Mujahidin's support was critical both to the newly formed parliament and to the provincial, departmental, and popular councils, especially the ones that were formed in the northern regions. The Mujahidin called for a program of land distribution and pressured the First Majlis into addressing the issue. In the early spring of 1907 the Majlis carried out a series of land reforms, including the abolition of *tuyul* land allotment. But these measures only boosted the authority of the central government and helped its depleted treasury rather than improving the situation of the peasants, who were conducting a campaign of resistance against landholders and government tax collectors in the northern provinces of Gilan and Azarbaijan.

After Muhammad 'Ali Shah's coup against the parliament in June 1908, Tabriz emerged as the new center of resistance. The Tabriz Anjuman and the Mujahidin, headed by Sattar Khan, controlled the city. A group of mainly Armenian social democrats, some of them revolutionaries from the Caucasus, were officers in the army of the Mujahidin and helped lead the resistance against Muhammad 'Ali Shah and the conservative clerics in 1908–9. By the fall of 1908, the social democratic leadership of the Mujahidin, the Tabriz Social Democrats, was divided in its assessment of the future direction of the movement. These divisions among Armenian and Muslim participants were not along ethnic lines, but rather represented political and ideological disagreements. Despite their small numbers, the Tabriz Social Democrats, especially the minority wing, would have an important influence on the course of events in Tehran once the constitutional order was reestablished.

In the second constitutional period, the Democrat Party, a coalition of liberals and social democrats with a social democratic program, was formed. The Democrat Party held a minority but vocal representation in the parliament and eventually entered a coalition government in the summer of 1910. The Democrat Party proposed a series of progressive laws and a minor land reform program. However, the reality of coalition politics with the more conservative Bakhtiari tribal leaders prevented the Democrats from carrying out these proposals, and instead further distanced them from the radical grassroots forces. Conflicts between the Democrats and some of the Mujahidin headed by Sattar Khan, who was now courted by the conservative Moderate Party, reached the breaking point. Once the Bakhtiari-Democrat government forcibly disarmed the Mujahidin, the coalition that made the conquest of Tehran possible fell apart. In November 1911, the Russian government, with extensive British support, gave an ultimatum that eventually resulted in a coup against the Majlis and the end of the constitutional order. The social, political, and ideological issues that the Constitutional Revolution had brought to the surface would not disappear, however. A decade later, they would resurface during the Jangali (forest) movement, which, together with the Russian revolution of 1917, would bring new momentum to the movement in Iran.

Notes

1. See Ann K. S. Lambton, *Landlord and Peasant in Persia: A Study of Land Tenure and Land Revenue Administration* (London: Oxford University Press, 1953); Charles Issawi, ed., *The Economic History of Iran, 1800–1914* (Chicago: University of Chicago Press, 1971); Nikki R. Keddie, "The Economic History of Iran 1800–1914 and Its Political Impact," pp. 119–136 in *Iran: Religion, Politics and Society, Collected Essays* (London: Frank Cass, 1980); Willem M. Floor, "The Merchants (*tujjār*) in Qājār Iran," *Zeitschrift der Deutschen Morgenländischen Gesellschaft* 126, no. 1 (1976): 101–35.

2. John Foran, "The Concept of Dependent Development as a Key to the Political Economy of Qajar Iran (1800–1925)," *Iranian Studies* 22, nos. 2–3 (1989): 5–56. Foran's essay is in part a response to an earlier study by Gad Gilbar in which Gilbar argued that the process of commercialization of agriculture brought higher yields for the economy as a whole and improved patterns of consumption for the majority of population, including the peasants, who now consumed more tea, sugar, opium, and tobacco. See Gad G. Gilbar, "Persian Agriculture in the Late Qajar Period, 1860–1906: Some Economic and Social Aspects," *Asian and African Studies* 12, no. 3 (1978): 313–65.

3. See Nikki R. Keddie, "The Origins of the Religious-Radical Alliance in Iran," *Iran: Religion, Politics, and Society, Collected Essays* (London: Frank Cass, 1980), 53–65. This essay was originally published in 1966.

4. Gad G. Gilbar, "The Big Merchants (*tujjār*) and the Persian Constitutional Revolution of 1906," *Asian and African Studies* 11, no. 3 (1977): 275–303.

5. Vanessa Martin, *Islam and Modernism: The Iranian Revolution of 1906* (London: I. B. Tauris, 1989).

6. Said Amir Arjomand, "The Ulama's Traditionalist Opposition to Parliamentarianism: 1907–1909," *Middle Eastern Studies* 17 (April 1981): 177.

7. Faridun Adamiyyat, *Fikr-i Dimukrasi dar Nihzat-i Mashrutiyyat-i Iran* (The idea of social democracy in the Iranian constitutional revolution) (Tehran: Payam, 1975); Mansureh Ittihadiyah Nizam Mafi, *Paydayish va Tahavvul-i Ahzab-i Siyasi-yi Mashrutiyyat: Daureh-yi Avval va Duvvum* (The formation and development of political parties in Iran: The first and second constitutional periods) (Tehran: Gustareh, 1982); Mangol Bayat, *Iran's First Revolution: Shi'ism and the Constitutional Revolution of 1905–1909* (Oxford: Oxford University Press, 1991).

8. See E. G. Browne, *Material for the Study of the Babi Religion* (London: Cambridge University Press, 1918), 22; E. G. Browne, *The Persian Revolution of 1905–1909* (Cambridge: Cambridge University Press, 1910); Nikki R. Keddie, "Religion and Irreligion in Early Iranian Nationalism," *Comparative Studies in Society and History* 4 (1962): 266–95; Nikki R. Keddie, *An Islamic Response to Imperialism: Political and Religious Writings of Sayyid Jamal ad-Din "Al-Afghani"* (Berkeley: University of California Press, 1983 [1968]).

9. Bayat, *Iran's First Revolution*, especially chap. 3.

10. By the term *Azari* I am referring to both Iranian Azarbaijanis and Muslims from the Russian Caucasus, present-day northern Azarbaijan, who were ethnically related and in many cases maintained familial ties with relatives in Iranian Azarbaijan. Such ties have been maintained to this day, though to a lesser extent than at the time of the Constitutional Revolution.

11. For an overview of these early *anjumans,* see Mangol Bayat, "Anjoman," in *Encyclopaedia Iranica,* vol. 2, ed. Ehsan Yarshater (London: Routledge & Kegan Paul, 1983), 77–88.

12. For a discussion of the Tabriz Anjuman, see Ahmad Kasravi, *Tarikh-i Mashruteh-yi Iran* (History of constitutionalism in Iran) (Tehran: Amir Kabir, 1984 [1951]). See also Mansurah Rafi'i, *Anjuman* (Tehran: Nashr-i Tarikh-i Iran, 1983). For a general discussion of the *anjumans,* see Janet Afary, "Grassroots Democracy and Social Democracy in the Iranian Constitutional Revolution, 1906–11" (Ph.D. diss., University of Michigan, Ann Arbor, Departments of History and Near East Studies, 1991).

13. See Hasan Hakimian, "Wage Labor and Migration: Persian Workers in Southern Russia, 1880–1914," *International Journal of Middle East Studies* 17, no. 4 (1985): 443–62.

14. See Kasravi, *Tarikh-i Mashruteh-yi Iran,* 245.

15. See Janet Afary, "On the Origins of Feminism in Early 20th Century Iran," *Journal of Women's History* 1, no. 2 (1989): 65–87; and Mangol Philipp Bayat, "Women and Revolution in Iran, 1905–1911," in *Women in the Muslim World,* ed. Nikki R. Keddie and Lois Beck (Cambridge: Harvard University Press, 1978), 295–308.

16. See *Anjuman,* May 28, 1907. All translations from non-English works in this chapter are my own.

17. Kasravi, *Tarikh-i Mashruteh-yi Iran,* 390–91.

18. Browne, *The Persian Revolution of 1905–1909.*

19. *Anjuman,* September 2, 1907.

20. See Adamiyyat, *Fikr-i Dimukrasi-yi Ijtima'i,* 65–92; Janet Afary, "Peasant Rebellions of the Caspian Region in the Iranian Constitutional Revolution," *International Journal of Middle East Studies* 23 (May 1991): 137–61.

21. *Majlis,* April 8, 1907.

22. For a summary discussion of the abolition of *tuyuls,* see Kasravi, *Tarikh-i Mashruteh-yi Iran,* 228–29.

23. See *Habl al-Matin,* January 13, 1908.

24. See "Statut de la Section Iranienne de l'Association de Mojahid Formée à Meched," in *La Social-démocracie en Iran,* ed. Cosroe Chaqueri (Florence: Mazdak, 1979), 161–74.

25. See the report in *Habl al-Matin,* December 28, 1907.

26. *Great Britain: Correspondence Respecting the Affairs of Persia,* Cd. 4581, no. 106 (February 28, 1908); *Great Britain: Correspondence Respecting the Affairs of Persia,* Cd. 4581, no. 107 (March 26, 1908).

27. Kasravi, *Tarikh-i Mashruteh-yi Iran,* 727.

28. See Andre Amuriyan, *Hamasah-yi Yiprim* (The Epic of Yephrem) (Tehran: Javidan, 1976), 28.

29. See Cosroe Chaqueri, ed., *La Social-démocracie en Iran* (Florence: Mazdak, 1979), 233.

30. See Georges Haupt and Madeleine Reberioux, *La Deuxième Internationale et l'Orient* (Paris: Cujas, 1967), 63–64.

31. Quoted by V. I. Lenin, "Events in the Balkans and in Persia," in *Collected Works,* vol. 15 (Moscow: Progress, 1978), 226.

32. See A. Chalangarian, "Iranians' Letter to Kautsky," ed. Cosroe Chaqueri, in *Lenin's Struggle for a Revolutionary International: Documents 1907–1916,* ed. John Riddell (New York: Monad, 1984), 60–61.

33. He made no mention of Marx's famous 1850 "Address of the Central Authority to the League," however, in which, after the defeat of the revolution, Marx emphatically called for the formation of an independent workers' party: see "Karl Kautsky's Reply," in *Lenin's*

Struggle for a Revolutionary International: Documents 1907–1916, ed. John Riddell (New York: Monad, 1984), 62–63; Karl Marx, "Address of the Central Authority to the League, March 1850," in *Marx-Engels Collected Works,* vol. 10 (New York: International, 1978), 277–87.

34. For a discussion of some of these differences among European social democrats, particularly during the 1907 London Congress of the Russian Social Democratic Workers Party, where the ramifications of the Russian revolution of 1905 were analyzed, and for Rosa Luxemburg's position, see Raya Dunayevskaya, *Rosa Luxemburg, Women's Liberation and Marx's Philosophy of Revolution* (Atlantic Highlands, N.J.: Humanities Press, 1982), 1–15, 199–206.

35. Cosroe Chaqueri, whose documentary collections have contributed much to our understanding of social democracy in this period, argues that they were the same person. See Chaqueri, "The Role and Impact of Armenian Intellectuals in Iranian Politics, 1905–11," *Armenian Review* 41 (Summer 1988): 1–51.

36. See "Protocole no. 1 de la Conférence des Social-Démocrates de Tabriz, 1908," in Chaqueri, *La Social-démocracie en Iran,* 35–36.

37. Ibid.

38. See "Khacaturijan à G. Plekhanov," in Chaqueri, *La Social-démocracie en Iran,* 39; "A. Tchilinkirian à G. Plekhanov," in Chaqueri, *La Social-démocracie en Iran,* 51. Throughout this chapter I have adopted the English rather than the French transliterations of these Armenian names.

39. See "Khacaturijan à G. Plekhanov," 38–43.

40. See Tigran Darvish, "Iran's Revolution," in *Asnad-i Tarikhi-yi Junbish-i Kargari, Susial Dimukrasi va Kumunisti-yi Iran* (Historical documents of the workers, social democracy, and communist movement in Iran), vol. 19, ed. Cosroe Chaqueri (Tehran: Padzahr, 1985), 31; originally published as "Die Persische Revolution," *Neue Zeit* 27, no. 20.

41. A. Chalangarian, "Iqtisad va Rishiha-yi Ijtima'i-yi Inqilabi-yi Iran" (Economic and social roots of the Iranian revolution), in *Asnad-i Tarikhi-yi Junbish-i Kargari, Susial Dimukrasi va Kumunisti-yi Iran* (Historical documents of the workers, social democracy, and communist movement in Iran), vol. 19, ed. Cosroe Chaqueri (Tehran: Padzahr, 1985), 62; originally published in *Neue Zeit* 28, no. 34.

42. M. Malikzada, *Tarikh-i Inqilab-i Mashruteh-yi Iran* (History of the Iranian Constitutional Revolution), vol. 6 (Tehran: Ilmi, 1979), 1335.

43. For documents confirming this close relation, see Iraj Afshar, ed., *Awraq-i Tazahyab-i Mashrutiyat va Naqsh-i Taqizadeh* (Newly found papers of the constitutional era and the role of Taqizadeh) (Tehran: Javidan, 1980), 239–40. See also Chaqueri, "The Role and Impact of Armenian Intellectuals," as well as the discussion of this issue in Afary, "Grassroots Democracy," chap. 8.

44. *Iran-i Nau,* March 10, 1911, 1–2.

45. Afshar, *Awraq-i Tazahyab,* 230–31, 207–8.

46. Ahmad Kasravi, *Tarikh-i Hijdahsaleh-yi Azarbaijan* (Eighteen-year history of Azarbaijan), vol. 1 (Tehran: Amir Kabir, 1978), 132–33.

47. *Great Britain: Further Correspondence Respecting the Affairs of Persia,* Cd. 5120, no. 173 (September 9, 1910).

48. Kasravi, *Tarikh-i Hijdahsaleh,* 139–44.

49. Isma'il Amirkhizi, *Qiyam-i Azarbaijan va Sattar Khan* (The uprising of Azarbaijan and Sattar Kahn) (Tehran: Tehran, 1960), 574.

Chapter 3

The Rise of Reza Khan

Michael P. Zirinsky

Modern Iranian history has been punctuated by a series of upheavals against strong royal power, including the tobacco boycott, the Constitutional Revolution, the Jangali movement, the Musaddiq era, and the Islamic Revolution. Despite the focus of these struggles on constitutionalism and their culmination in a republic, most of Iran's twentieth century was dominated by the royal dictatorship established by Reza Khan in 1926, which continued until his son, Muhammad Reza Shah, was overthrown in 1978–79. This raises an important question, then, for students of Iranian social movements: How did Reza come to the throne?

The history of Reza Khan has long been obscured by myth. Pro-Pahlavi accounts, such as that of Donald Wilber—Reza's only modern full-scale biographer—have focused on Iran's backward, chaotic condition after World War I and suggest that Reza was a champion sprung from the common people who rescued the country and brought it into the modern world. Wilber calls Reza's reign "the resurrection and reconstruction of Iran," implicitly referring his readers to both Persian and Western literature that frames history in cycles of decadence and renewal. Not surprisingly, Wilber wrote with the support of the Pahlavi family.[1]

Although they were not well publicized in the West before the 1978–79 Iranian revolution, critical views of Reza Khan reflect another mythology, that of Iran beset by alien tyrants. This theme in Iranian literature goes back at least to Firdausi's *Shahnameh,* the first major work in the modern Persian language, which recounts the epic struggle between Iran and Turan, good and evil.[2] Consequently, perhaps, Reza's detractors have sought to deny his legitimacy by implying he was a creature of alien powers, that he was put on the throne by England, that he established a brutal military dictatorship in order to further British policy.[3] Other critics, however, believe that the legend that Britain groomed Reza for royal dictatorship "completely overlooks Reza's own energy and efforts, the support given him by Iranian nationalists and modernists of various descriptions, and the mistakes made by his opponents. It also contradicts the evidence that the British Foreign Office was divided ... [and ignores Reza's] consistent Soviet support."[4]

Which myth, that of the savior sprung from the people or that of the foreign-inspired tyrant, best reflects Reza? This chapter will investigate his rise, seeking answers to several questions: What was the condition of Iran before he rose, out of which he emerged? What motivated him? What vision did he have for the future? What role was played in his rise by Iranian political forces, and how much domestic support did he really have? On the other side of the equation, what foreign help did he enjoy?

The facts of Reza's life seem simple. He was born in obscurity during the 1870s and was soon orphaned. His father had been an army officer, and his mother came from a family of refugees from the Russian-occupied Caucasus; several of his mother's family also followed military careers. At fifteen, Reza enlisted in the Russian-officered Cossack Brigade, where he grew well over six feet tall, strong, quick, and vigorous. Rising through the ranks, in 1911 he was promoted to second lieutenant, a machine-gun expert known as "Reza Khan Maxim." During World War I his rise continued, apparently because of both his military efficiency and his political subtlety. In 1918 he participated in the plot through which General Clergé, the Russian commander of the Cossack division, was removed by his second in command, Colonel Starosselsky, with the connivance of the shah and local British authorities. Reza's role was to assure the support of the Persian officers for the coup. After the British removed Starosselsky and the other Russian officers in 1920, Reza remained as one of the most important Cossack commanders. In February 1921 he provided military leadership for a coup d'état that seized power for pro-British newspaper editor Sayyid Zia al-Din Tabataba'i. Zia and Ahmad Shah named him army commander, and he provided a strong hand in the new government. He rose to minister of war (April 1921), to prime minister (1923), and, after an abortive 1924 attempt to create a republic, to the throne in 1925. As shah, he ruled Iran with absolute and increasingly arbitrary power until Britain and Russia deposed him in 1941. He died in exile in 1944.[5]

What sort of man was Reza? What motivated him? He is something of an enigma. There are very few records of his early years, and as shah he discouraged discussion of his origins. Clearly he played his cards close to his chest, keeping his own counsel and taking other players in the Iranian political game by surprise when he acted. So, lacking specific statements in his own words, the historian must infer his attitudes and motivations from his actions and career.[6]

On this basis, we may conclude that he was both a careerist and a patriot; as he aged, he distinguished less and less between his own person and the state, between his personal family and the nation. His background and education were military; he learned from his tsarist Russian officers that power came from the barrel of a gun. As an Iranian, he resented foreign domination of his country, and especially after 1918 he seemed to desire to rise in rank in order to take action to reduce foreign power in Iran. Also, he seemed to resent strongly any opposition by individuals and groups to central authority; as a military man as well as a patriot, he seems to have believed that such disorder led to national weakness.

It seems reasonable as well to conclude that Reza understood that central power in Iran commonly depended on two factors: first, the ability of government to balance competing and autonomous powers, both in the center of the country and on its edges; and second, government's willingness to act firmly, even ruthlessly, to remove rivals in time of crisis. Although the former factor may seem more important to his success, the latter tradition apparently loomed larger in Reza's own view.

Both factors seem to have shaped his actions as he rose to the throne. He was a fine politician, taking advantage of existing social movements and drawing many players in Iranian politics onto his team. He marshaled religious leaders, secularists, conservatives, liberals, altruists, and self-servers in his own cause, which he portrayed as the cause of Iran. He also used foreign powers (Britain, Russia, the United States, and others) just as nineteenth-century shahs had drawn European powers into Iran in a vain attempt to augment their own power. Above all, Reza sought to increase the institutional strength of central government, especially in military and financial affairs, in order to increase national power and to decrease government dependence on contending domestic and foreign factions. Reza used his allies in order to build a strong state. Given his own background and vision of the future, that state was a military dictatorship.

Iran before Reza's Rise

Iran's situation before Reza's rise was affected by several ideological movements, including modernization, nationalism, and Islamism. Modernization appealed especially to elite individuals exposed to Western ideas by education or travel; during the years of Reza's rise, these ideas often were called liberal, republican, or socialist. Modernists sought to adapt to Iranian conditions Western-style military organization and equipment, public administration, and urban structures.

Nationalism took different forms depending on group, education, and social orientation. During the year's of Reza's rise, Westerners described as nationalist those individuals and ideas that echoed Western secular nationalism, focusing on strong central government, militarism, the Persian language, and glorification of the pre-Islamic past. From the perspective of today, however, nationalism also seems to have included those who favored local and popular control and those whose worldview was framed by Islam.

Many patriotic Iranians, especially those Americans might call the "silent majority," made little distinction between Iran and Islam. For Islamists, the nation was both Iranian and Muslim. For a Muslim country beset by the Christian West, patriotism required both resistance to foreign foes and a buildup of national strength. Modernist patriots who saw the ulama as corrupt, ignorant, and consequently a source of national weakness often may have seemed anticlerical to Westerners, but they shared with Islamists a common goal: to strengthen Iran against a hostile world.

Events during the years 1921–26 were critical to Iran's survival as a sovereign state. Before the 1921 *putsch* the situation in Iran was disorganized. Central authority, weak throughout the Qajar period (1796–1925), in the early twentieth century seemed incapable of defending the state against Russia and Britain or even of maintaining order. Its only modern forces were the Russian-officered Cossack Brigade, established in 1879, and a Swedish-officered gendarmerie established in 1911.

Rivalry between civil authorities and the clergy added to the confusion. Within a century after the Safavids established Twelver Shi'ism as Iran's state religion in the sixteenth century, the public was beginning to identify Iran with Shi'a Islam. Some clerics saw secular power as usurpation of the Hidden Imam's authority. During Qajar times the ulama put themselves forward as protectors against civil tyranny. During the Iranian revolutionary movements of 1891–92 and 1905–11, the ulama also expressed hostility toward foreign influence—seemingly destroying Iran's autonomy—and mobilized mass support for national ideas. Nasir al-Din Shah withdrew the British tobacco monopoly and Muzaffar al-Din Shah accepted a constitution largely because the government could not resist ulama-supported demonstrations.

Foreign powers contributed to Iran's instability. During the Constitutional Revolution, national efforts to break Anglo-Russian control by establishing parliamentary government and pursuing a "third power" policy failed, in part because proconstitutional forces in the new Majlis split between liberal democrats and more traditional moderates. Also, central authority declined after liberal and tribal forces deposed Muhammad 'Ali Shah in 1909. By the end of 1911, Britain and Russia crushed Iran as they forced Morgan Shuster, the Majlis's American treasurer general, out of office and suppressed the assembly.

Efforts to resist Anglo-Russian power by supporting Germany and Turkey during World War I helped to make Iran a battlefield. With Iran overrun during and immediately after the war by Russian, Ottoman, German, and British forces, perhaps as much as a quarter of the Iranian population died, largely as a result of famine and diseases such as cholera, typhus, typhoid, and influenza. Following the collapse of Russia, the Ottomans, and Germany, English forces occupied much of Iran. Britain dominated Tehran's governments, subsidizing the shah, the cabinet, and the military. Not surprisingly, Tabriz, Rasht, and Mashhad resisted Tehran's orders, and the tribes (perhaps a quarter of Iran's population) ignored central authority.[7]

Underscoring the national crisis that Iran faced, there were frequent episodes of famine and massacre. Although these have not been extensively described in secondary literature, American missionary archives contain ample evidence of popular hardship. For example, hunger was so widespread in Tehran in 1918 that some poor families had only mother's milk to feed older children. Several episodes of cannibalism were recorded near Urmia in early 1919, and a May food riot there turned into a massacre.[8]

The political classes responded to Iran's crisis in several ways. Some Iranians collaborated with English efforts to take control of Iran. In 1919, at Lord Curzon's direction, British minister Sir Percy Z. Cox negotiated a treaty with the government of Mirza Hassan Vussuq al-Dauleh that proposed to give Britain control of Iran's finances and armed forces. As soon as Vussuq, Foreign Minister Firuz Mirza, and Finance Minister Akbar Mirza Saram al-Dauleh signed the Anglo-Persian Agreement on August 9, 1919, in return for a bribe of 131,000 pounds sterling, they put into force some of its most important provisions without waiting for Majlis ratification.[9]

In October, London named Sidney Armitage-Smith to take charge of the Iranian Ministry of Finance. Part of his job was to induce Iran to repay money Britain claimed Iran owed. Most of the millions of pounds in question had been paid to underwrite pro-British governments or to maintain British forces in the oil fields. Iran denied it owed Britain money, which it argued Britain had spent on its own behalf. By the time Armitage-Smith arrived in Tehran in May 1920, Iranian opinion had so turned against the agreement that he received no Iranian assistance.[10]

British officers tried to take command of Iranian forces. Major-General William E. R. Dickson, inspector general of the East Persia Cordon during World War I, led an Anglo-Iranian commission appointed to organize a uniform army. Iranians clearly opposed this effort. British-educated commission secretary, gendarmerie colonel Fazlullah Khan, killed himself on March 21, 1920, rather than see Britain take over Iran's military. Other Iranian officers, including Reza Khan, also strongly opposed an exchange of Russian or Swedish masters for Britons. They wanted independence.[11]

The most effective Iranian opposition to Britain was passive. Vussuq, for example, failed to convene a pliant Majlis. When this decision became unacceptable to England, British minister Herman Norman (Cox's successor) had Ahmad Shah name Mushir al-Dauleh (Hassan Pirnia) prime minister in June 1920. Mushir also did not convene a Majlis. Norman next had Muhammad Vali Khan Sipahdar put in charge in November. As long as Britain subsidized the shah and the Persian government, Norman could name cabinets almost at will, but Iranian resentment grew against British interference in Iranian politics.[12]

These apparently pro-British politicians had mixed motives. To some extent they must have believed that survival dictated bending before overwhelming power. They may also have accepted Curzon's claim that the treaty guaranteed

Iran's independence and territorial integrity. Certainly finance played a role: in addition to the bribe paid the treaty's Iranian signers, Britain promised Iran a loan of 2 million pounds sterling. These men also were landowners whose properties were endangered by revolutionary events in Gilan, which threatened to spread throughout Iran.

There were alternatives to collaboration. Not all Iranian leaders seemed to fall in with Britain's effort to establish hegemony in Iran. Some Iranians sought to restore equilibrium to Iran's foreign policy by improving relations with Russia. Moscow encouraged this effort by denouncing capitulations, concessions, and partitions. The government of Mushir al-Dowleh began negotiations for an Irano-Soviet treaty, which was finalized by Sayyid Zia's government on February 26, 1921.[13] Iranian aspirations were complicated by the Russian civil war. Under General H. B. Champain after Dunsterville's retirement, the British North Persia Force (Norperforce) tried to prop up anti-Bolshevik forces in the Caucasus. After the Reds defeated Denikin, Norperforce retired to Anzali, Rasht, and Qazvin. Baku fell in April 1920, and early in May Champain took over Denikin's Caspian Sea fleet at Anzali. Although the War Office, Treasury, and India Office had by this time determined the British army could no longer remain in such a weak position, Foreign Secretary Curzon feared British withdrawal would doom the 1919 agreement and blocked Champain's retreat. Alarmed by the threat of a continued White presence on the Caspian, the Soviets attacked, beating British forces at Anzali on May 18, 1920, and forcing Norperforce to evacuate Rasht on June 2 and fall back on Qazvin. This British humiliation doomed Curzon's hopes; Red forces occupied Gilan and Iran once again seemed partitioned between Russia and Britain.[14]

Under these circumstances, some Iranians sought to act against what they saw as a British puppet government in Tehran. Because they regarded restoration of balance as a means of restoring independence, they opened themselves up to charges that they favored Bolshevism. Muslim nationalist Mirza Kuchik Khan led one such revolt from Gilan. In 1915, he had launched the Jangali movement in favor of Iranian independence and in opposition to corruption. He accepted support from Ottoman pan-Islamic activists, who provided him with weapons used against Russia and Britain. He also accepted support from Iranian democrats and socialists such as Ahsanullah Khan. With the backing of both peasants and landlords, he established an Islamic government calling for democratic, social, and national reforms.[15]

Entering Gilan in 1918 on the way to Baku, Dunsterville pushed his way through the Manjil gap against Kuchuk Khan's forces. On July 20 the Jangalis burned the British consulate at Rasht, taking prisoners later exchanged for Democrat Sulaiman Mirza Iskandari (jailed by Britain in 1916). To avoid becoming tied down, Dunsterville worked out an agreement with the Jangalis, which Champain broke in March 1919 at Vussuq's urging. When the 1919 agreement was announced in August, the Jangalis gained wide support. Subsequently, the Red Army forced British forces from Gilan, and the Jangalis proclaimed a Soviet Socialist Republic at Rasht on June 4, 1920.[16]

This episode has been described as "the first Soviet experiment in Iran," an effort to separate Gilan from Iran, perhaps even to annex it to the Soviet Union.[17] Perhaps this was the objective of some of Kuchik Khan's more radical allies, such as Avetis Sultanzadah and Sayyid Ja'far Javad Zadeh Pishivari.[18] Kuchik Khan, however, and most of his supporters were motivated by Iranian patriotism and Shi'a Islamic values. The Jangali exchange of British prisoners for Sulaiman Iskandari and Kuchik Khan's support by Democrats, ulama, and Ahmad Shah — who hoped Jangali success would reduce British influence — support this interpretation.

Another revolt at this time was led by the clerical leader of the Azarbaijan democratic movement, Shaikh Muhammad Khiabani. In the Majlis in 1911 he had defended Morgan Shuster as a symbol of Iranian independence. He came into conflict with Ottoman officials during their wartime occupation of Azarbaijan; as a Shi'i leader and patriot he opposed both Sunni domination and pan-Turanism. Khiabani was the leading democrat in Tabriz during the postwar period. Opposing Vussuq's acceptance of the Anglo-Persian agreement, in April 1920 he cut ties with Tehran and decreed Azarbaijan an autonomous *azadistan* (land of freedom). Tehran plotted against his regime, inducing the Shahsavan tribe and the Shikkak Kurds under Ismail Agha Simko to attack him. On September 13, Cossacks seized Tabriz, shooting Khiabani two days later.[19]

The Gilan Republic also fell. Radical secular elements seized control of Kuchik Khan's government at the end of July 1920 and adopted policies to expropriate land and requisition food, transportation, and labor. These actions divided the Jangalis, mobilizing landlords, bazaaris, clerics, and peasants against the Soviet Republic. Kuchik Khan opposed most radical policies as anti-Islamic, but he could neither prevent them nor deter sharp infighting among the radicals themselves. The Red Army's limited presence in Gilan had acted as a shield for the Jangalis, inhibiting British and Iranian attacks. As a result of negotiations among the British, Soviet, and Tehran governments, however, the Russians and the British both left Iran. Norperforce withdrew in April 1921, as soon as the snows had melted sufficiently to permit withdrawal into Iraq, leaving its small arms, artillery, ammunition, and draft animals to the Iranian Cossacks. Soviet troops left shortly thereafter. Internal dissension having weakened the Jangalis, Reza Khan's Cossacks defeated them in October. Kuchik Khan fled into the mountains and froze to death, and an alternative to Reza's domination of Iran thus disappeared.[20]

Another option was pursued by still other Iranians who tried to reestablish a third-power policy, involving the United States in Iran as a counterweight to Britain. American hostility to the exclusion of Iran from the Paris Peace Conference and to the Anglo-Persian agreement encouraged this hope. Prominent Iranians associated with this policy included Vussuq's brother, Ahmad Qavam al-Saltaneh, governor of Khurasan in 1919–21 and twice prime minister between 1921 and 1923, and British-educated Hussain 'Ala, a member of Iran's abortive peace conference delegation. Qavam sent 'Ala to Washington as minister in 1921, to seek a loan, an oil concession for northern Iran, and technical assistance. 'Ala hired Morgan Shuster to act as Iran's agent with New York banking and oil firms. This initiative led to the 1922–27 Millspaugh mission. With American government cooperation, Iran privately hired State Department petroleum adviser Arthur C. Millspaugh to be administrator general of Iranian finances, charging him to streamline the collection and distribution of Iranian government revenue. Millspaugh's administration established new taxes, including excise taxes on tea and sugar and an income tax. Old taxes were rigorously raised and unpaid taxes were collected. Budgets were made and balanced. Millspaugh's success in creating regular sources of revenue for the Iranian government, without resorting to tax farming or foreign borrowing, essentially made Iran independent of foreign financial manipulation.[21]

Finally, Sayyid Hassan Mudarris of Isfahan, the most important cleric in the Majlis, had another response to the postwar crisis. During the Constitutional Revolution, Mudarris helped to organize the moderates; in World War I, he was a member of the anti-Allied powers Kermanshah government. Later he supported the Jangalis, hoping they would strengthen Iran against foreigners; as radicals came to dominate Gilan, Mudarris feared Soviet penetration and control. He opposed the 1921 Irano-Soviet treaty as too favorable to Russia (especially because it allowed Soviet invasion if Iran became a base for a hostile power); he opposed balancing British influence by making concessions to Russia. Like many patriotic Iranians afterward, in what was later popularized by Dr. Musaddiq as "negative equilibrium," he sought to check both Britain and Russia.[22]

These responses to the post-World War I crisis—pursuing balance in relations with great powers, seeking powerful friends, and opposing "foreign entanglements"—are enduring themes in Iran's search for a strong national policy. They grew out of the social movements of the early twentieth century, and they clearly affected Reza's rise. Following World War I, Iran was weak, its traditional foreign policy out of control. Efforts to restore Iranian control to relations with foreign powers, by improving relations with Russia, by bringing the United States and other "third" powers into the equation, or—irrationally, in the views of foreign "realists"—by standing strong against any foreign role within Iran, made it possible for Reza to rise from the military obscurity in which he had previously labored. Under more normal circumstances, his crude militarism might have repelled well-educated civilians, traditionalists and modernizers alike. Under the circumstances of the early 1920s, however, his forcefulness, strong sense of purpose, political expediency, and ability to channel force to achieve the social goals behind these enduring themes in Iranian policy made him an appealing instrument to many disparate politicians and patriots.

Foreign Contexts

Although Reza rose to power as a result of Iran's social movements and disorganization, foreign powers also affected events. Before we turn to British involvement in the 1921 coup, a few words are in order about Iran's place in Russian, American, and British policy.

Russia had long viewed Iran as an important border area and had expanded at Iranian expense during the nineteenth century. Challenged by Britain, in the late nineteenth century Anglo-Russian rivalry in effect made Iran a neutral buffer between the two empires. With the rise of German and Japanese power, however, Russia resolved its colonial disputes with Britain, partitioning Iran into spheres of influence in 1907 and 1915.[23]

Anglo-Russian cooperation ended with the Bolshevik revolution, which increased the Kremlin's sense that Britain was a dangerous rival in Iran. After the struggle between the Red and British armies was terminated by their mutual evacuation of Iran in early 1921, Soviet policy favored the development of an Iranian buffer against British expansion northward. Moscow supported the development of Reza's dictatorship after February 1921. Relations between the Kremlin and the Cossack barracks were often so close during the early 1920s that at times British officials were convinced Reza Khan was Moscow's man. Soviet relations with Reza possibly reached their peak in 1926, shortly after his coronation, when Moscow and Tehran exchanged ambassadors, giving the Soviet emissary personal access to the new king and precedence over the British minister. Subsequently relations cooled, as Reza Shah attacked the Iranian Communist Party and sought to improve relations with Nazi Germany.

Unlike Britain and Russia, the United States during these years did not regard Iran as important to its foreign policy. The United States saw Iran as primarily a British sphere of interest, but with two particular American concerns. Since the early nineteenth century, the U.S. State Department understood the activities of American Presbyterian missionaries in Iran to be the most important U.S. interest. There were more than one hundred American Protestant missionaries in Iran between the wars, and the Presbyterians owned considerable property. They ran hospitals and schools, providing some of the most modern medical and educational opportunities in the country. After World War I, the United States also hoped to participate in Iranian economic development, particularly with regard to exploiting northern oil reserves and building roads and railroads. Although these schemes did not immediately lead to substantial American economic penetration, they were the basis of Anglo-American sparring during 1919–

24. Arthur Millspaugh's financial mission of 1922–27, which laid the financial base of the Pahlavi government in Iran, was the most important result of these U.S. initiatives.[24]

Great Britain viewed Iran primarily as a buffer against Russian expansion toward India; after the discovery of oil, this too was important. For much of the nineteenth century Whitehall tried to maintain Iranian territorial integrity, but Germany's rise caused Britain to seek a Russian alliance, especially after Russia's defeat by Japan in 1905.[25] The resulting change in British policy toward Iran was not immediately clear. At the start of the Constitutional Revolution, Britain encouraged the constitutionalists, allowing them to protest inside the legation compound during the summer of 1906. In 1907, however, Britain and Russia divided Iran into spheres of influence, in effect proposing to transform it into a condominium. When World War I began, Iran became a theater of war on the eastern flank of the Ottoman Empire as Turkey invaded Russian-occupied Azarbaijan in January 1915. In order to maintain cooperation with Britain, Russia then agreed to transfer the neutral center of Iran, including the oil fields, to the British sphere.[26]

Anglo-Russian cooperation ended with the November 1917 Bolshevik revolution. After Soviet withdrawal from the war, Britain continued alone in the Iranian theater, in order to protect operations in Iraq, to prevent the Central Powers from taking the Caucasus, to stiffen resistance to the Bolsheviks, and—after the Ottomans signed the Armistice of Mudros in October 1918—to facilitate allied partition of Turkey and to safeguard British interests in Iran. Foreign Secretary Lord Curzon especially feared that Bolshevism might gain in India, and consequently pushed for the 1919 Anglo-Persian Agreement.

Despite Curzon's interest, Iran seemed unimportant to most Britons. London's financial position was weak; Whitehall did not have enough money to defeat the Soviets, suppress unrest in Iraq, occupy Iran, and subsidize the Tehran government. The Treasury, War Office, India Office, and Colonial Office therefore urged withdrawal. To Foreign Office chagrin, politicians and the public seemed not to care about preserving Britain's position in Iran; they were more concerned with matters nearer home (including relations with France, Germany, and Ireland, and labor unrest in Britain). Over Curzon's objections, the cabinet decided to withdraw the British Army from Iran in early spring 1921. The Foreign Office feared chaos would ensue, but a coup d'état during the night of February 20–21 secured Tehran.[27]

Britain's Role in the Coup

Was this a British-inspired coup? Whose idea was it? Tehran was taken by about 2,500 Cossacks led from Qazvin by Reza Khan, who thus came to national power. The shah named Sayyid Zia prime minister. Zia was a thirty-year-old journalist, editor of *Ra'ad* (Thunder), virtually the only Tehran newspaper to support the Anglo-Persian Agreement. Son of proconstitution cleric Sayyid 'Ali Aqa Yazdi, he studied in Paris in 1911–12. In 1920 Zia headed an Iranian diplomatic mission to Baku that sought to establish relations with independent Azarbaijan, Georgia, and the Caucasus. His relations with British officials were excellent, and his military attaché in Baku was a British protégé. Tehran rumor declared the coup a British enterprise. Britain denied involvement.[28]

Both Reza and Zia later claimed to have been the coup's chief architect. At the time, British and American observers saw the coup as Zia's. Reza's role seemed minor. Norman's first reports indicated that Reza was only one of three military leaders, that he acted on behalf of Zia, and that he had no political ambition. Reza later claimed to have been in charge, but this is not supported by contemporary evidence. After Reza became shah, Norperforce commander General Edmund Ironside claimed to have "engineered the *coup d'état*" on his behalf. Although there is no reason to doubt he recognized Reza's ability and encouraged him, his published diary does not contradict an interpretation that Reza was only one of several men plotting a coup.[29] But of all the conspirators, only Reza retained power.

British involvement with the coup included a number of different types of activity: preparation and technical aid, coordination, opening Tehran to the coup forces, and advocating support for the new regime. In terms of preparing the ground, it was Ironside's and Norman's advice that persuaded Ahmad Shah to remove the Russian Cossack officers in late October 1920. Ironside saw them as militarily incompetent, corrupt, and potentially Bolshevik; he sought to establish British command over Iranian armed forces as envisaged by the 1919 agreement. Norman cabled London, "Expulsion of ... Russian officers and virtual control by British officers of the only regular Military Force in Persia would make us practically independent of vagaries of Persian internal politics and in absence of external developments ensure gradual execution of [the 1919] agreement." In practice, however, this action also left Reza Khan as one of the highest-ranking remaining Cossack officers.[30] British officers were assigned to the Cossacks and gendarmerie to help prepare a national army. Lieutenant Colonel Henry Smyth tried to organize an Azarbaijan gendarmerie force; he was responsible for training Cossacks at Qazvin during the winter of 1920–21. Ironside took part in the process and singled out Reza for promotion. The Qazvin Cossacks, armed and outfitted from British stores, were paid with British money. Also, Ironside apparently discussed with Reza the possibility of using the Cossacks to bring a new political order to Tehran.[31]

Irked by Sipahdar's weakness toward the Soviets and by British cabinet pressure to evacuate Iran quickly, on January 15 Curzon told Norman, "The advent of a strong Cabinet would be welcome, either for purpose of conducting the affairs of the country from Tehran or, should evacuation of the capital become necessary, to provide a rallying point at Ispahan." Although the telegram referred specifically to Norman's earlier "proposal to consult Prince Firuz," the possibility that the coup resulted from Curzon's wish for a stable, pro-British government depends in part on how well subordinates internalized Curzon's desire. In any case, local British officials did aid the coup.[32] For example, Britons acted as intermediaries between Zia and the Cossacks. Contemporary accounts named Legation Oriental Secretary Walter A. Smart as "privy to the whole proceeding." In addition to Lieutenant Colonels Smyth and W. G. Grey, who admitted involvement, legation staffer Victor Mallet and Captain C. J. Edmonds also may have been involved.[33]

Furthermore, although Norman denied prior knowledge of the coup, he played a major role in introducing Reza's Cossacks into Tehran. He admired Smyth's work with the Qazvin Cossacks, which he reported to Curzon on January 24, 1921. Meeting Smyth on February 8, Norman suggested replacing the unruly Tehran Cossacks with a better-disciplined Qazvin force. He hoped that Tehran Cossack commander Sardar Humayun and his subordinate Sardar Makhsus could be removed from office at the same time. Norman reported, "Colonel Smyth approved the proposal and expressed the intention of sending General Reza Khan, one of his best officers, to Tehran with these reliefs."[34]

Norman also served as inadvertent midwife at the birth of Sayyid Zia's government. On February 20, 1921, having heard that Cossacks were nearing Tehran, Norman "sent for General Westdahl, the Swedish chief of police, and impressed on him the importance, in case the Cossacks should enter the town, of seeing that his men confined themselves to their proper duty of maintaining public order and did not become involved in any fighting which might take place." The next day, Reza and Zia having seized Tehran "practically without striking a blow," Norman cabled London, "I saw the Shah this morning, and advised him to enter into relations with leaders of movement and acquiesce in their demands, which is his only possible course. I was able to reassure him regarding his personal safety, and, though frightened, he did not talk of flight."[35] Ahmad Shah then appointed Sayyid Zia prime minister and Reza military commander (*sardar sipah*).

Norman eagerly supported the new regime. Despite Zia's immediate revocation of Curzon's agreement, signing a Soviet treaty, and arresting many pro-British Iranians, Norman reported that Zia's government "had been hailed with utmost satisfaction ... here as the most favourable to British interests which could possibly have arisen," and he appealed for support. Zia's apparently anti-British actions were already accomplished facts. The 1919 agreement was defunct: a pro-British government might gain support by denouncing it. Similarly, signing the Soviet treaty after British military failure actually limited Soviet influence in Iran by supporting British efforts to establish a buffer against Russian expansion toward Iraq, the Gulf, and India. Consequently, Norman argued, "Persia now has her last chance, and ... if it is lost nothing can save the country from Bolshevism." Nevertheless, his enthusiasm rings hollow. He was troubled by anti-British rumors that he had planned the coup,[36] rumors that threatened to weaken the Zia government and his influence over it, and he may have been trying to put the best face on a situation over which he had little control. His failure to report Zia's jailing of many notables remains unexplained. In any case, Norman believed that Zia's success, as well as his own position, depended on strong support from London.

Whitehall stalled. In reply to Norman's call for support of Zia, Iran desk officer George P. Churchill argued, "This would be all very well if there was any element of stability in the present regime at Tehran. In view of the uncertainty of the position it would ... be wiser to watch events for the present." Curzon wired Norman on the 28th that "formal denunciation ... is not disguised by statement that no hostility to Great Britain is implied." Two days later, Churchill noted, "These wholesale arrests, which Mr. Norman has not reported; the alleged hostility of the populace and the impression that the British are responsible for the coup d'état, lead to the belief that the present regime is not likely to be a success." London thus doubted that Zia could further Britain's interests; it refused him aid and adopted a "wait and see" attitude that contributed to his failure.[37]

In any event, Sayyid Zia could not retain power. Instead of giving him aid, Norperforce withdrew into Iraq, leaving its arms, ammunition, and draft animals to Reza's Cossacks.[38] Oblivious to his own weakness, Zia arrogantly tried to obtain revenue by arresting rich landowners. This provided fertile ground for alliances against him. In May, supported by the shah, landowners, and Soviet minister Theodor Rothstein, Reza forced Zia from office. Britain gave Zia refuge in Palestine, and Qavam al-Saltaneh came out of detention to become prime minister.[39]

Despite English help, the coup did not aid Britain. London knew nothing about it in advance, and Norman learned of Zia's and Reza's plans only after they were put into action. All Britain got from the coup was the reputation of having made it. In practice, it chiefly benefited Reza, whose position improved when Norperforce left him its arms. Over the next years he used his new position to work for policies he favored and to augment his wealth and power.

Reza Consolidates Power

Although it is tempting to conclude that Reza Khan was already a dictator,[40] his power was actually tenuous. During the next five years, taking advantage of Iranian political forces and with the support of foreign powers, he slowly increased his strength until he could crown himself shah.

During the Fourth Majlis (1921–23), Reza aligned himself with the Reformers' Party, heirs of the Moderates, whose landowner and ulama leaders included Qavam, Prince Firuz, and Mudarris. Reza liberated Zia's prisoners, including Qavam and Firuz, and openly aligned himself with the ulama. In 1923 he welcomed ayatullahs Shaikh Muhammad Husain al-Na'ini and Sayyid Abu al-Hasan al-Musavi al-Isfahani, expelled from Najaf and Karbala by the British. Reza also co-opted Prince Farmanfarma's nephew Dr. Muhammad Musaddiq, and prevailed upon him to serve as finance minister in Qavam's 1921 cabinet and as governor of Azarbaijan for Mushir al-Dauleh's government in early 1922.[41]

The reformers shared with Reza aims of reducing foreign power and ending separatist movements. They supported elimination of foreign officers from the Cossacks and gendarmerie. When efforts to bring the gendarmerie under War Ministry control led to revolts in Mashhad (October 1921) by Colonel Taqi Khan Pasian and in Tabriz (January-February 1922) by Major Lahuti Khan, who tried to mobilize local democrats against Tehran, the Majlis supported Reza. Likewise, his army ended Kuchik Khan's Jangali movement in November 1921, terminated the independence of Simko's Shikkak Kurds during the summer and fall of 1922, and suppressed the Sanjabi Kurds in 1923.[42]

Reza Khan also cooperated with the reformers in support of a third-power policy. The Millspaugh mission helped to build the army by tapping Iranian wealth; much of Millspaugh's success came at bayonet point. More than in Zia's time, Reza made good his February 20, 1921, brag to Walter Smart and Lieutenant Colonels Haig and Huddleston at Mehrabad that "there was plenty of money in Persia, and [we] well know where to find it." Although in the long run this revenue collection program alienated the elite, as Zia had done, in the short term Reza's alignment with the Reformers' Party shielded him from effective upper-class opposition. Under Millspaugh's management, half of the government revenue was expended on the army.[43] This accorded well with Reza's primary objective of building up the army. As early as May 1921, he indicated a desire to have an army of 100,000 men (nearly twenty times his existing force). In the waning days of the Fourth Majlis he broke with Mudarris over the conscription that would be necessary to recruit such a large army.[44]

In October 1923, after the Fourth Majlis ended, Reza forced the shah, who feared attack on his person or wealth, to name Reza prime minister, and at the same time exiled the shah to Europe. Ahmad Shah struck a deal with Reza, accepting banishment to France in return for expanding Reza's power.[45] Next, Reza used the army to rig elections for the Fifth Majlis (1924–25) in favor of secular reformers in the Tajaddud (Revival) and Socialist Parties, heirs of the Democrats, who supported Reza's objective of a modern, centralized Iran.

Tajaddud leaders included 'Ali Akbar Davar (educated in law at Geneva), Abdul Hussain Timurtash (educated in a Russian military academy and governor of Gilan when the Jangalis were suppressed), Sayyid Muhammad Tadayun, and Muhammad 'Ali Furughi (Zuka al-Mulk). These secular reformers aimed to erase ethnic diversity and autonomist movements; in 1921–26 they tried to create a strong central government that could introduce reform from above. Their program for national strength included creating a well-disciplined national army and an honest professional bureaucracy, ending capitulations, settling the nomadic tribes, expanding Western-style state-supported schools (including girls' schools), opening careers to talent, encouraging Iranian capital development, separating religion and politics, and making Persian the national language. They were disillusioned with universal suffrage, because giving equal votes to peasants and the urban poor had enabled conservative landowners and the ulama to dominate the Fourth Majlis. They opposed provincial autonomy and favored central government. Tajaddud and Socialist objectives meshed well with Reza's own, and the parties were willing to work under military leadership.[46]

Although Western observers sometimes called this reform program socialist, it seems to have owed more to the liberal ideals of the 1789 French Revolution and of American Presbyterian educators, teaching in Iran since 1835,[47] than to those of the Bolshevik revolution. Tajaddud support encouraged Reza to break with the Qajar past. His government levied new taxes, planned a railway to be financed entirely by Iranian money, built new roads, established a national system of weights and measures, introduced a solar-based *hijri* calendar, imposed conscription, abolished all aristocratic titles, and ordered the adoption of surnames. Tajaddud leaders also supported Reza's continuing military campaigns to unite the country (as did other Majlis groups). During 1924 the army successfully campaigned among the Bakhtiaris and the Lurs.[48]

The Independents (Munfaridin), including Mustaufi al-Mamalik, Mushir al-Dauleh, Taqizadeh, Yahya Daulatabadi, 'Ala, and Musaddiq, also supported Reza within the Fifth Majlis. These constitutionalists, whom Homa Katouzian calls "the Presbyterians of the Persian Revolution," hoped to tap Reza's energy, ability, and patriotism for Iran's progress. Reza met with them regularly, perhaps mainly to keep them quiet until he was able to do without them. In practice, if not intention, they helped him toward supreme power.[49]

Reza miscalculated in March 1924 when he tried to establish a republic. Just before the Majlis under Tadayun's leadership was to vote, Turkey ended the caliphate, galvanizing Muslim opinion against overthrowing the monarchy. While Mudarris filibustered, ulama-led demonstrations forced Reza to retreat. After a pitched battle between a crowd of 5,000 and two Cossack regiments in the Majlis garden on March 22, Reza withdrew to the country. On the 26th he went to Qum to confer with Ayatullahs Ha'iri, Na'ini, and Isfahani, after which they issued a joint statement that Islam prohibited a republic. Reza then resigned from the prime ministry in order to be restored by the Majlis.[50]

Rebuilding Reza's authority after this incident led to further violence. During summer 1924, the government encouraged an ulama-led anti-Baha'i pogrom. In early July, the opposition poet and newspaper editor Mir Zadeh 'Ishqi was murdered by an unknown assailant rumored to be a government agent. On Friday, July 18, American Consul Robert Imbrie was beaten to death by a crowd led by mullahs and largely composed of Cossacks. Reza weathered the diplomatic storm created by Imbrie's murder and used it to establish martial law in Tehran and to jail his opponents.[51] Then, in the fall, he departed for the south to complete the unification of the country by imposing his will on the previously autonomous British-supported Arab Shaikh Khazal of Muhammareh (Khurramshahr).

Once Khuzistan was subdued, Reza further consolidated his position. He cemented religious support, going to Najaf in January 1925 to confer with Ayatullah Na'ini before returning to Tehran. With the support of Mudarris and Musaddiq, the Majlis then voted him the position of commander in chief of the armed forces, formerly a royal power. During the next months he moved to depose the Qajars, which the Majlis voted on October 31, 1925. Only Taqizadeh, 'Ala, Yahya Daulatabadi, and Musaddiq voted no. Musaddiq's argument that it was not "to achieve dictatorship that people bled their lives away in the Constitutional Revolution" was ignored. A constituent assembly was hastily chosen to change the constitution, and by its vote on December 12, Reza finally achieved total power. Only three Socialist deputies, including Sulaiman Mirza Iskandari, abstained. No one opposed.[52]

Reformers, Tajaddudists, Socialists, and Independents all were political manifestations of movements referred to above that favored modernization, nationalism, or Islamism. Because of their natural antagonism and other weaknesses, however, they could not achieve their aims unaided. So these men of politics turned to Reza Khan, whose military strength they thought they could use. Instead, Reza manipulated them and discarded them.

Sir Percy Loraine: Appeasing Dictatorship

The crux of the charge that Britain made Reza shah may stem from his complex relationship with British minister Sir Percy Loraine. Contrary to previous British policy, Loraine favored Reza's efforts to create "a stable and self-dependent Persia, capable of maintaining herself unaided ... a new Persia disciplined and homogeneous."[53]

Before Loraine arrived in Tehran in mid-December 1921, Britain saw Iran as chaotic, a view caused in part by British bureaucratic disorganization. In addition to legation reports, London received often conflicting information on Iran from consuls, military attachés, the government of India, the Imperial Bank of Persia, the Indo-European Telegraph Department, and the Anglo-Persian Oil Company (APOC). In the cabinet, the Foreign Office had to defend its position against other departments whose arguments were strengthened by British public indifference to Iran. Treasury strictures minimized funds available for subsidies to the tribes and British forces. The Foreign Office denied funds to Qavam's government, which it regarded as hostile to British interests. Against Whitehall's advice, however, the Imperial Bank independently financed Cossack expeditions against autonomist movements. British confusion extended even to the key policy question of whether to support a strong central government or to favor regional autonomist movements. Affairs were not made easier by Curzon's angry reaction to Iranian repudiation of the agreement.[54]

As minister, Loraine developed great influence with the Foreign Office. He cultivated the foreign secretary's confidence, and Curzon usually supported his recommendations. Loraine acted much as Harold Nicolson later described the ideal ambassador: "the chief channel of communication between his own government and that to which he is accredited," trying to establish "that the word of command ... be delivered by a single voice only, and not by a chorus of discordant voices." Loraine's reputation as a brilliant manager of British interests was well established by the time Curzon fell from office in December 1923 following Conservative defeat in the general election. Consequently, Foreign Secretaries Ramsay MacDonald (Labour) and Austin Chamberlain (Conservative) continued to give him a free hand.[55]

Loraine's career flourished in part because of his relationship with the Eastern Department head, his cousin Lancelot Oliphant. Before the foreign secretary saw Loraine's communications, Oliphant almost invariably read and supported them. Oliphant was best man at Loraine's 1924 wedding, and the two men frequently exchanged long, personal letters. By modern standards, their correspondence suggests they were ethnocentric, arrogant, and acid-tongued. For example, when Loraine first arrived in Iran he described some Iranian officials in the Gulf as "smelly" and "shifty brutes." He also called U.S. minister in Tehran Joseph S. Kornfeld a "backwoods Rabbi." Similarly, Oliphant called the newly appointed Italian minister to Iran "as nearly white as one is likely to find among the ice creamers."[56] If, as seems to have been the case, they assumed less-than-civilized conduct from those not of their social caste, it seems likely that they saw no reason to discourage the growth of a military regime in Iran, if this regime could help achieve British security interests.

Loraine described his policy in a letter to British Resident A. P. Trevor at Bushire in mid-1922. After surveying the weakness of Britain's position and the depth of opposition faced, Loraine suggested:

> We must go very warily, draw in our horns ... and rebuild our platform of action slowly and laboriously, seeing that the bases of our post-war policy have been cut away from under our feet.... So I decline to interfere with Cabinet-making ... I decline to give a cent to the press, ... and my tack is to let natural forces operate, while trying to make the Persians realize and shoulder their own responsibilities, in order that they may realize from their own experience, firstly their own ineptitude and secondly that it is positively in their own interests to be on good terms with us.[57]

Nevertheless, Loraine did help Reza's rise in several ways. These included positive assessments of his rule, financial aid of various sorts, helping Reza become prime minister, allowing him to retake Khuzistan from a British ally, and support for the final assumption of the crown. Let us examine each of these in turn.

Loraine became Reza's advocate, describing him as

> a powerfully built, well set up, big boned man, well above the average height, with a quiet voice and a direct manner of speech which is most unusual in a Persian. He gets straight to what he has to say, and does not waste time in exchanging the delicately phrased but perfectly futile compliments so dear to the Persian heart.... he has never spoken for himself, nor for the Government of which he is a member, but only on behalf of his country.... an ignorant and uneducated man; nevertheless he betrays no awkwardness of manner, nor self-consciousness, he has considerable natural dignity, and neither his speech nor his features reveal any absence of self-control.[58]

Loraine judged Britain could deal with Reza, but felt Iranian opinion would reject him if Britain openly aided him. However, "if the conviction with which I have sought to imbue him, that England is the only real and disinterested friend of Persia, sinks into his mind, he will insensibly turn to us when difficulties arise for him, as they are bound to do, and we must then avoid any appearance of placing him under our protection."[59]

Financially, Loraine intervened with London to have the Imperial Bank of Persia advance money necessary to pay Reza's army. On February 6, 1922, he cabled, "We are just as much interested as the Persian Government in immediate suppression" of Lahuti Khan's rebellion, and he urged the Bank immediately to grant Reza Khan a 500,000 toman (approximately 100,000 pounds sterling) overdraft. Believing Reza preferable to any rule that might replace him, Loraine convinced London to smooth the way for regular provision of financial support for Reza's army and government.[60]

Loraine also shaped the 1922–27 American financial mission. Iran engaged Americans in order to break British hegemony, but Curzon endorsed the American mission after his own agreement failed, arguing, "The question by whom Persia is to be regenerated is of vastly less importance than that her regeneration should take place." Loraine encouraged Millspaugh to lay a financial base for strong government. "One day Persia may come to realize that her best chance of salvation lies in seeking the loyal aid ... of Great Britain," he wrote in May 1924, but "for the moment any chance of improvement centers around Reza Khan and the American advisers."[61] Loraine worked to prevent the Iranians from playing the United States against Britain. At the same time, he worked diligently to shape the American's view of the country. Loraine believed that, before coming to Iran, "Dr. Millspaugh was not friendly toward Great Britain, and ... was mainly instrumental in drawing up the indictment against England ... seeking to establish a practical monopoly of the world's supplies of mineral oil." Millspaugh's ideas, Loraine wrote, were "powerfully tinged by Mr. Morgan Shuster's notorious book, 'The

Strangling of Persia.' " Although Millspaugh sought to free Persia from British encroachments, Loraine argued that he never "desired and sought to undermine British practical influence in Persia"; he merely worked for "counterpoise to our influence." Loraine left him on his own, and by 1926 he had "convinced [Millspaugh] that British influence is never wantonly, unjustly or improperly used" and that "our silent sympathy and moral support ... [is] a definite asset to him in his task." "On the whole," he concluded, "such work as [the Americans] have done has been well and truly laid. They have certainly improved the administrative organization of the Ministry of Finance; they have tightened up the collection of revenue; they have established a much more effective control over expenditure ... and have steadfastly discouraged the favouritism ... of the rich and powerful."[62] In short, Loraine concluded the American mission had become an instrument of British policy, as Curzon intended, buttressing Reza's regime.

Supporting the consolidation of central authority, Loraine intervened with London to help Reza establish military monopoly. Loraine firmly supported Tehran's policy of disarming the tribes and rebellious military units. He discouraged any support for dissidents by London or Iraq. He encouraged Whitehall to have Reza's army acquire war surplus equipment (especially mountain guns), rebutting India and War Office arguments. Loraine also urged that Reza be given credit to buy new British trucks, airplanes, and armored cars. He encouraged London to withdraw Indian forces from the Gulf ports, leading to withdrawal from Bushire, occupied since 1778.[63]

Politically, Loraine took part in the events by which Reza strengthened his dictatorship at the end of October 1923, by making himself prime minister and exiling Ahmad Shah. In spring 1923 Loraine urged Whitehall to assist Reza to become head of government, arguing that Reza "would be an inconvenient opponent [and] he might be a very useful friend." Loraine believed that Reza had gone far toward unifying Iran, that his success was in Britain's interest. He asked for permission to suggest that the shah appoint Reza prime minister, "in such a way that refusal to entertain it would not commit us ... [to Reza should he fail]." The Foreign Office demurred and told Loraine to continue a policy of "complete disinterestedness."[64]

On September 1, 1923, Loraine again argued for intervention. Reporting instability and discontent with Millspaugh, he argued, "Minister of War is alone unshaken and maintains strong position." There was "growing conviction amongst Persians," he said, "of unpalatable necessity of coming to terms with Great Britain." Four days earlier the shah had demanded an interview with Loraine, who acted as His Imperial Majesty's "father confessor." The shah feared a coup, and Loraine reported that HIM "cared only for his [own] personal life and liberty." On September 3 Loraine reported that the shah feared Reza "means to be the Persian Kemal" and, anxious about his own safety, intended to leave for Europe. Curzon, fearing that "if the Shah were to desert his Kingdom, it would be the end of his dynasty," hinted "a douche of cold water on his idea of flight might invigorate his natural pusillanimity."[65]

The crisis came to a head on October 24, 1923. Loraine cabled that the Iranian government had resigned, Reza would become prime minister, and the shah would leave the country. Reza knew the risks of becoming prime minister, Sir Percy concluded, but believed that no one else could govern. "He wants and needs British friendship." Two days later Loraine again reported to London that the shah "cannot resist demand of Minister of War to become Prime Minister ... [and] cannot remain here with him." Loraine eased the shah's departure. "His Majesty is in such a state of nervous anxiety about himself that he would be quite useless even if he remained," he argued, "I ... will facilitate [a] solution ... and am seeing [the] Minister of War about it." On October 28, 1923, he cabled, "Shah behaved lamentably. Reza Khan sensibly. I think my intervention, though unusual, has had four good results, (1) prevented a deadlock, (2) preserved constitutional continuity, (3) earned gratitude of Shah, (4) placed new Prime Minister under an obligation."[66]

After the dust settled, Whitehall approved Loraine's action. Mallet noted that Iranian opinion supported Reza: "The fact that the terms 'nationalist' and 'democrat' ... have become almost synonymous may seem odd to those who see in the nationalist ebullitions of a Mussolini the antithesis of democracy. But in Persia they are not wholly incompatible." Oliphant approved Mallet's paper, noting that Reza "is patriotically minded and ... may consolidate [Iran] to a degree not hitherto attained."[67]

The most difficult part of Loraine's promotion of Reza was the destruction of Shaikh Khazal of Arabistan. Britain sacrificed Khazal as a "minor British interest" while Reza established "a stable and strong central government." After many years of captivity, in 1936 Khazal "died in suspicious circumstances while [still] under house imprisonment."[68] Britain had begun to establish special relations with tribal leaders in southwestern Iran when the Karun River was opened to navigation in 1888, increasing its presence in 1897 when the Lynch brothers built a road from Ahwaz to Isfahan. British presence again expanded with the oil industry after the turn of the century. Khazal succeeded his brother as shaikh in 1897; Britain reinforced its special relationship with him in 1902, 1907, and 1910. In 1919 Britain rewarded him with a river steamer "for his services during the war," and gave him "3,000 rifles and ammunition to enable him to protect the ... Oil Company and cover the withdrawal of British forces from Khuzistan."[69]

Reza moved slowly against Khazal. His initial goal, to collect taxes, required moving troops into Khuzistan. At first Britain opposed this plan, fearing loss of the oil fields. Loraine tried to mediate, and informed Khazal that British support depended on following British advice. Loraine advised Khazal not to resist

Tehran and to pay his taxes; he also asked Reza to confirm Khazal's autonomy and not to move troops southward. Although Reza replied in a conciliatory manner, his troops moved south.[70]

Reza's growing power forced Britain to choose between continued support of local autonomy and a strong central government. Advocates of the southern policy included Cox, Churchill, APOC manager Arnold Wilson, and Walter Smart, who doubted that "Reza Khan could last twenty years, reconsolidate and reform Persia," and who argued against "throw[ing] away these southern trumps."[71] The debate was already fully developed when Loraine cabled London on May 5, 1923. "To support Minister of War means the almost certain lapse of our local friendships of which the most important and difficult case is that of Sheikh of Mohammerah; but support might enable us to control Reza Khan to some extent and perhaps tie him down to definite assurances as regards Sheikh's position. Support would also strengthen bulwark against Russia." To oppose Reza, on the other hand, meant the "gradual collapse of our position and influence unless we uphold them and our friends by force; Thwarting the one chance that has appeared for decades of stability of Persia under Persian control; A period of intense friction with Persian Government almost certainly leading to a rupture; [and] Playing into the hands of Russia."[72]

At first the Foreign Office opposed Loraine. Churchill argued for "the policy already adopted," namely, "(a) support of the Bakhtiaris by financial means through the Anglo-Persian Oil Company ... and (b) support of the Sheikh of Mohammerah, even though such support may eventually lead to the dispatch of a gunboat to Mohammerah.... if Reza cannot be made to see the folly of his present course, it is possible for us to exert pressure upon him by withholding that financial assistance without which he will be utterly incapable of maintaining his army."[73]

On June 1, 1923, Loraine reported that Reza and Prime Minister Mustaufi proposed to send two hundred men to Shushtar but were willing to guarantee not to interfere with the shaikh. London considered the request, cabling Loraine to "insist as a *sine qua non* ... on previous written undertaking being given by Reza Khan ... and ... countersigned by Prime Minister."[74] In October, Loraine sent London a memorandum prepared by Military Attaché Sanders on the strength of the tribes and Reza's plans to disarm them. Loraine concluded, "There is no reason why Serdar Sepah should not be able to carry out the scheme of disarming the tribes.... I think the general result will be beneficial to British interests."[75]

During Loraine's leave in Britain, Reza provoked Khazal into rebellion. London sped Loraine back to Iran with instructions to "support Reza Khan and in the last resort throw over the Shaikh risking his total disappearance from Arabistan." As Reza's troops approached, Loraine flew to Ahwaz and got Khazal to apologize for his rebellion. Although he gave Khazal his word he would urge Reza to withdraw and cabled Tehran to that effect, Reza did not retreat. Instead,

Reza used the shaikh's Loraine-induced quiescence to tighten his grip on the entire province. On November 24, 1924, Reza informed Loraine that "the conditions ... for Khazal's pardon were unconditional surrender and his presence in Tehran." Four days later Khazal gave up, "ordered the disbandment of his forces ... and retired from Ahwaz to ... Mohammerah, where his yacht lay moored in the river." The next week Loraine mediated between Khazal and Reza at Ahwaz. Loraine tried to convince the shaikh to capitulate. Khazal still believed he could count on British protection, and Loraine found it "amazingly difficult to get a new idea into his head, ... even harder to dislodge an old one." In the end, however, he gained Khazal's agreement to temporary Iranian occupation of Khuzistan.[76]

Reza's troops never left; in April 1925 they arrested Khazal and took him to Tehran. Reza also seized his property. Despite legation advocacy, none was returned while Reza ruled. "The whole thing makes me very sad," Loraine wrote, "because I have personal affection for the old man in spite of his failings." Well it might have made him sad, for it was his advocacy that had removed Khazal's British support and thus made possible Reza's victory over him. Loraine's support for a strong Tehran government moved Britain to renege on earlier pledges to support local forces. Under Loraine's guidance, Britain appeased Reza, the emerging dictator. Loraine expressed pleasure at his achievement; Reza "is stronger and more popular than ever: he has understood for himself that our policy in the south is loyal and helpful and not disintegrating while Russian policy has been the reverse."[77]

Finally, Loraine helped remove Reza's doubts that Britain would permit him to seize the crown in 1925. After the failed attempt to create a republic in 1924, Reza hesitated to make himself chief of state. Perhaps he anticipated Dr. Musaddiq's later argument in opposition to the move: whereas as prime minister he could serve the country, as shah he would be responsible to no one. Perhaps, as Abrahamian suggests, Reza hesitated to lose left-wing support. Possibly he paused because of the promise given Ironside in 1921 "not to take or allow to be taken any violent measures to depose the Shah."[78] Much more important than this conceivable scruple was the question of whether Britain would permit him to take the throne: Reza seems to have believed Britain could prevent it. Certainly the British diplomatic record clearly shows that Reza tried to discover how Britain would respond to such a move. Loraine repeatedly reassured him that it was a purely Iranian affair. Once Loraine convinced him that Britain would do nothing, Reza moved to establish his own dynasty.

By 1925 the Foreign Office had no use for the Qajars. Victor Mallet (Churchill's successor at the Foreign Office) declared Ahmad Shah "a miserable creature entirely lacking in courage and quite untrustworthy." Oliphant agreed, noting on July 10 that "the Shah is a miserable and contemptible individual whose repeated statements that he is about to return to Persia no longer carry conviction with anyone." In October, Loraine cabled that Reza "must feel safe from interference in view of our repeated declarations of neutrality in internal affairs"; Mallet commented, "It would be madness for us to take any hand in this intricate and dangerous game now being played."[79]

Loraine could not escape being sounded. Iranian foreign minister Hassan Khan Mushar al-Mulk asked him on October 20 about the British government's attitude toward a change of dynasty. Loraine said Britain would not take sides. This was not clear enough for Reza. The next day, Mushar al-Mulk informed Loraine that Reza Khan "wants to get rid of [the] Kajars, but fears disapproval" of London; "he interprets silence as inconstancy." Loraine replied, "I did not myself see what Reza Khan could hope for more than our loyal and friendly attitude of strict non-intervention." Whitehall approved "Sir P. Loraine's [most judicious] language."[80]

This also eased Reza's doubts, and on October 29 he allowed Loraine "to understand that this time the issue with the dynasty will be pressed to a decision." Two days later the Majlis granted Reza headship of state until the meeting of a constituent assembly. Despite outspoken opposition by Musaddiq, Taqizadeh, and 'Ala, Loraine cabled that the changes were well received. The ulama in Qum and Najaf did not speak, and Mudarris abstained from the vote. The Foreign Office noted that "the revolution has passed off calmly." Loraine pressed London to recognize the new regime before any other state. On November 2, 1925, Britain granted "provisional recognition," which Reza received with the "liveliest satisfaction." Responding to this report, the Foreign Office noted that "the mutual understanding between Sir P. Loraine and Reza Khan is likely to be a valuable asset to us."[81]

The Foreign Office guardedly expressed pleasure at Reza's intention to become shah. Mallet noted, "On the whole a monarchy seems the best regime for Persia, and there seems no good reason why Reza Khan should not found a new dynasty. Persian history presents many examples of such changes; indeed the Kajars themselves came in on a revolution, while Nadir Shah rose ... in a very similar way." He added, "The Soviet [Union] will feel rather sore, if, having encouraged the elimination of the Kajars, they find another monarchy set up." Oliphant observed, "The world was a very different place when the Kajar dynasty was founded 150 years ago. While at the moment Reza Khan is clearly the only choice, it would be rash to cast a horoscope of his dynasty." The constituent assembly met in Tehran on December 6, 1925, and on December 12 voted to amend the constitution to grant the throne to Reza, now styled His Imperial Majesty Reza Shah Pahlavi. Muhammad Reza Pahlavi was named heir to the throne. The coronation took place on April 25, 1926.[82]

Loraine expressed only satisfaction with the success of his policy and the new regime. Was he realistic or merely self-congratulatory? His successor, Harold Nicolson, believed that Loraine's picture was far too rosy. As early as August 28,

1926, he wrote critically of "Loraine's 'hero-worship' of Reza," and a month later he wrote a long dispatch urging a policy review. Nicolson criticized Reza Shah, who he doubted had "the intellectual or moral calibre necessary for his high functions." Nicolson saw Reza to be "secretive, suspicious and ignorant ... wholly unable to grasp the realities of the situation or to realise the force of the hostility which he has aroused. His internal policy is apparently to discredit all possible rivals; his foreign policy is apparently to bribe his enemies and to abuse his friends."[83] The Foreign Office angrily rejected this criticism. Led by Oliphant, they defended Loraine and told Nicolson and Robert Clive, the next minister, to continue Loraine's policy of good relations and nonintervention. By the end of 1927, however, it became clear to the legation that Reza Shah "is one thousand times worse than Ahmad Shah in his love of money and land, and in the short two years that he has been proclaimed Shah, he has amassed a *huge, huge* fortune." Eventually, those in the Foreign Office turned to share Nicolson's assessment of Reza; by 1932 they referred to him as "a dull savage of the sergeant-major type," and a year later a "bloodthirsty lunatic." For better or for worse, however, Britain had helped make Reza shah.[84]

Conclusions

Reza Khan emerged from a complex history. He seems to have been his own chief promoter, taking advantage of opportunities and social movements as they developed. Whatever else may be said, in the years under discussion he seems to have been motivated by patriotism as well as by his own interests. For this reason he had wide domestic support. All politically aware Iranians seem to have detested Iran's weakness in 1919–21. Consequently, many different sorts of people supported Reza's efforts to build a strong central government. Because of their disappointment with recent events, Reza in fact gained support for his military rule from both religious and liberal nationalists.

Ulama opposed both foreign influence and anticlericalism. They supported efforts to strengthen central government and to reduce European financial and military influence, and they encouraged Reza's support of Islam. Ulama power was clearly demonstrated in the 1924 republican episode; their renewed support of Reza's rule helps to explain how Mudarris, so effective in stopping a republic, failed to prevent Reza's rise to the throne.

Reza also gained support from modernizing reformers, disillusioned by civilian weakness against British and Russian penetration and also by the results of universal manhood suffrage in the election of the Fourth Majlis. Understanding that under such a regime conservative landowners and the ulama would dominate elections, liberal reformers tied their fate to Reza's power in the hope that his force could achieve their program. Reza did impose many of their reforms, against popular wishes.[85]

Any view of Reza's rise to supreme power in the years 1921–26 is inevitably colored by understanding of how he acted as shah. How could a man who became so suspicious, intolerant of dissent, greedy, and brutal have had the wide support necessary to become shah? Yet contemporary accounts make clear that he carefully cultivated wide domestic support. Different groups supported him for their own reasons, often ignoring what in retrospect seem clear signs of potential for tyranny.

Obscuring the reality of this backing, critics have argued that Britain made Reza shah. This is a myth. For more than a century, England had regarded Iran as vital to its interests. British policy varied, sometimes seeking to keep Iran as a buffer against Russia, sometimes seeking to expand control. After World War I, England tried to take advantage of other powers' fragility by extending its holdings and met resistance from Arabs, Turks, and Iranians. London therefore adjusted its policy to accommodate nationalism. Britain recognized Faisal as king of Iraq in 1921 and unilaterally proclaimed Egyptian "independence" in 1922. At the 1922–23 Lausanne Conference Britain reluctantly accepted the Turkish nation-state.[86] And following the failure of the Anglo-Persian Agreement, Britain tried to come to terms with Iranian nationalism by supporting Reza Pahlavi.

Britain encouraged Reza's rise in two stages. Local agents gave help to the February 1921 coup, for the most part without London's knowledge. Seeing Soviet threat, British weakness, and Iranian chaos, individuals acted to nudge Iranian politics in a seemingly helpful direction. Whereas Ironside claimed to have acted on Reza's behalf, contemporary evidence suggests that Norman, Smart, and Smyth favored others, notably Sayyid Zia. For various reasons, including London's unwillingness to support the Zia government, the firepower left to the Cossacks by Norperforce, and his own single-minded pursuit of national unity, Reza Khan became the chief beneficiary of the coup.

After nine months of drift and indecision in British policy, Sir Percy Loraine arrived in Tehran and began to encourage Reza's rise. He understood that Britain in 1922 had little money and a government with no clear policy. He saw Britain's interests clearly: to keep Russia at bay and to protect the oil fields and Britain's positions in Iraq, the Gulf, and India. Early in his tenure, Loraine decided Reza was the strongest player in the Iranian game and that Britain did not have resources enough to impose a solution without him. Making virtue of necessity, he backed Reza to achieve order in Iran and thus secure British interests.

In retrospect, Loraine's policy seems to have been naive, self-serving, and ultimately futile. He disparaged cautionary voices, including Mudarris, 'Ala, and Musaddiq. He deprecated opposing views within the British establishment. Although Reza did keep Russia out of Iran, he soon ended the capitulations, made demands on the APOC, and made claims on the British position at Bahrain and on the Iraq boundary. These Iranian initiatives Loraine should have foreseen. More important for long-run Iranian stability, perhaps Loraine's most important objective in appeasing his rise, Reza weakened his own internal position by mistreating the Majlis and potential rivals. This too Loraine might have foreseen. Nevertheless, Loraine took pleasure in having picked a winner and backing him early on. This support, however, was a self-fulfilling prophecy, a part of the process by which Reza rose to the throne.[87] Other foreign powers also favored Reza's rise. Russian support, for example, was crucial. Had Moscow backed the opposition, Reza might not have been able to maintain domestic support for his rise to sovereignty. Instead, the Kremlin encouraged Reza's establishment of a strong Tehran regime, a regime that could reduce British influence along Iran's northern border. For Russia, as for Britain, Reza's rise coincided with a return to the late-nineteenth-century policy of maintaining an Iranian buffer between the Russian and British empires. Reza seems to have realized this and to have taken advantage of the opportunity it presented.

Although the United States was not yet a major power in Iran, it too played a key role in Reza's rise. After almost a century of missionary activity in their country, many Iranians hoped after World War I that the United States would take a third-power role, as a counterweight to Britain and Russia. The nominally private Millspaugh mission put government finances in order, enabling Reza to pay his forces with Iranian money. Quasi-official American assistance thereby freed Reza's new army from dependence on foreign subsidies.

Reza thus rose to total power with both domestic and foreign backing. Without downplaying the importance of this support, we should also note that Reza rose primarily by his own force of will, taking skillful advantage of political forces and social movements. Appalled by Iranian weakness, he used his personal strength and the army that he mastered to subdue opposition and become shah.

Notes

This chapter is based on research that led to my study, "Imperial Power and Dictatorship: Britain and the Rise of Reza Shah, 1921–1926," *International Journal of Middle East Studies* 24 (November 1992): 639–63. The research was supported by the Idaho State Board of Education, the National Endowment for the Humanities, and Boise State University, for which I am grateful. Also, I would like to thank the staffs of the Public Record Office, Kew; the National Archives, Washington, D.C.; the Presbyterian Historical Society, Philadelphia; and the British Library, the India Office Records, and the National Army Museum, London, for their essential help.

1. Donald N. Wilber, *Riza Shah Pahlavi: The Resurrection and Reconstruction of Iran* (Hicksville, N.Y.: Exposition, 1975). In his memoirs, Wilber asserts, "The fact of the matter is that I was the principal [CIA] planner for Operation AJAX" (the 1953 coup). Donald N. Wilber, *Adventures in the Middle East. Excursions and Incursions* (Princeton, N.J.: Darwin, 1986), 188. Other favorable accounts of Reza's rise may be found in L. P. Ellwell-Sutton, "Reza Shah the Great: Founder of the Pahlavi Dynasty," in *Iran under the Pahlavis,* ed. George Lenczowski (Stanford, Calif.: Hoover Institution Press, 1978), 1–50; Vincent Sheean, *The New Persia* (New York: Century, 1927); Amin Banani, *The Modernization of Iran, 1921–1941* (Stanford, Calif.: Stanford University Press, 1961); Joseph M. Upton,

The History of Modern Iran: An Interpretation (Cambridge: Harvard University Press, 1960), 36–80; Hassan Arfa, *Under Five Shahs* (London: John Murray, 1964). Like Wilber, Upton was an OSS agent in Iran during World War II.

2. *The Epic of the Kings: Shah-Nama, the National Epic of Persia by Firdowsi,* trans. Reuben Levy, rev. Amin Banani (London: Routledge & Kegan Paul, 1985). In a recent essay, Ahmad Karimi-Hakkak reminds us of the complex interrelationship between myth and politics in Iranian history; the onset of the "reign of the Ayatollahs" after the overthrow of the shah in 1979 was greeted by poet Ahmad Shamlu's attempt to reinterpret the tale of Kaveh's revolt, transforming Zahhak from Firdausi's vision of an alien tyrant into an Iranian folk hero who had tried to establish a classless society in place of a royal tyranny upheld by army and clergy. Shamlu viewed Kaveh's revolt not as the salvation of Iran, but as "a reactionary movement and a political rebellion in the service of an aristocracy severely wounded and deprived of its privileges by Zahhak." Ahmad Karimi-Hakkak, "Revolutionary Posturing: Iranian Writers and the Iranian Revolution of 1979," *International Journal of Middle East Studies* 23 (November 1991): 507–31.

3. See, inter alia, Malik al-Shua'ra Bahar, *Tarikh-i Mukhtasar-i Ahzab-i Siyasi-yi Iran* (A brief history of the political parties of Iran) (Tehran: Sipah, 1984); Husayn Makki, *Tarikh-i Bist Saleh-i Iran* (Twenty years' history of Iran) (Tehran: Nashr, 1983); Ervand Abrahamian, *Iran between Two Revolutions* (Princeton, N.J.: Princeton University Press, 1982), 102–65; Mohammad H. Faghfoory, "The Ulama-State Relations in Iran: 1921–1941," *International Journal of Middle East Studies* 19 (1987): 413–32; M. Reza Ghods, *Iran in the Twentieth Century: A Political History* (Boulder, Colo.: Lynne Rienner, 1989), 93–121.

4. Homa Katouzian, *Musaddiq and the Struggle for Power in Iran* (London: I. B. Tauris, 1990), 25.

5. Official accounts usually hold that Reza was born about 1878, but some observers believed he was much older; writing to his wife on March 16, 1941, the day after an official Iranian reception for Reza's birthday, British minister Reader Bullard noted, "He is officially about 62 but actually ten years or more older." *Letters from Tehran: A British Ambassador in World War II Persia* (London: I. B. Tauris, 1991), 46. Reza adopted the name "Pahlavi" in April 1925, long after he came to power. According to British minister Sir Percy Loraine, "Reza only assumed the family, and dynastic, name of Pahlavi" in order to become shah. Letter to the editor of the *Encyclopedia Britannica,* May 28, 1947, Loraine Papers, Public Record Office, FO 1011, 135. Wilber's account of Reza's early years in *Riza Shah,* 3–15 and passim, is detailed. In addition to the sources cited above, see also Shahrough Akhavi, *Religion and Politics in Contemporary Iran: Clergy-State Relations in the Pahlavi Period* (Albany: State University of New York Press, 1980); Nikki R. Keddie, *Roots of Revolution: An Interpretive History of Modern Iran* (New Haven, Conn.: Yale University Press, 1981); Peter Avery, *Modern Iran* (New York: Praeger, 1965); Michael P. Zirinsky, "Blood, Power, and Hypocrisy: The Murder of Robert Imbrie and American Relations with Pahlavi Iran, 1924," *International Journal of Middle East Studies* 18 (August, 1986): 275–92.

6. Homa Katouzian, *The Political Economy of Modern Iran: Despotism and Pseudo-Modernism, 1926–1979* (New York: New York University Press, 1981), 84 and passim.

7. Houshang Sabahi, *British Policy in Persia, 1918–1925* (London: Frank Cass, 1990), 11–58.

8. Presbyterian Historical Society, Record Group 91, 1918, Annual Report of the Tehran Station; United States National Archives (hereafter USNA), Record Group 84, Tabriz Consular Reports.

9. *Documents on British Foreign Policy 1919–1939* (hereafter *DBFP*), ser. 1, vol. 13 (London: Her Majesty's Stationery Office, 1963), 429–749; Parliamentary Papers, "Persia No. 1 (1919)," Cmd. 300; *Papers Relating to the Foreign Relations of the United States,* 1919, vol. 2, 703–7; Harold Nicolson, *Curzon: The Last Phase* (London: Constable, 1934). Curzon believed Iranian demands for payment to be "corrupt" and "odious." FO 371/7807, Foreign Office papers preserved at the Public Record Office, Kew. Cox obtained a "formal receipt" for the "backshish" from Saram al-Dauleh. Oliphant, FO 371/6401. See also Geoffrey Jones, *Banking and Empire in Iran: The History of the British Bank of the Middle East,* vol. 1 (Cambridge: Cambridge University Press, 1986), 191.

10. J. M. Balfour, *Recent Happenings in Persia* (Edinburgh: William Blackwood & Sons, 1922); Sabahi, *British Policy in Persia,* 11–32; Jones, *Banking and Empire in Iran,* 191.

11. Sabahi, *British Policy in Persia,* 45–46; Hassan Arfa, *Under Five Shahs* (London: John Murray, 1964), 88–92; Wilber, *Riza Shah.* According to two of Wilber's sources, General Amir Ahmadi and General Amanollah Jahanbani, both of whom knew him before the 1921 coup, Reza Khan first began to discuss politics *after* his first coup, the 1918 removal of Clergé from Cossack command; Wilber's records of his interviews and other notes made while writing *Riza Shah* are on deposit in the Department of Near Eastern Studies, Princeton University. It is likely that Reza's politicization dated from his reaction against the Russo-British manipulations of Iran during 1918–20.

12. Sabahi, *British Policy in Persia,* 46–53. Sabahi's excellent account is based on British government sources, many of which I have examined at the Public Record Office and the India Office Records.

13. Rouhollah K. Ramazani, *The Foreign Policy of Iran: A Developing Nation in World Affairs, 1500–1941* (Charlottesville: University Press of Virginia, 1966), 187–90; Nasrollah Saifpour Fatemi, *Diplomatic History of Persia, 1917–1923: Anglo-Russian Power Politics in Iran* (New York: R. F. Moore, 1952), 255–307, 317ff. As Iranian government envoy, Sayyid Zia had negotiated with the Caucasian Republics before they fell to the Red Army; he returned from Baku to Tehran in April 1920. Wilber, *Riza Shah,* 41.

14. Sabahi, *British Policy in Persia,* 61–73 and passim; Curzon to Loraine, May 30, 1922, Loraine to Curzon, August 2, 1922, FO 1011/49. Loraine believed "as early as our withdrawal from the Caucasus Vossugh made up his mind to throw over the agreement.... General Champain's retirement when the Russians landed at Enzeli clinched it."

15. Abrahamian, *Iran between Two Revolutions,* 112.

16. Ghods, *Iran in the Twentieth Century,* 52; Abrahamian, *Iran between Two Revolutions,* 111.

17. George Lenczowski, *Russia and the West in Iran, 1918–1948: A Study in Big-Power Rivalry* (Ithaca, N.Y.: Cornell University Press, 1949), 48–60.

18. On Sultanzadeh, see Cosroe Chaqueri, "Sultanzade: The Forgotten Revolutionary Theoretician of Iran: A Biographical Sketch," *Iranian Studies* 17 (1984): 215–36.

19. Ernest Bristow, consul at Tabriz, Annual Report for 1920, India Office Records, L/P&S/11/196, P. 1803; 'Ali Azari, *Qiyam-i Shaikh Muhammad Khiabani dar Tabriz* (The revolt of Shaikh Muhammad Khiabani in Tabriz) (Tehran: Safi 'Ali Shah, 1983).

20. Ghods, *Iran in the Twentieth Century,* 78–88; Ironside War Diary, 1920–21, National Army Museum, London (Lieutenant Colonel Smyth acted for the Cossacks); Sabahi, *British Policy in Persia,* 108–38.

21. *Foreign Relations of the United States* (hereafter cited as *FRUS*), 1919, vol. 2 (Washington, D.C.: U.S. Government Printing Office, 1934), 698–719. British diplomatic resistance in the United States helped to thwart oil concessions granted to Standard (1921) and Sinclair (1924), as well as the loans tied to them: see FO 371, 34 (Persia) files, 1921–24;

USNA, 891.51, 1921–24; Ghods, *Iran in the Twentieth Century,* 68–73; *FRUS,* 1927, vol. 3, 523–93; USNA, RG 59, 891.51 and 891.51A, includes copies of Millspaugh's quarterly reports; see also Arthur C. Millspaugh, *The American Task in Persia* (New York: Century, 1925). By 1922 the United States seemed to have modified the Wilson administration's support of Iran against British efforts to transform the country into a protectorate. Supporting British efforts to stabilize Iran internally and to check the expansion of Russian communism, the United States nonetheless continued to hope for oil concessions in northern Iran. The State Department's recommendation that Iran hire petroleum adviser Millspaugh as financial adviser strongly suggests that Washington hoped Millspaugh would enable Iran to hire American firms for northern oil exploitation. There also was a family continuity in U.S. policy toward Iran, despite the change in administration: President Harding's head of the State Department's Bureau of Near Eastern Affairs, Allan Dulles, was a nephew of Robert Lansing, Wilson's secretary of state.

22. Ghods, *Iran in the Twentieth Century,* 46–47, 91–98, 136, 158; Keddie, *Roots of Revolution,* 91–92; Katouzian, *Political Economy,* 86–91; Katouzian, *Musaddiq and the Struggle for Power,* 8–9, 22–24, and passim. Honored today as a forerunner of the Islamic Republic, Mudarris died under arrest in 1938; details of his death are given by Katouzian in *Musaddiq and the Struggle for Power,* 272 n. 25.

23. See Firuz Kazemzadeh, *Russia and Britain in Persia, 1864–1914* (New Haven, Conn.: Yale University Press, 1968); Ramazani, *Foreign Policy of Iran*; Edward Ingram, *The Beginning of the Great Game in Asia, 1828–1834* (Oxford: Oxford University Press, 1979); A. J. P. Taylor, *Struggle for Mastery in Europe* (Oxford: Oxford University Press, 1954). On the Anglo-Russian partitions of Persia, see J. C. Hurewitz, ed., *The Middle East and North Africa in World Politics: A Documentary Record,* 2d ed., vol. 1, *European Expansion, 1535–1914* (New Haven, Conn.: Yale University Press, 1975), and vol. 2, *British-French Supremacy, 1914–1945* (New Haven, Conn.: Yale University Press, 1979). On the August 1907 Anglo-Russian Convention by which Britain recognized the north of Iran as a Russian sphere of interest and Russia recognized the areas adjacent to India as a British sphere, see 1:538–41. On the eve of the outbreak of the 1914–18 war, the British government bought a controlling interest in the Anglo-Persian Oil Company. On March 20, 1915, there was a second partition of Iran: as part of the wartime secret diplomacy by which Britain recognized Russian paramount interest in Constantinople and the zone of the Straits, Russia agreed to "the inclusion of the neutral zone of Persia in the British sphere of influence"; see 2:16–21.

24. John Elder, "History of the Iran Mission," typescript preserved at the Presbyterian Historical Society (PHS); Zirinsky, "Blood, Power, and Hypocrisy"; Michael P. Zirinsky, "Harbingers of Change: Presbyterian Women in Iran, 1883–1949," *American Presbyterians: Journal of Presbyterian History* 70 (1992): 173–86; Millspaugh, *The American Task in Persia.*

25. Kazemzadeh, *Russia and Britain in Persia*; Ramazani, *Foreign Policy of Iran*; Ingram, *The Beginning of the Great Game*; Taylor, *Struggle for Mastery in Europe.*

26. See Vanessa Martin, *Islam and Modernism: The Iranian Revolution of 1906* (London: I. B. Tauris, 1989), 87–100.

27. Gordon Waterfield, *Professional Diplomat: Sir Percy Loraine of Kirkharle Bt. 1880–1961* (London: John Murray, 1973), 52ff., 61ff.; Nicolson, *Curzon: The Last Phase*; Sabahi, *British Policy in Persia,* 1–138.

28. On Zia, see Sabahi, *British Policy in Persia,* 27, 56, 58, 123–27, and passim; Katouzian, *Musaddiq and the Struggle for Power,* 17 and passim; Wilber, *Riza Shah,* 40–41ff.

29. On March 1, 1921, Norman asserted that Sayyid Zia "was probably the originator of the whole movement." D. 31, FO 371/6403; Jordan to Robert Speer, February 25, 1921, PHS, RG-91-3-18. The other military leaders of the coup were St. Cyr-educated gendarmerie major Masud Khan, minister of war in Zia's first cabinet, and Istanbul-educated Azari gendarmerie captain Qasim Khan (World War I veteran of the Ottoman army in Iraq), military governor of Tehran immediately following the coup. Norman, Tehran, March 1, 1921, D. 31, and March 3, 1921, D. 29, FO 371/6403. Masud and Qasim had been attached to Lieutenant Colonel Smyth to organize an Azarbaijan gendarmerie; Smyth brought them to Qazvin. Qasim had previously been military attaché in Sayyid Zia's embassy to Baku in 1919–20, where he and Zia both associated with Smyth and other British officers. Wilber, *Riza Shah*, 40–41. Masud and Qasim fell from power along with Zia in May 1921. In early 1922, Reza warned the press not to speculate about the coup, declaring, "I am the real plotter." Ramazani, *Foreign Policy of Iran*, 176; Elwell-Sutton, "Reza Shah," 18. Nikki Keddie argues that "from 1918 to 1921 Britain moved to consolidate control over Iran" and that "while there is no written evidence of British civilian involvement in the coup . . . the commander of British military forces in Iran, General Ironside, backed Reza Khan's rise to power in the Cossack Brigade and encouraged him to undertake a coup." Keddie bases her assertions on the work of Richard Ullman, *Anglo-Soviet Relations, 1917–1923*, vol. 3, *The Anglo-Soviet Accord* (Princeton, N.J.: Princeton University Press, 1972), 354–69, 383–89. Ullman in turn based his account on Ironside's diaries, Lord Ironside, ed., *High Road to Command: The Diaries of Major-General Sir Edmund Ironside 1920–1922* (London: Leo Cooper, 1972), 149, 160–61, which Keddie states is "the main document." Keddie, *Roots of Revolution,* 81, 87, 283 n. 9, and passim. It is not possible to tell from Ironside's published diary how much he wrote at the time and what he added later; Wilber's account, based in part on extensive interviews with Zia, highlights Zia's role as planner of the coup.

30. Norman, October 28, 1920, T. 711, C98884/56/34; *DBFP,* ser. 1, vol. 13, 618ff.; Ironside, *High Road to Command,* 135–46. Earlier, Reza quarreled with Cossack Commander Starosselsky, "had himself [urged his removal] and when word came of the dismissal he was exuberant." Wilber, *Riza Shah,* 12–15. Both Wilber and Avery agree that Reza played a key role in the 1918 removal of Colonel Clergé, Starosselsky's predecessor, winning over the Persian officers to Starosselsky's cause. See Avery, *Modern Iran,* 218. It seems clear that as early as 1918 Reza Khan had become a premier Persian Cossack officer, poised to take advantage of his position when the Russians were removed.

31. Norman, Tehran, March 3, 1921, D. 29, FO 371/6403; Ironside, *High Road to Command,* 147–78. Ironside made Captain Reza Khan Cossack commander. Lieutenant Colonel W. G. Grey gives an account of his role in the coup in "Recent Persian History," *Journal of the Royal Central Asian Society* 13, pt. 1 (1926), 29 and passim.

32. Curzon, January 15, 1921, E667/2/34; *DBFP,* ser. 1, vol. 13, 693–94, 698, and passim.

33. Oliphant, memorandum of conversation with Dickson, May 5, 1921. Dickson wrote Curzon on May 14, 1921, that Smyth himself told him of his role. FO 371/6427. Smart had a history of independent action; a student of E. G. Browne, in 1906 he was, according to Vanessa Martin, "friendly to what [he] saw as a liberal constitutional cause"; Martin believes it likely that, privately, he encouraged the *bastis* at Golhak. Martin, *Islam and Modernism,* 92; see also Emile Lesueur, *Les Anglais en Perse* (Paris: La Renaissance du Livre, 1922), 148–53; Grey, "Recent Persian History"; Denis Wright, *The English amongst the Persians during the Qajar Period 1787–1921* (London: Heinemann, 1977), 180–84. In a private letter to Norman, February 27, 1923, Oliphant chided Mallet for hosting Zia at a

private dinner; as Mallet had been in the legation during the coup, Oliphant argued that if his hosting Zia became public knowledge, Mallet's hospitality might persuade critics to believe rumors that the coup was planned by the British legation. FO 800, Oliphant papers, Pe/23/6. Proposed for Oriental secretary in Tehran, Edmonds was vetoed by Loraine, who noted, "Edmonds seems to have been mixed up in the Seyyid Zia coup d'état." FO 1011, 11, February 14, 1922.

34. Norman, Tehran, January 24, T. 56, and March 1, 1921, D. 31, FO 371/6403.

35. Norman, Tehran, February 21, T. 121, and March 1, 1921, D. 31, FO 371/6401, 6403.

36. Norman, Tehran, March 3, 1921, T. 135, FO 371/6401. Norman expressed his dismay to Dr. Samuel Jordan, president of the American College of Tehran, on February 25. Jordan to Speer, February 25, 1921, PHS, RG-91-3-18.

37. Curzon to Norman, February 28; Churchill, minute, March 2, 1921, reacting to an intercepted cable from U.S. Minister Caldwell to Secretary of State Hughes. FO 371/6401.

38. Ironside war diary, National Army Museum.

39. Ghods, *Iran in the Twentieth Century,* 71.

40. E.g., Ellwell-Sutton, "Reza Shah," 18–20; Keddie, *Roots of Revolution,* 88.

41. Abrahamian, *Iran between Two Revolutions,* 131; FO 371/9046, 9047; Faghfoory, "The Ulama-State Relations in Iran," 413–32; Akhavi, *Religion and Politics,* 27ff.; Muhammad Musaddiq, *Musaddiq's Memoirs,* ed. and trans. Homa Katouzian (London: Jebhe, National Movement of Iran, 1988), 5–10, 209–46.

42. Avery, *Modern Iran,* 254; Ghods, *Iran in the Twentieth Century,* 88; Ramazani, *Foreign Policy of Iran,* 180–81; India Office Records, London, L/P&S/11/210, file no. 573; Abrahamian, *Iran between Two Revolutions,* 120; Arfa, *Under Five Shahs,* 114–42.

43. Norman, Tehran, March 1, 1921, D. 31, FO 371/6403; *Fourth Quarterly Report of the Administrator General of the Finances of Persia* (Tehran, September 24, 1923), 84, preserved in USNA, RG 59, 891.51/328.

44. India Office Records, L/P&S/11/197, P.2545, Foreign Office correspondence with Henry W. R. Tarrant, secretary and manager, BSA Guns, Ltd.; Mahdi Farrukh, *Khatirat-i Siyasi-yi Farrukh* (The political memoirs of Farrukh) (Tehran, 1969), 222–25, cited by Abrahamian, *Iran between Two Revolutions,* 131; Akhavi, *Religion and Politics,* 37–38.

45. For a discussion of the British role in this drama, see below.

46. Abrahamian, *Iran between Two Revolutions,* 121–26, 132–33; Bahar, *Ahzab-i Siyasi-yi Iran,* passim; Muhammad Ali Jazayery, "Kasravi, Iconoclastic Thinker of Twentieth-Century Iran," in Ahmad Kasravi, *On Islam and Shi'ism* (Costa Mesa, Calif.: Mazda, 1990).

47. See Michael P. Zirinsky, "A Panacea for the Ills of the Country: American Presbyterian Education in Inter-War Iran," *Iranian Studies* 26 (Winter–Spring 1993); Zirinsky, "Harbingers of Change."

48. Abrahamian, *Iran between Two Revolutions,* 132–33.

49. Musaddiq, *Musaddiq's Memoirs,* 6–8; Katouzian, *Musaddiq and the Struggle for Power,* 23; Katouzian, *Political Economy,* 85 and passim. Musaddiq played a key role in Reza's election as commander in chief following suppression of Shaikh Khazal, cooperating with Mudarris. Ghods, *Iran in the Twentieth Century,* 94–97.

50. Faghfoory, "Ulama-State Relations," 416–18; Akhavi, *Religion and Politics,* 28–31; USNA, RG59, 891.00, 1262, 1268; FO 371/10145, file no. 455; in particular, note Oriental Secretary Havard's diary of events surrounding the failure of the republic, Tehran, April 1, 1924. Musaddiq was among those demanding Reza's return. Musaddiq, *Musaddiq's Memoirs,* 7; Katouzian, *Musaddiq and the Struggle for Power,* 23. Katouzian believes that Musaddiq and other "popular democrats still hoped that it would be possible to contain [Reza] within the constitutional framework."

51. Zirinsky, "Blood, Power, and Hypocrisy."

52. Loraine, Tehran, T. 398, December 12, 1925, FO 371/10840; Musaddiq, *Musaddiq's Memoirs*, 6–9; Katouzian, *Musaddiq and the Struggle for Power*, 24–25, Ghods, *Iran in the Twentieth Century*, 93–100; Faghfoory, "Ulama-State Relations," 419 and passim. Mudarris spoke against deposing the Qajars, asserting, "Even if you take a hundred thousand votes it would still be unconstitutional," but left the Majlis without voting. Neither he nor Musaddiq was elected to the constituent assembly. Mudarris, slapped during his filibuster against the republic on March 15, 1924, was shot on October 30, 1926; Tehran rumor held that the attack was commissioned by the chief of police on the direct order of the shah. Justice Minister Vussuq told British chargé Harold Nicolson that "all the evidence showed that the attempted murder was the work of the secret police." Havard, Tehran, April 1, 1924, FO 371/10145; Nicolson, Tehran, November 4, 1926, D. 527, FO 371/111481. Mudarris was imprisoned by Reza Shah in 1929 and killed in prison nine years later, strangled while at prayer. Keddie, *Roots of Revolution*, 91–92; Katouzian, *Musaddiq and the Struggle for Power*, 272 n. 25.

53. Chargé Harold Nicolson, Tehran, September 30, 1926, D. 486, FO 371/11483.

54. Norman, Tehran, May 25, 1921, and Churchill's response, FO 371/6404. The financial distress was general: see Martin Gilbert, *Winston S. Churchill*, vol. 14, 1916–22, *The Stricken World* (Boston: Houghton Mifflin, 1975), 531. The careers of Norman and Reginald Bridgeman, chargé d'affaires before Loraine's arrival, were ruined by Curzon, who revealed his frustration in a long letter to Loraine on May 30, 1922, ruing the "complete collapse of British prestige and influence ... and, as I judge, the universal execration of [our] friends." FO 1011; Waterfield, *Professional Diplomat*, 54–68.

55. Waterfield, *Professional Diplomat*, 1–9, 51–52; Harold Nicolson, *The Evolution of Diplomacy* (New York: Collier, 1962), 75, 111.

56. Oliphant to Loraine, March 6, 1923, FO 1011.

57. Loraine to Trevor, July 6, 1922, copy to Oliphant, FO 371/7807.

58. Loraine, Tehran, January 31, 1922, FO 371/7804.

59. Ibid.

60. Loraine, Tehran, T. 83, February 6, 1922, India Office Records, L/P&S/11; Foreign Office, Eastern Department, 34 (Persia) files, 1921–26; Jones, *Banking and Empire in Iran*; Sabahi, *British Policy in Persia*, 11–32, 108–40.

61. Curzon, March 1, 1922, *FRUS*, 1927, vol. 3, 524; Loraine, Tehran, May 24, 1923, FO 371/9024.

62. Loraine, Tehran, May 25, 1926, FO 371/11498.

63. Loraine, Tehran, June 12, 1923, FO 371/9024; Richard Cottam, *Nationalism in Iran* (Pittsburgh: University of Pittsburgh Press, 1979), 51–64, 102–17; Wright, *The English amongst the Persians*, 2–3, 62–74.

64. Loraine, Tehran, May 17, 21, June 1, 1923; Foreign Office, June 5, 1923, FO 371/9024.

65. Loraine, Tehran, September 1, 3, 8; Curzon, Foreign Office, September 6, 1923, FO 371/9024, 9025.

66. Loraine, Tehran, October 24, 26, 28, 1923, FO 371/9025.

67. Mallet, Oliphant, November 14, 1923, FO 371/9025.

68. Abrahamian, *Iran between Two Revolutions*, 150; Wright, *The English amongst the Persians*, 72.

69. The Foreign Office regarded the "Lynch Road" as an important British interest. Cottam, *Nationalism in Iran*, 111; see also *British Documents on Foreign Affairs: Reports and Papers from the Confidential Print*, pt. 1, *From the Mid-Nineteenth Century to the First World War*, ser. B, *The Near and Middle East*, David Gillard, ed., vol. 18, *Arabia, the*

Gulf and the Baghdad Railway, 1907–1914 (Frederick, Md.: University Publications of America, 1985), doc. 61, "British Assurances Given to the Sheikh of Mohammerah, 1899 and 1902–1910," 443–46; Wright, *The English amongst the Persians*, 71–72; Denis Wright, *The Persians amongst the English: Episodes in Anglo-Persian History* (London: I. B. Tauris, 1985), 150, 190ff.

70. Waterfield, *Professional Diplomat*, 68–70, is an account of a 1922 Anglo-Iranian dispute over an Iranian army defeat in Khuzistan; Loraine took the part of Khazal and the oil company against Prime Minister Qavam, believing Qavam was trying to waylay Reza.

71. Ibid., 78–79.

72. Loraine, Tehran, May 5, 1923, FO 371/9024.

73. Churchill, Foreign Office, May 9, 1923, FO 371/9024.

74. Loraine, Tehran, June 1, 1923; Foreign Office reply, June 5, 1923, FO 371/9024.

75. Loraine, Tehran, October 6, 1923, FO 371/9025.

76. FO 371, 34 (Persia) files, 1924; FO 1011, Loraine papers; Waterfield, *Professional Diplomat*, 83–98.

77. FO 371, 34 (Persia) files, 1925; FO 1011, Loraine papers; Waterfield, *Professional Diplomat*, 99–108; Loraine, Tehran, January 5, 1925, FO 371/10840.

78. Abrahamian, *Iran between Two Revolutions*, 135; Ironside, *High Road to Command*, 118, 161.

79. Mallet, March 3; Oliphant, July 10; Loraine, Tehran, October 13; Mallet, Foreign Office, October 15, 1925, FO 371/10840. Musaddiq believed "Ahmad Shah lost his throne because of his opposition to the Agreement. Honoured be a shah who would give up the throne for the good of his country." Musaddiq, *Musaddiq's Memoirs*, 200. If by this Musaddiq meant that Britain had written off the Qajars as useless to them by 1926, following their unenthusiastic response to the 1919 agreement, and had decided that Reza was Britain's man, surely he was right. Nonetheless, British officials were punctilious in making sure that their support of Reza was "deniable."

80. Loraine, Tehran, October 20, 21; Mallet, Foreign Office, October 22, 1925, FO 371/10840.

81. Loraine, Tehran, October 29, November 1; Mallet, Foreign Office, November 2, 1925; Loraine, Tehran, November 3; Mallet, Foreign Office, November 4, 1925, FO 371/10840; Akhavi, *Religion and Politics*, 30–32; Ghods, *Iran in the Twentieth Century*, 96–97; Avery, *Modern Iran*, 267.

82. Loraine, Tehran, November 3; Mallet, Oliphant, Foreign Office, November 4, 1925, FO 371/10840. For a brilliant description of the coronation, which perhaps cast the horoscope that Oliphant feared to do, see V. Sackville-West, *Passenger to Tehran* (London: Hogarth, 1926), 142–45.

83. Nicolson, Tehran, D. 486, September 30, 1926, FO 371/11484; this passage was omitted when, in 1968, the British government published the document in *DBFP*, ser. I A, vol. 2, 812–20.

84. FO 371/11484, file no. 92; Waterfield, *Professional Diplomat*, 134–38; James Lees-Milne, *Harold Nicolson: A Biography, 1886–1929* (London: Chatto & Windus, 1982), 243–320; minute, December 7, 1932, FO 371/16081; Sir Robert Vansittart, minute, December 17, 1933, FO 371/16942.

85. Sussan Siavoshi, *Liberal Nationalism in Iran: The Failure of a Movement* (Boulder, Colo.: Westview, 1990), 51–52.

86. Harry N. Howard, *The Partition of Turkey* (Norman: University of Oklahoma Press, 1931); Roderic H. Davison, "Turkish Diplomacy from Mudros to Lausanne," in *The Diplomats 1919–1939*, vol. 1 ed. Gordon A. Craig and Felix Gilbert (New York: Atheneum,

1965), 172–309; Aaron S. Klieman, *Foundations of British Policy in the Arab World: The Cairo Conference of 1921* (Baltimore: Johns Hopkins University Press, 1970).

87. Many years later, Loraine wrote to John Armitage, editor of the *Encyclopedia Britannica,* "Reza's rise to power obviously trod on a good many corns.... The big question was whether Reza would be able to pull Persia together. It is absolutely certain that no one else in the country had the will-power and the determination to tackle the job. Reza did it. But of course the nambi-pambies don't like that kind of man." Undated private letter, ca. 1950, Loraine Papers, FO 1011, 135.

Chapter 4

The Nationalist Movements in Azarbaijan and Kurdistan, 1941–46

Amir Hassanpour

World War II and the struggle against fascism changed the balance of forces throughout the world and provided favorable opportunities for the peoples of the world to assert their social, economic, and national rights, especially in Asia, Africa, and Europe. When the war started in 1939, Iran remained officially neutral under the iron fist of a hated dictator, Reza Shah Pahlavi. Germany and pro-Nazi sympathizers were active. Soon after the German offensive against the USSR, Allied forces — Soviets from the north and the British from the south — invaded Iran on August 25, 1941, deposed Reza Shah, and replaced him with his young son Muhammad Reza Shah. The United States dispatched noncombat forces in 1942.

The fall of Reza Shah's dictatorship, the reduced power of the new central government, and the presence of the Red Army in northern Iran contributed to the revival of social movements (of workers, peasants, nationalities, women) and the emergence of diverse political parties. In Tabriz in December 1945 the Azärbaycan Dimukrat Firqäsi (Democratic Party of Azarbaijan, or DPA) declared the formation of an autonomous government, known as the Democratic Republic of Azarbaijan. A month later the formation of the Kurdish Republic was announced in Mahabad. The two republics based their action on the Iranian Constitution and declared that their intention was not to secede from Iran.

The Allied forces had agreed to leave Iran by March 2, 1946. When the USSR refused to meet the deadline, Western pressure on Moscow through diplomatic channels and the newly created United Nations led to the internationalization of the conflict.[1] Some Western historians have claimed that the conflict marked the beginning of the Cold War between East and West.[2] The Soviet forces eventually left Iran in May 1946, and the Imperial Iranian Army attacked the two republics in December, overthrowing their short-lived rule.

The suppression of the two republics was brutal, with measures ranging from mass executions of leaders and participants to officially organized book burnings to a steady propaganda campaign against the nationalist movements that lasted until the fall of the Pahlavi dynasty in 1979 and has continued under the Islamic Republic. The date of the overthrow of the Azarbaijan republic was declared a national holiday—the "Return of Azarbaijan to the Motherland"—and was officially celebrated every year in the royal court, in government offices, and in schools, with the streets decorated for marching army units and students.

Historiography of the Two Movements

Whereas the two republics were a battlefield for numerous conflicting local, national, and international forces—such as peasants and landlords, Turks/Kurds and the central government, the USSR and the West—their historiography has also emerged as a site of methodological, theoretical, and philosophical struggles. This literature is diverse but is dominated by the conceptual and theoretical perspectives of Cold War, Western, positivist social sciences and Iranian monarchist historiographies. While Kurds and Azarbaijanis celebrate the achievements and the anniversary of the two republics, their adversaries continue to use this history against the legitimate demands of the two nations.[3]

The antimovement trend is dominant when measured by the quantity of published research. Under the Pahlavi regime, independent research on the two republics was not allowed. The published literature on the subject consists of memoirs by army officers and works by government-sponsored journalists.[4] Although these sources provide a number of carefully selected documents and some factual data, they were written primarily for propaganda purposes and constitute a monarchist historiography. Their main claims are as follows:

1. The Turks and Kurds of Iran are not distinct nations, they are "Iranians"; they do not have their own distinct or literary languages; their speech is a "local dialect" of Persian, the language of all Iranians. Their territory is an integral and eternal part of Iran; they love the institution of monarchy. Like other Iranians, they have sacrificed their lives throughout the centuries in order to protect the institution of the monarchy and the "territorial integrity" of the country. The demand for autonomy or self-determination is secessionist and communist inspired.

2. Those who set up the "puppet" governments in Kurdistan and Azarbaijan were a small band of communist and godless "rascals," "traitors," "aggressors," and "secessionists" led by a USSR interested in dominating Iran.

3. The people of Azarbaijan and Kurdistan hated the "puppet" governments and, responding to orders from the shah, rose up and overthrew the "secessionists."

Though this historiography is not based on serious research, it is important to examine it because it is virtually indistinguishable from Islamic and Western Cold War studies of the subject. It is also important to note that the approach to the two republics is not unique to the post-world war period; denial of the multinational character of the country is a paramount feature of monarchist and Western historiographies.

The emerging Islamic historiography on the two movements is a faithful replica of monarchist propaganda. In spite of their claim to the contrary, Shi'i clergymen have consistently promoted Persian nationalism and justified the national chauvinism of the monarchical regime. Khumaini frequently denounced nationalism as a Western phenomenon, declared that "Islam opposes nationalism," and argued that the great powers and their followers wanted to rule the Muslims by distinguishing a "Turkish nation, Kurdish nation, Arab nation, Persian nation."[5] When the shah's troops attacked the two republics in 1946, Sayyid Mahmud Taliqani (a future ayatullah) "found it appropriate to accompany the troops as far as Zanjan, stimulating their religious and patriotic sentiments."[6] In fact, an official Islamic history reproaches the shah's government for "irresoluteness" in putting a quick end to the two republics.[7] A serialized history of Iranian-British relations published in the daily newspaper *Jumhuri-yi Islami* can hardly be distinguished from Pahlavi propaganda literature.[8] This is not surprising, given that the clerical rulers inherited not only the monarchical state but also certain ideological tenets of the old regime. They tend to be Persian national chauvinists and etatists and centralists in politics, culture, economy, and language.[9]

The Iranian (Persian) nationalist historiography deviates to some extent from Pahlavi perspectives.[10] Unlike the monarchists, it admits the existence of injustice and misery in the two "provinces." However, it shares monarchist ideas such as denial of Turkish and Kurdish nationhood and their right to self-determination or autonomous rule, and is obsessed with explaining the two movements in terms of Soviet communist intentions.[11]

In spite of its methodological sophistication, Western historiography closely follows the conceptualization and problematization of the two movements as construed by U.S. foreign policy makers and the Iranian monarchist propaganda literature.[12] Thus, the political discourse of Western scholarship on Azarbaijan and Kurdistan is replete with Cold War concepts such as "communist takeover," "aggression," and "secessionism."[13] The main objective of this scholarship is to expose the "aggressive" policy of the USSR and to contrast it with the peaceful intentions of the "free world." In this worldview, the USSR always intervenes in the internal affairs of the country, but aggressive American/British interventions in support of what many Iranians consider their enemy (*istibdad,* "despotism" and *irtija',* "reaction") is normal and unproblematic.[14]

Western scholarship on the subject does not recognize Iran's Azarbaijani Turks and Kurds as distinct nations with legitimate rights of self-determination or self-rule. Although dozens of monographs have been produced on the Muslim nationalities of the USSR (even though their authors were not allowed to conduct fieldwork in the USSR),[15] not a single monographic work on the Baluchis, Kurds, Turks, or Turkmans of Iran, as distinct nations, has yet come forth. (And this in spite of the facts that Western researchers had easier access to Iran and that a number of American, British, and French research institutes operated in Tehran and had their own research libraries and facilities. It must be noted that there are several anthropological studies of Bakhtiari, Baluch, Turkish, and other *tribes.*) No doubt, Western scholars were not permitted (by the shah's government) to conduct research on ethnicity and non-Persian nationalisms. Although this was a serious form of intellectual repression, perhaps more damaging were the researchers' self-censorship and the limitations placed on them by the conceptual, methodological, and theoretical poverty of positivist social sciences.

Not surprisingly, compared with its Azarbaijani counterpart, the Kurdish Republic receives more sympathetic treatment because it was less radical (there was no land distribution and there were no communists in the leadership) and Soviet presence was less visible.[16] This portion of Western scholarship on the two republics is, thus, essentially a rehashing of U.S. and British foreign policy considerations. In spite of these limitations, a number of Western sources provide useful data on the Kurdish movement. Eagleton's book *The Kurdish Republic of 1946,* for example, is based on extensive interviews with some of the leading figures of the Kurdish Republic. Lieutenant Richard Mobley, focusing on Azarbaijani-Kurdish relations, conducted the first study to draw on the extensive diplomatic correspondence of the U.S. consulate in Tabriz as well as some issues of *Kurdistan,* the official newspaper of the Kurdish Republic.[17]

The above-mentioned trends are unified by the ideological and political perspectives of anticommunism and the protection of a monarchical system that was a stronghold of the West against the struggle of the peoples of Iran for democracy, independence, and freedom, and against the USSR. Opposing these perspectives can be found a smaller stream of sympathetic authors, particularly since the 1970s, who have dealt with the two movements as genuine national struggles. Thus sympathizers of the movement among the Tudeh Party, Democratic Party of Azarbaijan, and Kurdish historians treat the democratic movement of the people as a genuine force for social change. Although the Tudeh and DPA have not yet produced a detailed account of the two republics, they have furnished a considerable number of article-length writings in their periodical publications, such as *Dunya* and *Azarbaijan.* This literature is characterized by a listing of the achievements of the two republics and usually lacks detail. Soviet policy is always outlined in general and vague terms and without critical evaluation. This literature provides little information on and no critical analysis of the relations between the USSR and the leadership of the two republics or the Soviet role in the fall of the two republics.

Kurds were not allowed to conduct research on the topic in Iran or even in Iraq, where publishing in Kurdish was allowed but with very limited freedoms. The few Kurdish sources are informed by personal experiences of the writers or principal actors in the republic but are deficient because of lack of access to documents that have been destroyed. They treat the Kurdish republic as one of the most important events in Kurdish history because it was the first experience of modern state building since the overthrow of the last semi-independent Kurdish principalities by the Ottoman and Iranian governments in the mid-nineteenth century.[18] Among the Kurdish sources one may mention Kerim Hussami, one of the leading members of the Kurdish Democratic Party (KDP) and a member of the Tudeh Party.[19] Although it belongs to the tradition of Tudeh Party historiography, the work provides a certain amount of detail. Kurdish nationalists generally reproach the Soviet Union for abandoning the two republics. They explain this in terms of, among other things, Soviet self-interest and pressure from the West. One more critical recent work is by Mela 'Izzet, published in the liberated areas of Iraqi Kurdistan and reprinted in Sweden.[20]

Criticism of the two republics is not lacking, because the communist and nationalist movements are interested in learning from the experience. Since the 1960s, Iranian communists, both individuals and organizations, have produced a number of reappraisals of the two republics. This category includes works by writers opposed to the Tudeh Party and its Soviet "revisionist ideology," such as a pamphlet by Ali Riza Nabdil and the work of M. A. Javid.[21] Although these works celebrate the achievements of the two republics, they criticize the Democratic Party of Azerbaijan for downplaying or abandoning class struggle in favor of nationalist demands (reducing the struggle to linguistic and cultural issues) and for avoiding the Iranization of the democratic regime of Azerbaijan, in contrast with the constitutionalist revolutionaries of Azerbaijan earlier in the century. A well-documented treatment of the subject is provided by an Iranian democratic group, JAMI.[22] Another type of criticism comes from dissidents of the Tudeh Party such as Anvar Khami'i and Ardashir Avanisian.[23] Although they focus on interfactional conflicts within the party and between the Tudeh and DPA, they also engage in considerable critique of the dependence of the two organizations on the USSR and the problems of leadership and administration within the republic. Writing from a Trotskyist perspective, Javad Sadiq examines the class nature of the two republics and sees them as working-class regimes.[24] Criticizing this analysis, Azar Tabari argues that the Kurdish regime, unlike its Azari counterpart, was not working-class in composition or nature.[25] Both authors view "Stalinism" as a major factor in the defeat of the movements.

Among Western accounts, several critical approaches may be noted. Unaffected by either the foreign policy considerations of the Western powers or the "apolitical," "objective" social sciences are two French observers of the Kurdish nationalist movement, Bois and Kutschera, and an Arab scholar, Jwaideh.[26] Another type of research avoids advocacy of either side but treats the two movements as genuine struggles for social change. In this category belongs the work of Abrahamian, Foran, and Homayounpour.[27]

Although the rise and fall of the two republics are closely tied to developments in the world war, especially the Soviet occupation of northern Iran, the two movements cannot be reduced to or explained in terms of Soviet foreign policy. In this chapter I examine them as episodes in a long history of the development of the Turks and Kurds as *nations*. I attempt to provide a sketch of their histories as perceived by participants, taking the political discourse of the two movements seriously as central to their meanings.

The Formation of Turkish and Kurdish Nations

Iran is a multilingual and multinational country. No more than 50 percent of the population is Persian. The rest includes Azarbaijani Turks, Kurds, Baluchis, Turkmans, Arabs, and others. Throughout history, Iran has had no fixed borders. The borders were never determined by agreement among the various peoples but by the extent of the power of those who were able to rule over the territory. Within this mosaic of peoples, groups were usually ruled directly by their own tribal chiefs, khans, pashas, or kings and enjoyed either independence or semi-independence from any central government.

The Kurds have settled in Western Asia since ancient times, whereas the Azari Turks migrated to their present territory during the tenth to the eleventh centuries. Although they have mixed with the local populations, both peoples are distinct from the Persians and other neighboring peoples in language and culture (e.g., oral literature, dress, music). Between the eleventh and the nineteenth centuries, both peoples developed diverse forms of social organization, including tribal (nomadic and transhumant economies), feudal (rural agrarian), and urban structures. Historically, the tribal element gave way to sedentarization in villages, where a complex form of class differentiation, identified here as feudalism, emerged.[28] Prosperous villages supported numerous urban centers that were limited primarily by the productivity of an agriculture based on primitive technology. This feudal system of production was most dramatically manifest in a mosaic of principalities that were governed hereditarily by native rulers and were independent except when a powerful sultan, shah, or caliph was able to exact from them tax and military service. The tying of the majority of population to the land, the impressive permanence of the system of self-rule (until the mid-nineteenth century), and the emergence of a small intelligentsia contributed to the consolidation of Turkish and Kurdish cultures and languages. Although Persian and Arabic were used in the limited volume of correspondence, Persian was never spoken by the Kurds and Azarbaijanis. Even in this day of intensive state and media penetration into rural society, the majority of illiterate peasants and urban people in Iran do not speak Persian.

Under the conditions outlined above, Turks and Kurds developed their own literary traditions, which indicate deep-rooted linguistic and ethnic awareness. The Turkish written poetic tradition began in the thirteenth century and produced major figures, such as Fuzuli (1494?-1556). Poetry in the language was written by the rulers of the Qara Quyunlu dynasty (1400–1468) and some of the Safavid kings. The founder of the Safavid dynasty, Shah Isma'il I (1487–1524), has left a *divan* of Turkish poetry. The language continued to be used, alongside Persian, as a poetic medium in the courts of the Safavid and Qajar dynasties.[29] According to European travelers, Turkish was the dominant language of the court and high-ranking officials in Isfahan.[30]

Kurdish national and literary awareness began in the sixteenth century with the flourishing of a mosaic of powerful principalities and small kingdoms. The rivalry between the Ottoman and Iranian states to extend their rule over Kurdistan and their centralization policies led to a destructive war that lasted until the mid-nineteenth century. Kurdish principalities put up strong resistance to the two expansionist empires, and the unceasing wars led to numerous massacres, destruction (of cities, villages, farms, irrigation systems), the imposition of a war economy on Kurdistan for three centuries, the forced migration of entire tribes, and the resettlement of non-Kurdish tribes in Kurdistan in order to undermine Kurdish ethnic unity and territorial integrity. These events contributed to the rise of national awareness under conditions of feudal disunity in Kurdistan when political loyalties were owed to one's family, tribe, birthplace, and principality. This ethnic or national awareness is manifest in the emergence of literary Kurdish, the compilation of the first history of Kurdistan, the *Sharafname* (1597), and the ideas of the great Kurdish poet, Ahmade Khani (1650–1706). In his poetic narrative work, *Mem û Zîn,* a love story based on a Kurdish popular ballad, Khani clearly contrasted the Kurds with the Ottoman Turks, Arabs, and Persians, and strongly denounced the enslavement of the Kurds by these nations (*milel*).[31] He argued that the Kurds were superior to these three peoples in qualities of munificence, hospitality, and valor but were subjugated because they did not have their own king who could unite the discordant principalities. He argued that the formation of a unified Kurdish state required both the sword (military power) and the pen (a literary language). This apostle of Kurdish nationalism was a mulla, but he did not refrain from castigating Muslim Arabs and the Ottoman state as subjugators and oppressors of the Kurds.[32] The Ottoman and Persian states eventually divided Kurdistan in 1639. By the mid-nineteenth century, the last remaining principalities (two in Iran and four in Ottoman Turkey) were overthrown.

By this time, northern Azarbaijan had been annexed by tsarist Russia. Before the nineteenth century, Kurdish national feeling was clearly more pronounced than its Turkish counterpart. Monarchist and Western observers downplay the force of Turkish national feeling and claim that the Azarbaijani Turks consider themselves to be "Iranians" rather than Turks.[33] However, the remarkable phenomenon is not the attachment of the Turks to Iran, because they, in contrast to the Kurds, became rulers of Iran with the rise of Safavids to power. It is significant, rather, that the Turks of Azarbaijan were not Persianized but were able to Turkify an extensive territory to the west and southwest of the Caspian Sea that had been previously populated by non-Turkish peoples.

The latter part of the nineteenth century witnessed unprecedented changes in the development of Turkish and Kurdish societies. In Azarbaijan, the major social change was the growth of a mercantile class (or a bourgeoisie) bolstered by trade with Russia and other parts of Europe, the Ottoman empire, and the rest of Iran. This was accompanied by and in various ways related to other trends, including the rise of a working class, especially in the oil fields of northern Azarbaijan, which had ties to the social democratic movement in Russia; increasing social and economic differentiation in the rural society; peasant revolts; the publication of books, newspapers, and magazines in Turkish on both sides of the frontier; the founding of the first modern secular schools in Tabriz and other cities; the use of postal and telegraph services; and the export to Europe and the Ottoman empire of commodities produced in Azarbaijan and the rest of Iran.

Though social and economic change was occurring throughout the country, developments in Azarbaijan were unparalleled among other peoples of Iran, including the Persians. Tabriz was the most important city in Iran in the late nineteenth and early twentieth centuries. Not surprisingly, Azarbaijan was the heart of the Constitutional Revolution and the seat of another revolutionary movement in 1919–20 that declared Azarbaijan the Land of Freedom, *Azadistan,* under a radical autonomous government.[34]

Developments in Kurdish society were different but equally dramatic. The fall of the powerful principalities in the mid-nineteenth century did not put an end to Kurdish national awakening. In fact, this nationalism was revitalized further by the grafting on of a budding urban, middle-class social base. The major urban centers of the Ottoman empire—Istanbul, Baghdad, Cairo, and Damascus—became seats of political activism for an emerging Kurdish intelligentsia as well as the defeated princes or feudal nobility. Journalism and literature emerged as weapons of Kurdish nationalism at the close of the nineteenth century. The new middle-class nationalism found its most vocal expression in the enchanting poetry of the second apostle of Kurdish nationalism, Hacî Qadirî Koyî (1817?-1897). He not only attacked the Ottoman and Iranian states but also castigated the Kurdish feudal nobility, the shaikhs (heads of the Qadiri and Naqshbandi *tariqat*s), and the mullas whom he considered to be obstacles to Kurdish independence. Hacî called on the Kurds to acquire modern science, to develop their national language, and to liberate their country.[35]

World War I changed the balance of forces in the region and fanned the flames of the nationalist movement. In the wake of the Bolshevik revolution, northern Azarbaijan became an independent republic for a short period and, later, one of the autonomous Soviet republics.[36] The war dissected the Ottoman empire into numerous states under British and French rule. The Kurdish part of the empire was redivided between the newly formed states of Iraq (under British mandate until 1932), Syria (under French mandate until 1946), and Republican Turkey (after 1923). The Treaty of Sèvres, signed between the victors of the war and the Ottoman sultan in 1920, recognized the right to self-determination of the Kurds and Armenians and provided for the creation of an independent Kurdish state. However, the treaty was not implemented owing to, among other considerations, the recovery of a defeated Turkey under Kemal Ataturk.

Postwar conditions, especially the October Revolution, enhanced the revolutionary movement throughout Iran. In Gilan, a Soviet republic was formed in 1920 by a coalition of nationalist, communist, and radical religious forces that intended to extend their power throughout the country. In Azarbaijan, a liberation movement led by Shaikh Muhammad Khiabani succeeded in assuming power for a short period in 1919–20. Khurasan was the site of another movement against the state. In 1921, a coup d'état brought to power a military dictator, Reza Khan, who strengthened the power of the central government, suppressed the revolutionary movements, and by 1925 replaced the Qajars with his own Pahlavi dynasty. The Pahlavi state emerged as a centralist, etatist, and despotic power.[37]

Reza Shah Pahlavi's military dictatorship was supported by England and other Western powers interested in blocking Soviet influence in Western Asia. Reza Shah extended state control over all aspects of life—the economy, transportation, education, language, culture, media, foreign trade, and religion. Writing in non-Persian languages and speaking these languages in public places were declared illegal and were punished. With the imposition of Western dress throughout Iran, the national Kurdish dress was made illegal. Kurdish and Turkish music, dance, and other domains of cultural life were proscribed. Pre-Islamic culture and Persian language were officially promoted. The state's ideology advertised "Iranians" as a "pure Aryan race" superior to "savage" Arabs and Turks, whose rule over Iran was blamed for all the backwardness of the country. The coercive forces of the state—the police, gendarmerie, and army—implemented this racialist policy of Persian national chauvinism. According to the late Kurdish poet Hêmin, "Thousands of Kurds in schools and offices and even in the street were arrested, tortured, and disgraced on charges of speaking Kurdish."[38] Another poet, Hejar, wrote that in his village he and his father had to hide their few Kurdish books in a box and bury it every night after they finished reading.[39] Persianization was conducted in a situation where Kurdish linguistic and cultural rights were recognized and promoted in the neighboring USSR, while in Iraq the Kurds enjoyed the right to read and write, and native-tongue education was allowed in some primary schools. In the Azarbaijan Soviet Socialist Republic, Turkish was the official language of the state and was used in all functions. Radio broadcasting began in Turkish and Kurdish in the USSR in the 1920s and in Kurdish in Iraq in 1939 before it started in Persian in Iran in 1940.

The Persianization ideology and practice of the Pahlavi state fanned the flames of a nationalism that was already in full swing in both Azarbaijan and Kurdistan. A whole body of oral and written literature denouncing Pahlavi tyranny emerged in Kurdish and Turkish. A Kurdish popular song ran:

> Don't assent, Oh [God] don't assent
> Don't assent to the Pahlavi [king's tyranny],
> May God topple your throne,
> May your highness be turned [upside] down.

> Heĺnegrî wey heĺnegrî,
> Heĺnegri le pehlewî,
> Yaxwa textit weřgeřê,
> Bĺîndit lê bin newî.[40]

When the Soviet forces advanced on Kurdistan and Azarbaijan, the people welcomed the disintegration of the Pahlavi coercive forces and moved to assert their right to self-rule.[41] The bombs and leaflets that were dropped in order to warn the Imperial Army of Iran and to inform the people of the approaching Soviet Army were hailed in Kurdish folk songs and poetry. The bombs were called by a nationalist Kurdish poet *bombi rehmet,* "bombs of mercy," and one of the poems that spread by word of mouth asked:

> Which airplanes? [They were] statutes of happiness
> Who was in them? The angel of freedom. . . .
> With the dropping of two leaflets [from Soviet airplanes],
> The Imperial Army [of Iran] disintegrated,
> The shah, who was a lion in hunting the destitute
> Was, I saw, like a mouse under Stalin.

> Çi fiřokêk? Mucesemey şadî
> Kêy têda bû? Firiştey Azadî....
> Be bilaw bûnî dû peř agahî
> Bû biław erteşî şahenşahî
> Şa ke şêr bû le rawî miskên da
> Dîm mişke le jêr stalîn da.[42]

A similar celebration of the fall of Reza Shah's despotism occurred in Azarbaijan. In the absence of a strong central government, Turkish culture and language flourished; native-tongue journalism, book publishing, theater, and music changed the face of Azarbaijan. Workers and peasants continued their struggle for a decent life and soon were organized under the leadership of the Tudeh Party. However, the shah's civil and military apparatus was still able to suppress the movement regularly, if ineffectively.[43]

The Formation of the Two Republics

The Allied forces invaded Iran on August 25, 1941, ostensibly in order to forestall German advances in the region and to assist Soviet forces, which had stopped the advancing Nazi army not far from the strategically vital oil fields of Baku. At this point, the USSR's main concern was to defeat the invading forces. The Soviets promoted anti-Nazi activism in northern Iran but openly discouraged the Kurdish and Turkish nationalist struggles against the central government in the early years of occupation.[44] Under Soviet occupation, the shah's police, gendarmerie, and army were weakened but remained largely intact. They supported the *irtija'i* (reactionary) groups (landlords, capitalists, and other proregime groups, individuals, and publications) and continued to harass the emerging social movements.

The weakening of the coercive forces of Reza Shah led to the rise of both spontaneous and organized activism of all social classes, nationalities, and religious and ethnic groups. Peasant revolts occurred in Azarbaijan, and peasant demands against the system of serfdom were raised throughout the country. Political organizations of all persuasions emerged. Marxist activists, released from prison, soon formed the Tudeh Party (Party of the Masses, known in the West as the communist party), which became the best organized and persuasive group in the country. The party quickly organized workers, leftist intellectuals, youth, women, and, to a limited extent, the peasantry. In Azarbaijan, a nationalist organization, the Azarbaijan Society, was formed in the fall of 1941 and published a Turkish-Persian bilingual journal named *Azarbaijan,* which exposed the Pahlavi dictatorship and was banned in Tehran and wherever the government was in firm control.[45] Tudeh Party activism in Azarbaijan began in the fall of 1942.

In Kurdistan, an underground political party, Komeley Jiyanewey Kurdistan (Organization for the Revival of Kurdistan), better known as Komeley J. K., was formed in 1942.[46] Komele published a clandestine magazine, *Niştman* (Homeland), and evolved as a widely respected political organization. Membership in the group was considered an honor, not only for the members but also for their families. The party called for the establishment of an independent Greater Kurdistan.

Throughout Iran, workers demanded better wages, improved living conditions, housing, unions, and a decent life. Peasants demanded land and the abolition of feudal dues and bondage. Women were fighting for equality and nationalities called for linguistic and cultural rights. In spite of occasional slogans to the contrary, the Tudeh Party never took a revolutionary stand against the monarchy. It remained an essentially reformist party and demanded democracy, freedom, and independence within the framework of a constitutional monarchical system. Preventing the restoration of Reza Shah's dictatorship and supporting the antifascist struggle were among the priorities of the party. It declared adherence to Marxism-Leninism, supported the USSR, and was in turn aided by Moscow.

Under the Tripartite Treaty of Alliance (January 29, 1942), Britain and the USSR agreed to respect the sovereignty and political independence of Iran and its territorial integrity. In fact, during the occupation, the new shah was not a disinterested ruler; the state apparatus acted in the interests of Britain, the United States, the dominant classes (landlords, tribal chiefs, the wealthy, and the capitalists in the cities), and reactionaries of all persuasions. The army, gendarmerie, and police both directly and indirectly, through their armed gangs and club wielders, suppressed but failed to silence demonstrations, labor unions, peasant activists and their families, and the opposition press.

In a country occupied by three world powers, the destinies of both the social movements and their adversaries were bound up with great power interests and their rivalries. Before defeating German forces in 1943, the USSR aimed primarily at making northern Iran free of any German threat and ensuring the peace and order necessary for receiving logistical aid dispatched via Iran by Britain and the United States. To achieve this goal, the USSR actually *discouraged* the Turkish and Kurdish nationalist movements. For instance, Kurdish nationalists had to print the literary and political Kurdish magazine *Niştman* clandestinely in Tabriz and distribute it secretly. Even in July 1945, Soviet authorities did not allow Kurdish nationalists to perform a theatrical play unless they changed its anti-Iranian message.[47] The nationalist Azarbaijan Society and its journal *Azarbaijan* came under increasing attack by the central government, leading to the paper's closure within six months.

Britain, a major power in Iran long before the arrival of the Americans, dominated the oil industry and had vital interests in Iraq, the Persian Gulf region, and India. The American and British confidential correspondence of the period documents the stiff competition between the two nations in Iran, the United States to establish and extend its influence and Britain to protect its empire. They shared, however, an overriding policy of saving the region from communism and the USSR.

Iranians, especially leftists and many nationalists, opposed Britain as a colonial power, and similar attitudes toward the United States had already formed among the populace. The shah and reactionaries of various persuasions looked to the United States and Britain for their survival. While the DPA, KDP, and Tudeh Party relied on the USSR as an ally, the monarchy, religious leaders, and many Iranian nationalists viewed Moscow as their enemy. These political alignments, more or less clear-cut, are vividly recorded in the press and literature of the period and in the diplomatic correspondence of the United States and Britain.

The End of the War

The conflicts between the two sides — social movements and the shah's regime — became aggravated by late 1943, when the balance of forces in the war had changed radically against the Axis powers. Both sides were now preparing for the postwar struggle. As early as July 27, 1944, Ja'far Pishivari, the future leader of autonomous Azarbaijan, predicted:

> The bloody World War will come to an end. With the end of the war, our coun-
> try too will face a dilemma. The Iranian nation will have to choose one of two
> roads. There is no middle road.... One is the renewal and revival of [Reza
> Shah's] dictatorship, oppression, encroachment, killing, crime, and adversity,
> the other is freedom, evolution, progress, and justice.... If reaction wins and
> leads us down the first road, the result would be nothing other than the wreck-
> age of the nation and the destruction of the country's independence. If we could
> take the second road, we would reach the shores of salvation.[48]

Most worried and perhaps most prepared were Britain and the United States. They began to reinforce their foothold in Iran soon after their forces entered the country in 1941 and 1942, respectively. In spite of their rivalries, both countries aimed at consolidating the shah's power by strengthening his coercive forces, establishing or reinforcing their economic, military, and political bases in Iran, and suppressing the independence and radical democratic movements throughout the country. While the stunning defeats of the German army in Stalingrad, Kursk, and other fronts in the winter of 1943 were officially celebrated in London and Washington, they signaled a new phase in the conflict among the Allied powers.

The USSR not only did not disintegrate, as had been hoped for in 1938 and 1939,[49] it emerged politically as a more powerful, prestigious, and inspiring force in the eyes of activists in revolutionary movements. This was the result, in part, of the driving of German forces out of Eastern Europe, the success of the communist parties in the Balkans and Eastern Europe in defeating fascist and Nazi aggressors, and the gains of communist forces in China, Indo-China, and other parts of Asia. From the perspective of Western states, the Nazi enemy was being defeated but the communist enemy had grown stronger throughout Asia and Europe.[50] A backlash against the social movements in Iran and elsewhere was to be expected.

As early as 1942, the United States and Iran concluded a series of agreements for American aid to the Iranian police, gendarmerie, and army. From 1942 to 1946, U.S. military advisers "reorganized, trained, armed, and commanded Iran's 20,000 rural police/paramilitary force from the Gendarmerie headquarters in Tehran."[51] By December 1944, the U.S. embassy in Tehran informed Washington that the reorganized army and gendarmerie were "capable of dealing effectively with any disorders and violence" in urban centers and in the countryside.[52] At

the same time, a number of American oil companies that had sought oil concessions in Iran since the 1920s continued their push for concessions in the north
(close to the Soviet border and its Azarbaijani oil fields). The USSR considered
these moves a threat to its security and, to counterbalance the Americans, proposed in October 1944 a more favorable bid for developing the oil resources of
northern Iran (a fifty-year contract on a 51–49 percent division of shares). The
Iranian government, supported by the United States, opposed these concessions
to the USSR. As a result, granting concessions to foreign companies was delayed
until the end of the war.

Under the circumstances, the Soviet policy of containing the Kurdish and Turkish nationalist movements changed. The USSR now actively supported the Turkish and Kurdish nationalist aspirations for self-rule within Iran. Why did this
happen? Cold War historiography explains Soviet policy simply as part of the
overall communist aggression aimed at "reaching the warm waters of the Persian Gulf" and exploiting the resources of the country. It explains Western policy
simply as one aimed at defending the sovereignty and territorial integrity of Iran,
a noble aim motivated by the desire to defend the "Free World."[53] The Allied
forces had agreed to withdraw from Iran within six months after an armistice
with the Axis powers. The war in Europe ended with the surrender of Germany
on May 8, 1945. In late May, Iran called on the three powers to withdraw their
forces from the country. Tehran's demand was supported by Britain and the United
States, but the USSR did not agree to an early withdrawal, preferring to wait until the total end of the war, which came with the defeat of Japan on September 2.
The transparent purpose of the Anglo-American-Iranian demand was to achieve
an early Soviet evacuation, which they considered a precondition for the consolidation of the shah's regime and putting an end to the social movements directed
against the shah and Anglo-American neocolonialism.[54] Obviously, the evacuation of Anglo-American troops would not have weakened their position, as the
Americans were already firmly involved in organizing and arming the shah's
armed forces and Britain was in control of the most important resource of Iran,
the oil industry. The evacuation deadline was then set for March 2, 1946.

The shah's efforts to consolidate his power in Azarbaijan continued in 1944.
The fourteenth parliament, dominated by monarchists, had already refused to
accept the two representatives from Tabriz, Imami Khu'i and Pishivari, elected in
1943. State-sponsored attacks on the movement further escalated in the summer
of 1945. Throughout the country, but especially in Azarbaijan, the gendarmerie
outposts armed the landlords, whose henchmen attacked and killed peasant activists; in Tabriz, a massacre of political prisoners who were mostly peasant activists took place and seven were killed.[55] The Ministry of the Interior refused to
sanction the elected members of the Municipal Council of Tabriz because they included popular and democratic figures. In the village of Liqwan, the landlord attacked Tudeh Party members, resulting in six casualties. A major showdown was

brewing between Tehran and Azarbaijan. On August 12, 1945, a telegram signed by participants in a Tudeh-led rally in Tabriz warned the central government: "Atrocities committed in Azarbaijan recently are based on a reactionary plot and aim at killing and strangling freedom.... The freedom fighters are able at any time to put down the bloodthirsty reactionaries."[56] The telegram demanded the disarming of the landlords and prosecution of army and justice officials who had cooperated with them. It warned that if these demands were not met, the people of Azarbaijan would directly take action.

On September 3, 1945, Ja'far Pishivari, a prominent communist leader, together with other veteran Azeri revolutionaries, formed the Azärbaycan Dimukrat Firqäsi (Democratic Party of Azarbaijan).[57] They argued that the parliamentarian and reformist policies of the Tudeh Party were inappropriate for revolutionary change and that the DPA was necessary in order to carry out the national-democratic revolutionary tasks. Soon the Tudeh Party and its labor union, together with the remnants of the Azarbaijan Society, joined the DPA. It is widely believed that the Soviet Union was instrumental in the formation of the DPA.[58] Unlike the Tudeh Party, which was a national pro-Soviet political organization, the DPA restricted its activism to Azarbaijan only and pressed for the rights of the Turkish people. The DPA moved to expand its organization and to implement the portions of the Iranian constitution that stipulated a measure of provincial self-rule but had remained on paper. On November 16, 1945, the DPA sent an open letter to the consulates of foreign governments in Tabriz and Iranian government authorities and cited 102 repressive acts committed by (pro)government forces, including the cutting of lips and tongues, stabbings, floggings, rapes, shootings, and setting fire to the harvest in Azarbaijan. Meanwhile, elections for the DPA congress were conducted amidst popular excitement and participation. Azarbaijan once more felt as it had in the days of the Constitutional Revolution; "a truly mass movement was going on."[59] When the DPA allowed the peasants to defend themselves against the landlords, they quickly rounded up the gendarmerie posts and took over the villages. The city of Mianeh, which had born the brunt of gendarmerie brutality, collapsed first, followed by Sarab and Maragheh, and a number of tribes armed by the central government changed sides. Isma'il Purvali, a journalist for *Iran-i Ma* who was in the region, reported that "one feels in this environment that power is now completely in the hands of the barefooted.... the fire which has blazed in Azarbaijan does not seem to be extinguishable.... I feel that its warmth will reach Tehran and from there to all over Iran."[60] Tehran decided to send troops to subdue the movement, but Iranian army units were stopped by Soviet troops near Qazvin. On December 12, the formation of the Azarbaijan autonomous government was announced. A day later, the army garrison at Tabriz surrendered, and the garrisons and other military and gendarmerie outposts were either captured or gave up within a week.[61]

In parts of Kurdistan to the north of the British occupied territory, the Komeĭey J. K. changed into the Kurdish Democratic Party in August 1945. The changes involved, among other things, abandoning the establishment of Greater Kurdistan in favor of autonomy within the borders of Iran. Another significant development was the toning down of the antifeudal and antitribalist agenda of Komeĭey. This change in political line occurred, like that of the DPA, after negotiations between Komeĭey leaders and Soviet authorities.[62] The Kurdish autonomous government was announced on January 22, 1946, in the capital city of Mahabad; despite the initial opposition of the DPA and Moscow to the formation of a Kurdish autonomous regime, Kurdish leaders refused to be incorporated into the Azarbaijan republic.

Achievements of the Two Movements

Many observers of the two movements have noted that they achieved in one year what had been impossible under the Pahlavi regime in twenty years. Azarbaijan introduced reforms that were far more radical than those of the Kurdish republic. A popular army was formed to defend the autonomous regime. The use of Turkish as the official language of the government was accompanied by legislation punishing administrative corruption. Peasants saw the formation of a peasant congress, abolition of feudal dues, and the division among them of agrarian land belonging to absentee landlords and the state. Women received suffrage rights. In education, the first provincial university in Iran was formed, native-tongue education became the norm on all levels, and compulsory primary education was introduced. Workers obtained a comprehensive labor law that favored them by setting a minimum wage and maximum hours of work and legalizing collective bargaining. A radio station and publishing houses were established; Turkish culture, especially in arts such as music and theater, was promoted; Pahlavi Street was renamed after Sattar Khan, a hero of the Constitutional Revolution. Numerous construction projects included the founding of factories, hospitals, health clinics (including itinerant ones serving the villages), orphanages, houses for the elderly, and the paving of streets. And, not least, ethnic, linguistic, and religious minorities were granted equal rights.[63]

Similar reforms were undertaken in Kurdistan, although on a more limited scale. Education was promoted, but no institution of higher learning was set up. Land reform was not initiated, in spite of peasant demands. The urban economy flourished, however, especially because of the lifting of the state monopoly on tobacco. Kurdish nationalists from Iraq helped as teachers, printers, and army officers and soldiers. The national army was reinforced with Barzani Kurds, who were battle tested in guerrilla warfare against the Iraqi government. The Kurds of Iraq, Turkey, and Syria viewed the republic as the realization of their dreams.

The difference between the two movements can be explained by contrasting the leaderships of the two movements and the states of social and economic development of the two societies. Composed largely of nationalist intellectuals and notables of Mahabad and Bokan, the Kurdish Democratic Party was less radical than the DPA; a number of nationalist-minded landowners became cabinet ministers, and many opportunistic tribal and feudal lords were appointed to sensitive positions. Qazi Muhammad, president of the republic and leader of KDP, was a nationalist judge and a member of the wealthiest family of Mahabad. By contrast, the DPA and the Azarbaijan government were led by an experienced revolutionary and leader in the Iranian communist movement, Ja'far Pishivari. Less developed in terms of urbanization and industry, the western and northern areas of the Kurdish republic were still under the rule of tribal chiefs. The capital city, Mahabad, had a population of only 19,000. There was no trace of an industrial working class or a trade union movement.

The reforms implemented by the two governments were popular and were seen by opposition forces throughout Iran as a model of progress under a democratic regime.[64] The existence of the two autonomous regimes was therefore contributing to the further isolation and delegitimation of the Pahlavi monarchy, which had come to power as a result of a British-sponsored coup d'état and had remained without a popular social base. In order to neutralize the impact of the two republics, the central government conducted a vast propaganda campaign and extensive sabotage activities. Accusing Azarbaijan of "secessionism," "communism," and "betraying" the independence of the country was a common theme in the propaganda campaign. An economic blockade was also applied.

Monarchist and Cold War Western accounts distort the history of the two movements by accusing them of being Soviet "puppets" that were hated by the people. The weight of the evidence, however, demonstrates that the two republics were certainly popular and their reforms were planned not by the USSR but by their own leadership. This is best reflected in contemporary eyewitness accounts by Iranian journalists, British and American diplomatic dispatches from Tabriz, and other reports after the fall of the two governments.[65] To cite one example from an opponent, U.S. Supreme Court Justice William Douglas wrote in 1951:

> I had assumed from press reports that Pishevari was not only a Soviet stooge but a bumbling and ineffective one as well. I learned from my travels in Azerbaijan in 1950 that Pishevari was an astute politician who forged a program for Azerbaijan that is still enormously popular. . . . Events intervening since the Pishevari government collapsed have made this program increasingly attractive to the people as they view it in retrospect. . . . Pishevari's program was so popular—especially land reform, severe punishment of public officials who took bribes, and price control—that if there had been a free election in Azerbaijan during the summer of 1950, Pishevari would have been restored to power by the vote of 90 per cent of the people. And yet not a thousand people in Azerbaijan out of three million are Communists.[66]

Equally popular was the Kurdish republic, the anniversary of whose foundation (*dûy rêbendan,* January 22) is celebrated by Kurds throughout the world. The national anthem of the republic has been adopted as the national anthem of the Kurds, and the grave of Qazi Muhammad, the president of the republic, became a shrine. Douglas found out in his trip that

> the grave of Qazi Mohammed is indeed a shrine; hundreds of Kurds flock there each week to worship. The hanging of this Kurdish hero killed only the man, not the idea of Kurdish independence. His death in fact gave the idea new impetus. In the eyes of the simple peasants who walk hundreds of miles to pay homage to his memory, Qazi Mohammed was a good man who gave his life that their dream might come true.[67]

The Fall of the Republics

In spite of their popular social base, the two republics collapsed soon after the offensive by the shah's army in December 1946. The defeat of the two movements was the product of a complex web of contradictions on the local, national, regional, and international levels. On the international level, the Western powers, especially the United States, used their influence in the United Nations to force the USSR into withdrawal of its troops (other pressures are discussed below).[68] On the national level, the shah's regime was in a very weak position. Trade unions in the oil industry and elsewhere, urban and rural masses, intellectuals, youth, and women organized by the Tudeh Party were a formidable force that was kept in check only by the reformist policies of the Tudeh leadership. The masses were more revolutionary than their leaders, not only in Azarbaijan and Kurdistan, but in other parts of Iran. Prime Minister Ahmad Qavam al-Saltaneh, an old politician known for his reactionary and pro-British politics, took a "progressive" stance in the summer of 1946, relaxed police repression of the movement, conducted negotiations with the two republics, traveled to Moscow, and negotiated a number of concessions to the USSR and the Tudeh Party that, in concert with pressures from the United States, Britain, and the United Nations, ensured the withdrawal of Soviet forces. The Soviet Union was promised an oil concession in the wake of withdrawal and on the condition of ratification by a future parliament. Three Tudeh members were allowed into the cabinet. The party was especially powerful in the oil fields, the Caspian region, and the central provinces.[69]

Once the Soviet forces were evacuated, Qavam set the scene for repression of the movement. Tribes in the south led by a Qashqa'i chief captured a number of towns in September 1946, demanding autonomy similar to that of Azarbaijan and Kurdistan, and calling for the dismissal of Tudeh members from the cabinet in order to save the country from communism and atheism. The opposition forces considered this revolt orchestrated by the central government as a pretext to suppress the Azarbaijan and Kurdistan and other movements throughout Iran.[70] In mid-October, Qavam dismissed the Tudeh ministers and governors, reached an agreement with the tribal chiefs in the south, and formed a new cabinet. He soon began the suppression of the Tudeh Party, the trade unions, and the leftist press and declared martial law in a number of provinces. Qavam announced that nationwide elections would take place for the National Assembly in December and indicated that troops would be sent to Azarbaijan and Kurdistan to supervise these. This announcement alarmed the political parties on the left, who considered the sending of troops a final offensive to overthrow the two republics. Although the DPA continued negotiations with Qavam for a peaceful resolution of the crisis, Azarbaijan braced for the central government's offensive.[71]

Pishivari assured the people of Azarbaijan that there would be "death but no return" to the rule of despotism. On December 3, he told the people of Tabriz that Sattar Khan had successfully defeated Tehran's army with a limited force, whereas the DPA had an organized and extensive army.[72] He said on Azarbaijan Radio that once more, as in the Constitutional Revolution, Azarbaijan would defend freedom and move toward Tehran in order to spread freedom all over Iran.[73] On December 10, Qavam, assured of the "unwavering" support of the United States,[74] dispatched the army to Azarbaijan. The first confrontation occurred in Mianeh on two fronts. In spite of losses in one sector, the *fada'i* and partisan forces repulsed the attack and advanced toward Zanjan.[75] Only two days later, however, the DPA decided to give up resistance and allow the army into Azarbaijan.

The movement was not defeated militarily. In fact, the shah's dilapidated army was not able to crush the two movements. The defeat was political. By the time army units were sent out, the DPA was being pressured by the USSR to give up the struggle.[76] In the Central Committee of the DPA, Pishivari opposed the Soviet demand and argued against surrender and in favor of resistance.[77] He had to give up, however, because other committee members followed the Soviet line. Pishivari left for the USSR and was replaced as general secretary of the DPA by another committee member. Soon, the DPA ordered its defenders on all fronts to abandon the resistance. On December 12, DPA leaders announced in a rally in Tabriz that the Iranian army would be allowed to enter Azarbaijan peacefully. Qavam and the shah were informed of the decision in telegrams sent by the Central Committee.

Assured of the surrender of the DPA, the army and the armed gangs of the landlords conducted a savage attack on the people of Azarbaijan and Kurdistan.[78] Three years later, William Douglas recounted the stories he had heard in his trip to Azarbaijan:

> When the Persian Army returned to Azarbaijan it came with a roar. Soldiers ran riot, looting and plundering, taking what they wanted. The Russian Army had been on its best behavior. The Persian Army—the army of emancipation— was a savage army of occupation. It left a brutal mark on the people. The beards

of peasants were burned, their wives and daughters raped. Houses were plundered; livestock was stolen. The Army was out of control. Its mission had been liberation; but it preyed on the civilians, leaving death and destruction behind.[79]

In Kurdistan, a "war council" formed to deal with Tehran's offensive decided to engage in armed resistance. Soon, however, a telegram sent to Mahabad by the DPA announced Azarbaijan's decision not to resist.[80] Left in the lurch, the KDP decided to follow suit and abandoned resistance. However, armed Barzani Kurds of Iraq, who had joined the Kurdish republic, refused to surrender. They returned their families to Iraqi Kurdistan but were forced to enter Iran again under the pressure of the Iraqis. Refusing to lay down their arms, they successfully defeated Iranian troops in a number of confrontations, crisscrossing the Iranian, Iraqi, and Turkish borders several times, fighting all three armies, and eventually taking refuge in the USSR. The successful military operations of the Barzanis against the three armies and the tribes armed by Tehran is further testimony to the strength of the movement and the weakness of the central government.

The defeat of the DPA and KDP, the organizational embodiments of the two nationalist movements, provides a striking example of how subjective conditions (the nature of the leadership) lagged behind objective conditions (the weakness of the government and the strength of popular forces). The people were ready and willing to fight for the overthrow of the monarchy, but their leaders followed a policy of seeking freedom and democracy within the framework of the despotic Pahlavi state. Being essentially reformist parties, the DPA and Tudeh tied their destinies to the USSR. Instead of maintaining their political and ideological independence and relying on the more powerful forces of the people, the two parties relied on the USSR, which was more interested in protecting its borders than in promoting the cause of Iranian peoples. The weight of the evidence shows that the Tudeh and the DPA usually acted as obstacles to the revolutionary actions of the masses.[81] They tied the destinies of the workers, peasants, and other mobilized people to their dealings with the Pahlavi monarchy (sharing power in the cabinet and in the parliament) and the Allied powers.

On the international level, the reformist policies of the two parties reflected a rightward trend in the international communist movement, including in the Soviet Communist Party. Instead of attempting to seize power even when the movement was at its peak, the communist parties followed a policy of capitulation for the purpose of "maintaining peace and democracy" and "defending the socialist Soviet Union." The prime example in Europe was Greece, where the revolutionary forces had liberated the country in 1944, but, instead of establishing a democratic state, the communist leadership delivered the country to Britain and its government-in-exile composed of conservatives. Other examples include France and Italy, where the mass movements were betrayed by the reformist communist leadership.[82] Only a few parties, including those of Albania, Vietnam, Korea, and China, rejected the reformist line.

The betrayal of the two movements by the USSR was thus not motivated by Soviet need for Iranian oil or other material gains. The Soviet demand for oil concessions in northern Iran was primarily based on a policy of maintaining the security of its southern borders by preventing the United States from establishing bases there. The USSR did not realize that a democratic regime established in Azerbaijan and Kurdistan and throughout Iran would have ensured more secure borders, because Iran would not have turned into a major base against the USSR, as it actually became under the shah's alliance with the United States. The Soviet leadership was no doubt preoccupied with internal postwar difficulties (the loss of eighteen million lives, a totally destroyed country) and intimidated by an aggressive anticommunist U.S. foreign policy based on extending the American empire throughout the world. Historians have sometimes referred to President Truman's March 1946 ultimatum to Stalin to withdraw Soviet forces from Azerbaijan; whether the ultimatum was real or not,[83] the threat of nuclear attack on the USSR was a major news topic at the time. Responding to an American journalist's question about a possible American nuclear attack on the USSR in August 1946, Mao Zedong did not deny the threat, but indirectly criticized the capitulationist trend in the Soviet leadership and the world communist movement. He argued that although the United States was using nuclear arms to intimidate freedom fighters, "all reactionaries are paper tigers."[84]

Conclusions

What light does the experience of the two movements shed on modern Iranian history? The two nationalist movements were powerful engines of social change in the multinational country of Iran. They were an inseparable link in the successive struggles for democracy, freedom, and independence—the Babi movement (1848–53); the tobacco movement (1890–92); the Constitutional Revolution (1905–11); the revolutionary struggles of Azerbaijan, Gilan, and Khurasan (1918–21); the oil nationalization movement of 1951–53; the 1967–68 uprising of Kurdistan; the 1978–79 revolution; and the autonomy movement of Kurdistan (since 1979). The two movements were distinguished from their predecessors by their distinctively nationalistic character.

Both experiences showed the inability of the leadership to take the mass movement to victory. At times of enemy offensive, when effective leadership became most crucial, the leaders turned into obstacles against the further unfolding of the struggle. This allowed their strategically weaker opponents, the Pahlavi state and its colonialist backers, to defeat the movement. In both cases, the masses of people were disarmed and forced into surrender by their leaders rather than by their enemies. Without a Soviet presence, the two movements arguably might have been able to march on Tehran, as was the case during the Constitutional Revolution. The extremely corrupt and weak regime of the shah was not able to continue the war, even with British and American aid.[85] This was borne out seven years later when the monarch had to flee Iran in spite of years of modernization of his armed forces by the United States. He was able to regain his throne as a U.S. puppet only because of a CIA-organized coup, the betrayal of the movement by the Tudeh Party, and the reformist policies of the National Front.

The analysis put forward in this chapter rejects many propositions of the mainstream historiography of contemporary Iran. The nationalist movement of the Turks, Kurds, and other nationalities of Iran are genuine struggles rooted in the histories and cultures of these peoples. Religion did not occupy any visible place in the two movements. In fact, secular Kurdish nationalism, which emerged as early as the sixteenth century, was formulated by two mulla poets, one of whom castigated the traditional, nonnationalist, clergy. The idea of Iran as a monolithic Persian state is a construct of Persian national chauvinism that has served the ideological and political hegemony of the Qajar and Pahlavi dynasties.

The history of these two movements deserves more adequate study because, combining a direct and complex involvement of numerous local, national, regional, and international forces, it provides enormous opportunities for a better understanding of the dynamics of social change in contemporary Iran.

Notes

1. See, e.g., Richard van Wagenen, *The Iranian Case 1946* (New York: Carnegie Endowment for International Peace, 1952).

2. Louise L'Estrange Fawcett, *Iran and the Cold War: The Azarbaijan Crisis of 1946* (Cambridge: Cambridge University Press, 1992).

3. For example, the semiofficial Tehran newspaper *Kayhan Havai* attacks the commemoration of the Azarbaijan republic in Baku: see *Kayhan Havai,* January 16, 1991, 2, 8; *Kayhan Havai,* December 23, 1992, 8. The political discourse of these pronouncements is faithfully monarchist, declaring the DPA "secessionist" and "disbanded" (*munhalli*) and labeling the movement a "disturbance" (*gha'ili*).

4. See, for example, Sarlashkar Ahmad Zangani, *Khatirat-i az Ma'muriyyatha-yi man dar Azarbaijan* (Memoirs of my assignments in Azarbaijan) (Tehran: n.p., 1974). Examples of journalists' work include Najafquli Pisyan, *Az Mahabad-i Khunin ta Karaniha-yi Aras* (From bloody Mahabad to the banks of the Aras) (Tehran: Bungah-i Matbu'ati-yi Imruz, 1949); and Najafquli Pisyan, *Marg bud, Bazgasht ham bud* (There was both death and return) (Tehran: Bungah-i Matbu'ati-yi Imruz, 1949).

5. Ayatullah Ruhullah Khumaini, *Dar Justuju-yi Rah az Kalam-i Imam: Daftar-i Yazdahum: Milligara'i* (In search of the path from the word of the Imam: Book eleven: Nationalism) (Tehran: Amir Kabir, 1984), 50, 73. All translations from non-English works in this chapter are my own.

6. Hamid Algar, "Introduction," in Ayatullah Sayyid Mahmud Taleghani, *Society and Economics in Islam: Writings and Declarations of Ayatullah Sayyid Mahmud Taleghani,* trans. R. Campbell (Berkeley, Calif.: Mizan, 1982), 12.

7. Sayyid Jalal al-Din Madani, *Tarikh-i Siyasi-yi Mu'asir-i Iran* (Contemporary politi-

cal history of Iran), vol. 1 (Qum: Daftar-i Intisharat-i Islami, Jami'i-yi Mudarrisin-i Hauzi-yi 'Ilmi-yi Qum, 1982), 146.

8. "Murur-i bar Tarikhchi-yi Ravabit-i Iran va Inglis" (A review of the history of relations between Iran and England), pt. 27, *Jumhuri-yi Islami,* 5 Azar 1363/1984, 13.

9. Amir Hassanpour, *Nationalism and Language in Kurdistan, 1918–1985* (San Francisco: Mellen Research University Press, 1992), 130–32.

10. E.g., Faramarz Fatemi, *The U.S.S.R. in Iran* (New York: A. S. Barnes, 1980).

11. The semiofficial *Kayhan Havai,* June 30, 1993, 7, approvingly reprinted an article published in the monarchist *Kayhan,* no. 452 (London), that argues that among the four principal political currents—monarchists, Islamists, nationalists (followers of Dr. Musaddiq), and leftists—only the leftists have threatened the "territorial integrity of Iran under the rubric of defending 'the rights' of oppressed nationalities."

12. "Western" scholarship or historiography, as used here, is not a geographic or racial concept. It refers, rather, to the methodological, theoretical, and philosophical perspectives of positivist social sciences and humanities as developed in Western Europe and the United States. This type of research is conducted by both Westerners and non-Westerners, including Iranians.

13. See, inter alia, Major William Andrews, "The Azarbaijan Incident: The Soviet Union in Iran, 1941–46," *Military Review* (August 1974): 74–85; Rouhollah Ramazani, "The Autonomous Republic of Azarbaijan and the Kurdish People's Republic: Their Rise and Fall," in *The Anatomy of Communist Takeovers,* ed. Thomas Hammond (New Haven, Conn.: Yale University Press, 1975), 401–27; Martin Sicker, *The Bear and the Lion: Soviet Imperialism and Iran* (New York: Praeger, 1988); S. Enders Wimbush, "Divided Azarbaijan: Nation Building, Assimilation, and Mobilization between Three States," in *Soviet Asian Ethnic Frontiers,* ed. W. O. McCagg and B. D. Silver (New York: Pergamon, 1979), 61–81; Kuross A. Samii, "Truman against Stalin in Iran: A Tale of Three Messages," *Middle Eastern Studies* 23 (January 1987): 95–107; Manoucher Vahdat, "The Soviet Union and the Movement to Establish Autonomy in Iranian Azarbaijan" (Ph.D. diss., Indiana University, 1958); and especially George Lenczowski, "United States' Support for Iran's Independence and Integrity, 1945–1959," *Annals of the American Academy of Political and Social Science* (May 1972): 45–55. A specialist on the topic, Bruce Kuniholm, admits that the Azarbaijan movement "was not created solely by Soviet pressures" but refrains from conceptualizing the Azarbaijanis and Kurds as nations and reduces their nationalist movements to "a concern for identity within their own communal groups." The USSR's long-run goal is identified as "access to warm water ports" in the Persian Gulf. Bruce Kuniholm, "Azarbaijan. V. History from 1941 to 1947," in *Encyclopaedia Iranica,* vol. 3, ed. Ehsan Yarshater (London: Routledge & Kegan Paul, 1989), 231–34.

14. The concepts *despotism* and *reaction*—borrowed from the French Revolution—have become an inseparable part of the political discourse of Iranians. They are found in political writings, poetry, fiction, and the arts. As used in Iran, these terms have more or less exact referents, and they are more adequate than the "neutral" or "objective" conceptualizations of positivist social sciences, which, as far as many Iranians are concerned, are biased in favor of the enemies of the social movements. *Despotism* refers to the exercise of power by the monarchs and their state, and, recently, for some, the Islamic regime; *reaction* refers to the monarchs, the feudal class, the big and dependent merchant class, and individual groups or organizations opposed to democracy, freedom, and independence.

15. See, for example, the Hoover Institution on War, Revolution and Peace series titled "Studies of Nationalities in the USSR," which includes books on the Crimean Tatars, the Volga Tatars, the Kazakhs, Georgians, Uzbeks, Estonians, and Azarbaijani Turks.

16. See, for example, Archie Roosevelt, "The Kurdish Republic of Mahabad," *Middle*

East Journal 1, no. 3 (1947): 247–69; William Eagleton, *The Kurdish Republic of 1946* (London: Oxford University Press, 1963). This treatment is not unique to the academy: American media, with their claims to "objectivity" and "freedom," follow a similar approach to social and political movements around the world — anticommunist groups, organizations, and movements receive sympathetic treatment, whereas leftist, anti-Western movements are depicted negatively. See, e.g., Noam Chomsky, *Necessary Illusions: Thought Control in Democratic Societies* (Montreal: CBC Enterprises, 1989).

17. Richard A. Mobley, "A Study of Relations between the Mahabad Republic and the Azerbaijan Democratic Republic: The Turbulent Alliance and Its Impact upon the Mahabad Republic of 1946" (unpublished seminar paper, Department of History, Georgetown University, 1979).

18. Another experiment in autonomous rule was the Kurdish government established in Sulaimania (now in Iraqi Kurdistan) in the wake of World War I. The head of the state was Shaikh Mahmoud, who declared himself the king of Kurdistan.

19. Kerim Hussami, *Komarî Dêmokratî Kurdistan yan Xudmuxtarî?* (The Kurdish Democratic Republic or autonomy?) (Sweden: Binkey Çapemenî Azad, 1986).

20. Mahmoud Mela 'Izzet, *Komarî Millî Mehabad* (The National Republic of Mahabad) (Iraqi Kurdistan: Ibrahîm 'Ezo, 1984; reprinted in Sweden in 1986). Mela 'Izzet has also published a rare collection of the internal official correspondence of the Kurdish Republic: *Dewletî Cimhûrî Kurdistan: Name u Dokûmênt* (back cover: Mahmud Mulla Izzat, *The Democratic Republic of Kurdistan [Correspondence and Documents]*, vol. 1 [Sweden: Binkey Çapemenî Azad, 1992]).

21. E.g., *Tudeh*, no. 21 (Mordad 1350/1971), 37–43; Ali Riza Nabdil, *Azarbaijan va Mas'ali-yi Milli* (Azarbaijan and the national question) (n.p.: 1352/1973); M. A. Javid, *Dimukrasi-yi Naqis: Barrasi-yi Salha-yi 1320–32, Daftar-i 2–3: Azarbaijan* (Incomplete democracy: A survey of the years 1941–53: Azarbaijan) ([Europe]: Union of Iranian Communists, [1977?]).

22. JAMI (Jibhi-yi Azadi-yi Mardum-i Iran), *Guzashteh Chiragh-i Rah-i Ayandeh ast* (The past is the light on the path to the future) ([Europe]: 1976; reprinted in Iran in 1979).

23. Anvar Khami'i, *Fursat-i Buzurg-i az Dast Rafteh* (The great lost opportunity), vol. 2 (Tehran: Hafteh, 1983); Ardashir Avanisian, *Khatirat-i Ardashir Avanisian* (Memoirs of Ardashir Avanisian) (Köln, Germany: Hizb-i Dimukratik-i Mardum-i Iran, 1990).

24. Javad Sadiq, *Milliyat va Inqilab dar Iran* (Nationality and revolution in Iran) (New York: Intisharat-i Fanus, 1973).

25. Azar Tabari, *Bibin Tafavat-i Rah az Kuja ast ta beh Kuja!* (See how far the difference is!) (n.p., 1974).

26. Father Thomas Bois (Le Père Thomas Bois O.P.), a Dominican priest familiar with and sympathetic to the Kurds, published *Les Kurdes et le Droit* under the pseudonym Lucien Rambout (Paris: Les Editions du Cerf, 1947). The book provides a pro-Kurdish picture of the nationalist movement and is critical of U.S. policy toward the two republics. Not surprisingly, a reviewer in the *Middle East Journal* 2 (July 1948) assessed the book as "largely communist propaganda" (p. 356). See also Thomas Bois, "Mahabad: Une éphémère république kurde independante," *Orient* 29 (1964): 173–210; Chris Kutschera, *Le movement nationale kurde* (Paris: Flammarion, 1979); Wadie Jwaideh, "The Kurdish Nationalist Movement: Its Origins and Development" (Ph.D. diss., Syracuse University, 1960).

27. See John Foran, *Fragile Resistance: Social Transformation in Iran from 1500 to the Revolution* (Boulder, Colo.: Westview, 1993); Ervand Abrahamian, "Communism and Communalism in Iran: The *Tudah* and the *Firqah-i Dimukrat*," *International Journal of Middle East Studies* 1 (1970): 291–316; Ervand Abrahamian, *Iran between Two Revolutions* (Princeton, N.J.: Princeton University Press, 1982); Parviz Homayounpour, *L'Affaire*

d'Azarbaidjan (Lausanne, Switzerland: n.p., 1967). Homayounpour is less enthusiastic than the other cited authors about the nationalist component of the movements. Two useful studies were published in late 1993 while this book was in press. On Kurdistan, see *Newşîrwan Mistefa Emîn, Ḧikûmetî Kurdistan, Rêbendanî 1324-Sermawezî 1325[:] Kurd le Gemey Sovêtî da* (back cover: Noshirwan Emin, The Government of Kurdistan, 22 January-17 December 1946: The Kurds in the Soviet Game) (Utrecht, The Netherlands: KIB, 1993). This book is based largely on the newspaper *Kurdistan,* the official organ of the Kurdish Democratic Party in 1946. In spite of its subtitle, the focus of the book is not the Soviet role in the republic. The other work, on Azarbaijan, is Touraj Atabaki, *Azerbaijan: Ethnicity and Autonomy in Twentieth-Century Iran* (London: British Academic Press, 1993).

28. Like other social science concepts, *feudalism* is controversial. It is indispensable, however, for the purposes of this study. The term refers, here, to a social and economic system in which the landowners (the feudal class) own the land (and usually water and pasture) and the tillers of the land, the peasants, work on the land, usually with their labor, tools, draft animals, and seed (the peasant may not own the last two). The nonproducing feudal class appropriates a portion of the total product because of its ownership of the land and associated social, political, and military power. The peasant (family) is tied to the land and personally dependent on the feudal lords or their representatives. Every productive activity of the peasant is subject to taxation by the dominating class. The peasant does not enjoy the right to travel, move, or, usually, marry without the consent of the lord.

29. For a brief review of the literature and language, see H. Javadi and K. Burrill, "Azerbaijan. X. Azeri literature in Iran," in *Encyclopaedia Iranica,* vol. 3, ed. Ehsan Yarshater (Costa Mesa, Calif.: Mazda, 1989), 251–55.

30. Audrey Altstadt, *The Azerbaijani Turks: Power and Identity under Russian Rule* (Stanford, Calif.: Hoover Institution Press, 1992), 5, 233.

31. Though the seventeenth-century meaning of *milet* in the Ottoman empire did not imply the European notion of "nation," Khani's use of the concept is strikingly similar to the modern concept. See Hassanpour, *Nationalism and Language,* 98–99.

32. Ibid., 49–67, 83–90.

33. See, for example, Wimbush, "Divided Azerbaijan," 74–75.

34. John Foran, "Social Structure and Social Change in Iran from 1500 to 1979" (Ph.D. diss., University of California at Berkeley, Department of Sociology, 1988), 503–8.

35. Hassanpour, *Nationalism and Language,* 90–94.

36. Altstadt, *The Azerbaijani Turks,* 89–107.

37. Foran, "Social Structure and Social Change," 503–18.

38. M. Hêmin, "Sereta" (Introduction), in Hesen Qizilcî, *Pêkenînî Geda* (The beggar's laughing) (n.p.: Binkey Pêşewa, 1972), 6.

39. A. Hejar, "Le meř jiyan û beserhatî Hejar bwêjî Kurd" (On the life and biography of Hazhar, the Kurdish poet), in *Kurdskii Dialekt Mukri,* (The Mukri Kurdish Dialect), comp. Karim R. Eiiubi and Iraida A. Smirnova (Leningrad: Nauka, 1968). On the repression of Turkish, see JAMI, *Guzashteh,* 236–40.

40. Quoted in Hussami, *Komarî Dêmokratî Kurdistan,* 28. On oral and written literature, see also 'Ebdul Qadir Debbaẍî, *Raperînî "Komeley" Jê - Kaf: Welamêk be Namêlkey: "Jê Kaf Çi bû?"* (The uprising of "Komeley" J. K.: A response to the pamphlet: "What was J-K?") (n.p.: Kurdish Democratic Party of Iran: n.d.; written in March 1982).

41. My evidence includes numerous stories told to me by adults when I was a child growing up in Mahabad, as well as accounts in published memoirs.

42. These are lines from a longer poem first published in *Hawarî Kurd,* Rezberî 1324/ September–October 1945, 25. According to Debbaẍî, "Raperînî," 16, the nationalist poet

Hejar composed the piece in Bokan in 1322/1943. It is interesting that the magazine *Hawarî Kurd* used ellipses in place of the words "imperial," "the shah," and "Stalin." This was apparently to appease Soviet authorities, who tried to tone down anti-Tehran sentiments.

43. See JAMI, *Guzashteh,* 236–66.

44. According to U.S. diplomatic dispatches from Iran (November 1941), there was widespread sympathy for the creation of an autonomous Azarbaijan. Bertel E. Kuniholm, U.S. consul at Tabriz, reported that "a soviet could be established overnight in Azarbaijan if the Russians gave the word." Memorandum prepared by the Division of Near Eastern Affairs, State Department, Washington, January 23, 1943, in *Foreign Relations of the United States: Diplomatic Papers,* 1943 (hereafter *FRUS*) (Washington, D.C.: U.S. Government Printing Office, 1964), 4:333.

45. JAMI, *Guzashteh,* 240–41.

46. Eagleton, *The Kurdish Republic,* 33–39.

47. Ibid., 40.

48. *Azhir,* July 27, 1944, quoted in JAMI, *Guzashteh,* 220.

49. It must be noted that, before the war, British, French, and American policy in 1938–39 aimed at directing Nazi power against the USSR, exhausting the two enemies, and getting rid of both.

50. C. R., "On the Outcome of World War 2 and the Prospects for Revolution in the West," *The Communist* (Chicago) 2, no. 2 (1978): 61–65.

51. Thomas Ricks, "U.S. Military Missions in Iran, 1943–1978: The Political Economy of Military Assistance," in *U.S. Strategy in the Gulf: Intervention against Liberation,* ed. Leila Meo (Belmont, Mass.: Association of Arab-American University Graduates, 1981), 38.

52. Quoted in ibid., 40.

53. See, among others, David Nissman, *The Soviet Union and Iranian Azarbaijan: The Use of Nationalism for Political Penetration* (Boulder, Colo.: Westview, 1987).

54. JAMI, *Guzashteh,* 225.

55. Javid, *Dimukrasi-yi Naqis,* 17.

56. JAMI, *Guzashteh,* 245–46.

57. On the history of the DPA, see Abrahamian, "Communism and Communalism."

58. See, e.g., JAMI, *Guzashteh,* 147, 271–74. See also note 62 below.

59. Ibid., 277–78.

60. Quoted in ibid., 279.

61. Ibid., 290–92.

62. Contrary to the claims of their adversaries, the DPA and KDP were not created by the USSR. Although much remains unknown, the Tudeh Party, closely tied to Moscow, was not informed or consulted during the formation of the DPA: see Iraj Iskandari, *Khatirat-i Siyasi* (Political reminiscences) (Tehran: Intisharat-i 'Ilmi, 1989), 128. Once they realized that the Soviet policy of discouraging nationalist struggle had changed to encouragement and support, the KJK and DPA negotiated their program with the USSR, as both an occupying force and an ally. However, far from fanning the flames of revolution in Azarbaijan, Kurdistan, or throughout Iran, the USSR did its best to harness them. The KDP, for example, had to enter into alliance with feudal and tribal chiefs who were not sympathetic to the cause, and the DPA and KDP were not allowed to extend their struggle beyond Azarbaijan and northern Kurdistan, and were enjoined to avoid a radical confrontation with Tehran. This subjection of the interests of their peoples to the demands of the Soviet Union by Azeri and Kurdish leaders helped bring the two movements to a tragic end.

63. Two primary sources on these developments are the newspaper *Azarbaijan* and the book *Sahrivarin Onikisi* (The twelfth of Sharivar/September 3), published by the DPA in

Tabriz in 1325/1946 on the occasion of the first anniversary of the formation of the DPA; the Persian translation is *Davazdahum-i Shahrivar* (Italy: Intisharat-i Babak, 1978).

64. See, among others, Abrahamian, "Communism and Communalism," 313; Homayounpour, *L'Affaire d'Azarbaidjan,* 135–46; and the eyewitness accounts of journalist Abul-Hasan Nuri, *Azarbaijan-i Dimukrat* (Democratic Azarbaijan) (Tehran: Dad, 1946).

65. Reports from Tabriz dispatched by the British consul (quoted in Abrahamian, *Iran between Two Revolutions,* 409) and a less enthusiastic American consul (Rossow to Secretary of State, Dispatch 242, Secret, January 4, 1946, 891.00/1–1446) confirm the popularity of Azarbaijan and its reforms. By the fall of 1946, economic difficulties, including food shortages resulting from bad weather and poor harvests, as well as political and financial uncertainties, confronted the government with serious problems that were handled with tough bureaucratic measures such as overtaxation, discipline, and even cuts in benefits to workers. These measures led to discontent, especially among the bazaaris and other wavering supporters. However, contrary to its adversaries' accounts, the people did not rise up against the democratic regime. On the popularity of the movement, see also Nuri, *Azarbaijan-i Dimukrat.*

66. William O. Douglas, *Strange Lands and Friendly People* (New York: Harper & Brothers, 1951), 43, 45, 50.

67. Ibid., 64. Fearing the continuing impact of the Kurdish republic, the shah's regime removed the grave of Qazi Muhammad and two hanged leaders in the late 1950s on the pretext of "forestation" of the cemetery. The graves were restored by the people of Mahabad after the fall of the monarchy in 1979.

68. At a social gathering celebrating the fall of the two republics, the shah paid a "fulsome and even embarrassing tribute" to American support. Others at the party referred to Azarbaijan as "the Stalingrad of the western democracies" and the "turn of the tide against Soviet aggression throughout the world." Ambassador Allen to the secretary of state, secret telegram, December 17, 1946, in *FRUS,* 7:563.

69. See Foran, *Fragile Resistance,* 280.

70. JAMI, *Guzashteh,* 374–97.

71. Ibid., 398–400. According to an American missionary returning from Tabriz, Azarbaijani forces "are digging trenches in front of Zenjan and give every appearance of intending to put up strong resistance." U.S. Ambassador Allen to secretary of state, secret telegram, November 8, 1946, in *FRUS,* 7:545.

72. *Azarbaijan,* December 3, 1946.

73. *Azarbaijan,* December 9, 1946.

74. See U.S. Ambassador Allen's secret telegram to the secretary of state, November 8, 1946, in *FRUS,* 7:545; and the acting secretary of state's top-secret telegram to Allen, ibid., 546–47, indicating diplomatic and military support for Tehran.

75. JAMI, *Guzashteh,* 415.

76. Although there is no documentation, it is unanimously believed by those in the movement that the Soviets pushed for nonresistance. See, among others, Abul-Hasan Tafrishian, *Qiyam-i Afsaran-i Khurasan 1324* (The uprising of the Khurasan officers, 1945/46) (Tehran: Intisharat-i 'Ilmi, 1980), 79; JAMI, *Guzashteh,* 416–19.

77. JAMI, *Guzashteh,* 416–17. See also Ambassador Allen's telegram to the secretary of state, December 12, 1946, in *FRUS,* 7:560.

78. See JAMI, *Guzashteh,* 419–22, for a short account.

79. Douglas, *Strange Lands and Friendly People,* 45. For a similar assessment, see Homa Katouzian, *The Political Economy of Modern Iran: Despotism and Pseudomodernism, 1926–1979* (New York: New York University Press, 1981), 155.

80. Eagleton, *The Kurdish Republic,* 111; JAMI, *Guzashteh,* 418; M. Hêmin, *Tarîk û Rûn* (Twilight) (n.p.: Binkey Pêşewa, 1974), 26–28.

81. The DPA regularly prevented the *fida'ilar* forces from engaging in offensive action. To cite a few examples, Pishivari admitted that after the coming to power of Qavam, who offered reconciliation with Azarbaijan, the DPA prevented their forces from advancing on Astara, Bandar Pahlavi, and Qazvin, whose people wanted to join Azarbaijan. *Azarbaijan,* April 21, 1946, quoted in JAMI, *Guzashteh,* 425, 359. When Qavam argued that Khamseh was not administratively part of Azarbaijan and asked the DPA to return its administration to the central government, the people and *fida'ilar* forces refused to obey, but the DPA disarmed the dissident forces. JAMI, *Guzashteh,* 401; see also 416–17, 419, 429. The policy of compromise was also evident when an agreement between Azarbaijan and Tehran was signed. *Azarbaijan,* July 5, 1946, wrote, "Until today, we struggled with arms in order to meet our demands; from now on we continue our struggle with pens and with our organization." Quoted in JAMI, *Guzashteh,* 428.

82. C. R., "On the Outcome of World War 2," 77–102.

83. Although Truman has confirmed the sending of the ultimatum (see J. Philipp Rosenberg, "The Cheshire Ultimatum: Truman's Message to Stalin in the 1946 Azerbaijan Crisis," *Journal of Politics* 41 [1979]: 933–40; Samii, "Truman against Stalin"), some historians deny it. See James A. Thorpe, "Truman's Ultimatum to Stalin on the 1946 Azerbaijan Crisis: The Making of a Myth," *Journal of Politics* 40 (February 1978): 188–95; Turaj Atabaki, "Afsaneh-yi yik Ultimatum" (The myth of an ultimatum), *Chashmandaz* 3 (Autumn 1987): 54–68.

84. Quoted in C. R., "On the Outcome of World War 2," 104–8.

85. The leaders of the two movements believed that the shah's army was a cowardly force propped up by foreign powers. This view is best reflected in Qazi Muhammad's letter to the Iranian military commander in Saqqiz. He referred to the following couplet by the great Iranian epic poet, Firdausi: "Hameh sar bih sar tan bih kushtan dahim / Az an bih kai kishvar bih dushman dahim" (We would much rather die one by one / Than give our country to the enemy) and told the army commander, "You are the officers of an army which, at the time of fighting and risking lives, take to your heels and traduce Firdausi's great lines of poetry thus: 'Hameh sar bih sar pusht bih dushman konim / Az an bih kai khud ra bih kushtan dahim' (We turn our backs to the enemy one by one / Rather than die for our country)." Quoted in Eagleton, *The Kurdish Republic,* 125. According to confidential diplomatic correspondence of the U.S. ambassador in Tehran, army commanders were panicked, and plans for the defense of Tehran and even the removal of the capital to Isfahan were being considered. Ambassador Murray's telegram to the secretary of state, November 28, 1945, in *FRUS,* 8:464–65. Even Britain wavered in the confrontation with Azarbaijan. According to a secret memo sent to Washington by American Ambassador Allen on September 28, 1946: "There are some additional indications that British are envisioning possible severance of Azarbaijan from Iran as an alternative to continuance of present situation, which they fear will result in incorporation of larger part of country into Soviet sphere. Idea seems to be that it would be preferable to cut off rotten part of apple rather than let it infect remainder" *FRUS,* 7:517.

Chapter 5

The Oil Nationalization Movement, 1949–53

Sussan Siavoshi

Between 1949 and 1953, Iran experienced the emergence, ascendence, and ultimately failure of a movement that had a profound impact on the future course of its history. The oil nationalization struggle started as a protest against British control over the oil industry, but soon developed into an expression of a genuine popular desire for Iran's dignity as an independent nation-state. It attracted support from large sections of different urban social classes with diverse ideological leanings and led to the formation of the National Front, which became its organizational instrument. The leader of the movement was the liberal and charismatic Muhammad Musaddiq, who aspired not only to sovereignty for his country but also to the establishment of a truly democratic polity.

Unfortunately for the Iranians, the odds against the long-term victory of the movement, as we will explore in this chapter, were huge. In retrospect, the combined hostile forces of foreign powers and their domestic allies, the dependent and weak nature of the Iranian economy, and the internal tensions within the movement itself made its defeat easy to predict. The purpose of this chapter is to analyze the factors that brought about the brief victory of the nationalistic struggle and then led to its ultimate defeat.

There were multiple interpretations about the nature of the groups and factors involved in the 1949–53 phenomenon as it was unfolding. These ranged from the initial verbal reactions of the leftist Tudeh Party to the interpretation presented by conservative Iranians and the principal antagonist of the movement, Great Britain. As time passed, other approaches to the movement were put forth by students of Iranian history and politics. A brief summary of these various approaches will precede the interpretation undertaken in this study.

As intellectuals of a Marxist-Leninist party, the Tudeh theoreticians believed that a genuine revolutionary potential existed in the downtrodden classes of workers and peasants and that the post-World War II economic situation in Iran had encouraged the actualization of this potential.[1] The problem, however, lay with the bourgeois leadership that took over the budding movement. By its nature,

106

the bourgeois class was ultimately less frightened of imperialism than of a true national movement that would struggle against not just foreign domination but also internal exploitation.[2] Based on this worldview, the activities of the National Front and the Musaddiq administration, which initially included gestures of co-operation with the United States in fighting against British domination, were harshly criticized.[3] Tudeh newspapers such as *Razm* and *Bisu-yi Ayandeh* labeled Musaddiq and other leaders of the oil nationalization movement as antiprogressive and agents of American colonialism. The National Front was considered a fake reformist political current beguiling the masses away from a correct and radical social struggle.[4]

The Tudeh Party's views went through various changes, particularly after tension arose between the U.S. administration and Musaddiq's government in 1952. However, an official theoretical revision occurred only after the 1953 coup d'état. Through a soul-searching process, a new interpretation of the 1949–53 movement evolved that parted from its predecessor, most importantly over the character of the national (non-Western-connected) bourgeoisie and its representatives during the oil nationalization struggle.[5] The new analysis focused on the anti-imperialist tendencies of the national bourgeoisie and the important role played by the National Front in leading an anticolonial struggle from 1949 to 1953.[6]

Overall, the assessment of leftist Iranian intellectuals has been that during the oil nationalization period a revolutionary situation existed in Iran and that the liberal national bourgeoisie was in the position to assume the leadership of the emerging movement and to make a valuable contribution by attacking British imperialism. But because the struggle between liberation movements on the one hand and imperialism and its domestic allies (foreign-linked compradors, feudal elements, and conservatives) on the other was a life-and-death battle, anything short of a complete eradication of the hostile forces would ultimately result in failure. The National Front, owing to its lack of resolve, which itself was a result of its class interest, failed to push the struggle to its logical conclusion (it attacked only British imperialism and not U.S. imperialism or domestic reactionaries) and therefore lost in the end.[7]

The conservative Iranian analysis of the movement can be found in Muhammad Reza Pahlavi's interpretation of Musaddiq and the oil nationalization era. Considering himself a proponent of nationalization, the shah nonetheless judged the movement and its leader with contempt. Admitting that there was frustration with British control over oil, the shah, however, had nothing to say about any genuine nationalistic or revolutionary movement. In fact, his analysis was focused on the actions of Musaddiq. The shah depicted Musaddiq as a power-hungry, irrational leader, and believed that Musaddiq was personally responsible for plunging the country into ruin by not positively responding to British or American proposals to reach a settlement. The overthrow of Musaddiq, then, was not the defeat of a nationalistic movement seeking independence for Iran, but rather the triumph of rational and positive nationalism led by the shah over the fanaticism and negativism of Musaddiq and his supporters.[8]

A similar interpretation was provided by British politicians and the British press. The British parliamentary debates recorded throughout the nationalization period are quite revealing. Echoing the sentiments of the politicians, the British press (with few exceptions) also lashed out at Musaddiq and the public mood in Iran. Typical of such analysis was a book called *Abadan,* written by a BBC correspondent. The Anglo-Iranian Oil Company (AIOC) had been generously compensating Iran for exploitation of its oil. However, corrupt politicians and greedy landowners had prevented wealth from trickling down and therefore had created a crisis in a half-civilized, poor land.[9] The crisis had led to a vicious alliance between the communists and rabble-rousing fanatical religious leaders. Inflamed by the accusations made by the landowning class, who blamed Iran's misfortune on the foreigners, the AIOC had become a scapegoat.[10] Meanwhile, the right-wing demagogue Dr. Musaddiq, "the anxious vulture of the oil industry," had taken advantage of the situation and declared the nationalization of the "company's resources."[11]

On this account the entire nationalization movement could be reduced to the malicious intention of xenophobic rabble-rousing leaders who used an "obscure sense of popular discontent" and directed it against the generous and civilizing mission of the AIOC. Like the shah's account, the basic British position was to ignore the existence of a genuine movement and to attribute the whole crisis to the irrational actions of a few men and their blinded and emotional followers. Given that the movement was irrational, its defeat should be considered a rational and even natural outcome of the "progressive" movement of human history. These views were later echoed by the American mass media as well.[12]

The assessment of the oil nationalization movement by academics has also ranged from negative to positive. For example, Peter Avery's book *Modern Iran* portrays the movement as destructive and vengeful.[13] Emphasizing Iranians' attraction to "self-immolation," Avery contrasts, in subtle ways, Iran's apparently "irrational" behavior with the "cautious" and "rational" reaction of the British. Like the British press and government, Avery describes Musaddiq as a power-hungry, frightened, and inconsistent man. Seeing the whole crisis as the work of basically one man with some help from demagogues such as "Mulla Kashani," Avery emphasizes the ability of Musaddiq to excite a frustrated mob that for the time being was mobilized and acted according to its cruelest instincts.[14] The hooligans who provided the rowdy bodies for street demonstrations struck fear in the hearts of those rational and responsible men who wanted to voice their opposition to Musaddiq's action, both in the press and in the parliament. To Avery, the Musaddiq phenomenon therefore was not only economically detrimental to Iran but also eroded parliamentary institutions and was therefore in essence antidemocratic.[15]

A different interpretation of the movement has been given by other students of Iranian society and politics. Nasrollah Saifpour Fatemi, a scholar and an important government official during the oil nationalization period, saw Iran as a case study of the Third World countries that were going through two revolutions: a political revolution against foreign domination, and a social and economic revolution against poverty.[16] The reason for the failure of the movement, according to Fatemi, was a combination of British intransigence and arrogance, the inability of Iranian leaders to unite, and underestimation of several important factors by Iranian politicians. One of these underestimated factors was the British government's ability to influence the American administration. Another was AIOC leverage with big American oil companies, which led to the latter's refusal to help Iran with oil production and marketing. This underestimation was intensified by overestimation of Iran's ability to develop the oil industry without outside support.[17]

Richard Cottam likewise considers the oil nationalization movement the genuine expression of nationalist aspirations, an example of Third World liberation struggles. Unlike Avery, Cottam believes that the movement was led predominantly by democratic intellectuals and that Musaddiq, who gave the Iranian nationalist movement its direction and mission, was a true liberal.[18] Cottam regards the middle class as the core support group for the movement, with a large percentage of the urban lower classes joining the movement in early 1952.[19] In essence, then, the movement was basically one of the middle class, with lower-class support in its struggle against foreign influence and the domestic oligarchy. As such, it elaborated revolutionary programs that aimed at the destruction of all aspects of the oligarchical-imperial alliance through the elimination of the AIOC.[20] However, the leaders who were able to work together and directed the movement in its early days were ideologically divergent, and not all shared the same vision about the future of the Iranian polity and society. The right, left, and centrist tendencies within the National Front made the reaching of a coherent plan for a new order a difficult task, one that only a decisive leadership could have overcome.

As the reason for the defeat of the movement, Cottam cites the concerted efforts of Britain and the United States to topple the Musaddiq administration. However, he also focuses on the problems that plagued the movement itself, one of which was perceptual. In contrast to Fatemi, Cottam explains the perceptual factor in terms of the overestimation of British influence by Musaddiq and therefore the underestimation of his own power in creating a radically different polity in Iran. Cottam's conclusion rests on the assumption that despite great odds against the movement its defeat was not inevitable if Musaddiq had exercised continued skillful political leadership by breaking the stalemate in the oil dispute (accepting the World Bank oil proposal) and therefore shifting his attention to domestic issues.[21]

Other serious academic interpretations of the events follow in varying degree the general outlook set by Cottam. Homa Katouzian's line of analysis, for example, seems different from Cottam's in terminology but not in essence. Katouzian rejects the label of nationalism in characterizing the movement and asserts that nationalism is the ideology of despotism.[22] But a careful reading of Katouzian reveals that his substantive characterization of what he calls the "democratic" or "popular" movement is similar to Cottam's depiction of the movement in terms of its nature, aspirations, and direction.[23]

Another noteworthy study of the period has been done by Fakhreddin Azimi, whose reading of the movement demonstrates agreement with both Cottam and Katouzian. The only major difference between Azimi and the latter two regards the causes of the movement's failure. In analyzing the defeat, Azimi puts emphasis on structural factors and considers the outcome almost inevitable, whereas both Cottam and Katouzian see the nonstructural, political factors as crucial elements in explaining the same phenomenon.[24]

This brief review of literature points to the complexity of the oil nationalization era and the difficulty in both the conceptualization and the interpretation of the movement it entailed. What follows is an attempt first to outline an alternative conceptual approach, calling the movement *liberal nationalist,* and then to describe certain key trends and events that led to the rise of the movement, and ultimately to its failure.

The Oil Nationalization Movement as a Liberal Nationalist Movement

Faithful to the aspiration of its predecessor, the Constitutional Revolution, the oil nationalization movement was preoccupied with two interrelated goals: the destruction of internal dictatorship and the establishment of a truly sovereign country. The struggle against dictatorship entailed not only individual freedom from the absolutist rule of the state but also social legislation promoting the socioeconomic equality essential for a dignified life. These are the essence of modern liberalism adhered to by social democrats, as opposed to laissez-faire or classical liberalism, which has been primarily a bourgeois ideology. It should be mentioned that the movement contained illiberal elements (including some of the leaders of the National Front), but Musaddiq and his close associates in charge of running the nationalist government held liberal values.

There has been reluctance on the part of many to label the oil nationalization movement a nationalist movement. Part of this reluctance stems from the negative connotation attached to the concept of nationalism after the experience of Nazism in Germany and fascism in Italy. Racial supremacy and an aggressive foreign policy were the essential ingredients of this notion of nationalism. However, there is no necessary connection between the expression of nationalism in many societies (especially in the Third World) and what symbolized Nazi and fascist nationalism. In fact, for Iranian liberal nationalists, like many other Third World nationalists, nationalism was and is closely associated with liberation from the dominance of imperialism and the creation of a truly sovereign country. If freedom from foreign oppression is the main goal of nationalism, as the term is defined in this study, then the 1949–53 movement should definitely be labeled a nationalist movement.

The rise and fall of the oil nationalization movement can be attributed to a variety of factors, including the internal characteristics of the movement, Iran's structural and political dynamics, and the global power configuration. Politically, the organization, leadership, and mobilizational capacities of the National Front and those of its internal and external challengers probably played the most important role in the rise and fall of the movement. Structurally, Iran's economic dependency and its social structure set the parameters within which the expansion and effectiveness of the movement were confined. However, the failure of the movement did not result from the domestic factors alone. Globally, the structural demands of an ever-expanding world capitalist system and the advent of the Cold War and its impact on the Third World nationalist or nonaligned movements challenged the oil nationalization movement every step of the way and dealt it a fatal blow.

A Historical Overview

When oil was discovered by British subject William Knox D'Arcy in Iran in 1908, the country, never a direct colony, was subject to British control in the south and Russian control in the north. The D'Arcy oil agreement allocated a very small proportion of the oil revenues to Iran. According to the terms of the agreement, Iran was to receive 20,000 pounds sterling in cash, 20,000 pounds in shares, and 16 percent of the profits. Politically and economically weak, Iran did not have much influence in setting the terms of the oil concession that was to be in effect until 1961. As a result, not only was the Iranian share of the oil revenues insignificant, but several incidents were used as pretexts by the British-owned oil company to deny Iran part of those revenues.[25] The terms of the concession and the company's actual behavior concerning Iranian demands and interests testified to the dismal position of Iran in its relations with both foreign governments and powerful foreign interests.

The 1921 coup d'état that brought Reza Khan to power laid the foundation for the making of a strong central state. Reza Khan, later crowned as the founder of the new Pahlavi dynasty, succeeded in bringing internal order to Iran. Despite his achievements in dealing with domestic issues, Reza Shah failed to demonstrate any meaningful control over the Anglo-Iranian Oil Company. The events that led to the conclusion of a new agreement with the company in 1933 proved Iran to be as weak in its relation to foreign powers as in the early 1900s. The agreement, which was supposed to address Iranian grievances with the previous concession, extended the control of the British company over oil resources until 1993 without any significant change in Iran's income.[26] It should come as no surprise that the terms of this new concession were silently resented by Iranian nationalists. This resentment had no outlet until Reza Shah's abdication and the subsequent breakdown of the tight control of the state over civil society, precipitated by the Allied occupation of Iran in 1941. The emergence of a free press and several political parties were products of this era.

Nationalist grievances over the oil issue found an opportunity to surface when Iran demanded a revision of the 1933 concession. The response of the AIOC was to propose a "Supplementary Agreement" with minor changes in Iran's favor. However, compared with the arrangement of other foreign oil companies such as the Arabian-American Oil Company with the government of Saudi Arabia,[27] this supplementary proposal fell far short of any real improvement for Iran.[28] The terms of the proposal became the subject of heated parliamentary debates toward the end of the term of the Fifteenth Majlis.[29] The impressive resistance shown by a few of the deputies, such as Hussain Makki and Muzafar Baqa'i, to the Supplementary Agreement prevented the taking of a vote on the bill, and the task of dealing with the oil industry was left to the Sixteenth Majlis.

The fiery debates in the Majlis and Iranian press set the tone for the demand for the nationalization of the oil industry. Meanwhile, the 1949 election of the Sixteenth Majlis drew the public's attention. However, despite government assurances regarding the honesty of the elections, it soon became obvious that they had been rigged. To protest the conduct of the elections, in October 1949 Musaddiq and nineteen other influential individuals took sanctuary in the shah's palace and demanded an investigation. With no immediate success, the protesters left the palace grounds after four days. However, during those four days, the protesters founded the National Front, which became the organizational expression of the nationalist movement.[30]

Another result of that protest was its impact on public pressure on the government for new elections. After the assassination of Hazhir, the shrewd and influential court minister, the government retreated partially, declaring Tehran's elections null. The new elections brought eight National Front candidates from Tehran to the Majlis, including Musaddiq, Ayatullah Kashani, and Muzafar Baqa'i. From the outset it was clear that sooner or later the issue of oil would be addressed in the parliament. The government of 'Ali Mansur, itself taking a noncommittal stand, presented the Supplementary Agreement to the Majlis. On June 26 a special committee chaired by Musaddiq was created to study the issue and to make a recommendation to the Majlis.

In the meantime, Mansur's administration was replaced by that of General 'Ali Razmara in June 1950. Razmara's assumption of power was not received kindly by the National Front, which considered him unsuited for the job and characterized his administration as a military dictatorship.[31] Despite this protest, Razmara was confirmed by the Majlis and quickly proposed several bills on domestiç issues and pursued an active foreign policy.[32] Still, like his predecessor, Razmara did not take an official stand with regard to the Supplementary Agreement, leading to a request for the interpellation of the government by the National Front deputies.[33] Government response to the pressure was confusing. Razmara, who had received a new offer for 50/50 profit sharing from the AIOC, did not reveal this. In order to consolidate his power he decided to wait for an opportune moment. In the meantime, Razmara gave two contradictory speeches to the Senate and the Majlis. In his address to the Senate, he supported the Supplementary Agreement. However, in his next day's speech in the Majlis, he failed to indicate his approval of the agreement. Musaddiq pointed out the contradiction and the activities of the special oil committee intensified.[34] The committee ultimately rejected the Supplementary Agreement on December 10, 1950, and reported its decision to the Majlis.[35] Its recommendation was widely publicized throughout Iran and gave momentum to the eventually successful call for the nationalization of the oil industry.[36] Next, both houses of the parliament, the Majlis on March 15, and the Senate on March 20, unanimously approved the recommendation of the oil committee for nationalization of oil. What remained to be done was to find methods to implement the measure. A two-month extension was given to the special oil committee to come up with a solution.

Meanwhile, there were changes in the government. Razmara was assassinated in March, creating an atmosphere of intimidation and fear among those members of the political elite who up to then were contemplating resistance to the public mood and the nationalization of oil. The next administration, headed by Hussain 'Ala, was short-lived. On April 26, the special oil committee approved the recommendation of a subcommittee of seven regarding a nine-point implementation plan. Caught between a rock (the AIOC) and a hard place (the strong nationalist leadership in the Majlis supported by the public), 'Ala elected to throw in the towel. On April 29, 1951, Musaddiq's premiership was recommended by the Majlis and received royal confirmation. On the same day, the Majlis approved the nine-point plan and the Senate followed suit on April 30. The nationalization of the oil industry brought the wrath of Britain, which showed its indignation through boycott, blockade, threat of military force, and refusal to make oil payments to Iran.

The Nature of the Movement

Leadership

What gave the oil nationalization movement its character was the leadership that guided it during the fateful years of 1949–53. This leadership was vested in the person of Musaddiq and a few other individuals who joined him in directing the movement through the organization of the National Front. Who were these leaders, what did they stand for, how did they organize their activities, and what were their relations to the rank and file of the movement? Answers to these fundamental questions shed much light on the character of the movement.

Muhammad Musaddiq was born to an aristocratic family in 1882.[37] His privileged position placed him among the minority of well-educated Iranians. After receiving his doctorate in law in Switzerland, he came back to Iran in 1914, where he taught and wrote for a year and, as a socially conscious intellectual, advocated sweeping government reforms. During these early years, his efforts for reform did not bring tangible results, and once again he left for Europe. From abroad, Musaddiq opposed the treaty of 1919, which if ratified would have made Iran a virtual British colony. In 1920 he was back in Iran, taking up various government positions, such as the governorship of Fars province.[38] The rise of Reza Khan to power and his tightening grip over the polity was a major factor in Musaddiq's decision to leave the government and challenge its authority as an elected Majlis deputy.[39] However, the ever increasing power of Reza Shah made the Majlis virtually useless and led to Musaddiq's temporary retirement from politics and to his eventual house arrest.

After the breakdown of the Reza Shah regime in 1941, Musaddiq resumed his political activity and became the first deputy from Tehran to the Fourteenth Majlis. It was there that his famous policy of national independence known as "negative equilibrium" was consistently presented and acquired credence.[40] Musaddiq's nationalistic credentials, manifested in his relentless opposition to granting concessions to foreign entities, made him the natural leader for the brewing movement. However, Musaddiq was not just a nationalist. His value system included essential liberal elements such as belief in human dignity and tolerance, and a whole series of operational measures such as freedom of expression and association. Liberalism was an important factor in shaping his vision about how the movement should act and where it should go.

Several other individuals played crucial roles in influencing and mobilizing support for the movement. Among them were Ayatullah Kashani, Muzafar Baqa'i, and Khalil Maliki. Although a religious figure, Abulqasim Kashani was a this-worldly and political man. Influenced by the nineteenth-century pan-Islamist Jamal al-Din Afghani, Kashani saw a tactical alliance with secular forces as a necessary step in emancipating the Islamic world from foreign domination. He was in tune with many of Musaddiq's ideas, such as nonalignment and the necessity to fight British control over the political economy of Iran.[41] This affinity with the nationalistic aspirations of the time persuaded Kashani to join the National Front in 1950. The alliance was natural as long as efforts were concentrated on the negative program of elimination of British influence. However, Kashani's vision about what Iran's future should look like and how it should be built was different from that of the secular and liberal Musaddiq. As a religious man and

Musaddiq's political rival, Kashani occasionally aspired to link politics and religion.[42] In addition to ideological differences, the frustration of Kashani's political aspirations for himself and his close relatives by Musaddiq contributed to a growing rift between the two men that culminated in Kashani's split from the National Front in early 1953.

Muzafar Baqa'i was another influential figure of the National Front who, before his break with Musaddiq, made valuable contributions to the cause of the movement. Baqa'i came from a politically involved family. His father, a founder of the Ijtima'iyun (Socialist) Party, served in the Fourth and Fifth Majlises as a deputy from Kirman. Adding modern education (he studied in Saint Cloud in Paris and later was awarded a doctorate by the Iranian Ministry of Education) to the training received from his father, Baqa'i developed into a person of impressive political ability.[43] He was an ambitious man who chose to enter into the turbulent political currents on the side of the opposition to the status quo. He successfully ran for the Majlis in three consecutive elections, starting with the Fifteenth Majlis.

Baqa'i was an ardent advocate of the nationalization bill and mobilized support for the bill outside the Majlis. His connections with the bazaar and his ability as an orator made him one of the most popular figures of the movement and gave him the impression that he could challenge Musaddiq without losing his status within the movement. As events showed, he was wrong. But his personal ambitions were not the only reason for the rift between him and Musaddiq. He was an anticommunist, and was wary of what he perceived as the Tudeh Party's penetration of Musaddiq's administration.[44] Through his newspaper *Shahid,* Baqa'i also criticized Musaddiq and his administration for lack of resolve in pushing for far-reaching reforms.

Khalil Maliki was an Azarbaijani who, like his father, closely identified with Iranian nationalism. He came from a middle-class family, but was sensitive to the plight of the poor. His government-sponsored trip to Germany, cut short before he finished the final phase of his studies, opened his eyes to the contrast between Europe and Iran. Like many of his peers, Maliki concluded that the solution to Iran's problems lay in socialism, and he therefore joined the Tudeh Party. A few years later, in 1948, Maliki split from the party, disillusioned by its submissive attitude toward the Soviet Union.[45] Maliki gradually came to the conclusion that the focus should be on the problems faced by Iran and not on the elusive notion of international communism. This realization made him a nationalist, with socialist values, and a natural ally of Musaddiq and his movement. Maliki collaborated with Baqa'i in forming the Toilers' Party, and the party soon joined the National Front. Baqa'i and Maliki, with complementary talents, the first an outgoing person and a man of action, the latter a man of ideas with a sensitive and contemplative personality,[46] made the Toilers' Party a dynamic force that mobilized support for the movement from different strata of the population. However, this union did not last, and when Baqa'i left the National Front, Maliki and his supporters split from the Toilers' Party and formed the Third Force. They remained as part of the National Front and stayed loyal to Musaddiq to the end.

There were other leaders in the National Front who served the movement to various degrees, but none enjoyed the mobilizing ability of men such as Kashani and Baqa'i, or the intellectual vigor of Maliki, or the popularity and political courage of Musaddiq. It was the combination of certain essential resources for mobilization, at the disposal of these leaders, that transformed the movement's potential into actuality.

Organization

Musaddiq was a truly charismatic figure, and his charisma was probably the most valuable asset of the movement. However, he did not have organizational ties with any of the National Front parties. In fact, he was against the transformation of the National Front from an umbrella organization consisting of a more or less loose coalition of different parties into one centralized structure, a belief that he held even regarding the second National Front.[47] Musaddiq's ability for mobilization lay in his direct appeal to an attentive public, who saw in him the personification of Iranian dignity and independence. His beliefs and his record made him a trustworthy leader, and his call for action drew an immediate and enthusiastic mobilized response.

Musaddiq's charisma was not the only mobilizing asset of the movement. The Front consisted of formal and informal left, right, and centrist organizations that contributed to the viability of the movement. Among these organizations were the Iran Party, the Pan-Iranist Party, the Toilers' Party, the Society of Muslim Warriors, and the Organization of the Milli Group.[48] The Iran Party, a center-left organization, adhered to a mild Fabian-style socialism. It advocated full rights for minorities and women, political equality for all citizens, and elimination of tension between the haves and the have nots. It appealed to the well-to-do section of the modern intelligentsia, such as lawyers, university professors, and the professional cadre of the civil service in urban areas such as Tehran, Rasht, and Isfahan. The Iran Party never developed into a mass party. The character of its base of support was naturally responsible for its preoccupation with administrative reforms. Throughout the 1949–53 period the party remained loyal to Musaddiq.

The Pan-Iranist Party appealed to the nationalistic emotions of urban youth. It focused on the grandeur of Iran and the return of parts of Iranian territories that were carved away during the nineteenth century. Unlike the Iran Party, the Pan-Iranist Party did not join its nationalism to liberal values. In fact many influential members of the party had fascistic tendencies. However, the party eagerly joined the National Front soon after the latter's inception. The party's social base was relatively small, made up especially of high school students. The fascistic tendencies of the party and its anticommunist stand made the organization a "street" party most apt for fighting the Tudeh supporters. The pan-Iranian tendency of the party was a source of tension between it and the mainstream of the National Front. This tension ultimately led to a split within the party once the differences between the court and Musaddiq began to crystalize. Dariush Furuhar, the leader of the pro-Musaddiq faction, reorganized his supporters into the Iranian People's Party and remained in the National Front. Under the leadership of Muhsin Pazishkpur, the other faction sided with the court.

The Toilers' Party came closest to being a mass party. The union of Baqa'i and Maliki that led to the founding of the party in 1950 was instrumental in drawing a variety of different segments of the population to the party. On the one hand, there were part of the modern intelligentsia, particularly the university students and segments of the professional government employees who were attracted to Maliki and his vision of a good society. On the other hand, there were many bazaaris who knew and trusted Baqa'i as an assertive leader. This latter group was able to bring a fair number of the politically inarticulate into the street, first in support of and later against the movement.

The Toilers' Party was a party of the left, with a socialist but anticommunist outlook. The socialism of the party appealed to the supporters of Maliki, whereas its anticommunist stand made the party attractive to the followers of Baqa'i. But the party was never able to acquire significant support from the labor movement.[49] In 1952, Baqa'i publicly withdrew his support from Musaddiq and subsequently the Toilers' Party split. Maliki and his followers who remained loyal to Musaddiq formed the Third Force. Despite or perhaps because of its small size, the Third Force under the leadership of Maliki became the most organized and disciplined group within the National Front.

The Society of Muslim Warriors was a religiously oriented group that supported Ayatullah Kashani and his views on how a legitimate future polity should be organized. Its members were nationalists who attacked all aspects of Western domination, particularly Western cultural influence. The group itself was quite small and never developed into a political party; its importance came from the influence of leaders such as Kashani with the masses. In the first two years of the movement, Kashani used this influence in support of Musaddiq. However, once he broke with the National Front, his ability for mobilization was employed to undermine the nationalist movement.

The Organization of the Milli Group was a secret organization that was founded by a handful of army officers in 1952. This group never developed into a significant entity, and at its peak it consisted of a minority of military men who were in agreement with Musaddiq. The major goal of the organization was to assist Musaddiq in putting the military under civilian control as a step toward achieving democratic reforms.[50] But the organization had no clear program of action and therefore remained inconsequential. It lost a great deal of its potential to influence events when one of its leaders, Mahmud Afshartus (Musaddiq's chief of police) was murdered in early 1953. Its other influential member, Taqi Riahi (Musaddiq's army chief of staff) failed to support Musaddiq on August 19, 1953, the day of the successful coup d'état.

The ideological characteristics, social bases, and leadership of the above-described groups and parties made them diverse enough to render sustained solidarity problematic among the constituent elements of the National Front. As we will see, this problem dealt a serious blow to the movement.

Musaddiq's Premiership: Opportunities and Challenges

As prime minister, Musaddiq was faced with great obstacles in fulfilling his goal of creating a democratic and sovereign nation invested with liberal values. On the eve of his assumption of power, Iran was both an economically and politically dependent and weak country. At home, conservative and reactionary forces had a deep hold on many state institutions, such as the army. Outside the state itself the oligarchical social system exerted a good deal of influence on the socioeconomic structure. Political and economic power, as much as it could be exercised by Iranians, was vested in a traditional elite, many of whose members had close ties with foreign powers. Foreign influence was not new to Iranians in the mid-twentieth century. The history of modern Iran is rich in terms of continuous indirect influence and episodes of blatant and direct foreign intervention in the country's affairs.

The influence of the two traditional foreign powers, Russia and Britain, stemmed from both geopolitical and economic sources. In addition to the objective factors of their military and economic might, forcing dependency on the Iranian political economy, there was a subjective element that fostered dependency even further. The history of Iran's international relations was responsible for the creation of a worldview in which the omnipotence of foreign powers was a central pillar. The overestimation of the power of Britain or Russia was logically linked to a feeling of political impotence for many Iranians and therefore could lead easily to compliance. Such multifaceted dependency made the rise to power of independent and nationalist political figures very difficult, and their long-term hold on power even more problematic.

However, several developments made the ascendence of Musaddiq in the period of 1949–53 relatively easier than in other periods. One was the change in character of the Iranian polity since the breakdown of the Reza Shah dictatorship. Muhammad Reza Shah, as an inexperienced king, did not enjoy the influence of his father and could not restore the grip that his predecessor had on the Iranian polity. During World War II, the fact that the occupying forces came from several countries, each having influence with different political groups or individual politicians, created a system with no clear and dominant center of power. This characteristic of the post-Reza Shah period was accompanied by an attempt to revive the constitution.

There were many reasons why a genuine democracy was not fully institution-alized in the 1940s. The meddling of foreign powers, now also including the United States, could be cited as one factor. In addition, there were procedural, le-gal, and institutional characteristics of different branches of government that made the fulfillment of true democracy quite problematic.[51] However, several features of liberal democracy, such as freedom of speech and assembly, were present. Criticism of the past regime was tolerated. Political censorship was by and large curbed. Many, including part of the modern intelligentsia who had either actively or passively supported Reza Shah, became professed supporters of the newly in-stituted freedoms. Many political parties and associations, ranging from the com-munist left to the extreme right, were founded. Such a context provided an edu-cational atmosphere for citizens to learn both about the fundamental ills of the society and alternative ways to address them. What made nationalism a rallying point for a majority of the political groupings and the attentive public was the start of a debate about the terms of the 1933 oil agreement. This debate provided the public with a tangible issue that, in the context of a long and painful history of foreign intervention and a newly emergent atmosphere of freedom, created the necessary ingredient for a movement to be born. The sufficient element for the actualization of the movement was vested in the person of Musaddiq, a leader with an active and positive record and an ability to manipulate nationalist symbols.

There is no doubt that Musaddiq was the most popular prime minister in the modern history of Iran. His charisma created an unprecedented opportunity to effect change. As far as his nationalist goals were concerned, Musaddiq had the support of the majority of the politically active urban population. The cause of nationalization of the oil industry was pursued by all the constituent elements of the National Front. Powerful and influential individuals such as Ayatullah Kashani and the bazaar community were behind Musaddiq. Support for this goal was so intense that the opposition felt quite powerless and therefore had no choice but to submit to the initiatives of Musaddiq and his nationalist followers. Even the punitive and threatening actions of Britain, which in the absence of such support for nationalistic goals would have been enough to break the resolve of any gov-ernment, did nothing but foster Musaddiq's popularity.

Economic Challenges

As time passed, opportunities were replaced with more and more challenges, chief among them the absence of a resolution to the oil dispute with Britain. None of the several attempts at negotiations produced results. There were several rea-sons for such a deadlock. The most obvious was that Britain had to forgo the control of the huge oil reserve of Iran and experienced a cut in its profits. Beyond that was the fear of Iran setting a frightening precedent for other Third World countries to nationalize British economic and strategic interests. Related to the issue of economic interest was British concern with its declining prestige as a world power and its contempt for entering into a meaningful dialogue with "inferior and irrational orientals."[52] There was also a wide perceptual gap between the British and the Iranians with regard to what was the most important aspect of the dispute. For the British the issue was mainly conceptualized in economic terms, and therefore any negotiations had to concentrate on those terms. For the Iranians, on the other hand, the nationalization of the oil industry was first and foremost a political act, and therefore no dialogue was possible without the acceptance by all parties of the fundamental principle of Iran's right to the control of its oil.[53] Thus, for example, a sticky point during most of the negotiations was Iran's insistence on a non-British general manager for the industry. Such insistence was interpreted by the British and eventually by the Americans as an irrational demand of fanatical nationalists.[54]

The failure to reach an agreement had two detrimental effects on Musaddiq's ability to govern. The first was Musaddiq's preoccupation with the dispute, which took time and leadership resources away from dealing with pressing domestic socioeconomic issues.[55] The second was the economic difficulty resulting from drastic cuts in Iran's oil revenues. Mid-twentieth-century Iran was a poor country in dire need of reform and development. In Iran, as in many Third World countries, the state had to be the principal agent of development and reform. The social structure and the configuration of power were such that the emerging modern middle class, the natural engine for socioeconomic development, encountered serious obstacles in effecting change. Its size was small and its power did not penetrate deeply enough to mobilize adequate human, administrative, political, and financial resources for the cause of development. In contrast, the forces that favored the status quo, such as the landlords, part of the traditional merchant class, and more generally the majority of the wealthy families, exerted a substantial amount of control over all the above-mentioned resources. In such a context no speedy change would be possible unless the state interfered. Musaddiq's administration, despite the aristocratic background of its leader, represented the aspiration for reform and, as such, had the support of the middle class.[56]

In normal circumstances the popularity of Musaddiq and the enthusiasm of his core support group, the middle class, would probably have been enough to shake the foundation of the traditional power elite and to introduce the necessary socioeconomic reforms. But circumstances were extraordinary. A state seriously dependent on oil revenues was stripped of those revenues because of the British boycott and the cooperation of big American oil companies with the AIOC.

In the crucial year of 1952, Iran's oil revenues were almost nonexistent. In addition, Britain froze Iranian assets, which prevented Iran from using part of its foreign exchange for economic development. Financial aid from the United States did not materialize. The Soviet Union not only did not offer help but refused to pay back its World War II debt to Iran. The Musaddiq administration's options were thus severely limited. Determined to overcome these difficulties, the government decided on a developmental path known as the "oil-less economy."

The essential purpose of this strategy was to free Iran from oil dependency through promotion of nonoil production and export.[57] It was designed to encourage self-sufficiency in both foodstuffs and key imported products through an increase in agricultural production and promotion of domestic industries such as textiles and sugar refining. In both these areas certain successes were achieved. Cutting imports was accompanied by an increase in nonoil exports that achieved a positive balance of trade with an amazingly insignificant contribution from petroleum. However, with an oil-related annual deficit of 3.5 billion rials for the year 1951–52, the oil revenue shortage had a severe impact on the government budget.[58] Both fiscal and monetary measures were employed to deal with the budget problem. The most important fiscal weapon was an increase in taxation, which was ultimately not fully realized. Monetary measures included the printing of new bank notes and the issuing of government bonds. Unfortunately for Musaddiq and his movement, economic restrictions on the government, lack of support from many administrative institutions, and divergent views on economic issues within the movement itself were serious enough not to leave room for any further policy of socioeconomic reforms.

The political implications of the overall economic policy of the nationalist government were mixed. Import substitution, also known as "national production," was welcomed by those groups, such as sectors of the bazaar, that would benefit from promotion of domestic production. The purchasing of government bonds, mostly by the middle and lower-middle classes, was also an indication of support for and confidence in the government. However, those wealthy merchants who were engaged in the import sector experienced cutbacks in their business activities. In addition, because of strict limitations on the importation of luxury goods, the wealthy sectors of society suffered inconveniences in sustaining their accustomed mode of life. Conservative groups in general were against higher taxation, and the army opposed a cut in the military budget as a measure to deal with the overall budget deficit. Moreover, the absence of substantial redistributive reform policies that would specifically address the plight of the poor and the working class brought criticism of the government from leftist groups such as the Tudeh Party.

The dissatisfaction of these powerful groups had serious political implications for the Musaddiq government. The economic factor thus became an important element in the weakening of Musaddiq's effectiveness and control over the polity. However, in the absence of other internal and external problems, the economic situation in itself would hardly have made the failure of the movement inevitable.

Political Challenges

When Musaddiq became prime minister, his charisma and the popularity of his cause were such that any direct confrontation with him and his policies would have required a tremendous amount of confidence and willingness to take risks on the part of the challenger. The traditional elite, the conservative opposition, lacked these necessary characteristics. The only group that openly and vocally criticized Musaddiq was the communist Tudeh Party, whose role will be analyzed later. But, overall and at least on the surface, Musaddiq had the support of the overwhelming majority of the politically relevant groups within civil society. Considering the historical political passivity of the peasantry, this support was confined to the urban areas of Iran. There was, however, one major nonurban support base, the powerful nomadic Qashqa'i tribe, led by Nasir Khan and Khusrau Khan Qashqa'i.[59]

When it came to important institutions, such as the court, the army, the Majlis, and the Senate, however, Musaddiq proved to be less popular. As a constitutionalist, Musaddiq believed that the shah's power over the polity should be curbed. He took several steps to put limits on the actions of the shah and his family, in particular the shah's ambitious twin sister, Ashraf. Logically, the court did not appreciate these steps and, as is well documented, became actively involved in undermining Musaddiq. In general the army, too, was a royalist institution, and many of its highest officers were not amused by Musaddiq's attempt to put the military under the control of the government. As mentioned above, there were also budgetary reasons for the army's opposition to Musaddiq. Such dissatisfaction led to the collaboration of many influential army officers in conducting the August 19, 1953, coup d'état.

It is true that intense popular support for Musaddiq intimidated many conservative members of the Majlis to vote in favor of most of Musaddiq's measures. But the social background and political affiliation of the majority of the members of the Sixteenth Majlis and to a lesser degree its successor were such that if the opportunity had presented itself the Majlis would have been more than eager to get rid of Musaddiq.[60] The Senate was conservative by its very nature, given that half of its deputies were selected directly by the monarch.

The dragging on of the oil dispute put the government in a vulnerable position that provided the closet opposition with opportunities to undermine the nationalist government. It is ironic that those in the Majlis opposition, such as Jamal Imami, Ghulam Hussain Ibtihaj, Imad Turbati, and Abdul Qadir Azad, many of whom had close ties with foreign powers, felt compelled to use nationalist or democratic rhetoric in their attacks on the government.[61] That in itself was an indication that nationalist symbols were still the most powerful weapons for mobilizing support, and as no one could match Musaddiq's ability in doing so, the vocal opposition within the Majlis for the most part remained a minority. Musaddiq's popularity discouraged most of those among the parliamentary opposition from taking antigovernment stands.

The open parliamentary debates by the vocal opposition were accompanied by other means (mostly covert) to topple the nationalist government. There were many individuals who in secret collaboration with Britain tried to undermine Musaddiq through lobbying the shah (who was generally indecisive, despite his conservative inclinations), launching media campaigns, and sowing discord within the National Front coalition.[62] These attempts intensified in July 1952. After months of activities and secret negotiations with the foreign powers, the conservative opposition ultimately agreed on Ahmad Qavam, an influential former prime minister, as the possible successor to Musaddiq. All they had to do was wait for an opportunity, which presented itself on July 16, 1952. On that day Musaddiq, who had the constitutional prerogative to appoint the minister of war, demanded the right to supervise the ministry himself. The shah challenged Musaddiq, and the latter submitted his resignation. The shah accepted the resignation and Qavam, who was hastily elected by the conservative members of the Majlis as the successor, became the prime minister. The National Front urged the population to take a stand, and for the next few days the major cities of Iran were the scenes of huge demonstrations against the new government. After many bloody clashes between demonstrators and the army and police, the shah finally gave in and asked Musaddiq to form his second government on July 21. Ironically, this episode not only demonstrated Musaddiq's extraordinary appeal but also greatly contributed to the process of weakening his control over the polity and over his own original support groups. During those few days the National Front leaders, who had increasingly been showing signs of disunity, put their differences aside and collectively took the side of Musaddiq against Qavam. But once Musaddiq resumed the premiership and the immediate crisis was over, disagreements among the nationalist coalition resurfaced with a greater force than before.

The Role of the Tudeh Party

A major reason for the intensification of the process of disintegration within the National Front was the role played by the Tudeh Party. The Tudeh Party, the best organized political force in Iran, never joined the National Front. Because the party was an illegal organization it could not officially join the National Front, but it could have entered into a working coalition with the latter. However, this course of action was not taken, and instead tensions rose between the party and the nationalist leadership. Throughout the period of 1949–53, the Tudeh Party pursued contradictory policies toward the movement and Musaddiq.[63] The initial position of the Tudeh Party on the oil issue was to oppose the National Front's proposal for nationalization of the oil industry.[64] There were two reasons behind the Tudeh's opposition: first, the party was fearful that nationalization of the oil industry would only lead to the replacement of British control by a more forceful and energetic American imperialism in Iran; second, as an organization with close ties to the Soviet Union, the Tudeh Party was worried about the consequences of oil nationalization for Soviet designs on Iran's northern oil. Once the oil was nationalized, the party's street demonstrations and its press criticism contributed to the frustration of attempts to reach a settlement with the AIOC. In domestic affairs also the Tudeh Party opposed some major policies, such as the issuance of government bonds. In fact, for all practical purposes the Tudeh Party and the conservative opposition acted in harmony to undermine the Musaddiq administration. Musaddiq's attitude toward the Tudeh Party was affected by both his nationalism and his liberalism. On the one hand, because of the dependence of the Tudeh Party on a foreign power (the Soviet Union), the nationalist Musaddiq could not trust and therefore ally himself with the party. Moreover, many of the National Front elements were quite anticommunist and therefore emphatically against a rapprochement with the communist Tudeh Party. On the other hand, the liberal Musaddiq believed in freedom of association and was therefore reluctant to suppress the party by force. Musaddiq's attitude was thus for the most part one of ignoring the confrontational posture of the Tudeh Party.

After a long period of attacks on Musaddiq, the Tudeh Party changed its attitude from overt hostility to a half-hearted and conditional support for Musaddiq following the July 1952 uprising.[65] The role of the Tudeh Party during the uprising is still a matter of controversy. Ervand Abrahamian argues that through demonstrations and strikes the pro-Tudeh forces played a significant role in bringing victory to the National Front.[66] On the other hand, Homa Katouzian is of the opinion that the Tudeh press attacked Musaddiq throughout the uprising, and that the party did not participate in the July events.[67] However, no matter which interpretation is closer to the truth, the fact remains that after the July uprising there were signs of reduced tension between Musaddiq and the Tudeh Party.

The dynamic of the relationships among Musaddiq, the other National Front leaders, and the Tudeh Party, in the context of an active pursuit of the Cold War by the British and American administrations, and the Soviets' practical indifference and inactivity toward the nationalist movement of Iran made both the initial Tudeh hostility and its later somewhat softer attitude toward Musaddiq quite problematic for the success of the movement. There is still controversy about who or what should be blamed for the damaging effect of this relationship between the National Front and the Tudeh Party. After the coup, the leaders of the party admitted that some of their own mistaken tactics had led to their tense relationship with Musaddiq and the National Front. But they also heavily blamed

Musaddiq and Kashani for the initial round of the confrontation.[68] Defectors from the Tudeh Party, on the other hand, put the blame squarely on either the entire or at least part of the leadership of the party. For example, Anvar Khami'i, depicting the Tudeh Party as a mere agent of the Soviet Union, states that from the very beginning the Tudeh leadership was sabotaging the nationalist cause for its own opportunistic goals.[69] Another defector, Faridun Kishavarz, who saw the party as faction-ridden, believes that the party was split on the issue of supporting Musaddiq. According to him, the faction that dominated the party was anti-Musaddiq. Kishavarz asserts that in the last stage of the nationalist struggle, on August 19, 1953, Kianuri, the leader of the dominant faction, betrayed both the party and the nation by remaining a passive spectator of the coup.[70]

Regardless of the question of which interpretation is more valid, the important point is that the Tudeh Party's later more or less cooperative spirit had mixed consequences. On the one hand, it mobilized a new and organized force in support of the movement. On the other, it accelerated the gradual disintegration process of the National Front as a unified force. As an umbrella organization the National Front included diverse ideological forces, many of which were anticommunist. Any form of cooperation between the National Front and the Tudeh Party was a source of tension and a potential cause for the defection of the right-wing supporters of the National Front. The cooperation between the two organizations also added strength to the argument of the pro-coup d'état faction within the U.S. foreign policy-making apparatus.[71]

The National Front and Internal Challenges

The Tudeh Party was not the only contributor to the problem of unity in the National Front. In fact, the most essential difficulty lay in the character of the National Front itself. The front was not a political party, and had neither a solid structure nor a comprehensively unified ideology. It was an umbrella organization consisting of diverse groups, each with its own worldview and agenda. Many of its constituent groups were mainly vehicles for fulfilling the desires of their leaders. What brought them together was the broad notion of nationalism and Iran's gaining control of its own destiny. The differences among the member groups surfaced over the goals and strategies that should shape that destiny. There were liberal as well as illiberal, socialist as well as capitalist, religious as well as secular tendencies within the Front. Once it came to formulating positive socioeconomic policies, all these conflicting ideological inclinations made attempts at retaining unity, a herculean endeavor. For example, there was pressure from the left wing of the National Front for assertive socioeconomic measures, including land reform. On the other hand, many people associated with the right wing of the organization were uncomfortable with talk about the need for sweeping reforms.

As Musaddiq's second term started in July 1952 an additional cause for concern developed, besides the Tudeh's conciliatory gestures toward Musaddiq, when the new administration began to show a more assertive approach to domestic issues. In addition to a series of political moves that targeted the court and the army, there were economic measures, such as a land reform program that would oblige the landlords to return a large percentage of their annual income to the villagers. There was also a progressive tax policy. Although most of these measures would hurt the traditional opposition, they were not comforting to the wealthier supporters of the movement either.

On the cultural front, the secular attitude of the government frustrated the religiously oriented followers of the National Front. Their demand for policies such as a ban on alcohol and other religiously sanctioned measures, including no concessions on the issue of women's rights, either went unimplemented or were in danger of being ignored. The threat of the Tudeh Party was seen not only in terms of the socioeconomic influence of the collectivist ideology, but also in the cultural aspect of the materialist worldview of the Marxist party. These cultural issues strained relations between the government and the religious community as a whole. The majority of the clergy followed the example of Ayatullah Muhammad Hussain Burujirdi, who was initially apolitical, but ultimately sided with the shah.[72] These differences also contributed to the widening gap between Musaddiq on the one hand and Kashani and other leaders of the Society of Muslim Warriors on the other.

Ideological issues aside, there existed personality conflicts among the National Front leaders. Both Kashani and Baqa'i had leadership ambitions far greater than the opportunities afforded them. As two of the most popular and influential leaders of the movement, they demanded more extensive roles in appointing officials and formulating policies. Musaddiq, who was both ideologically and temperamentally more akin to the Iran Party (demonstrated in his choice of cabinet ministers) than to other National Front groups, frustrated Baqa'i and Kashani. On more than one occasion, Baqa'i used the Majlis tribune to accuse Musaddiq's government of nepotism.[73] The official influence of both these leaders was basically confined to their position in the Majlis. As long as the Majlis remained a key institution, the power gap between Baqa'i and Kashani and Musaddiq was not critical. But because of pressing economic issues, Musaddiq asked for and was granted emergency powers for six months in August 1952; these powers were extended again in January 1953. The consequence of these developments for the Majlis was obvious. In addition to its executive powers, the government now had the power to legislate independent of the Majlis. The diminishing power of the parliament was not welcomed by many deputies, including Baqa'i and Kashani, who openly opposed the extension of the emergency powers in January 1953 as dictatorial. However, their official defection from the National Front did not occur until February 1953.

It is worth noting that despite their own independent source of power, and the government's inability to solve many pressing problems, once Kashani, Baqa'i, and others broke with Musaddiq, their own popularity began to wane. Throughout 1952 and early 1953, public support for Musaddiq was enthusiastic and, despite more or less open tension among the leaders, many of the traditional allies of Baqa'i and Kashani expressed unequivocal support for Musaddiq. However, the defection of Baqa'i and Kashani ultimately hurt the movement. In the case of Baqa'i, the damage was more in terms of his participation in plots, such as the murder of Afshartus, and collaboration with the court and the army in toppling the government.[74] Kashani's defection was more serious because of his greater influence in mobilizing the masses for street demonstrations.

Meanwhile, the situation in the Majlis was deteriorating. The defection of early supporters of the movement was not limited to Baqa'i and Kashani. Hussain Makki, Shams Qanatabadi, Abdulhassan Ha'irizadeh, and some of the initial members of the National Front coalition also withdrew from it for personal, political, or religious reasons.[75] The decreasing support for the National Front in the Majlis encouraged the opposition to take a more active role. Resorting to obstruction and preventing a quorum became frequent and normal practices.[76] The Majlis, once an asset, now became a liability for Musaddiq in carrying out his program.

Ironically and sadly, the democratic-minded prime minister saw no other choice but to resort to tactical authoritarian measures, such as declaration of martial law, assumption of extraordinary power, and ultimately calling for a referendum for the dissolution of the paralyzing Majlis. But for authoritarian measures to succeed, one must have both an authoritarian resolve and the support of the coercive organs. Mussadiq possessed neither. Temperamentally, he was a liberal who did not believe in suppression of freedom and resorting to violence as a means to resolve conflict. As testified to by his behavior toward Baqa'i, who was involved in the murder of the chief of police, or General Zahidi, who was taking part in plots to overthrow him, Musaddiq deeply respected ideas such as parliamentary immunity or protection for those who took sanctuary. Letting such men go free to engage in their unlawful activities did nothing to help the process of democratization, and it actually contributed instead to the success of a coup that gave life to the undemocratic regime that would rule Iran for the next quarter of a century.

As far as control over coercive institutions was concerned, Musaddiq was in a weak position. The most important of these, the army, was by and large loyal to the shah. Despite the appointment of General Riahi, a supporter of Musaddiq, as the army chief of staff, many influential army officers, including the members of the powerful retired army officers club, were in the ranks of the opposition. Their resolve to topple the government intensified as the tension between the shah and Musaddiq increased in 1953. On August 16, a coup d'état to replace Musaddiq with General Fazlullah Zahidi as the new prime minister was attempted. In addition to some of the army officers, the plotters included Loy Henderson, the U.S. ambassador to Iran, CIA agent Kermit Roosevelt, Princess Ashraf, and some of Musaddiq's former allies, such as Baqa'i. However, the plot was discovered and reported to Musaddiq. Precautionary measures were subsequently taken by the government and the section of the army that had remained loyal to the government, resulting in the failure of the coup. But Musaddiq did nothing to prepare for the predicted next attempt, and the section of the army that opposed him played a major role in carrying out the August 19 coup while the pro-Musaddiq Riahi remained inactive.[77]

Foreign Powers and the Fate of the Movement

By its very nature, the nationalist movement involved the foreign powers. British behavior, from beginning to end, was not surprisingly hostile. After all, the movement challenged both its economic interests and its political prestige. Its goal therefore was to crush the movement. Britain's incessant undermining of the nationalist government is well documented. The American response to the movement was more complex. At the outset, the U.S. administration showed some sympathy for the cause of nationalization of the oil industry. Henry Grady, the American ambassador to Iran from July 1950 to September 1951, was particularly understanding of Iran's position. The reasons for this initial U.S. support were a mixture of ideological conviction and American economic interest in Iran, which would have been furthered by breaking Britain's monopoly on Iranian oil.[78] Ironically, this oil interest became partly responsible for a change in U.S. policy from mild support for the nationalist government to violent intervention aimed at overthrowing Musaddiq: a genuine nationalization of oil would have set an example for other oil-rich countries such as Saudi Arabia to challenge American oil companies.

But more important than oil in determining the U.S. foreign policy agenda was the perceived communist threat. After the conclusion of World War II, the United States was eager to set aside its traditional semi-isolationalist policy and expand its global influence. The communist Soviet Union also emerged as a competitive superpower. Rivalry between the two global giants led to the emergence of the Cold War. In the early 1950s, it seemed that communist forces were in ascendance. In Vietnam, Korea, Burma, and Malaysia, they were actively challenging the interests of the capitalist world. In the meantime, the Truman administration was replaced by that of Eisenhower. Two Cold Warriors, John Foster Dulles and his brother Allen Welsh Dulles, became secretary of state and CIA chief, respectively. The Cold War outlook divided the world into dichotomous camps of friends and foes. Nonalignment, the path that Musaddiq wished to adopt, had no realistic place in this worldview. The apparent rapprochement between the Tudeh Party and the nationalist government, from the point of view of the Cold Warriors, was enough proof for the soundness of their analysis. It was in such a perceptual context that the U.S. administration, through its financial and intelligence support, initiated the August 1953 coups in Iran.

Conclusion

The oil nationalization movement was one of the most important and promising phenomena in modern Iranian history. Its importance lay in the fact that a weak country decided to withstand the wrath of powerful foreign forces to demand what was rightfully its own. It was also promising because it produced a trusted and popular leader who held democratic and liberal values and who was willing to put these values into operation through building the proper institutions. What gave life to the movement were, however, first and foremost national aspirations. Despite the fact that the movement started as a middle-class phenomenon, the nationalist demands were simple and tangible enough to mobilize the less literate lower classes. The participation of huge numbers of people from different walks of life testified to the broad salience of nationalistic symbols. Added to the importance of the message was the charisma of the messenger. Musaddiq captured the imagination of a nation that entrusted its fate to his judgment. These factors, in the context of a relatively relaxed political atmosphere, an activated civil society, and a defensive state, created the opportunity for the rise of the nationalist movement. In the absence of serious threats from the weak and disoriented state, and enjoying the necessary leadership and mobilizing resources, the movement took a measure of power.

The defeat of the movement was caused by a combination of domestic and foreign factors. Internally, the continuation of the nationalist struggle jeopardized the interests of powerful groups and individuals whose privileged positions were in one way or another tied to the political and economic influence of the outside powers. The constitutional and democratic measures of the triumphant nationalist government broadened the ranks of the conservative opposition to the movement. The leftist opposition attacked the government for its mild manners and its attempts to solve the oil problem through negotiations, exacerbating the already tense foreign relations situation. Despite certain achievements, the Iranian economy remained vulnerable and dependent and added an important dimension to the political problems faced by the Musaddiq administration. Although a major part of the movement's social base willingly made certain economic sacrifices, the prolongation of the economic crisis and uncertainty dampened their enthusiasm and decreased active support for the government. They remained passive during the fateful day of August 19, 1953, when the army and the mob, which was mobilized by Tehran toughs and paid by the CIA, stormed the streets of the capital.

The character of the National Front itself made the movement vulnerable to discord and disunity. Ideological and political differences among the leaders led to several defections and eroded the effectiveness of the movement to a dangerous degree. Most of the groups and parties that remained faithful to Musaddiq lacked the necessary mobilizing resources. Despite his charisma, Musaddiq himself had no systematic and organized link to his support base. Temperamental as he was, Musaddiq preferred to be asked to rule and not to request it. Therefore, when his supporters did not show up in the streets on August 19, he did not appeal to them, leaving the initiative in the hands of his enemies.

There would probably have been no coup in 1953 without the active participation of the foreign powers. As mentioned above, the historical experience of Iran created a perception, particularly among the traditional elite, that the implementation of any major change required the blessing of foreign powers. Considering the popularity of Musaddiq in the oil nationalization period, the necessity of foreign participation for the success of a coup against the nationalist government was felt more intensely than before by the opposition. It is quite unlikely that in the absence of the British and American intrigues and financial support, the domestic opposition would have taken the risk. There were important internal factors that weakened the possibility of the long-run success of the liberal nationalist movement, but the movement had a chance and Iran could have seen the fruits of its democratization process were it not for the hostile response of the two most powerful countries in the "free" world.

Notes

1. Abdul Samad Kambakhsh, *Nazari beh Junbish-i Kargari va Kummunisti dar Iran* (A look at the workers' and Communist movement in Iran), pt. 2 (Stockholm: Tudeh Party, 1975), 6, 32.

2. *Asnad-i Tarikhi-yi Junbish-i Kargari, Sosial Dimukrasi va Kummunisti-yi Iran* (Historical documents of the workers', social democratic and communist movement of Iran), vol. 1 (Tehran: Ilm, n.d.), 352.

3. *Asnad-i Tarikhi,* 350–56.

4. Cited in JAMI (Jibhi-yi Azadi-yi Mardum-i Iran), *Guzashteh Chiragh-i Rah-i Ayandeh ast* (The past is the light on the path to the future) (Tehran: Quqnus, 1983), 583–85.

5. See Noureddin Kianouri, "The National Bourgeoisie, Their Nature and Policy," *World Marxist Review* 2 (August 1959): 61–65.

6. "Report of the Executive Board of the Tudeh Party Central Committee on the Central Committee Vast Plenum" (1957), cited in *Asnad-i Tarikhi,* 361–64.

7. See Kambakhsh, *Nazari,* 97–111; for a leftist but non-Tudeh interpretation, see Bizhan Jazani, *Capitalism and Revolution in Iran* (London: Zed, 1980), 25–33.

8. Muhammad Reza Pahlavi, *Answer to History* (New York: Stein & Day, 1980), 79–92.

9. Norman Kemp, *Abadan* (London: Allan Wingate, 1953), 19.

10. Ibid., 24–26.

11. Ibid., 26.

12. See articles in different issues of *Newsweek,* such as July 28 and August 4, 11, and 18, 1952. See also *Time* weekly magazine, especially January 7, 1952, 18–21. For an analysis of U.S. media reports on Iran during the oil nationalization period, see William A. Dorman and Mansour Farhang, *The U.S. Press and Iran: Foreign Policy and the Journalism of Deference* (Berkeley: University of California Press, 1987), 31–62.

13. Peter Avery, *Modern Iran* (London: Ernest Benn, 1964), 419–20.

14. Ibid., 432.

15. Ibid., 429.

16. Nasrollah Saifpour Fatemi, *Oil Diplomacy: Powderkeg in Iran* (New York: Whittier, 1954), 381–82.

17. Ibid., 365–81.

18. Richard Cottam, *Nationalism in Iran* (Pittsburgh: University of Pittsburgh Press, 1979), 259, 264.

19. Ibid., 264.

20. Ibid., 268.

21. Ibid., 284–85.

22. Homa Katouzian, *The Political Economy of Modern Iran: Despotism and Pseudo-Modernism, 1926–1979* (New York: New York University Press, 1981), 171.

23. Ibid., 164–92. See also Homa Katouzian, *Musaddiq and the Struggle for Power in Iran* (London: I. B. Tauris, 1990).

24. Fakhreddin Azimi, *Iran: The Crisis of Democracy* (New York: St. Martin's, 1989), 257–344.

25. L. P. Elwell-Sutton, *Persian Oil* (Westport, Conn.: Hyperion, 1976), 15, 26–35.

26. Ibid., 80–87.

27. For an analysis of the origin of the 50/50 agreement between Aramco and the Saudi government, see Irvine H. Anderson, "The American Oil Industry and the Fifty-Fifty Agreement of 1950," in *Musaddiq, Iranian Nationalism, and Oil,* ed. James Bill and Roger Louis (Austin: University of Texas Press, 1988), 143–59.

28. See the text of the Supplementary Agreement in Hussain Makki, *Kitab-i Siyah* (The black book) (Tehran: n.p., n. d.), 38–43.

29. For a list of the points raised in the Majlis against the proposed agreement, see Fatemi, *Oil Diplomacy,* 334–35.

30. Karim Sanjabi, *Umidha va Na-Umidiha* (Hopes and Disappointments) (London: Nashr-i Kitab, 1989), 97.

31. See the communiqué published by the National Front cited in Union of Islamic Students Associations, *Musaddiq va Nahzat-i Milli-yi Iran* (Musaddiq and the national movement of Iran) (Europe: Union of Islamic Students Associations, 1978), 71–73.

32. For a summary of Razmara's and his administration's achievements and failures, see Azimi, *Iran,* 226–45.

33. For the text of the interpellation's proposal, see Makki, *Kitab-i Siyah,* 387–583.

34. See Muhammad Musaddiq, *Nutqha va Maktubat-i Dr. Musaddiq* (Dr. Musaddiq's speeches and correspondence) vol. 1, no. 4, 2d bk. (n.p.: Musaddiq Publications, 1969).

35. Makki, *Kitab-i Siyah,* 624–25.

36. See Elwell-Sutton, *Persian Oil,* 201–9.

37. For a detailed biography of Musaddiq's early years, see Farhad Diba, *Mohammad Mosaddegh: A Political Biography* (London: Croom Helm, 1986), 1–63.

38. For information about Musaddiq's activities during these years, see Muhammad Musaddiq, *Khatirat va Ta'alumat-i Duktur Musaddiq* (Dr. Musaddiq's memoirs and sorrows) (n.p.: National Front Sympathizers Outside the Country, 1986), 115–67.

39. Ibid., 167.

40. For a sample of Musaddiq's speeches on the "negative equilibrium policy," see *A Collection of Musaddiq's Historical Speeches* (Europe: Iran-i Azad, Organ of Organizations of the Iranian National Front in Europe, 1967), 17–52.

41. For a survey of Kashani's ideas and actions, see M. Dihnavi, ed., *Majmu'a-yi az Mukatibat va Payamha-yi Ayatullah Kashani* (A collection of Ayatullah Kashani's correspondence and messages) (Tehran: Pakhsh, 1982–83), various volumes.

42. See the interview with Kashani cited in the daily newspaper *Bakhtar-i Imruz,* September 29–30, 1951; and Dihnavi, *Majmu'a,* 4:35.

43. For detailed and varied information on Baqa'i, see the following sources: Center for Middle Eastern Studies, Harvard University, *Iranian Oral History Project,* transcript of the interview with Baqa'i, 1986; Muzafar Baqa'i, *Ankeh Guft Na* (The one who said no) (Franklin Lakes, N.J.: Mansur Rafizadeh, 1984); *Asnad-i Laneh-i Jasusi* (The spy nest documents), no. 23 (Tehran: n.p., n.d.); Muhammad Turkaman, *Asnad Piramun-i Tuti'-yi Rubudan va Qatl-i Shahid Afshartus* (Some documents concerning the plot for the kidnap and murder of Martyr Afshartus) (Tehran: Organization of the Cultural Services of Rasa, 1984).

44. Muzafar Baqa'i, *Shinakht-i Haqiqat* (Understanding the truth) (Kirman: Toilers' Party, 1979), 109–11, 117–19, 133–41.

45. See Homa Katouzian, ed., *Khatirat-i Siyasi-yi Khalil Maliki* (Khalil Maliki's political memoirs) (Hannover, Germany: Kushish Bara-yi Pishburd-i Nahzat-i Milli-yi Iran, 1981), 58–80.

46. For succinct insights into Maliki's personality, see Jalal Al-Ahmad, *Dar Khidmat va Khianat-i Rushanfikran* (On the Intellectuals' Service and Betrayal) (Tehran: Ravaq, n.d.), 369–70.

47. Although Musaddiq, being under house arrest, did not participate in the revival of the National Front in 1960, he made his view about its organizational characteristics perfectly clear. See *Mukatibat-i Musaddiq: Talash Bara-yi Tashkil-i Jibhi-yi Milli-yi Sivvum* (Musaddiq's correspondence: Attempts for formation of the third National Front) (n.p.: Musaddiq Publications, 1976), no. 10.

48. For a brief description of these organizations, see Sussan Siavoshi, *Liberal Nationalism in Iran: The Failure of a Movement* (Boulder, Colo.: Westview, 1990), 68–74.

49. Ibid., 70.

50. For more information on the Organization of the Milli Group, see Ghulam Reza Musavar Rahmani, *Khatirat-i Siyasi-yi Bist-u Panj Sal dar Niru-yi Hava'i-yi Iran* (Political memoirs of twenty-five years in the Iranian Air Force) (Tehran: Ravaq, n.d.), 100–140.

51. For an analysis of these issues, see Azimi, *Iran,* 6–31.

52. On the British attitudes toward negotiating with Iran during the oil nationalization period, see Roger Louis, "Musaddiq and the Dilemma of British Imperialism," in *Musaddiq, Iranian Nationalism, and Oil,* ed. James Bill and Roger Louis (Austin: University of Texas Press, 1988), 228–60.

53. See Musaddiq's speech to the Sixteenth Majlis in *Nutqha va Maktubat,* vol. 2, no. 5, 1st bk., 31–36, 41–44.

54. On the differences between Iranian and British interpretations of the issue, see Richard Cottam, *Iran and the United States: A Cold War Case Study* (Pittsburgh: University of Pittsburgh Press, 1988), 95–98.

55. Musaddiq admitted this shortcoming in his speech on the second anniversary of

his premiership. See Parsa Yamgani, *Karnameh-i Musaddiq va Hizb-i Tudeh* (The record of Musaddiq and the Tudeh Party) (Tehran: Ravaq, 1979), 138.

56. For an analysis of middle-class support in this era, see Cuyler Young, "The Social Support of Current Iranian Policy," *Middle East Journal* 6, no. 2 (1952): 125–43.

57. For the major aspects of the "oil-less economy," see Homa Katouzian, "Oil Boycott and the Political Economy: Musaddiq and the Strategy of Non-Oil Economics," in *Musaddiq, Iranian Nationalism, and Oil,* ed. James Bill and Roger Louis (Austin: University of Texas Press, 1988), 208–25.

58. Ibid., 214.

59. For a description of Nasir Khan Qashqa'i and his tribe's role during the nationalization era, see the daily memoirs of Muhammad Nasir Saulat Qashqa'i, *The Years of Crisis in Iran: 1950–1953* (Houston: Book Distribution Center, n.d.).

60. On the social background of the Majlis deputies, see Ervand Abrahamian, *Iran between Two Revolutions* (Princeton, N.J.: Princeton University Press, 1982), 261, 269.

61. See, for example, Azad's outbursts during reports given by Musaddiq or other members of the cabinet to the Seventeenth Majlis on August 4 and September 7, 1951, cited in *Nutqha va Maktubat,* vol. 2, no. 5, bk. 1, 44–45, 71.

62. For a brief description of British interference in the internal affairs of Iran through its Iranian collaborators, see Mark J. Gasiorowski, "The 1953 Coup d'Etat in Iran," *International Journal of Middle East Studies* 19 (August 1987): 263–66. For a more detailed account of the same process, see Azimi, *Iran,* chaps. 18–20.

63. For interpretations of the activities of the Tudeh Party during the oil nationalization period, see Sepehr Zabih, *The Communist Movement in Iran* (Berkeley: University of California Press, 1966), 166–207; Abrahamian, *Iran between Two Revolutions,* 318–25.

64. See the Tudeh newspapers *Mardum,* October 15, 1950; *Naysan,* October 19, 1950; and *Bisu-yi Ayandeh,* November 16, 1950; all cited in Anvar Khami'i, *Az Inshi'ab ta Kudeta* (From the split to coup d'état), vol. 3 (Tehran: Hafteh, 1984), 281.

65. F. M. Javanshir, *Tajrubi-yi Bist-u Hasht-i Murdad* (The experience of the 28th of Murdad/August 19) (Tehran: Tudeh, 1980), 196–204.

66. Abrahamian, *Iran between Two Revolutions,* 320.

67. Katouzian, *Musaddiq and the Struggle for Power,* 125.

68. See Javanshir, *Tajrubi-yi Bist-u Hasht-i Murdad,* 79–97.

69. Khami'i, *Az Inshi'ab ta Kudeta.*

70. Faridun Kishavarz, *Man Mutaham Mikunam: Kumiti-yi Markazi-yi Hizb-i Tudeh ra* (I Accuse the Central Committee of the Tudeh Party) (London: Jibhi Newspaper Publications, n.d.), 134–44.

71. See Kermit Roosevelt, *Countercoup: The Struggle for the Control of Iran* (New York: McGraw-Hill, 1979), chap. 1.

72. For an analysis of the position of the religious community in the oil nationalization era, see Shahrough Akhavi, "The Role of the Clergy in Iranian Politics, 1949–1954," in *Musaddiq, Iranian Nationalism, and Oil,* ed. James Bill and Roger Louis (Austin: University of Texas Press), 91–117.

73. Baqa'i, *Shinakht-i Haqiqat,* 117–19.

74. See Turkaman, *Asnad Piramun-i Tuti'-yi Rubudan.*

75. On the defection of Ha'irizadeh and Makki, see Katouzian, *Musaddiq and the Struggle for Power,* 162–65. Shams Qanatabadi was a close ally of Kashani in the Majlis, and his defection was connected to Kashani's deteriorating relationship with Musaddiq.

76. For a comprehensive account of the conflict between the Majlis and the government, see Azimi, *Iran,* 309–30.

77. For accounts of the plans and the executions of the August coups, see Roosevelt, *Countercoup*; Gasiorowski, "The 1953 Coup d'Etat in Iran"; Katouzian, *Musaddiq and the Struggle for Power,* 188–93.

78. See James Bill, "America, Iran, and the Politics of Intervention, 1951–1953," in *Musaddiq, Iranian Nationalism, and Oil,* ed. James Bill and Roger Louis (Austin: University of Texas Press, 1988), 267–74.

Chapter 6

Mosque of Last Resort: State Reform and Social Conflict in the Early 1960s

Misagh Parsa

There are at least four theoretical perspectives that can be employed to explain social conflicts and collective action. They include the social breakdown model, Davies's J-curve, Marx's theory of revolution, and resource mobilization. With the exception of resource mobilization, these theories are insufficient to explain the conflicts and collective actions of the 1960s in Iran.

The social breakdown model claims that large-scale social transformations such as commercialization, urbanization, or industrialization tend to erode traditional values and authority relations and generate conditions in which conflicts arise. The Iranian revolution in 1979 and the rise of fundamentalism have often been interpreted using this model.[1] When this model is applied to the political mobilization in Iran during the 1960s, two key problems become evident. At that time, Iranian society had not yet experienced any of the large-scale social transformations that purportedly lead to anomie. Instead, Iran was in the throes of an economic decline, which was harming broad segments of the population. It was not the erosion of traditional values or the failure of the market, but rather the adverse effects of government economic policies, combined with a set of pre-existing conflicts unresolved by the 1953 coup d'état and attempts at political liberalization, that set the stage for conflict and collective action. A second problem concerns the options for mobilization: Why did the mobilization and collective actions that marked early June 1963 erupt during Islamic holy days, and why were they channeled through religious institutions? It is important to note that throughout the conflicts of the early 1950s, major social groups mobilized through the secular National Front and the Tudeh Party. The coup of 1953 practically eliminated the Tudeh Party and weakened the National Front. The liberalization of the early 1960s allowed the Front to mobilize again and demand political changes. But by June 1963, when popular protests erupted, a combination of repression and internal divisions had drastically limited the Front's capacity to mobilize. At that time, the political opposition had no option remaining but to mobilize within the mosque and religious structures. These facts do not lend support to the theory of anomie and social breakdown.

James Davies's J-curve would explain the mobilization in terms of sudden economic decline, which contradicted the population's rising expectations.[2] Marx's analysis would point to the economic crisis and its adverse effects on social classes, leading to class conflict. But neither of these explanations is sufficient. Davies's J-curve assumes the existence of organizations and solidarity structures necessary for mobilization and collective action. This assumption is highly problematic. Adversely affected social groups very often lack the resources and solidarity structures to mount sustained mobilization and collective action. Marxian class analysis suffers from two problems. First, it assumes that economically structured classes inevitably organize and engage in revolutionary social conflicts. Applied to the conflicts of the early 1960s, it becomes apparent that the peasantry and the working class were the least mobilized of all classes in Iran and, in fact, did not participate in national-level political processes. Furthermore, Marx's theory assumes that the state plays no autonomous role, but is rather an instrument of upper-class domination. In the Iranian case, this analysis is faulty because the state is the most important actor with interests of its own that may contradict those of the upper class. Skocpol's reformulation is more successful because it assigns potential autonomy to the state and stresses the significance of divisions between the state and the dominant class.[3] Yet her analysis does not fully explain why the conflicts of the early 1960s in Iran did not culminate in revolution, although segments of the upper class did defect from the state at that time.

I shall argue that the conflicts and collective actions of this period can be explained more satisfactorily by a broader perspective that draws on the resource mobilization model.[4] The explanatory strength of this model lies in its focus on a number of significant variables, including interests, organization, repression, facilitation, and opportunity for action, among others. *Interests* are defined in terms of shared advantages or disadvantages that accrue to a group in interaction with other groups. By *organization* is meant the extent of a common identity and unifying structure among individuals in the group. *Repression* refers to the cost of collective action, whereas *facilitation* refers to actions that reduce the cost of collective action. *Opportunity* for collective action is defined as the extent of vulnerability of the groups that are the targets of attack.

To be fully effective, this model must incorporate the state as a principal actor, because many political conflicts in developing countries during the twentieth century have derived in part from state policies designed to bring about social change and economic development. Such policies set the stage for conflicts by redistributing resources and power and by providing opportunities for collective action and conflict. In Iran, most of the conflicts of the twentieth century have emerged within the context of political and economic crisis involving the state, social groups and classes, and external forces emanating from powerful nations.

The economic crisis of the early 1960s and divisions within the dominant class—specifically between landlords and bureaucratic state managers—set the stage for mobilization and conflict. This condition increased the state's vulnerability and provided a favorable opportunity for mobilization and collective action. In addition, external pressure from the United States to liberalize reduced the cost of repression and facilitated mobilization. The reduction of repression also provided a favorable opportunity for mobilization and the emergence of unifying structures. Finally, economic crisis and state policies adversely affected the interests of broad segments of the population, thereby increasing the likelihood that they would act collectively.

At the conclusion of the conflicts of June 1963, the shah was the sole winner. Weaknesses within the opposition and the lack of effective coalition formation enabled the government to repress the opposition. This repression effectively put an end to popular mobilization and collective action until the revolutionary period of 1977–79. The shah centralized his power at the expense of other social groups, in particular the landed upper class, his traditional basis of support.

Although a number of other scholars have studied this period, no analyst has presented a theoretical explanation of the social movements of the early 1960s.[5] The aim of this chapter is to examine the causes and outcomes of these conflicts of the early 1960s. What were the economic and political conditions that set the stage for conflict? Who were the participants in the short-lived but dramatic uprising of June 1963? Why did the uprising fail? The answers to these questions can, by implication, illuminate the reasons why the same groups that participated in this rebellion were more successful a decade and a half later.

The Stage

Following World War II, Iran's economic development became a matter of central concern to the United States. American policy makers viewed economic development as a crucial aspect of anticommunist and anti-Soviet struggles. In their view, economic failure would invite revolution and perhaps even communism. Either a nationalist or a communist victory in Iran would deprive Western oil corporations of Iran's oil, which they had managed to control after the 1953 coup. For the shah, too, economic development was attractive during the 1950s because it would expand the basis of his support within the country. Given that his rule had been initiated in 1941 and rescued in 1953 by external forces, economic development would increase his popularity and hence assure his political survival. The state he had inherited from his father was already highly interventionist and hyperactive in promoting economic growth and development. American aid and rising oil prices would provide the means through which the state could further stimulate economic development.

Intensified development efforts by the government, however, contained the seeds of economic decline and financial crisis. Toward the end of the 1950s, as domestic and international credit expanded rapidly, so did government expenditures on the Second Seven-Year Development Plan (1955–62). Although oil revenues kept increasing, the ambitious Seven-Year Plan, combined with increasing military expenditures, forced the government to resort to deficit financing and borrowing from abroad. As Abrahamian notes, "Deficit financing, compounded by a bad harvest in 1959–1960, forced the cost-of-living index, which had been fairly stable in 1954–1957, to climb over 35 percent between 1957 and 1960."[6]

The government had also eased monetary and fiscal controls, freely issued import permits, and imported foreign goods on an enormous scale. By 1959, Iran's imports had jumped more than sixfold from their 1954 level.[7] Despite increases in oil revenues, the rapid growth of imports along with the necessity of repaying foreign loans created a trade imbalance and reduced foreign exchange to nothing. On the recommendation of the International Monetary Fund and with the support of the World Bank, the government implemented a stabilization program in September 1959 that forbade luxury imported items, raised import tariffs on nonessential goods, and restricted both bank credit and the sale of foreign exchange. These policies had negative effects on the private sector and resulted in a number of bankruptcies and bank failures. The tight control of credit led to an increase in the unofficial interest rate within the business sector to 30 percent. Urban land values fell drastically, by 500 percent.[8] At the same time, the stringent economic measures stabilized the economy to the point of complete stagnation for nearly three years and provided conditions that favored the emergence of conflict.[9]

Within the context of these economic difficulties,[10] a number of additional pressures emerged. Rising inflation provoked workers' strikes, made possible in part by the lifting of martial law in 1957, although such strikes were still considered illegal. Abrahamian notes, "The number of strikes, which had totaled no more than three in 1955–1957, jumped to over twenty in 1957–1961."[11] Another source reports that between 1957 and 1960, workers struck on at least fourteen separate occasions.[12] Government policies also produced growing bankruptcies and economic stagnation in the bazaars, creating a favorable climate for mobilization and collective action. Inflation, in combination with low salaries, also generated economic problems for the new middle class, particularly teachers, who launched a strike for more pay.

Along with these internal developments, some external changes pressured the Iranian government toward reform. On July 14, 1958, a revolution overthrew the government of Iraq, sensitizing both the United States and Iran to the prospect of political instability. A few months later, on January 1, 1959, another revolution in Cuba intensified these concerns. Toward the end of the year, the United States began encouraging the shah to bring about some measure of ameliorative social change. During a brief stop in Tehran on December 14, 1959, President Eisenhower remarked, in an address to the members of the Iranian parliament: "Military strength alone will not bring about peace with justice. The spiritual and economic health of the free world must be likewise strengthened."[13]

In response to internal economic conditions and external political pressures, the shah announced a series of reforms in the summer of 1960 that represented a dramatic departure from past policies. These measures, which included permitting opposition groups to participate in upcoming elections, eventually led to growing mobilization and collective action, a realignment within the dominant class, and, in particular, a significant undermining of the position of both landlords and the Islamic clergy.

Limited Liberalization

In early 1960, the shah announced that the upcoming Majlis elections would be open to independent candidates. He planned to control parliament and undermine the position of the landed upper class by introducing two parties with connections to the royal court. The candidates of these parties were largely drawn from the ranks of professionals and civil servants. Responding to the possibility of a political opening, several independent candidates also announced their intention to run for seats in the Majlis; they included Hussain Makki, 'Ali Amini, and several members of the second National Front, notably Allahyar Saleh. The second National Front, founded on July 21, 1960, the eighth anniversary of the uprising that restored Musaddiq to the premiership, began to prepare for the elections to the Twentieth Majlis. The government took measures to ensure that National Front candidates faced difficulties in campaigning. Prime Minister Iqbal even declared publicly that supporters of former Prime Minister Musaddiq would not be allowed to run for office.[14] The elections in August were obviously rigged, with the government interfering everywhere to ensure the victory of its favored candidates. Public outcry overwhelmingly repudiated the results and obliged the shah to nullify the outcome, and Iqbal was forced to resign on August 27. In early September, to forestall protests by the opposition, the government prohibited people from assembling publicly without specific authorization.[15]

In the repeat elections held for the Majlis in January 1961, the shah was forced to compromise with the incumbent representatives.[16] Saleh was the only opposition candidate from the second National Front allowed to win. The obvious repetition of electoral fraud was met with renewed protests by the Front. On January 30, 1961, a group of Front leaders staged a sit-in at the Senate to protest the elections. University students and bazaaris organized a number of demonstrations on behalf of the Front. The protests were so intense that the government was obliged to close down Tehran University.[17]

Two major events of this period contributed to the opening of a new phase in the country's development: the teachers' strike in Iran and the election of John F. Kennedy to the U.S. presidency. In particular, the teachers' strike, discussed below, garnered a great deal of support from other social groups and, within the context of growing mobilization, escalating conflicts, and external pressures, succeeded in bringing down the government of Prime Minister Sharif Imami. The shah was obliged to proceed in new directions and, reluctantly, to initiate radical reforms.

Reforms from Above: An Opportunity for Opposition Mobilization

During this period, the United States played an important role in pressing the shah to install a reformist government. While still a senator, Kennedy, among other leading Democrats, had expressed dissatisfaction with U.S. policy toward corrupt regimes in the Third World, particularly Iran.[18] As president, Kennedy became concerned with Iran's political instability, first in April of 1961, when Soviet Premier Nikita Khrushchev stated to Walter Lippmann that Iran was headed for a revolution.[19] According to former U.S. ambassador Armin Meyer:

> The Kennedy administration was very concerned about Iran and immediately set up a task force.... The result of that task force was to instruct our ambassador that we would provide $35 million in aid in return for which we would expect from the Iranians various steps which we considered necessary for progress, including even suggestions as to the prime ministerial candidate we considered best qualified to administer the proposed reforms.[20]

In response to U.S. pressure and growing internal conflicts, notably the teachers' strike, the shah appointed 'Ali Amini as prime minister. Amini, a relative of Musaddiq and finance minister in his administration, had been in favor of land reform since the mid-1940s. Upon taking office, he dissolved the newly elected Twentieth Majlis; exiled General Bakhtiar, the head of SAVAK; granted freedom of the press; allowed the National Front to resume public activities; and, most important, appointed as minister of agriculture Hassan Arsanjani, a radical journalist with socialist views who had advocated land reform since the early 1940s.

A key feature of the new cabinet was land reform. The shah's decision to accept land reform was extraordinarily complex, both economically and politically. As the country's largest landowner, the royal family would have been significantly affected by any reforms that might reduce their economic interests and resources for political maneuvering.[21] A 1951 survey showed that the holdings of the royal family were extensive. They included 300,000 acres under cultivation, 131,000 acres of arable but uncultivated land, and 494,000 acres suitable for cultivation with proper irrigation. There were 49,117 families living on the royal estates.[22] The 1953 removal of Musaddiq had restored the landed upper class to its politically dominant position; its grateful members continued to constitute the shah's main social base of support. Of the representatives to the Nineteenth Majlis, convened in 1959, 61 percent were from the landed upper class; two years later, 58 percent of the representatives still came from the landed upper class.[23] Moreover, politically powerful elements of the clergy also controlled extensive landholdings and were certain to be alienated by any land reform program.

At the same time, there were distinct benefits that would accrue from implementing agrarian reform. Hooglund has suggested that these benefits were primarily political. First, the central government could extend power into rural areas traditionally dominated by large landowners. Second, the shah could present the appearance of a reformer, interested in his people's welfare. Third, land reform would create a new base of popular support among the peasantry. And fourth, land redistribution would be received favorably by the Kennedy administration in the United States, which was pushing for land reform in the Third World.[24]

At the same time, broader economic considerations were also extremely persuasive, as Najmabadi has pointed out: "Certain key features of land reform measures, such as the exemption of all mechanized farming regardless of size, or the exclusion of large sections of the rural population from the benefits, would be incomprehensible or even counterproductive if the primary goal of such reforms had been to create social stability and to break up large holdings of land."[25] Najmabadi has argued further that although the exact timing of land reform is for the most part a political decision in every country in which it is undertaken, political explanations of land reform fail to account for many of its important features. For example, interpreting land reform as an attempt to reduce social tension and effect political stability ignores the fact that reform programs were compatible with and in fact required by the needs of economic development.

Najmabadi has suggested that the reasons behind land reform are rooted in economic development and broad international factors. The agricultural sector was envisioned by Third World reformers not only as the source of surplus to be used for accumulation, but also as a labor supply and an internal market for developing industry. Toward this end, precapitalist agrarian relations were to be dismantled, monetary relations enlarged, and production stepped up.[26]

The explanations of Hooglund and Najmabadi are not incompatible. Both perspectives shed much light on the reasons behind Iranian land reform. Political considerations go a long way toward explaining agrarian reform programs, especially when the dominant classes are deeply divided among themselves. For example, in the early 1950s, there had been conflict between Iranian royalists and liberals, with each attempting to gain the upper hand. Distribution of crown land by the shah would have generated a measure of political support for the monarch in the countryside, an outcome certain to be opposed by the National Front. The

National Front objected to the procedure, demanding that the lands be distributed by the government, not by the shah himself. The Front argued that the lands had originally belonged to the people and were illegally appropriated by Reza Shah.

Economic factors also help account for the Iranian land reform. After World War II, the United States demonstrated an interest in Iran's economic development. At that time, the U.S. government established a large-scale agricultural extension program in Iran to encourage rural development. The distribution of crown lands seems to have been encouraged by the United States in 1950.[27] The shah himself often expressed his commitment to land reform and to setting a limit on landholding in order to achieve economic development. In a press conference held on January 25, 1959, shortly after the Cuban revolution, he declared:

> As I have repeatedly stated, I would have liked to see the work of land distribution over and done with overnight. But unfortunately it takes time. Undoubtedly, after the distribution of Crown and State lands, it will be time for limitation of [private] land-ownership, limitation and not elimination. We want to limit ownership and to increase the number of owners. We will then investigate the local situation, we will see how much land each person is able to cultivate. What we aim at is a situation whereby each owner should be in a position to manage his own land. This system in which landlords sit in Tehran, New York and Paris and the local manager delivers their land revenues to them annually should be eradicated. In this system neither the land-owner benefits from his land, nor does the sharecropper. But perhaps if the landlord himself manages part of his estate directly his income will increase many fold.[28]

Although the shah's statement reflects his concern with development and the positive impact of reform, the timing of the statement indicates his concern with political instability as well. The fact that in September of the same year the government contracted with the U.S. Agency for International Development mission in Iran to draw up an agrarian reform act may also evidence concerns with political instability in the wake of the Cuban revolution.

The resulting plan, which would have limited holdings of agricultural land to 200 irrigated hectares or 600 hectares of rain-fed land, was never implemented.[29] The landlord-dominated Majlis drastically modified the original reform bill, making it extremely difficult to implement. By the time the legislation was passed in 1960, the limits on landholdings had been raised to 400 irrigated hectares and 800 rain-fed hectares. Further modification of the original legislation permitted landlords to transfer any holdings beyond their limit to their legal heirs within two years; additional land could be sold to others as long as the owners paid a 50 percent sales tax. Finally, time-consuming surveys were required that would have prolonged the procedure for years, making it practically irrelevant to the country's agrarian problems.

Two factors in 1961 favored a renewed interest in reform and encouraged the shah to take more serious steps toward some kind of land reform. Ayatullah Burujirdi, leader of Iran's Shi'is and a chief opponent of land reform, died in March 1961, thus removing an obstacle to the program. The second was the Kennedy administration's concern with Iran's stability, which was to be attained through development. Even then the shah, as the largest single landlord, was unwilling to carry out radical land reform. He favored only a selective redistribution against those landlords who competed with him. Finally, the shah wanted to receive credit for the reforms.[30]

Amini and the Second National Front

Amini had hoped to fulfill his program and limit the shah's power with the cooperation of the National Front. He had also hoped to use the power of the National Front to carry out his reforms, particularly land reform. He even held a private meeting with the Front's leading members to explain that he had no personal quarrel with them. He argued that he was serious about land reform and had accepted the premiership only on the condition that the shah dismiss the Majlis. He could not, he explained, hold elections before implementing land reform because otherwise the landlords and the shah's men would once again dominate the process. Amini told the Front's leaders that the economy was in desperate shape and that any further deterioration would play into the shah's hands. Finally, he argued, if the shah managed to remove him, the National Front would be eliminated as well. Although the Front's leaders responded sympathetically, no formal or informal agreement was reached between the two parties.[31]

As a gesture of goodwill, Amini initiated some liberalizing reforms, such as allowing Musaddiq's picture to appear in the Iranian press on May 7, 1961.[32] He also permitted the nationalists to hold a mass meeting at Jalalieh Field on May 18, in which 80,000 people participated. The national press, which had been forbidden even to acknowledge the existence of the second National Front, began competing to publish the views and policies of the Front.[33]

The National Front, however, did not support Amini in his reforms. Even at the Jalalieh meeting, speakers such as Karim Sanjabi attacked him, declaring that the Iranian people did not want a prime minister imposed by America.[34] In the next several months, the Front intensified its attacks on Amini's government. National Front supporters at Tehran University called for Amini's resignation, and the Front's own demand was for "immediate general elections."[35]

The Front was not united in its approach to Amini, but divided instead into radical and moderate wings. The radical wing preferred mass mobilization and confrontation with the shah. The elder statesmen who represented the moderate faction favored discrete negotiations with the shah and hoped that U.S. pressure would lead him to turn to them.[36] The radical wing wanted to take advantage of division between Amini and the shah by strengthening Amini. Those in the moderate wing had no interest in confronting the shah, but favored attacking Amini instead. Their principal demand was for free elections, which were not in Amini's power to guarantee.

In the absence of National Front cooperation, compounded by rising social conflicts and growing popular mobilization, the shah's forces began moving against the Front and Amini. On January 21, 1962, Tehran university students who supported the National Front demonstrated against the expulsion of two high school students for political activities. The demonstration was attacked by paratroopers. This attack was intended to demobilize the students and perhaps bring down Amini's government. In response to the commando raid on the university, the chancellor of Tehran University, Dr. Ahmad Farhad, resigned his post. In his resignation, he noted: "I have never seen or heard so much cruelty, sadism, atrocity, and vandalism on the part of the government forces. Some of the girls in the classrooms were criminally attacked by the soldiers. When we inspected the University buildings we were faced with the same situation as if an army of barbarians had invaded an enemy territory."[37]

For his part, Amini hastily denied that he had anything to do with the repression. Nevertheless, his government lasted only a few months more, until July 17, when, after fourteen months in office, he resigned in a dispute with the shah over the amount of military expenditures. Although this issue triggered Amini's resignation, his administration had failed to attract the support of the public and three major actors. His implementation of the IMF-recommended stabilization program adversely affected most social groups and classes. The shah was suspicious of Amini and threatened by his independence; he also disliked the prime minister's flirtation with the Front. The National Front refused to cooperate with him unless he dissolved SAVAK and held free elections. Finally, Amini had failed to obtain U.S. support in his disagreement with the shah over military expenditures.[38] He expected that the United States would come to his aid, but this backing did not materialize. On his trip to the United States, the shah had already cut his deal; U.S. officials realized that Amini lacked a social base of support and that he could not establish political authority in the face of challenges from landlords, the National Front, and the shah and his military.[39]

To succeed Amini the shah appointed Asadullah 'Alam, a close friend, as prime minister. Although Arsanjani was kept on as minister of agriculture for another year, the shah decided to water down the land reform program, while at the same time introducing several other reforms. He labeled this package the White Revolution, later also known as the "Revolution of the Shah and the People." The reforms were contained in six points: (1) agrarian reform, (2) nationalization of pastures and forests, (3) public sale of state-owned factories to finance land reform,

(4) profit-sharing in industry, (5) enfranchisement of women, and (6) establishment of a literacy corps.

A plebiscite was scheduled for January 26, 1963, to approve the six-point program proposed by the shah. Both the clergy and the National Front opposed it and called for a strike in protest. The bazaar closed down on January 22 for three days. The Front also called for a demonstration on January 25, which was banned by the government. That day most of the leaders of the National Front were arrested. The number of Front leaders in prison eventually reached four hundred.[40] The government announced that except for 4,115 people out of more than five million voters, the nation had fully endorsed the referendum. Yet, within the space of a few months, the regime had to contend with popular protests.

Conflicts and Collective Action

A number of factors had contributed to economic decline and a political crisis, mutually reinforcing each other and setting the stage for mobilization and conflict. Three groups in particular were adversely affected and, as a result, mobilized and acted collectively: the bazaaris, whose economic position was jeopardized; the clergy, who played a major role in the events of June 1963; and teachers. Let us begin with the mobilization and collective actions of teachers.

The Teachers' Strike

Schoolteachers were a social group that played a brief but significant role in the conflicts of the early 1960s. The unique position of teachers gives them the potential to influence political processes through their contact with students, who are often very active politically in developing societies. Student networks have linkages with other elements of society and can be activated during times of conflict. These networks are often critical in forming coalitions and escalating conflicts.

Reduced repression, a political opening, and the promise of freedom for political activities, combined with a severe economic crisis and deteriorating living conditions for low- and fixed-income groups, prompted teachers in the elementary system and high schools to organize a nationwide strike in the spring of 1961. The vast majority of teachers received monthly salaries equivalent to $40-$65. In mid-April, teachers in Tehran circulated leaflets and called for a nationwide strike on May 2, while the government prepared to control an anticipated wave of demonstrations and protests. On the designated day, teachers throughout the country walked off the job.[41] In Tehran, thousands of striking teachers marched through the streets and assembled in front of the Majlis in Baharistan Square to make speeches and choose representatives to meet with the parliament. When the demonstrators began shouting their demands, the government sent in fire-fighters with hoses to disperse them. At the same time, the armed forces arrived and arrested many of the demonstrators. They opened fire, killing Dr. Khanali, a high school teacher, and wounding three other teachers and a student.[42]

Given the context of other conflicts and rising mobilization against the government within which this repression occurred, the event was quickly politicized, and mobilization and collective action multiplied rapidly. University students struck in support of teachers and participated in Dr. Khanali's funeral on May 3. During the funeral, the teachers demanded punishment for those responsible for his death. On the third day of their strike, the teachers led a sit-in of 30,000 people in front of the Majlis, demanding that the government be dismissed. They sent six representatives to discuss the issues with members of parliament. On May 6, thousands of teachers gathered at the Mihrigan Club to hear a speech by Muhammad Darakhshish, head of the Society of Teachers. To forestall further mobilization and politicization, parliament members promised to investigate the teachers' demands.

Because of the economic crisis and the government's stringent economic policies, the teachers received sympathy from other segments of the population in Tehran. Universities closed down in support of their strike, and bazaaris and some workers also backed the walkout. Several workers' syndicates in Tehran issued statements of support. Bazaaris in Baharistan Square closed their shops in support of the teachers, and demonstrations were held in front of the central bazaar. On the seventh day following Dr. Khanali's death, thousands of teachers, students, bazaaris, and workers went to the cemetery to pay tribute. The bazaar's representative declared, "Bazaaris have vowed to continue their support of the teachers and their demands."[43]

The coordinated, nationwide strike by teachers and the support expressed by other social groups forced the government into a defensive posture. As soon as the strike began, the shah proclaimed his intention to improve conditions for teachers. The Ministry of Culture immediately announced that 30 million rials had been allocated to supplement teachers' wages, which averaged less than 6,000 rials (about $75) per month. In addition, the authorities promised that teachers would be given insurance, a salary increase, a new hospital, and priority in government housing.[44] At the same time, however, the government proceeded to arrest many teachers and students in the provinces.

Neither the shah's promises nor the arrests brought an end to the walkout. Teachers vowed to continue their strike until all their demands had been won. On the fourth day of the strike, in the midst of growing politicization and demonstrations, Prime Minister Sharif Imami resigned along with his government and was replaced by 'Ali Amini. The new prime minister met several times with the teachers and finally accepted their demands, including higher salaries and punishment within six months of those responsible for Dr. Khanali's death. The government also promised to establish a bank for teachers and to provide housing loans. On May 13, thousands of teachers gathered at the Mihrigan Club and voted to end their twelve-day strike.

Beyond the economic concessions the teachers won, their strike had two significant political consequences. First, it challenged the government of Sharif Imami and accelerated his replacement by 'Ali Amini. In addition, it facilitated the mobilization of other social groups that also opposed the government.

Bazaaris' Mobilization

Bazaaris have consistently played a crucial role in the political conflicts of twentieth-century Iran because of the particular structure of the central bazaars and their resources. The bazaar generates a strong solidarity structure because of its spatial concentration and trade specialization. In most large cities, the central bazaar is clustered in a single location down a string of narrow alleys, which facilitate interaction and communication. Within bazaars, the production or sale of a single line of goods is centered in the same street or alley. Although closeness and dependence on specialized commodities may generate competition under ordinary conditions, they can also create a common fate with respect to market conditions, the rise of new competitors outside the bazaar, and powerful actors such as the state. In addition, bazaaris possess significant resources. In the early 1960s, Tehran's central bazaar covered six square miles and controlled the bulk of the nation's domestic and foreign trade. Several hundred moneylenders located in the bazaar controlled a part of private sector credit. The combination of these factors enabled various segments of the bazaaris, in contrast with other groups and classes, to mobilize and act collectively to defend their interests.

As in earlier times, bazaaris mobilized for collective action in the conflicts of the early 1960s. Their collective actions can be explained in terms of the resource mobilization model discussed above. The government's policies in the early 1960s adversely affected bazaaris' interests, setting the stage for their mobilization. Partial liberalization and reduced repression facilitated actions by bazaaris. Finally, the formation of the second National Front and clerical opposition to the government in June 1963 provided opportunities for coalition formation and opposition. Let us review the collective actions of bazaaris.

As part of the stabilization program imposed in 1960, the government reduced credit and loans to bazaaris, alleging that money bazaaris borrowed from banks was lent out to others at higher rates. The government also imposed tight controls on certain imports, which were met with disapproval by bazaar importers.[45] With the assistance of progovernment merchant guilds, the government designed a new rate of taxation for the bazaar, over the protests of rank-and-file bazaaris. According to shopkeepers and artisans, the burden of taxation was being transferred to poorer elements of the bazaar, while the leaders of the merchants' guilds were assessed little in taxes.[46] In protest, they refused to pay taxes for more than three years, and complained that the government did nothing to promote commerce.[47]

The stabilization program, the recession it produced, and the government's restrictions forced increasing numbers of bazaaris into bankruptcy.[48] Despite bazaar dissatisfaction with the government's policies, it was organizationally weak and little able to mobilize for collective action. The bazaar lacked both leadership and autonomous organizations. The Society of Merchant Guilds and Artisans, which had been central in mobilizing against the shah in the 1950s, had been dissolved, and a new merchants' guild had taken its place. This latter organization was under government control and hardly an autonomous bazaar organization. Because of their weak organization, bazaaris were unable to act in the absence of favorable opportunities. Such an opportunity did arise briefly in the early 1960s, owing to reduced repression and the partial liberalization that had led to the formation of the second National Front. In February 1961, when several dozen leaders of the Front organized a sit-in at the Majlis, demanding that free Majlis elections be guaranteed, bazaaris joined this mounting political opposition and closed down their shops to support the students and the second National Front, which they fully backed.[49] They also sided with striking teachers in May 1961 during their protest. In October 1961, hundreds of bazaaris organized the Union for the Safeguarding of the Constitution and Individual Rights and expressed their opposition to the reform cabinet and the suspension of parliament. Significantly, they demanded that the government's new economic policies be scrapped.[50]

In January 1963, when the shah's White Revolution reforms were up for approval in a referendum, both the second National Front and the clergy boycotted the referendum and were supported by bazaaris, who closed down for three days to protest the voting. Thirty-two protesters were arrested, including the entire leadership of the second National Front and most bazaari activists, notably Mahmud Maniyan and Muhammad Shanehchi.[51] With the National Front leadership in jail, bazaari supporters cooperated with the clergy, who also opposed the government. As an example, Abulqasim Labaschi, a bazaari member of the National Front who had been forced into hiding, traveled to Qum to obtain antigovernment leaflets put out by the clergy for distribution in Tehran.[52]

A new round of attacks was directed against bazaaris by the government. In May 1963 the government began investigating individuals who were delinquent in their taxes. In Tehran alone, 300,000 cases of refusal to pay taxes were discovered, the majority of which involved merchants, artisans, and small shopkeepers.[53] Furthermore, the government warned of an antiprofiteering campaign against bazaaris who refused to lower prices in the midst of mounting inflation.[54] Price controls were slapped on bakers and butchers at the end of April and again in mid-May.[55] Attacks and restrictions such as these further threatened the situation of broad segments of bazaaris within the commercial sector.

These developments set the stage for bazaar opposition to the government in

June. Bazaaris were unorganized, however, and did not respond to these threats in a unified fashion. Shopkeepers and artisans actively protested the government's actions, but merchants refrained from open opposition. In a sample of 579 individuals arrested or killed in the protests, shopkeepers and artisans constituted the largest group; only one was a merchant.[56] Once demonstrations turned violent and shots were fired, the bazaaris among the protesters rapidly withdrew.[57] Outside the central bazaar, some shopkeepers did not join in the actions at all, and as a result their shops were smashed and even looted.

In sum, mobilization and collective action by bazaaris during this period derived from several factors, including their economic interests, an organizational vacuum or weakness, and the opportunity for collective action. Bazaari interests were directly challenged by the policies and actions of the government. With a reduction in repression, bazaaris mobilized against these policies, but their collective action was promptly extinguished by an upsurge in government repression.

The Clergy and the State

Relations between the state and the clergy began to sour in December 1959, when the shah proposed land reform. Most clergy opposed land reform, which would have considerably reduced the holdings of both mosques and some individual clerics. At least one high cleric, Ayatullah Burujirdi, openly expressed dissatisfaction with the land reform proposed by the government, but he died in March 1961, before the reforms were put into effect.[58] In May 1961, the shah ordered the government to introduce a program of reforms, including land reform. At the same time, he dissolved the Majlis, which was dominated by landlords. In October 1962, the government approved a bill that would have formed local councils throughout the country. The same bill contained other measures that many clergy found objectionable, including women's suffrage. In a reversal of previous statutes, the bill also declared that candidates and voters were not required to adhere to Islam, nor were elected councillors obliged to swear their oath of office on the Qur'an.[59] Most clerics regarded this bill as contrary to Islam and pointed to the constitution of 1906, which prohibited any law that was against Islam. Ulama mounted a protest by means of telegrams and petitions sent to Prime Minister 'Alam. The latter ignored the rising protests until November 1, when the clergy called for nationwide prayer and protest. In the early hours of that day the government capitulated, contacting religious leaders in Qum and Tehran and announcing that the local council's bill had been suspended.[60]

The government did not, however, discard all provisions of the bill. In particular, it retained those measures providing for land reform and women's franchise. These items were later incorporated into the White Revolution and submitted to popular approval in January 1963. After the voting, the government declared that the reforms had received the overwhelming support of the people.

The clergy's response to the reforms was divided. Only a small clerical minority that maintained ties to the government supported the shah; they included Ayatullah Mahdavi, Allamah Vahidi, and the Imam Jum'eh of Tehran.[61] Most of the clergy opposed both land reform and the vote for women, but they assumed differing stances on the issues. In some areas, notably Azarbaijan, Isfahan, and Kirman, the clergy were large landholders who stood to lose under the proposed reforms. Land belonging to mosques and religious institutions was also slated to be confiscated. For some preeminent clerics, including Ayatullahs Shari'atmadari and Muhammad Reza Gulpaigani, women's franchise was unacceptable, and they specifically asked the shah to withdraw this proposed reform. Still other clergy, including Ayatullahs Taliqani, Zanjani, and Mahallati Shirazi, adopted a radically different position. They criticized the shah's dictatorship and the capitulation laws and instead advocated justice for the poor.[62]

Ruhullah Musavi Khumaini was among the preeminent clerics, although relatively young and unknown in the early 1960s. His vociferous opposition to the shah and the proposed reforms soon made him well known. He condemned virtually all the features of the White Revolution and their broader implications for Iran's place in the world. A central theme of many of these attacks was Khumaini's concern for the position of the clergy and Islam, both of which he believed to be threatened by the reforms. Women's suffrage and equality were rejected as a Baha'i principle.[63] Land reform was opposed in part because of a lack of support for it within the agrarian sector, and in part for its perceived negative economic consequences.[64] Even the referendum organized by the shah was condemned as against the interests of the nation. Khumaini opposed the government's policies because he believed they would fortify Iranian Baha'is, Israel, and American imperialism, all of which were potential threats to Islam. Khumaini was alone among Iran's preeminent religious leaders in going beyond strictly religious matters and issuing statements that took up the causes of other social groups, thus facilitating coalitions with other forces opposed to the shah. He denounced Iran's economic penetration by Israel and the United States, the loss of Iranian markets, and bankruptcies among farmers and bazaaris.[65]

Most important, and a point that has been ignored in other analyses of the period, Khumaini was the only political or religious leader at this time who actually called for the overthrow of the shah's regime. In preparation for the Persian New Year in March 1962, Khumaini called for a time of mourning rather than of celebration, "to awaken Muslims and the country to the dangers that are ahead."[66] In this message, Khumaini demanded that the "despotic government," which had violated the constitution, be overthrown and replaced by a new government that respected Islam and cared for the Iranian people. On the second day of the new year, clerical students in the Faizieh clerical school in Qum organized a ceremony commemorating the martyrdom of Imam Ja'far al-Sadiq. They were attacked by the army, and a number of students were killed and wounded. Khumaini's response was a vehement denunciation of the ruling apparatus and its "Ghengis Khan-like nature. With this crime, the tyrannical regime guaranteed its own failure and destruction."[67] In the months that followed, Khumaini repeatedly criticized the shah's regime, specifically its reforms, its violation of Islam and the constitution, and its economic policies, which adversely affected bazaaris. His complete rejection of the government and unwillingness to compromise made him well known and respected within some sections of Iranian society, especially within a segment of the bazaar.

The Shi'i mourning month of Muharram took on a highly political tone in May and June 1963. This observance is marked by public religious ceremonies of mourning characterized by large-scale processions of men marching through the streets, beating their breasts with their arms and chanting. These religious rituals provided a unique opportunity for the expression of political opposition and protest against the government. On June 3, 1963, the actions of participants in the 'Ashura processions were highly politicized. Although organizers tried to block the slogans from targeting the shah, anti-shah slogans were shouted as the marchers reached the Marble Palace.[68] The day after the peak of the mourning ceremonies, on June 5, Khumaini was arrested along with a number of other clerics throughout the country. Within a few hours of Khumaini's arrest, popular protests erupted in Tehran, Qum, Mashhad, Isfahan, Shiraz, Tabriz, and Kashan. This uprising lasted for three days, from June 5 through June 7, and was met by brutal repression. In the end, the uprising failed to dislodge the regime, and in fact, decisive repression solidified the power of the government and the shah. But the price was the breakup of the loose alliance that had existed between the monarch and the clergy since the shah first came to power during World War II.

The Failure of the Uprising

The mourning ceremonies and arrests of Ayatullah Khumaini and a number of other clerics sparked an uprising that presented a unique opportunity for broad segments of the population to voice their opposition to the regime. The movement was unable to bring about a political change, however, largely because of organizational weaknesses and the lack of a strong coalition.

Specifically, two major factors contributed to the uprising's failure. One was the weakening of all opposition organizations in the aftermath of the coup d'etat against Prime Minister Musaddiq in 1953. The Tudeh Party was virtually eliminated at that time, and the National Front lost some of its capacity to mobilize. The other factor was the absence of a coalition among major segments of the population. As a result, the military forces were able to repress and eliminate the opposition for more than a decade. Both of these can be illustrated by examining the second National Front and its inability to mobilize broad segments of the population before and during the June uprising.

The second National Front was organized in July 1960, following the shah's announcement permitting opposition groups to participate in the election. In the three-year period between July 1960 and June 1963, the National Front was unable to regain its formerly prominent position within the opposition to the shah. The Front's failure was rooted in a number of political changes that had taken place in the country and within the National Front itself.

In the early 1960s, the Pahlavi state was in a stronger position vis-à-vis the opposition than it had been a decade earlier. Having eliminated Musaddiq and his supporters, the state, with the partial exception of the period of Amini's prime ministership, was more consolidated and able to act more consistently against its opponents. Increased oil revenues, along with economic and military aid from the United States, had strengthened the Iranian army and hence the shah's position as well. The formation of SAVAK contributed to the repressive capacity of the state, raising the cost to the opposition of mobilization and collective action.

In clear contrast to the state, the National Front had undergone decline in its resources and capacity for mobilization. In the early 1950s, the Front had been part of the power structure and was able to use government resources such as Iranian radio, the main media instrument in the country, to mobilize opposition against conservatives and royalists alike. By the early 1960s, the Front and its members no longer had access to such resources. This lack combined with government repression to curtail sharply the Front's networks within the country and, hence, their influence in the provinces. Musaddiq continued to be under house arrest and was unable to participate in National Front activities. Without a powerful, popular, and nationally known leader, the Front had great difficulties in mobilizing broad segments of the population. Musaddiq's absence also created a vacuum within the organization, which lacked the unity and effective leadership to fill it.

Internally, the Front was divided into two factions. The first was supported by the central council's influential leaders, including Allahyar Saleh, Karim Sanjabi, and Shahpur Bakhtiar. This faction advocated the formation of a unified organization as a single party to oppose the dictatorship within a legal framework. The second faction favored the existence of the Front as a coalition of political parties and political groups. Many within this faction argued for confrontational rather than legalistic tactics in opposing the existing regime. This second faction was represented primarily by the younger generation, especially university students, along with the Liberation Movement of Iran, led by Mehdi Bazargan, a member of Musaddiq's cabinet, and Ayatullah Taliqani, a loyal supporter of Musaddiq who did not waver after other religious leaders such as Kashani shifted sides. Throughout the period under review, the first faction, represented heavily in the central council, prevailed.[69]

The Front was unable to present a unified program beyond demanding free elections, a democratic government, and adoption of a neutral foreign policy. Anything more was too internally divisive. The Front boycotted the Majlis elections in the winter of 1961 mainly because the members could not agree on a list of candidates.[70] The organization was also very cautious on the issue of land reform. The Front's High Council was composed in part of a number of major landlords. According to Katouzian, the Front admitted Amir Taimur (Kalali), a conservative large landowner, to its High Council in return for his contribution of 200,000 rials ($2,500).[71] Nor did the Front want to antagonize high-ranking clerics, many of whom opposed land reform.[72] The Front went so far as to publish a pamphlet in the fall of 1962 that argued that because Iran had never had feudalism there was no need for land reform.[73]

More fundamentally, the National Front's internal structure was itself undemocratic. The High Council possessed a great deal of power, which it exercised arbitrarily. For instance, the council blocked the membership in the Front of Maliki's Socialist Society, supported by many university students, and the Liberation Movement, formed in 1961 and supported by religious elements. The addition of these groups would have enhanced the Front's own capacity for broader mobilization. In addition, seats in the Front's congress were undemocratically allocated to various member organizations without regard to the size of their membership. Although the Organization of University students constituted nearly half of the total membership in the National Front, it had only 30 of the 160 or 170 delegates in the congress.[74] Furthermore, out of 160 members, 100 were elected as representatives of various organizations, and 60, including party leaders, had seats as individuals.[75] The Front even expelled some 90 students from its youth organization on ideological grounds because they were leftists, an action that reduced the organization's support among university students. These policies led Mehdi Bazargan and his allies to break away from the second National Front altogether by abruptly walking out of the congress in December 1962.[76]

Another factor that reduced the capacity of the National Front to mobilize people effectively was government repression. Although the group managed to obtain a house at 143 Fakhrabad Avenue in Tehran, meetings there were often broken up by government agents. Eventually, in 1961, the headquarters of the National Front were closed down by the police. Repeated arrests of Front leaders reduced their capacity for mobilization. For example, in the aftermath of the attack of January 21, 1962, on Tehran University students, the government arrested some of the organization's leaders, although they had had nothing to do with the student rally.

As prime minister, even Amini put constraints on the Front. When Front leaders, particularly Bakhtiar and Sanjabi, attacked the prime minister in their rally, he ordered the arrests of a large number of them. That rally was the sole legal event sponsored by the second National Front. Amini did not permit the Front to commemorate the anniversary on July 21, 1961, of Musaddiq's return to power in 1952. The Front decided to proceed with its plans regardless, but with police intervention the event turned into a riot. In response, the government arrested many of the leaders and closed down their club.[77]

By the time of the uprising in June 1963, repression had for all intents and purposes paralyzed the second National Front. By that time approximately four hundred leaders and activists of the Front were in jail. The repression and imprisonment of its leaders ensured the Front's absence from the ensuing conflicts.

In contrast to the National Front, the clergy had greater resources for mobilization. They had a national network of mosques with regular members and attendance. In addition, the state had not yet repressed the clergy on a large scale, although clerical students had been attacked in Qum. The clergy, however, failed to utilize fully their resources against the government. A major problem was national divisions, which prevented the development of a unified program of action. With the exception of Ayatullah Khumaini and a few others, the vast majority of the clergy were not concerned with the broader social, political, and economic issues of the time. Ayatullah Khumaini was the only cleric who actually demanded the overthrow of the government. The divisions within the clergy are reflected in the fact that Khumaini's arrest led to protests in only half a dozen cities. In Tehran, a number of social groups did not participate in the protests. University students, who had opposed the shah's regime on a broad scale, did not (with some individual exceptions) actively join the demonstrators. Instead, they remained on the university campus and prominently displayed a banner that proclaimed, "The murderous and bloodthirsty shah spills the blood of the people." Students also shouted slogans against dictatorship and in favor of Prime Minister Musaddiq.[78]

Other groups whose participation in the uprising was relatively minor (again with individual exceptions) were industrial workers, white-collar employees, and the peasantry. In the sample cited earlier, only 2.9 percent of the Tehran participants were factory workers. More significantly, no workers' strike or factory shutdown of any sort occurred anywhere in the country, and white-collar employees showed up at their jobs without interruption. Nor did teachers take part in the protests, as they had earlier mobilized successfully against the government and won all their demands. Even more conspicuous was the absence of the peasantry from the political scene. With the exception of peasants from Varamin, ninety miles east of Tehran, who participated in the Tehran demonstrations, peasants elsewhere refrained from political action. Inactivity by these classes and groups prevented the opposition from consolidating their actions and facilitated the success of repression.

The various ethnic minorities, including the Kurds, Turkoman, Arabs, Bakhtiaris, and Baluchis, abstained from the political opposition of this period. The explanation is in part geographic, as most of these groups are located on the peripheries of the country, whereas the opposition was confined to a few major cities. Another reason had to do with the presence of a separate mosque network among the Sunni ethnic groups, who do not observe the Shi'i holy month of Muharram.

The absence of industrial workers from the events was in part a result of the fact that they lacked independent organizations, which would have enhanced their capacity to act collectively. Another reason for workers' inaction was that the shah's reforms promised to institute profit sharing for industrial workers. The government claimed that several industrial sectors had already been covered under this plan by early 1963.[79] The government's promise of improved wages and income might well have been taken seriously by workers, who therefore abstained from antigovernment mobilization. Moreover, some workers and white-collar employees probably regarded the government's policies of implementing land reform and women's suffrage as just and progressive policies in the interest of the working classes, particularly because the Tudeh Party and, to some extent, elements within the National Front had advocated agrarian reform in the 1950s.

The reasons for the peasantry's absence from the political conflicts are complex. To begin with, the Iranian peasantry as a whole has not manifested a high degree of politicization. Major peasant revolts have been almost nonexistent in the twentieth century.[80] The lack of peasant organizations also contributed to their inaction. Finally, the government's promise of land reform and redistribution likely reduced peasant interest in political action. The government actually began to redistribute land to peasants as early as March 1962, starting in Maragheh.[81] Although segments of the clergy opposed land reform, peasants went their own way and took the land that was offered by the government. There is no evidence of peasants refusing any land redistributed by the government.

The absence of white-collar employees and professionals, industrial workers, peasants, and students from the demonstrations and strikes in early June 1963 was critical. Formation of a broad coalition among these groups and classes along with bazaaris and clergy might have rendered the state incapable of acting decisively. Such a broad coalition might have generated divisions and factionalism within the army, creating a revolutionary situation as did indeed occur fifteen years later. Without a consolidated opposition, however, government repression was successful in quashing the uprising and dispersing the regime's opponents. The defeat of this rebellion marked the cessation of popular collective action until the revolutionary period of 1977–79.

In conclusion, the political and economic developments of the early 1960s led to realignment within the system and set the stage for the conflicts of the 1970s. With land reform, the landed upper class lost some of its power; more important, a small group consisting of industrial-financial interests, along with the military and state bureaucracy, became the beneficiary and the new basis of support for the state. In the countryside, the reforms reduced the power of the landed upper class and extended state control over the peasantry. At the same time, land reform created a new class of small landlords, while eliminating landless laborers and pushing them to urban areas. Finally, the state became more interventionist in the economy, eventually rendering the government more vulnerable to attack and challenge in the late 1970s.

After the 1963 events, with the dissolution of the parliament, land distribution, and the repression of popular protests and the political opposition, including the clergy and the second National Front, the shah was able to concentrate power in his own hands. He controlled all the major centers of power in the country, including the army, government bureaucracy, the cabinet, parliament, and political parties. He personally made every important political decision. He appointed all the top-echelon officials of the government and bureaucracy. Political parties were never able to gain independence from him, and all political candidates had to be approved in order to run for office. Furthermore, he made all the important economic decisions, including national planning. Even major investments in the private sector needed the consent and often participation of members of the royal family. The entire media and the press came under the strict control of the government. The government also expanded its control over religious establishments and the clergy.[82] All these changes were made possible because the shah also commanded the army and SAVAK, which played a growing role in the affairs of the country.

Mobilization during the period from 1960–63 differed from that of the early 1950s. Earlier, political mobilization proceeded largely through political parties, the universities, and workplaces such as bazaars and factories. By the early 1960s, opposition political parties as well as the National Front had been drastically weakened, and state repression prevented the effective mobilization of broad segments of the population. Much of the mobilization that did occur was limited to the universities and the bazaar and was eventually directed through the mosque. The same pattern of mobilization occurred in 1977. Secular political groups, including the National Front, mobilized politically long before the clergy engaged in collective action. Once again, a combination of internal weaknesses and government repression eventually channeled mobilization through the mosque, the only institution with relative autonomy from the state, a national network, and a secure space for expressing grievances, broadcasting news of government repression, and organizing for collective action. Although the mosque was crucial for mobilization, both in 1963 and 1978–79, it was not the mobilization option that determined the outcome of the conflicts. To explain the revolutionary outcome in 1979, other variables must be taken into account.

Notes

I would like to thank John Foran, Gene Garthwaite, and an anonymous reviewer for helpful comments on an earlier draft of this chapter.

1. Said Amir Arjomand, "Iran's Islamic Revolution in Comparative Perspective," *World Politics* 38 (1986): 383.

2. James C. Davies, "Toward a Theory of Revolution," *American Sociological Review* 27 (1962): 5–19.

3. Theda Skocpol, *States and Social Revolutions: A Comparative Analysis of France, Russia and China* (Cambridge: Cambridge University Press, 1979).

4. Charles Tilly, *From Mobilization to Revolution* (Reading, Mass.: Addison-Wesley, 1978), 54.

5. Ervand Abrahamian's seminal work, *Iran between Two Revolutions* (Princeton, N.J.: Princeton University Press, 1982), discusses some of the events of the early 1960s, but offers no theoretical explanation. Similarly, Nikki R. Keddie's *Roots of Revolution: An Interpretive History of Modern Iran* (New Haven, Conn.: Yale University Press, 1981) covers the period descriptively. H. E. Chehabi's *Iranian Politics and Religious Modernism: The Liberation Movement of Iran under the Shah and Khomeini* (Ithaca, N.Y.: Cornell University Press, 1990) presents no theoretical perspective on the mobilization and collective action of this period. Sussan Siavoshi's book, *Liberal Nationalism in Iran: The Failure of a Movement* (Boulder, Colo.: Westview, 1990), contains a limited analysis of the National Front, but does not cover the broader social, political, and economic issues. James Goode's "Reforming Iran during the Kennedy Years," *Diplomatic History* 15 (Winter 1991): 13–29, is entirely descriptive.

6. Abrahamian, *Iran between Two Revolutions*, 421–22.

7. Homa Katouzian, *The Political Economy of Iran: Despotism and Pseudo-Modernism, 1926–1979* (New York: New York University Press, 1981), 206.

8. Ibid., 229.

9. Julian Bharier, *Economic Development in Iran, 1900–1970* (London: Oxford University Press, 1971), 95.

10. The degree of severity of economic downturn has been questioned by Katouzian, who uses aggregate data to argue that the economy was depressed but not stagnant. Katouzian, *The Political Economy*, 229.

11. Abrahamian, *Iran between Two Revolutions*, 422.

12. M. Ivanov, *Tarikh-i Nuvin-i Iran* (Modern history of Iran), trans. (from Russian) Hushang Tizabi and Hasan Qa'im Panah (Stockholm: Tudeh, 1356/1977), 205–7.

13. Quoted in Yonah Alexander and Allen Nanes, eds., *The United States and Iran: A Documentary History* (Frederick, Md.: University Publications of America, 1980), 247.

14. Chehabi, *Iranian Politics*, 144.

15. Mark Gasiorowski, *U.S. Foreign Policy and the Shah: Building a Client State in Iran* (Ithaca, N.Y.: Cornell University Press, 1991), 178–79.

16. Hossein Bashiriyeh, *The State and Revolution in Iran, 1961–1982* (New York: St. Martin's, 1984), 20.

17. Gasiorowski, *U.S. Foreign Policy*, 180.

18. Katouzian, *The Political Economy*, 213.

19. James Bill, *The Eagle and the Lion: The Tragedy of American-Iranian Relations* (New Haven, Conn.: Yale University Press, 1988), 132.

20. Ibid., 143.

21. The shah's father, Reza Shah, enriched his holdings by confiscating substantial tracts of land from landlords who no longer enjoyed royal favor. Although Reza Shah himself had come from a family of small landowners, by 1941 his family owned roughly 2,000 villages or portions thereof. See Ann K. Lambton, *The Persian Land Reform* (Oxford: Clarendon, 1969), 49–50.

22. Alexander and Nanes, *The United States and Iran*, 248–49.

23. Z. Shaji'i, *Namayandigan-i Majlis-i Shura-yi Milli dar Bist-u yik Daureh-i Qanun guzari* (Members of parliament in twenty-one legislative sessions) (Tehran: Tehran University Press, 1965), 173.

24. Eric Hooglund, *Land and Revolution in Iran, 1960–1980* (Austin: University of Texas Press, 1982), 50.

25. Afsaneh Najmabadi, *Land Reform and Social Change in Iran* (Salt Lake City: University of Utah Press, 1987), 11.

26. Ibid., 9–10.

27. Ibid., 66.

28. Mohammad Reza Pahlavi, *Collection of Speeches, Messages, and Interviews of His Majesty Mohammad Reza Shah Pahlavi* (Tehran, 1962), quoted in Najmabadi, *Land Reform*, 82.

29. Najmabadi, *Land Reform*, 74.

30. Bill, *The Eagle and the Lion*, 145.

31. Katouzian, *The Political Economy*, 220.

32. Bill, *The Eagle and the Lion*, 142.

33. Katouzian, *The Political Economy*, 221.

34. Chehabi, *Iranian Politics*, 64.

35. Katouzian, *The Political Economy*, 221.

36. Chehabi, *Iranian Politics*, 147.

37. Quoted in Bill, *The Eagle and the Lion*, 146–47.

38. Abrahamian, *Iran between Two Revolutions*, 423–24.

39. Katouzian, *The Political Economy*, 224.

40. Chehabi, *Iranian Politics*, 175.

41. *Ittila'at*, May 2, 1961.

42. *Ittila'at*, May 3, 1961.

43. Quoted in *Ittila'at*, May 9, 1961.

44. *Ittila'at*, May 2, 1961.

45. *Ittila'at*, May 20, 1963.

46. *Ittila'at*, April 30, 1963.

47. *Ittila'at*, May 21, 1963.

48. *Ittila'at*, May 7, 1961.

49. Interview with Abulqasim Labaschi, conducted by Habib Ladjevardi, February 28, 1983, tape 2, p. 7. This tape recording is part of the Iranian Oral History Collection, Houghton Library, Harvard University.

50. Bashiriyeh, *The State and Revolution*, 23.

51. *Ittila'at*, January 24, 1963.

52. Labaschi, interview, tape 2, p. 9.

53. *Ittila'at*, May 19, 1963.

54. *Ittila'at*, April 21 and 23, 1963.

55. *Ittila'at*, April 29 and May 16, 1963.

56. Mansoor Moaddel, "The Shi'i Ulama and the State in Iran," *Theory and Society* 15 (1986): 544. According to a sample of 579 individuals in Tehran who participated in the uprising of June 1963, 22.1 percent were workers (9 percent were industrial workers, but only 2.9 percent of these were factory workers), 12.4 percent were students, 9 percent were clergy, 3.8 percent were peasants, 2.8 percent were unemployed, 0.9 percent were housewives, and 0.2 percent were merchants. The largest group were those Moaddel labels the "petty bourgeoisie," which made up 43 percent and included ice cream sellers, vegetable sellers, shoemakers, blacksmiths, grocers, and tailors. Their apprentices constituted an additional 5.9 percent. In terms of the occupational structure of the population of Tehran, virtually all groups except these were underrepresented.

57. Bizhan Jazani, *Tarh-i Jama'eh Shinasi va Mabani-yi Stratijy-i Junbish-i Inqilabi-*

yi Khalq-i Iran (Sociological sketch and fundamentals of the strategy of the revolutionary movement in Iran) (Tehran: Maziar, 1979), 144.

58. K. S. McLachlan, "Land Reform in Iran," in *The Cambridge History of Iran,* vol. 1, *The Land of Iran,* ed. W. B. Fisher (Cambridge: Cambridge University Press, 1968), 690.

59. Shaul Bakhash, *The Reign of the Ayatollahs: Iran and the Islamic Revolution* (New York: Basic Books, 1984), 24.

60. Ibid., 25.

61. Shahrough Akhavi, *Religion and Politics in Contemporary Iran: Clergy-State Relations in the Pahlavi Period* (Albany: State University of New York Press, 1980), 103.

62. Ibid., 101.

63. Ruhullah Khumaini, *Sahifeh-i Nur,* 16 vols. (Tehran: Ministry of Guidance, 1983), 1:56.

64. Ibid., 1:70, 1:152–53.

65. Ibid., 1:112.

66. Ibid., 1:27.

67. Ibid., 1:38.

68. Chehabi, *Iranian Politics,* 178.

69. Siavoshi, *Liberal Nationalism,* 100–101.

70. Chehabi, *Iranian Politics,* 151.

71. Katouzian, *The Political Economy,* 221.

72. Chehabi, *Iranian Politics,* 164.

73. Katouzian, *The Political Economy,* 222.

74. Siavoshi, *Liberal Nationalism,* 102.

75. Chehabi, *Iranian Politics,* 167.

76. Ibid., 184.

77. Ibid., 164.

78. Ibid., 130–31.

79. *Ittila'at,* May 20, 1963.

80. Farhad Kazemi and Ervand Abrahamian, "The Nonrevolutionary Peasantry of Modern Iran," *Iranian Studies* 11 (1978): 259–304.

81. *Ittila'at,* March 20, 1962.

82. Akhavi, *Religion and Politics,* chap. 5.

Chapter 7

The Iranian Revolution of 1977–79: A Challenge for Social Theory

John Foran

The mass upheaval that swept Iran in the course of 1978 startled almost all observers, from journalists and diplomats to Iran scholars and theorists of Third World social change. By the time the shah left his country in January 1979 and Ayatullah Khumaini returned a month later, the first accounts of the events were being published. Now, more than a decade later, the literature on the causes and nature of the Iranian revolution has achieved sizable proportions, although a number of controversial issues remain unsettled and the theoretical implications of the case of Iran for social theorizing about revolution have yet to be fully drawn. It is thus a good moment to pursue and take stock of the intersection of three sets of literature: existing theories of revolution, explanations of the Iranian revolution, and the primary data and secondary accounts that form the raw material of the story. My purpose in the present chapter is to bring these literatures into mutual contact, identifying certain puzzles and controversies along the way, and offering a set of theoretical concepts for making sense of the Iranian case that make it comparable with other instances of Third World social revolutions, a task that I pursue in the final chapter of this volume.

Theories of Revolution, Perspectives on Iran

It is of course impossible in a short space to do more than sketch in some leading approaches to revolution in the social science literature.[1] Karl Marx and Alexis de Tocqueville between them raised most of the issues that still interest theorists today: the analysis of classes and coalitions, the role played by the state, international pressures, and the relative weight of ideas, among others.[2] In the 1920s and 1930s, comparative historians Lyford Edwards, Crane Brinton, and George S. Pettee worked out elaborate sequences of stages that they felt all major revolutions passed through; their "natural histories" highlighted such factors as the desertion of the intellectuals from the old regime, efforts by the state to implement reforms, crises brought on by state fiscal problems rather than opposition efforts, and a process of radicalization during revolutions that ended with military leadership. A good number of their insights can be applied to the Iranian case, yet the standard critique of their work is that it offers *descriptions* of revolutions rather than telling us why they occur.[3]

American social science entered the lists in the 1960s under the sign of structural functionalism and social psychology. Neil Smelser and Chalmers Johnson looked for disequilibria in the relationships among the economic, political, and cultural subsystems of society; Ted Robert Gurr and James C. Davies examined frustrated expectations and relative deprivation as sources of revolt. The fit of Davies's "J-curve," positing a period of increasing prosperity followed by a sudden economic decline, has been noted by some observers as applicable to the bust in Iran's oil boom after 1975, but it is doubtful that a single factor can explain the outbreak, and most of these models suffer from reducing collective action to psychological states that are hard to observe or measure. They are also cast at a very high level of abstraction that makes it hard to see why revolutions are so rare, given that discontent presumably always exists among some sectors of a population.[4] On the positive side, they do take participants' beliefs and sentiments seriously, which was not the case with their structuralist successors in the 1970s (except Tilly, to a degree). Barrington Moore's *Social Origins of Dictatorship and Democracy* (1966) and Eric Wolf's *Peasant Wars of the Twentieth Century* (1969) set the stage for a series of later works by Jeffery Paige, Charles Tilly, and Theda Skocpol that used comparative methods to search out structural keys to the causes of revolutions.[5] These were found in such factors as the impact of the commercialization of agriculture on monarchies, nobilities, and peasants (Moore and Wolf), the economic organization of export-oriented agriculture (Paige), the mobilization of political resources and organizational capacities by challengers to state power (Tilly), and the stresses caused by falling behind more powerful international competitors while being constrained by agrarian social relations or productivity levels (Skocpol).

It is generally acknowledged that these works moved the study of revolutions to a new plane (even if it is not always recognized that they have essentially revived the concerns of Marx and de Tocqueville). The Iranian revolution, however, played a role in revealing some of the limits of the structuralists' analyses. Skocpol, for example, who had boldly claimed, "Revolutions are not made, they come," in 1979, had to admit three years later that Iran's was one revolution that was "deliberately and coherently made."[6] Nor did the shah's Iran fit the model by coming under severe outside pressure such as defeat in war or falling behind economically more dynamic rivals. The absence of a peasant component in the Iranian revolutionary coalition flew in the face of the arguments of Moore, Wolf, Paige, and Skocpol. And culture or ideology, in the form of religious and secular challenges to the regime's authority, had played a role out of all proportion to the scant attention accorded it by any of the structuralist theorists. Finally, the relative absence of armed force and the strategies of general strike and massive, peaceful demonstrations fit almost no one's conception of how revolutions succeed. The question for social theory in the 1980s became: Is the Iranian revolution to be treated as a uniquely deviant case of revolution, or should the causality of social revolutions generally be reexamined in light of the evidence from Iran?

Before turning to more recent developments in the theory of revolution, let us survey the literature on Iran by the leading area specialists. How have those who know the case most intimately chosen to make sense of it? There are many cross-cutting ways to characterize this literature—no matter what schema is chosen, some violence is inevitably done to the subtlety of many of these works, almost all of which are valuable.[7] Keeping this in mind, we may identify explanations stressing (1) the cultural significance of the revolution, (2) political economy and structural disequilibrium, (3) politics-oriented resource mobilization approaches, and (4) conjunctural, multicausal analyses, of various emphasis.

The cultural explanation of the revolution is put forward by some of the actors themselves, beginning with Ayatullah Khumaini:

> They [the left] did not contribute anything. They did not help the revolution at all. Some of them fought, yes, but only for their ideas, only for their goals, only for their interests. They were not decisive for the victory.... [The people who were killed by the thousands died] For Islam. The people fought for Islam.[8]

On this view, which was shared by the post-1979 ruling Islamic Republican Party (IRP) and enshrined in the preamble to the 1979 constitution by Ayatullah Bihishti, the causes of the revolution were not economic; rather, the shah was overthrown for not adhering to Islam. This approach is shared by Muslim scholars in Iran such as 'Ali Davani and Hamid Algar in the United States, who argues, "The Iranian revolution has been, among other things, an implicit repudiation of Marxism as a revolutionary ideology and as a doctrine relevant to the problems of Iranian society or valid for humanity at large."[9] Paradoxically, one of the IRP's staunchest critics, sociologist Said Amir Arjomand, also considers the ideological significance of the revolution—its "value-relevance"—as its central defining feature. Treating the relationship of the shah to the ulama as the key to the revolution, his several excellent pieces on the revolution downplay the role of the working class and stress the Islamic outcome as brought about less by the disintegration of the army than by the collapse of the shah's legitimacy orchestrated by the "reactionary radicals" among the ulama.[10] Theda Skocpol's reflections on Iran also emphasize ideology and the role played by Shi'a Islam. The Iranian case evidently pushed her to rethink the basic definition of a social revolution to include ideological as well as state and class transformation: "This remarkable revolution forces me to deepen my understanding of the possible role of idea systems and cultural understandings in the shaping of social action."[11] Though Arjomand pays passing attention to socioeconomic causes, and Skocpol retains her characteristic emphasis on various structural features, the danger in all such accounts is overemphasizing the cultural factor, reducing it to "Shi'a Islam," and privileging the role of the clergy (and sometimes their bazaar allies) over all other social forces.

The diametrically opposed theoretical tack of stressing political economy and/ or social structure in the causality of the revolution is taken by a number of scholars, among them M. H. Pesaran:

> Contrary to what might appear at first, the February Revolution came about not because of a sudden and dramatic Islamic resurgence, but largely as a result of socio-economic conditions and ever-rising inequities as well as political suppression by the old regime that became intolerable as soon as the masses realized that it was possible to avoid them.[12]

It was not so much the rapidity of modernization as the form this took in Pahlavi Iran. A variant is Ervand Abrahamian's thesis of a structural disequilibrium between economic and political development (itself an echo of Huntington's "gap theory"):

> The failure of the Pahlavi regime to make political modifications appropriate to the changes taking place in the economy and society inevitably strained the links between the social structure and the political structure, blocked the channeling of social grievances into the political system, widened the gap between new social forces and the ruling circles, and, most serious of all, cut down the few bridges that had in the past connected traditional social forces, especially the bazaars, with the political establishment.[13]

This argument is sometimes combined with a "vacuum" theory of the ulama's ascendancy during the revolution: because all secular opponents of the shah were closely monitored, the clergy emerged from the relative sanctuary of the mosque to lead the movement.[14]

A focus on politics has been pursued by a related set of scholars, whose most original representative is Misagh Parsa. Parsa uses resource mobilization theory (associated with Charles Tilly, William Gamson, John McCarthy, and Mayer Zald) to explain the emergence of a revolutionary coalition based on class and group interests, communication networks, organizations, resources, and leadership. The result is an outstanding account of the activities of such key groups as the bazaar classes, workers, and the clergy in the making of the revolution.[15] Resource mobilization theory is at its best in studying the dynamics of social movements, rather than as a theory of the causes of revolution per se, either on the macrostructural level of development or on the cultural/ideological motivational level of the actors themselves. Another useful approach to the revolutionary coalition is that of Val Moghadam, among others, on *populist* politics. Moghadam argues that as Islamization set in well *after* February 1979, the revolution of 1977–79 must be seen as a populist, rather than an Islamic, social revolution, in terms of its diverse social bases and antidespotic and anti-imperialist discourse. Moghadam argues, as I do, that broad-based coalitions have the best potential to succeed, but tend to splinter after power has been won, as in post-1979 Iran, when the ulama, secular intellectuals, merchants, artisans, workers, the urban poor, the peasantry, and ethnic minorities and women across various social classes began to struggle for their own interests.[16]

Growing out of some of these analyses of a multiclass populist coalition is a final set of approaches to the causes of the revolution. Some theorists—including a few already mentioned under one or another heading above—have insisted that the causes of the revolution were multiple, that they had to occur together (i.e., they were conjunctural), and that they operated along economic, political, and cultural/ideological axes.[17] A prescient early statement was offered by Michael Fischer: "The causes of the revolution, and its timing, were economic and political; the form of the revolution, and its pacing, owed much to the tradition of religious protest."[18] This lead, which was not systematically developed by Fischer himself (most of his book discusses the religious cultures of Iran), was followed up by other scholars. Two years later, British Marxist Fred Halliday maintained, "The main reason why the revolution occurred was that conflicts generated in capitalist development intersected with resilient institutions and popular attitudes which resisted the transformation process."[19] Halliday identifies five principal causal areas of the revolution: (1) rapid and uneven capitalist development, (2) the political weakness of the monarchy, (3) the broad coalition of opposition forces, (4) the mobilizing role of the Islamic religion, and (5) the ambivalent international context. This is an excellent list, and it squares fairly closely with the analysis I shall offer below; what are needed in addition are historical and theoretical explanations of where these factors came from and a sharper focus on the political cultures that underpinned the events.

Recently, political scientist Farideh Farhi has offered a compelling synthesis that is rooted in current theorizing about revolutions and compares the Iranian with the Nicaraguan revolution. Building on Skocpol's concept of the autonomy of the state, Farhi adds two other foci: "the changing balance of class forces occasioned by uneven development of capitalism on a world scale" and a "broader understanding of ideology," building on the work of Gramsci, Therborn, and others.[20] Social structure is analyzed in terms of state intervention, export of primary products and rapid urbanization, but

> since most of the economic and social factors arising from a disadvantaged economic position are present in almost all peripheral formations, they cannot

be considered as the crucial trigger for these revolutions. The factor that differentiated Iran and Nicaragua was the type of state that oversaw these societies.[21]

These states—personalist and authoritarian—were particularly vulnerable to crises brought on by a combination of internal and external factors. The ulama and other middle-class groups (Farhi calls them the "prominent classes") were mobilized through religious beliefs that identified the shah as the source of Iran's ills. The ulama made skillful use of their mosque and bazaar networks to gain ascendancy in the revolutionary coalition, spurred on by historical memories of past errors in sharing power with secular groups in the Constitutional Revolution and the oil nationalization movement.

Farhi's admirable theoretical and empirical accomplishment represents a major statement on the Iranian revolution. It can be criticized and improved upon in several areas, however. In terms of the structural features of the analysis, Farhi emphasizes the state at the expense of social structures.[22] She presents no holistic class analysis, and sees social structure too much in terms of the state and too little in terms of dependency in the world-system. In Farhi's analysis, the middle classes are the main revolutionary protagonists, rather than artisans, workers, or urban marginals. Farhi's excellent theoretical scaffolding of cultural analysis is weakened somewhat by her attention to a hegemonic Islam rather than the varying cultures that were tapped by diverse groups, or the other overarching themes of nationalism and populism.

My own theoretical approach is broadly consonant with Farhi's, though worked out independently in my own early work on social change in Iran, and incorporating other recent advances (along with hers) in the theory of revolutions.[23] Third World social structure can be conceptualized in terms of the intersection of ongoing precapitalist modes of production internally with external economic, military, and political forces brought to bear on it by the core powers of the world-system.[24] Over time, this leads to ever more complex class structures (now capitalist and precapitalist combined in various ways) and, in the more dynamic economies and periods, a process of accumulation that may be termed *dependent development*. Both sides of this concept must be grasped together: development occurs in the sense of industrialization, increased foreign trade, and rising GNP, but it is limited by the structure of the world-system and entails significant social costs in education, health, housing, unemployment, inflation, income inequality, and other highly negative consequences.[25] To maintain social control in societies wracked by the rapid change and attendant ill effects of dependent development, repressive states with strong foreign supporters are often the only functional form capable of keeping the lid on social unrest, if only for a time. We have now specified a structural setting of state and society found in a distinct subset of Third World cases such as Brazil, Mexico, South Korea, Taiwan, Iran, and a few others at various times in their histories. Recent research on Third World revolutions has identified as particularly vulnerable personalist, authoritarian, repressive states that are exclusionary in the sense of autocratic rule without allowing participation by most social groups.[26] This narrows the set of cases to include Nicaragua under Somoza, Mexico under Díaz, Iran under the shah, and Cuba under Batista (though it includes other cases where revolutions have not occurred, such as Mobutu in Zaire and Taiwan under Chiang Kai-shek, or where dictators were toppled but not by full-fledged social revolutions, such as Duvalier in Haiti, Marcos in the Philippines, Stroessner in Paraguay).

To these structural features must be added agentic and conjunctural factors. I incorporate culture into the model with the notion of political cultures of opposition and resistance: dependent development and state repression constitute salient realities of everyday life for numerous groups and classes who experience and interpret them in terms of ongoing values, beliefs, and cultural elements. At the level of ideology this may take the form of religion, nationalism, socialism, or populism.[27] At the level of shared sentiments, it may entail anger and resentment rooted in the violation of norms of justice and what it means to act as a human being. It is important to look at both levels (although, practically, more evidence is available on the first). It is also important to acknowledge and map the variety and complexity of political cultures of opposition throughout a population, as well as to search for the unifying factors that broad sectors can agree upon. Finally, Third World social revolutions have been touched off by the combination of internal economic downturns and what I call a *world-systemic opening*. The first entails a discernible worsening of (often already difficult) conditions for large groups in society, which acts as a kind of final straw on the back of long-standing grievances. The second refers to the *letting-up* of external controls by the dominant core power in the equation. This may be the result of distraction (e.g., tsarist Russia's 1905 uprising and defeat in war with Japan as a favorable setting for the launching of the Iranian Constitutional Revolution in 1905–6) or of rivalries among core powers (also a factor in the Constitutional Revolution, and during the course of the Mexican revolution), or, finally, as in the cases of Iran and Nicaragua in the late 1970s, may come about when the core power criticizes (however mildly) repression by its client, and then is itself paralyzed by policy splits when a rebellion occurs.[28]

The model thus posits that the constellation of dependent development, exclusionary personalist regime, elaboration of effective political cultures of resistance, internal economic downturn, and favorable world-systemic opportunity will touch off broad, multiclass coalitions of social forces with excellent prospects for success. In the analysis that follows I apply this schema to late Pahlavi Iran, using as data many of the excellent secondary accounts already introduced above, as well as such primary materials as newspaper articles, oral histories, and archival documents.

How the Crisis Arose: Four Factors

Dependent Development

The deep structure of the revolution should be sought in the changes experienced in Iranian society between the 1940s and the 1970s, a process best characterized as dependent development, in which the chief actors were the various classes, the state's policies, and external powers, led by the United States. Even after the centralizing modernization project of Reza Shah Pahlavi from 1926 until his forced abdication by the Allies in 1941, the social structure of Iran remained essentially that of earlier in the century. The rural population was divided between a pastoral nomadic mode of production of tribal chiefs and tribespeople living off their flocks (just 7 percent of Iran's 14.6 million people in 1940, owing to Reza Shah's ruthless sedentarization campaign), and a peasant crop-sharing mode of production consisting of private, clergy-administered, and royal landed elites and sharecropping tenants, with a landless underclass (in all, accounting for up to 70 percent of the population, its numbers swelled by settled tribespeople). The urban sector was likewise bifurcated between a long-standing petty-commodity mode of production in the bazaar sector involving the ulama, merchants, artisans, day laborers, and urban marginal classes (at perhaps 13.5 percent of the population) and a slowly growing capitalist production sector with state, local, and foreign owners and a working class accounting for some 10 percent of the population.[29]

Once Muhammad Reza Shah was secured on his throne after the CIA coup of 1953, he embarked on a policy of land reform and rapid industrialization fueled by oil revenues. A few basic indicators illustrate the "development" side of this: population grew from 14.6 million in 1940 to 33.6 million by 1976, and GNP rose much faster, from $3 billion in 1953 ($166 per capita) to $53 billion in 1977 ($1,514 per capita), raising the country from the ranks of the periphery of the world economy to a claim on the semiperiphery, in world-systems parlance. Foreign trade skyrocketed from $162 million in 1954 to $42 billion by 1978; gross domestic product grew at 10.8 percent annually between 1963 and 1978, a figure surpassed by only two or three countries in the world.[30]

In what senses was Iran *dependent,* then, and what were the negative consequences of this growth? The centerpiece of rural development was the shah's land reform of the 1960s, prompted by American encouragement, criticism from a revived nationalist opposition, and his own desire to weaken landlords' traditional power and bind a grateful peasantry to the state. In fact, more than 90 percent of former sharecroppers received some land; however, the half of the peasantry who had been landless received nothing, the half who received land found themselves mostly on plots too small to support their families, and up to one-half of all land remained in the hands of large landlords. Low income, poor health, and limited education remained the lot of those who stayed on the land, while millions migrated to the cities in the late 1960s and 1970s. Inadequate state support and inefficient foreign agribusiness operations slowed growth in the new capitalist agricultural sector to 2–3 percent a year (stagnant, given gains in population), while food imports rose to $2.6 billion in 1977. Agriculture was thus a disaster area in itself and contributed heavily to urban discontent through migration as well. Tribal social structure meanwhile was severely affected by the shah's centralization policies and military controls, making life increasingly hard in Kurdistan, Baluchistan, Khuzistan, and Fars.[31]

The underside of the showcase sector of modern industry also reveals much about dependent development. Despite impressive growth rates in both the import-substitution and heavy sectors, high tariffs, guaranteed profits, and inflation-driven wage bills meant that very few manufactured goods could be exported. Foreign capital, technology, and management dominated most growth industries, which were either petroleum derivatives or "screwdriver"-type, simple assembly of imported parts. Oil and gas had accounted for 77 percent of all exports already in 1963; this rose to an incredible 98 percent by 1978, leading to complete dependence on oil revenues to keep the economy functioning, and a corresponding disincentive for the state to tax income effectively. A small but wealthy private sector of capitalists arose, squeezed between the twin leviathans of the state and multinationals, while the working class more than doubled in twenty years to 600–900,000 in factories with more than ten workers, a million in construction, 280,000 in transport and communications, 88,000 in oil and mining, and 65,000 in utilities (in all, 20–25 percent of the labor force). Pay rose with the oil boom, but work conditions, hours, and urban life generally were still very hard. Another key sector, the educated middle class of professionals, civil servants, and technical workers, also swelled with industrialization and the growth of the state itself. Although salaries and opportunities rose, so did inflation and housing costs, with few formal channels open for political participation.[32]

The petty-commodity urban sector of the bazaar economy contracted somewhat, but persisted in straitened circumstances. Guild artisans were affected by cheap imports and state controls, whereas the more well-to-do merchants remained important in retail trade but also suffered from the onslaught of chain outlets and modern shopping areas, combined with state persecution for their supposed role in causing inflation. The nearly 100,000 members of the ulama lost influence as modern education expanded at their expense, but they continued to draw income from religious taxes and property. Worst off in the cities were the urban marginals, who took unskilled work when they could find it (most often in construction), while unemployment, poor diets, and crowded housing made life desperate.[33]

By the late 1970s, then, significant quantitative and qualitative change had occurred in the hothouse of dependent development. The rural modes of production's share of the work force declined from approximately 77 percent to as little as 32 percent, the capitalist sector had expanded in both agriculture and urban activities, the tribes had been largely settled, peasants were migrating, the bazaar was hard-pressed. Income inequality was already the worst in Asia in 1970, and deepened as the oil boom skewed it further; inflation rose from less than 4 percent annually for 1968–72 to 15.7 percent a year from 1973 to 1977; infant mortality of eighty per thousand and life expectancy of fifty-one years had improved, but only to the level of India; undernourishment afflicted 64 percent of city dwellers and 42 percent of the peasantry; illiteracy, at 65–70 percent, was higher than in India.[34] While the elite enjoyed spectacular luxuries, the middle classes strove to maintain recent gains and the vast majority still suffered widespread hardships in the 1970s at the height of Iran's modernization. This was the dark underside of dependent development, and it traces the contours of a social structure with deep, if varying, grievances.

The Repressive, Exclusionary State

Muhammad Reza Pahlavi emerged after 1963 as a monarchic dictator in his country. This role had roots in his father's strongman repressive reign in the 1930s, but it was not a smooth, unchallenged process: Iran experienced a round of more democratic politics during the Allied occupation in the 1940s; nationalist prime minister Muhammad Musaddiq almost gained control of the government in 1953, only to be toppled by splits in his movement and the covert American intervention that restored the shah to the throne; a coup plot was uncovered in 1958; and finally, a religious uprising was quelled bloodily in June 1963. It was only after this that the shah solidified the institutions of his rule, which, in descending order of functional significance, consisted of the oil revenues, the instruments of repression and social control, the bureaucracy, and the party system.

Oil revenues underpinned the shah's position atop the state and social structure. The formation of OPEC in 1960 and the Iranian threats to boycott Western markets after the 1967 and 1973 Arab-Israeli wars did more to raise Iran's income than the nominal nationalization of oil by the shah in 1954. Revenues jumped almost a thousand times, from $22.5 million in 1954 to $20 billion in 1977. This income both paid for state activities and enriched the shah, royal family, and court. The sixty-three princes, princesses, and cousins of the royal family were worth between $5 billion and $20 billion; by one estimate the Pahlavis controlled one-fifth of the private assets of Iran, with shares in 207 companies involved in agriculture, housing, hotels, autos, textiles, insurance, and publishing companies, among others. This siphoning off of the country's economic surplus, and the attendant bribery and corruption throughout the upper echelons of society, was one material basis of the shah's power and secured the nominal allegiance of his associates to the state and to his person.[35]

Protecting this wealth was the army and the hated intelligence organization,

SAVAK. The armed forces grew from 191,000 in 1972 to 413,000 in 1977 (fifth largest in the world), absorbing 25–40 percent of the budget, almost $10 billion in 1978/79. This army was used internally for social control, alongside the police and intelligence services, all trained, armed, or supplied by the United States. SAVAK censored the media, controlled the civil service and government unions, and intimidated political dissidents. Amnesty International estimated there were between 25,000 and 100,000 political prisoners in 1975, reporting: "No country in the world has a worse record in human rights than Iran.... The Shah of Iran retains his benevolent image despite the highest rate of death penalties in the world, no valid system of civilian courts and a history of torture which is beyond belief."[36]

Behind the institutions of wealth and force lay the government proper: a cabinet and ministries beholden to the shah, who delegated little authority; 304,000 civil servants and 800,000 civilian state employees in all; and the Majlis (parliament). The Majlis was made up of two pro-shah parties popularly referred to as the "Yes" and "Yes Sir" parties (their formal titles were the Milliyun, or National Party, and Mardom, or People's Party) until 1975, when the shah set up a single ruling party (Rastakhiz, or Resurgence). The shah claimed legitimacy as a progressive, national-minded modernizer; the reality in the popular imagination was a repressive, U.S.-dominated dictator.[37] In class terms, the Pahlavi state was hegemonic in relation to the dominant classes, locked in an uneasy relationship with the industrialists, large landowners, high bureaucrats, and military officers that it selected as partners. Objects of impotent resentment by other members of the elite and potential targets of social movements from below, the shah and the state were *autonomous* within Iranian society, but dangerously so from the standpoint of their long-term survival.

The World-Systemic Opening

The United States emerged after the 1953 coup as the undisputed core power in Iran, taking over from Great Britain. In the 1950s and 1960s a "special relationship" was forged between the two countries based solidly on the economic, political, and strategic significance of Iran as a major oil exporter on the Soviet border. Cemented by U.S. aid, oil profits, and investments, this relationship reached a new level in the early 1970s with the Nixon doctrine of sponsoring strong regional allies to secure a favorable economic and political atmosphere in various parts of the Third World. In a May 1972 secret agreement, President Nixon committed the United States to supply Iran with any nonnuclear weapons it wanted, an unparalleled degree of cooperation that led to $10 billion in arms sales by 1977 and $40 billion in bilateral trade (mostly arms for oil) projected for 1976–80.[38]

Jimmy Carter would upset this alliance in subtle ways after 1976. As a candidate, he criticized American arms policy toward Iran. As president, he announced his intention to base U.S. foreign policy in part on respect for human rights abroad, instructing the State Department to work with human rights organizations to moderate the shah's repression. The shah took all of this quite seriously, reportedly remarking to an aide, "It looks as if we are not going to be around much longer."[39] In 1977 the shah "liberalized" his rule to a slight degree by releasing some political prisoners, and the new atmosphere encouraged the writing of critical open letters by dissident intellectuals, as well as a series of public gatherings and protests that heralded the first distant early warning signals of the impending revolution. Despite this, Iran was too important strategically and economically for the special relationship to be abandoned. The flow of arms continued, despite some obstruction by Congress. Improbably, Carter developed a strong personal rapport with the shah, toasting him in Tehran on December 31, 1977, just one week before serious clashes broke out: "Iran under the great leadership of the Shah is an island of stability in one of the more troubled areas of the world. This is a great tribute to you, Your Majesty, and to your leadership, and to the respect, admiration and love which your people give to you."[40] As late as May 1978, U.S. ambassador William Sullivan cabled home that Iran was stable and there were no serious outstanding issues between the two countries. In September, Carter himself made a much-publicized phone call of support to the shah right after the Bloody Friday massacre of demonstrators. The shah, however, now ill with cancer, continued to doubt that he had full American backing in the crisis.

This mutual ambivalence would continue with even more serious consequences as the revolution unfolded. While Sullivan became increasingly aware of the strength of the revolution in the fall of 1978, Secretary of State Cyrus Vance did not see it, and National Security Adviser Zbigniew Brzezinski advocated the firm hand of repression. Special reporter George Ball advised Carter in December that the shah was finished as an absolute monarch; Brzezinski sent General Robert Huyser to Tehran early in 1979 to hold the military together and help make a coup to save the system if necessary. Carter was ultimately paralyzed by this conflicting advice and his feelings toward the shah, lending "moral" support long past the point of no return (and thus inflaming the opposition), but not enough clear counsel or material support to the shah to deter the revolution.

This *nonaction* of the key world power in the Iranian equation opened the door to the full play of the internal balance of forces, and this did help the revolution from its earliest to its final phases, just as the special relationship of America with the shah from 1953 to 1978 undermined his legitimacy in the first place. The world-system conjuncture, then, was favorable to the success of the revolution in the sense that the core world power did not aggressively intervene to prevent it. One may plausibly contend that the revolution would have succeeded regardless, but the cost in human terms would surely have been higher, and unforeseen historical alternatives might have opened up (coup, intervention, different internal coalitions, and so forth).

Economic Downturn

The final factor at play in the creation of the revolutionary crisis was the downturn that struck the economy after 1976. This had several interlaced contributing causes: the boom and bust cycles of dependent development, internal economic bottlenecks and mismanagement, and the impact of the worldwide recession on Iran. In the euphoria following the fourfold OPEC price rises of 1973–74, the five-year plan for the economy was revised radically upward and enormous amounts of state expenditures flooded the country. By early 1975, in consequence, "the Iranian economy was almost completely out of control.... Less and less was being achieved at greater and greater cost."[41] Bottlenecks arose in infrastructure (ports and roads), human capital (skilled and managerial labor), and technological capacity to absorb the military and industrial modernization. Then the oil boom burst around 1975, when world demand fell sharply in an international recession in part brought on by the high price of oil itself. Iran's oil exports had fallen 20 percent by the end of the year, leaving a shortfall of $2.7 billion in revenues. The regime fell $3 billion behind in payments on contracts by March 1976; by October the shah was warning: "We have not demanded self-sacrifice from people, rather we have covered them in soft cotton cloth. Things will now change. Everyone should work harder and be prepared for sacrifices in the service of the nation's progress."[42] Two telling indicators at this point were the erosion of business confidence, resulting in capital flight of more than $100 million a month by 1975–76, and steady increases in consumer prices from 9.9 percent in 1975 to 16.6 percent for 1976 and 25.1 percent by 1977 (rents in Tehran rose astronomically, by 200 percent in 1974–75 and 100 percent the next year).

Thus, 1977 would prove to be a hard year. Industrial growth was still positive, but contracted from 14.4 to 9.4 percent. This raises the question of whether the downturn was one of absolute stagnation or merely relative slow down in the economy; Halliday has argued, "There was no widespread hardship, but the slowing down [of the economy] had political effects."[43] But the effects were real in many sectors: private investment fell 6.8 percent, agricultural production declined 0.8 percent, the state budget was cut by $3.5 billion, and borrowing from the West resumed. In January 1977 oil production fell 1.5 million barrels per day as Iran insisted on selling oil for 5 percent more than Saudi Arabia and the United Arab Emirates, cutting exports and earnings by 30 percent. Unemployment rose as contracts and projects were canceled or scaled back, affecting urban unskilled labor in particular. The official rate in 1977–78 was 9.1 percent (900,000 out of 9.9 million); rural unemployment ran at 20–30 percent, affecting approximately

1–1.5 million people. Ulama subsidies were cut, adding to grievances among this crucial group. Bazaar shopkeepers continued to be scapegoated and fined for inflation. The new prime minister, Amuzigar, responded to inflation by slowing the economy further, compounding unemployment and other problems of the recession.

These trends underlay the first protests of mid-1977 on, and though moderating somewhat in real terms (if not in the popular imagination) in early 1978, the revolutionary year, political protests would magnify them with strikes, property damage, and growing business disquietude, domestically and internationally. The economic downturn was thus the final structural condition that undermined the shah and touched off the crisis.

How the Coalition Succeeded

Political Cultures of Opposition

In this final section, we take up the causes and dynamics of Iran's multiclass populist revolutionary coalition, beginning with a look at the political cultures that inspired the actors involved in it. In the first part of this chapter, I argued that value orientations are of crucial importance in translating structural conditions conducive to revolution into actions. Ideology and culture act as filters through which groups order their experience of injustice and mobilize themselves to correct it. Owing to the difficulty of knowing what is in the minds of millions of relatively anonymous social actors, we will here study the critiques of identifiable leaders and organizations in the Iranian setting, and attempt to discern the social base of each as a first step in this direction. We will see that, rather than a homogeneous Shi'ism, at least five distinct value orientations refracted the growing criticisms of various groups in Iranian society. These may be labeled Khumaini's militant Islam, Shari'ati's radical liberation theology, Bazargan's liberal-democratic Islam, the guerrilla groups' socialism (with Islamic and secular variants), and secular nationalism (both socialist and democratic in form). Taken together, these ideologies mobilized the various elements composing Iran's multiclass, populist revolutionary coalition.

Ayatullah Ruhullah Musavi Khumaini (1902–89) emerged as the leader of the revolutionary movement in the course of 1978. He had made his reputation as a critic of the government during the agitation over the shah's White Revolution reforms at Qum in 1963, speaking out against "the political and economic exploitation by the West on the one hand ... and the submission of the regime to colonialism on the other.... The regime is bent on destroying Islam and its sacred laws. Only Islam and the Ulama can prevent the onslaught of colonialism."[44] From exile in Iraq, he issued his 1971 work on Islamic government, an ideological bombshell in that it challenged the legitimacy of monarchy and advocated direct rule by qualified Islamic jurists. Much better known than these ideas were his many criticisms of royal corruption and dictatorship, Western domination, and the economic problems of Iran. Khumaini's militant brand of Islam may also be characterized as populist, because it combined progressive and traditional elements and appealed to diverse social strata. With a primary social base among lower-ranking ulama, theology students, and sectors of the bazaar, Khumaini's anti-imperialist bent attracted secular intellectuals, leftists, and workers as well, whereas his religious idiom appealed to the marginal urban and rural populations whom he extolled as the *mustazafin* (the dispossessed masses). He had the organizational support of a fiercely loyal network of students and ulama in and outside of Iran, including the clerics who were members of the Ruhaniyun-i Mubariz (Organization of Militant Ulama), many of them rising to prominence after the revolution. Together with his uncompromising opposition, personal integrity, and political astuteness, these advantages helped Khumaini emerge as the leader once the movement began.

The chief ideologue of the revolution, along with Khumaini, is generally considered to have been 'Ali Shari'ati (1933–77). A student of sociology, history, and literature at the Sorbonne from 1960 to 1964, he returned to Iran to teach high school English and then history at the University of Mashhad. After being dismissed for his politics in 1971, he gave enormously popular lectures in Tehran before his arrest, exile, and death in England in June 1977, on the very eve of the revolution. His work was an attempt to fashion a radical, activist Islam, fusing politics, social analysis, and religious inspiration. Critical of quietist and status quo ulama, he elaborated a theology of liberation, arguing: "Islam's most basic tradition is martyrdom, and human activity, mixed with a struggle against oppression and establishment of justice and protection of human rights."[45] Recognizing Marxism's utility for analyzing society and history, he felt Islam held the solution, calling ambiguously for an Islamic government that would be a popular, but "directed," democracy. The social base for his ideas lay first among radical university students and intellectuals, but extended also to the more popular urban classes of workers, migrants, and marginals. His writings provided many of the slogans chanted in demonstrations and written on walls in 1978, further proof of his mass appeal, which was second only to Khumaini's.

A third, less influential, but still important trend within Islam was the liberal, democratic version espoused by Mehdi Bazargan (1905-) and the Liberation (or Freedom) Movement of Iran (LMI) (Nahzat-i Azadi-yi Iran). A Paris-educated engineer and physicist, Bazargan had been an associate of Musaddiq in the oil nationalization movement. He is regarded as the founder of Islamic modernism in Iran; his works included praise for constitutionalism, democracy, and a mild socialism within a devoutly Islamic framework. He criticized large landownership, called for meeting the needs of the people, and tried to bring progressive ulama and secular forces together, to overcome the weaknesses of the Musaddiq era. Banned in 1963, the Liberation Movement's social base lay in the middle-class strata of merchants, civil servants, students, and professionals.[46]

Similar in social composition were the secular liberal nationalists left over from the National Front, which had been severely repressed after the 1953 coup, re-emerged in the 1960–63 anti-shah agitation, and was driven underground again. Calling for a democratic alternative to autocratic monarchy and an independent foreign policy, its base was limited to a part of the bazaar, white-collar workers, and professionals. Resurfacing again in 1977–78, it ultimately subordinated it-self to Khumaini's leadership. To its left, the Tudeh (Communist) Party had also suffered a harsh repression after 1953 but managed to carry on clandestinely and abroad, where it claimed 38,000 members. Its political positions included support for the Soviet Union, calls for a democratic republic, real land reform, re-jection of violence, and support for progressive clergy, especially Khumaini. Its social base inside Iran was limited to a portion of the intelligentsia, and in the 1978 strikes it proved to have some supporters in the factories, particularly in the oil industry.[47]

More radical and effective in the anti-shah struggles of the 1970s were the left-wing guerrilla organizations, most notably the Islamic Mujahidin and the Marxist Fada'ian. The Mujahidin grew out of the Liberation Movement in the 1960s, dissatisfied with peaceful methods. Linking Islam and revolutionary activ-ity, they declared their respect for Marxism in 1973 and split over this issue in 1975, with the Islamic wing influenced by Shari'ati retaining the name Mujahidin. Engaging in assassinations and bombings, severely repressed by the regime, the Islamic Mujahidin lost seventy-three members through death after 1975, the Marxists thirty, including almost all of the original leadership. The Fada'ian were a Marxist-Leninist counterpart that left the Tudeh and, like the Mujahidin, were based among university students. The Fada'ian too split in 1975–77; they too lost many leaders, and 172 members in all, at the hands of the regime. The Fada'ian were influential in the Iranian Students Association in the United States and had some 5,000 members and many more supporters on the eve of the rev-olution. Through the Mujahidin and the Fada'ian, many students and intellectu-als, and some workers, came to embrace revolutionary and socialist ideas, and a nucleus of armed fighters would be available to staff the final uprising in Febru-ary 1979.[48]

Out of these several political cultures, then, came the ideas that would mobi-lize millions of Iranians in 1977–79: nationalism, democracy, socialism, Islamic fundamentalism, radicalism, and liberalism all appealed in sometimes complex and overlapping fashion to the various constituencies—young ulama, merchants, students, artisans, intellectuals, urban marginals—that would loosely coalesce into an urban populist social movement. Without these orientations it is hard to see the shape that a revolutionary movement could have taken; their presence, then, is a significant causal factor in the making of the revolution.

Phases of Mobilization, 1977–79

Dating the precise start of the movement is a matter of some debate, but there is no question that a series of important protest activities occurred in 1977, well before anyone realized where they might lead. On the heels of the shah's mini-liberalization and the economic downturn, a series of open letters critical of human rights and constitutional violations were addressed to the government by writers, poets, judges, and lawyers. The newspaper *Kayhan* received more than 40,000 letters when it asked, "What is wrong with Iran?" In April, Bazargan addressed 14,000 people at a Tehran mosque; during the spring and summer, the Liberation Movement, National Front, Tudeh Party, Fada'ian, and Mujahidin all agitated publicly. In June and again in August the shantytown dwellers of Tehran resisted forced evictions and a number were killed in clashes with security forces. Poets and writers organized a series of cultural nights in mid-October that grew over ten days from 3,000 to 15,000 listeners in demonstrations against censorship. In November, Khumaini's son Mustafa died mysteriously in Iraq, and there were clashes at his mourning ceremonies. In the United States, meanwhile, the shah's visit resulted in confrontations between 8,000 protestors and 1,500 pro-shah demonstrators (reportedly paid $100 each by the Iranian embassy). By the beginning of December, most of Iran's twenty-two universities were closed or on strike; Tehran students and shopkeepers turned the Muharram religious gatherings into demonstrations against government economic policy. Thus, at the end of a year in which Carter toasted Iran as "an island of stability," it is retrospectively possible to see the start of a mass protest from diverse sources, involving intellectuals, students, urban marginals, workers, ulama, and bazaaris.[49]

The revolution per se may be considered to have begun on a continuous basis in the first half of 1978, when Fischer's "religious timing" marked a series of cyclical protests at regular forty-day mourning intervals. These were touched off by a slanderous article against Khumaini on January 7, 1978, in the semiofficial newspaper *Ittila'at,* which led to clashes involving 4,000 to 10,000 people (ulama, bazaaris, seminarians) at Qum, with ten to seventy being killed. On February 18 there were large commemorative processions in twelve cities that turned violent in Tabriz after police shot a young man, provoking demonstrators to attack banks, hotels, liquor and TV stores, pornographic cinemas, fancy cars, and the Rastakhiz offices — all symbols of the regime and Western influence. This event produced the first cries of "Death to the Shah!"; as many as one hundred people died. On March 28–30, demonstrations occurred in some fifty-five places, notably in Yazd, where up to a hundred were killed in a clash that was tape-recorded; the tape was subsequently distributed throughout the country. Between May 6 and 10, violence broke out again in thirty-four cities, with fourteen to eighty deaths (as always, government and opposition estimates varied widely). The shah made public apologies and promised further liberalization, and through June and much of July there seemed to be a lull in protest activity. This was shattered in August during the fasting month of Ramazan. The shah's promise of free elections on the sixth was countered by a march of 50,000 in Isfahan four days later in which one hundred people were killed. Then, on August 19, at the oil terminal of Abadan, 400 were burned to death in the Rex Cinema under murky circumstances in which SAVAK was widely blamed. The rest of the month was marked by more demonstrations and deaths and the appointment of a new prime minister (Ja'far Sharif-Imami) who promised numerous reforms.[50]

The events of September, which witnessed the massive demonstrations and start of a general strike that sealed the escalation of the conflict, marked the point of no return for the revolutionary process. Ramazan ended September 4 with a march of 250,000 in Tehran; a half million called for the end of the dynasty three days later. On September 8, known as Bloody Friday, troops fired on crowds around the city; the government claimed eighty-six dead, but bodies in the Tehran morgue numbered more than 3,000. From September 9 onward, a series of strikes broke out in the oil industry. These continued into October and spread to the railroads, post offices, newspapers, hospitals, government ministries, and numerous factories. Demands turned increasingly political—for freedoms and the overthrow of the dynasty. Khumaini was forced from Iraq on October 6, but landed in Paris, where his communications links to Iran and the world were even greater. By late October, oil production had fallen from 5.7 million to 1.5 million barrels a day. November witnessed the closing of universities and the declaration of a martial law government by the shah but under the old and moderate General Azhari rather than a hard-liner. Some strikers were forced back to work. The month of December—coinciding with Muharram, the emotionally charged mourning period for Shi'is—proved decisive for the opposition. Millions defied martial law to take to the streets, strikes shut down the economy, American support for the shah finally wavered, and the shah himself seemed to lose his remaining resolve.[51]

A period of revolutionary dual power came into effect in January 1979 during the new government of Shapur Bakhtiar, a National Front member who was denounced by that organization for accepting the prime ministership. He was greeted by a continuing general strike and large demonstrations. The shah finally announced on January 11 that he would leave the country on a "vacation," and did so as crowds celebrated wildly on January 16. The next day, Khumaini announced the formation of the Council of the Islamic Revolution; on January 19 in Tehran a million people adopted a resolution dethroning the shah and demanding "a free Islamic Republic." Khumaini's return was blocked by the army on January 24, but as more huge demonstrations demanded it, this was allowed on

February 1, with three to four million people, perhaps the largest crowd in world history, lining the streets. Khumaini announced a provisional government under Bazargan on February 5, opening a complex round of negotiations with the army and its American advisers. A final armed uprising of air force technicians, members of the guerrilla organizations and ordinary citizens challenged the army between February 9 and 11. The high command then decided to abandon Bakhtiar, who quietly slipped out of the country. At 6 p.m. on Sunday, February 11, the radio declared: "This is the voice of Tehran, the voice of true Iran, the voice of the revolution. The dictatorship has come to an end."[52]

Social Forces: The Multiclass Coalition

It remains to assess the social bases of these events, which have attracted diverse hypotheses. Most scholars have acknowledged that it took a coalition to make the revolution. For Abrahamian, this assumed the form of an alliance between traditional middle classes (ulama, merchants) and modern middle classes (intelligentsia, students), with workers and lower urban classes acting as "battering rams." Keddie emphasizes the urban poor from February to September 1978, the middle and working classes joining in the fall. Bazargan gives a good account of the social composition of the crucial December 10–11, 1978, demonstrations:

> Members of the urban middle class, especially young high school and university students, constituted the majority of the participants, next came the Bazaaris (craftsmen and tradesmen), shopkeepers and civil servants who were also numerous. The workers and peasants who were present constituted a very small minority. Religious students (*talaba*) and clergymen did participate but in proportion to their number in society at large, they were less represented. Young women ... were present, without the veiled ones having the majority.[53]

Ashraf and Banuazizi perceptively break the revolution down into five stages, each with its own actors and modes of struggle: an opening act from June to December 1977 of nonviolent mobilization led by students and intellectuals; a second stage of cyclical riots from January to July 1978, in which the ulama and bazaar classes became involved; followed by a third phase of mass demonstrations in August and September with the above plus urban middle and marginal classes; stage four in the fall of 1978, carried by mass strikes of blue- and white-collar workers; and a final period of dual sovereignty from December 1978 to February 1979 in which all these classes were united against the shah's regime. To these observations I would add that the 1977–79 revolution was made by yet another instance of Iran's urban, populist, multiclass alliance, as in the Constitutional Revolution and oil nationalization movement before it. The present essay has attempted to show the roots of this coalition in the process of dependent development, state repression, and political cultures of opposition of the 1960s and 1970s. In the context of Iran's class structure, ulama, merchants, artisans, intellectuals, workers, and urban marginals composed the populist alliance. Women and religious minorities cut across class lines to participate. Peasants and tribespeople had at best supporting roles. These was also a pro-shah coalition ranged against the revolution. Let us conclude this study by briefly analyzing each in turn.

The peasants and tribespeople of the countryside were largely outside the main lines of the movement before February 1979. Those peasants who lived close enough to large cities, especially if they worked in the city, took part in some of the large marches of late 1978, and brought news of the movement back to their villages. Many were skeptical or ambivalent in attitude toward Khumaini because they could see rural elites ingratiating themselves with the movement. Tribespeople were even less well placed to be active, although settled groups in Kurdistan, Baluchistan, and Turkaman Sahra took advantage of the unrest to renew claims against the state, processes that continued after the revolution against the new government.[54]

A section (but by no means all) of the ulama, the religious students, and the bazaar classes of merchants and artisans that supported them financially, clearly played a key role in the revolution. Khumaini's network emerged as crucial leaders and coordinators in 1978, touching off the Qum protests, organizing the subsequent fortieth-day mourning processions and the Ramazan and Muharram demonstrations, and setting up Islamic *komitehs* (committees) in neighborhoods throughout Iran toward the end of 1978. They received key financial support from bazaar merchants, and artisans were numerically significant in the series of fortieth-day protests in January, February, March, and May 1978.[55]

The secular intelligentsia also aspired to a leadership role, and students and professionals were an important mass base. Intellectuals were most prominent in the earliest protests of the prerevolutionary year of 1977 (open letters, poetry nights). Students struck on their campuses and demonstrated heavily throughout 1978, and together with young professionals (who helped paralyze the private and state sectors of the economy in the fall of 1978), suffered the most casualties relative to their numbers. Intellectuals and students were the backbone of the National Front, Tudeh, Mujahidin, and Fada'ian, organizing demonstrations, agitating in factories, and (in the case of the guerrilla groups) delivering the coup de grâce to the army in February 1979.[56]

A critical component of the mass movement was the workers whose more or less spontaneous strikes gradually coalesced into the general strike of late 1978. Economic demands had increased over the course of 1977; by the summer of 1978 some of the strikes were political in nature. The oil workers, who said, "We will export oil only when we have exported the shah," and the employees of banks, hospitals, communications, transport, and many industrial sectors, definitively affected the outcome by weakening the regime. Their actions delegitimated it internally and hamstrung its repressive capacity (for the army needed fuel, the government communications) and convinced the United States that the shah could no longer guarantee the flow of oil, much less provide the stability needed to attract investments. Motivated by Khumaini, Shari'ati, the Mujahidin, and the Marxists, their factory councils displayed diverse ideological tendencies by early 1979. The general strike was central to the revolution's success; Khumaini could not have taken power (or would have had an unimaginably more difficult job of it) without it.[57]

The most important supporting mass role played by the lower classes was that of the urban marginals. Their resistance to evictions in the summer of 1977 had shown that the regime could be challenged. In 1978 they swelled the ranks of the huge demonstrations, facing the army's guns and suffering many of the revolution's estimated 10,000 to 12,000 deaths. Poor urban youth often emerged as neighborhood leaders. Less active than the settled poor were the squatters, one of whom told a reporter that to demonstrate, "you have to have a full stomach"; another said he had no time to demonstrate, but "things will get better once the King goes."[58]

Finally, women and religious and ethnic minorities also contributed to the revolution, in most cases along their respective class lines. The large demonstrations often featured thousands of chador-clad women in the front ranks in spite of—and to reduce—the danger. Keddie considers these primarily "bazaari women"; the urban lower classes and students should be counted among them as well (and Bazargan, quoted above, noted the unveiled participants as numerous). Women also participated in the workers' councils in some cases (presumably roughly proportional to their fewer numbers in the work force). The religious minorities—Christians, Jews, and Zoroastrians—tended to be involved as members of the populist coalition along occupational lines. Although naturally more concerned about the shape of an Islamic Republic, they too sought the overthrow of the shah; Jews and Zoroastrians (and probably Christians as well) put out communiqués stressing solidarity with the movement.[59] There was also a regional, ethnic dimension to the conflict, with strong centers of resistance emerging in the historical opposition areas of the Azeri-speaking northwest, Gilan, and Kurdistan, the scope of which goes beyond what can be documented here.

Faced with such opposition, the shah nevertheless did not roll over and quit in 1978. Particularly in the early months, the state tried to mobilize its own social bases of support. The official press reported pro-shah demonstrations of 50,000 at Tabriz on January 18, 200,000 in Khuzistan a day later, and 300,000 in Tabriz on April 9, claiming the support of numerous organizations and classes, including ulama, students, workers, bazaaris, women, professionals, and peasants. Paramilitary groups such as SAVAK's Underground Committee of Revenge and the Rastakhiz Party's Resistance Corps paid members of the marginal classes, workers, and some peasants to harass demonstrators and opposition organizations. But the shift from voluntary to coercive forms of "mass support" only reflected the deteriorating legitimacy of the regime. The shah himself showed remarkable ignorance of the true situation in the crisis (he told a British journalist in September 1978 that there were no slums in Tehran). This was compounded by his own indecisiveness and wavering between repression and concessions, and his battle with cancer. By the end of the year, reality seems to have sunk in: "When asked by a foreign correspondent where his supporters were, he shrugged his shoulders and replied, 'Search me.'"[60] Under these circumstances the last bastion of defense was the army. Arjomand considers that it remained intact until the shah left in mid-January, but Bill points out that defections numbered a thousand a day by early December 1978 and Halliday notes that it became demoralized at having to confront unarmed crowds motivated by Islam. The top officers were corrupt and, like U.S. policy, divided between hawks and doves; the conscripts eventually lost the will to fight.[61] Iran's isolated, untested army could not alone stem the tide of revolution against a regime in economic, political, and ideological crisis. The "autonomous" Iranian state, despite the absence of elite contenders or military defeat, proved in the end extremely fragile in the face of a massive, populist alliance of aggrieved social forces acting under favorable circumstances.

Conclusions

The Iranian revolution, I have argued, is not an anomaly, although it has provoked considerable rethinking about the causes of Third World social revolutions. As I will argue in the concluding chapter of this volume, its deep causes are to be sought in the same processes of dependent development, state repression, political cultures of resistance, economic downturn, and world-systemic opening that underlay other successful revolutions in Mexico, Cuba, and Nicaragua.[62] Its lessons include the need to restore coequal attention to social structure alongside the state, subjective agency alongside objective conditions, culture alongside political economy. The revolution of 1977–79 takes its place in Iranian and Third World history as yet another massive, courageous social upheaval, regardless of the disasters that followed (see chapter 8). Indeed, in some telling senses these these flow from the complexities of holding multiclass coalitions together and the continuing legacies of economic dependence, political cultural diversity, and outside intervention as favorable world contexts gave way to hostile ones. As in most of the Third World to date, the results have been imperfect, yet the stakes of real development and citizen participation remain high enough to justify future attempts, perhaps with better chances of success.

Notes

1. For good overviews, see Jack A. Goldstone, "Theories of Revolution: The Third Generation," *World Politics* 32 (April 1980): 425–53; Jack A. Goldstone, "The Comparative and Historical Study of Revolutions," *Annual Review of Sociology* 8 (1982): 187–207;

Michael S. Kimmel, *Revolution: A Sociological Interpretation* (Philadelphia: Temple University Press, 1990); John Foran, "Theories of Revolution Revisited: Toward a Fourth Generation?" *Sociological Theory* 11 (March 1993): 1–20.

2. Both are discussed in Kimmel, *Revolution*. Marx's writings on revolution are found in various of his works; de Tocqueville's 1856 masterpiece is *The Old Regime and the French Revolution*, trans. Stuart Gilbert (Garden City, N.Y.: Doubleday, 1955).

3. See Crane Brinton, *The Anatomy of Revolution* (New York: Vintage, 1965 [1938]); Lyford P. Edwards, *The Natural History of Revolutions* (Chicago: University of Chicago Press, 1927); George S. Pettee, *The Process of Revolution* (New York: Harper & Row, 1937); and Goldstone's critiques in "Theories of Revolution" and "The Comparative and Historical Study." Bashiriyeh has used Brinton's phases to "explain" the course of the Iranian revolution. Hossein Bashiriyeh, *The State and Revolution in Iran 1962–1982* (New York: St. Martin's, 1984).

4. See Neil J. Smelser, *Theory of Collective Behavior* (New York: Free Press, 1963); Chalmers Johnson, *Revolutionary Change* (Boston: Little, Brown, 1966); Ted Robert Gurr, *Why Men Rebel* (Princeton, N.J.: Princeton University Press, 1970); James C. Davies, "Toward a Theory of Revolution," *American Sociological Review* 27 (1962): 5–19. Samuel Huntington's *Political Order in Changing Societies* (New Haven, Conn.: Yale University Press, 1968) is an insightful transitional work of this period. Critiques of these "general theories" can be found in Goldstone, "Theories of Revolution" and "The Comparative and Historical Study"; Rod Aya, "Theories of Revolution Reconsidered: Contrasting Models of Collective Violence," *Theory and Society* 8 (July 1979): 39–99. The fit of Davies's J-curve to Iran has been observed by Sepehr Zabih, *Iran's Revolutionary Upheaval: An Interpretive Essay* (San Francisco: Alchemy, 1979), 76; Bashiriyeh, *The State and Revolution*, 85, 198 n. 84; and Nikki R. Keddie, "Iranian Revolutions in Comparative Perspective," *American Historical Review* 88 (June 1983): 589–91.

5. Barrington Moore, Jr., *Social Origins of Dictatorship and Democracy: Lord and Peasant in the Making of the Modern World* (Boston: Beacon, 1966); Eric R. Wolf, *Peasant Wars of the Twentieth Century* (New York: Harper Colophon, 1969); Jeffery M. Paige, *Agrarian Revolution: Social Movements and Export Agriculture in the Underdeveloped World* (New York: Free Press, 1975); Charles Tilly, *From Mobilization to Revolution* (Reading, Mass.: Addison-Wesley, 1978); Theda Skocpol, *States and Social Revolutions: A Comparative Analysis of France, Russia, and China* (Cambridge: Cambridge University Press, 1979). To reduce each of these richly complex studies to a brief phrase is of course a gross — if necessary — simplification of their arguments.

6. Theda Skocpol, "Rentier State and Shi'a Islam in the Iranian Revolution," *Theory and Society* 11 (May 1982): 267.

7. For just two alternative approaches to the literature, see M. H. Pesaran, "The System of Dependent Capitalism in Pre- and Post-Revolutionary Iran," *International Journal of Middle East Studies* 14 (November 1982): 501–22. Pesaran distinguishes among fundamentalist, liberal, left, and conservative accounts. See also Misagh Parsa, *The Social Origins of the Iranian Revolution* (New Brunswick, N.J.: Rutgers University Press, 1989), 6–10. Parsa contrasts models of social breakdown with models of social movements.

8. Khumaini, quoted in Oriana Fallaci, "An Interview with Khumaini," *New York Times Magazine,* October 7, 1979, 30. Compare this with Khumaini's speech to radio workers: "I cannot believe and I do not accept that any prudent individual can believe that the purpose of all these sacrifices was to have less expensive melons, that we sacrificed our young men to have less expensive housing.... No one would give up his life for better agriculture." Radio Tehran, September 8, 1979, text in *Foreign Broadcast Information Service,* September 10, 1979. Elsewhere, he admits that "others took part — university professors, intellec-

tuals, merchants, students—but it was the religious leaders who mobilized the whole people." Imam Khomeini, *Islam and Revolution: Writings and Declarations of the Imam Khomeini,* trans. and anno. Hamid Algar (Berkeley: Mizan, 1981), 338.

9. Hamid Algar, "Preface," in Ali Shari'ati, *Marxism and Other Western Fallacies: An Islamic Critique,* trans. R. Campbell (Berkeley, Calif.: Mizan, 1980), 12. See also 'Ali Davani, *Nahzat-i Ruhaniyun-i Iran* (Movement of the clergy of Iran), vol. 8 (Tehran: Bunyad-i Farhangi-yi Imam Reza, 1981).

10. Said Amir Arjomand, "The Causes and Significance of the Iranian Revolution," *State, Culture and Society* 1, no. 3 (1985): 56–58, 60; Amir Arjomand, *The Turban for the Crown: The Islamic Revolution in Iran* (New York: Oxford University Press, 1988), 189–91, 196, 205.

11. Skocpol, "Rentier State and Shi'a Islam," 268.

12. M. H. Pesaran [Thomas Walton, pseud.], "Economic Development and Revolutionary Upheavals in Iran," *Cambridge Journal of Economics* 4 (September 1980): 271, see also 288. See related positions in Nikki R. Keddie, *Roots of Revolution: An Interpretive History of Modern Iran* (New Haven, Conn.: Yale University Press, 1981), 177; Hans-Georg Müller, "Remarks on the Role of the State Capital Sector and National Private Capital in the Evolutionary Process of Capitalism in Iran up to the End of the 1970s," in Iran: From Monarchy to Republic, *Asia, Africa, Latin America* 12, special issue, ed. Günter Bartel (1983): 85, quoting M. Massarrat, *Iran—von der ökonomischen Krise zur socialen Revolution* (Offenbach, 1979), 31.

13. Ervand Abrahamian, "Structural Causes of the Iranian Revolution," *MERIP (Middle East Research and Information Project) Reports* 87 (May 1980): 21; see also Ervand Abrahamian, *Iran between Two Revolutions* (Princeton, N.J.: Princeton University Press, 1982), 427. This approach is also taken with varying nuances by Amin Saikal, *The Rise and Fall of the Shah* (Princeton: Princeton University Press, 1980), 203–4; Jerrold D. Green, *Revolution in Iran: The Politics of Countermobilization* (New York: Praeger, 1982); Mehran Kamrava, *Revolution in Iran: The Roots of Turmoil* (London: Routledge, 1990), 8–13.

14. See, among others, Mohammed Amjad, *Iran: From Royal Dictatorship to Theocracy* (Westport, Conn.: Greenwood, 1989), viii. Amjad considers various factors in his model and makes a number of astute observations.

15. Parsa, *The Social Origins.* Resource mobilization is also deployed by Yadollah Alidoost-Khaybari, "Religious Revolutionaries: An Analysis of the Religious Groups' Victory in the Iranian Revolution of 1978–79" (Ph. D. diss., University of Michigan, Department of Sociology, 1981). Zabih basically emphasizes political factors as well in *Iran's Revolutionary Upheaval.*

16. Valentine M. Moghadam, "Populist Revolution and the Islamic State in Iran," in *Revolution in the World System,* ed. Terry Boswell (Westport, Conn.: Greenwood, 1989), 147–63; and, on an earlier period, John Foran, "The Strengths and Weaknesses of Iran's Populist Alliance: A Class Analysis of the Constitutional Revolution of 1905–1911," *Theory and Society* 20 (December 1991): 795–823. Populism, in one guise or another, is also invoked by, among others, Zabih, *Iran's Revolutionary Upheaval,* 20; Kambiz Afrachteh, "The Predominance and Dilemmas of Theocratic Populism in Contemporary Iran," *Iranian Studies* 14 (Summer-Autumn 1981): 189–213; and Edmund Burke III and Paul Lubeck, "Explaining Social Movements in Two Oil-Exporting States: Divergent Outcomes in Nigeria and Iran," *Comparative Studies in Society and History* 29 (October 1987): 663–65.

17. The most theoretically inclusive of the works already mentioned are Bashiriyeh, *The State and Revolution*; Skocpol, "Rentier State and Shi'a Islam"; Mohsen M. Milani, *The Making of Iran's Islamic Revolution: From Monarchy to Islamic Republic* (Boulder, Colo.: Westview, 1988); Moghadam, "Populist Revolution and the Islamic State." Keddie's works, espe-

cially *Roots of Revolution,* are always illuminating and subtle, though as a historian Keddie wears her theory more lightly than the social scientists do.

18. Michael M. J. Fischer, *Iran: From Religious Dispute to Revolution* (Cambridge: Harvard University Press, 1980), 190.

19. Fred Halliday, "The Iranian Revolution: Uneven Development and Religious Populism," *Journal of International Affairs* 36 (Fall-Winter 1982–83): 193.

20. Farideh Farhi, *States and Urban-Based Revolutions: Iran and Nicaragua* (Urbana: University of Illinois Press, 1990), 9–10. See also her "State Disintegration and Urban-Based Revolutionary Crisis: A Comparative Analysis of Iran and Nicaragua," *Comparative Political Studies* 21 (July 1988): 231–56.

21. Farhi, *States and Urban-Based Revolutions,* 26.

22. This should be clear from earlier passages, despite (or in addition to?) the disclaimer: "It is important to note I am not contending that the state is the sole causal agency bringing about revolutions." Ibid., 134.

23. See John Foran, "Social Structure and Social Change in Iran from 1500 to 1979" (Ph. D. diss., University of California, Berkeley, Department of Sociology, 1988); John Foran, "A Theory of Third World Social Revolutions: Iran, Nicaragua, and El Salvador Compared," *Critical Sociology* 19, no. 2 (1992): 3–27; John Foran, *Fragile Resistance: Social Transformation in Iran from 1500 to the Revolution* (Boulder, Colo.: Westview, 1993); Foran, "Theories of Revolution Revisited."

24. On the world-system, see the three-volume work by Immanuel Wallerstein, *The Modern World-System* (New York: Academic Press, 1974, 1980, 1989). On modes of production, see Aidan Foster-Carter, "The Modes of Production Controversy," *New Left Review* (January-February 1978): 47–77. For applications of each to Iran at an earlier period, see my essays, "The Making of an External Arena: Iran's Place in the World-System, 1500–1722," *Review* (Journal of the Fernand Braudel Center) 12 (Winter 1989): 71–119; and "The Modes of Production Approach to Seventeenth-Century Iran," *International Journal of Middle East Studies* 20 (August 1988): 345–63.

25. The best work in the dependency literature—rarely cited by analysts of Iran—is the classic study of Fernando Henrique Cardoso and Enzo Faletto, *Dependency and Development in Latin America* (Berkeley: University of California Press, 1979). For an important study of Third World revolutions as linked to processes of underdevelopment, consult John Walton, *Reluctant Rebels: Comparative Studies of Revolution and Underdevelopment* (New York: Columbia University Press, 1984). I have applied this model to nineteenth-century Iran in "The Concept of Dependent Development as a Key to the Political Economy of Qajar Iran (1800–1925), *Iranian Studies* 22, nos. 2–3 (1989): 5–56.

26. See Robert H. Dix, "Why Revolutions Succeed and Fail," *Polity* 16 (Summer 1984): 423–46; Jeff Goodwin and Theda Skocpol, "Explaining Revolutions in the Contemporary Third World," *Politics and Society* 17 (December 1989): 489–509; Timothy P. Wickham-Crowley, "Understanding Failed Revolution in El Salvador: A Comparative Analysis of Regime Types and Social Structures," *Politics and Society* 17 (December 1989): 511–37; Richard Snyder, "Explaining Transitions from Neopatrimonial Dictatorships," *Comparative Politics* 24, no. 4 (1992): 370–99. A major recent work applying the concept of the autocratic, modernizing state to Iran is Tim McDaniel's *Autocracy, Modernization, and Revolution in Russia and Iran* (Princeton, N.J.: Princeton University Press, 1991).

27. For an argument that has influenced me, see A. Sivanandan, "Imperialism in the Silicon Age," *Monthly Review* 32 (July-August 1980): 24–42; this article was first published in *Race and Class* (Autumn 1979). The works of James Scott also bear on these issues.

28. The original notion of a "permissive world context" was introduced into the litera-

ture by Walter L. Goldfrank, "Theories of Revolution and Revolution without Theory: The Case of Mexico," *Theory and Society* 7, no. 1 (1979): 135–65.

29. These calculations are based on Foran, *Fragile Resistance,* chap. 6. Many figures for the whole period through the 1970s should be treated as rough indicators only, because of technical problems and political biases.

30. On population, see Fred Halliday, *Iran: Dictatorship and Development* (New York: Penguin, 1979), 10. On GNP and income, see Abrahamian, "Structural Causes," 22; Pesaran, "The System of Dependent Capitalism," 504; Homa Katouzian, *The Political Economy of Modern Iran: Despotism and Pseudo-Modernism, 1926–1979* (New York: New York University Press, 1981), 325 table 16.2.

31. On rural Iran, see Eric J. Hooglund, *Land and Revolution in Iran, 1960–1980* (Austin: University of Texas Press, 1982); Grace Goodell, *The Elementary Structures of Political Life: Rural Development in Pahlavi Iran* (New York: Oxford University Press, 1986); Afsaneh Najmabadi, *Land Reform and Social Change in Iran* (Salt Lake City: University of Utah Press, 1987). On the tribes, see Lois Beck, *The Qashqa'i of Iran* (New Haven, Conn.: Yale University Press, 1986); Gene R. Garthwaite, *Khans and Shahs: A Documentary Analysis of the Bakhtiyari in Iran* (Cambridge: Cambridge University Press, 1983).

32. On the industrialization process, see the works of Katouzian, Abrahamian, Halliday, and Keddie, as well as M. S. Ivanov, *Tarikh-i Nuvin-i Iran* (Modern history of Iran), trans. (from Russian) Hushang Tizabi and Hasan Qa'im Panah (Stockholm: Tudeh, 1356/1977); Manizheh Zavareei, "Dependent Capitalist Development in Iran and the Mass Uprising of 1979," in *Research in Political Economy: A Research Annual,* ed. Paul Zarembka (Greenwich, Conn.: JAI, 1982), 139–88; Assef Bayat, *Workers and Revolution in Iran: A Third World Experience of Workers' Control* (London: Zed, 1987); Wilfrid Korby, *Probleme der industriellen Entwickling und Konzentration in Iran* (Wiesbaden: Dr. Ludwig Reichert Verlag, 1977); Massoud Karshenas, *Oil, State and Industrialization in Iran* (Cambridge: Cambridge University Press, 1990).

33. For data on all these classes, see Foran, *Fragile Resistance,* chap. 8 and the references therein.

34. See Pesaran, "Economic Development," 33; Kamran M. Dadkhah, "The Inflationary Process of the Iranian Economy: A Rejoinder," *International Journal of Middle East Studies* 19 (August 1987): 389 table 1; Abrahamian, *Iran between Two Revolutions,* 431, 446–47; Katouzian, *The Political Economy,* 271–72; Ivanov, *Tarikh-i Nuvin,* 254, 297; Halliday, *Iran,* 13, 164.

35. See Robert Graham, *Iran: The Illusion of Power* (New York: St. Martin's, 1979), 152–63; Dilip Hiro, *Iran under the Ayatollahs* (London: Routledge & Kegan Paul, 1985), 253; Abrahamian, *Iran between Two Revolutions,* 437–38. See also interviews with Sir Peter Ramsbotham, 'Ali Amini, and Ahmad Ghoreishi, Iranian Oral History Collection, Houghton Library, Harvard University.

36. Amnesty International, *Annual Report 1974–75* (London: AI Publications, 1975), 8. On the repressive apparatus, see, among many others, Graham, *Iran,* 140–49, 163, 168–83; Halliday, *Iran,* 87–88, 90–96; Reza Baraheni, *The Crowned Cannibals: Writings on Repression in Iran* (New York: Vintage, 1977), 131–218.

37. Farhi, *States and Urban-Based Revolutions,* 87–88; Katouzian, *The Political Economy,* 192–93, 197, 234–35, 241–42; Graham, *Iran,* 133–38; Abrahamian, *Iran between Two Revolutions,* 419–21, 438, 440–41; Saikal, *The Rise and Fall,* 63, 90–91, 190.

38. On the United States and Iran, see Halliday, *Iran,* 83, 91–95, 153 table 2, 248, 254–56, 339 n. 1; Saikal, *The Rise and Fall,* 51, 56–58, 205–7; Zavareei, "Dependent Capitalist Development," 170, 172, 174; and the overviews by James A. Bill, *The Eagle and the*

Lion: The Tragedy of American-Iranian Relations (New Haven, Conn.: Yale University Press, 1988); Richard Cottam, *Iran and the United States: A Cold War Case Study* (Pittsburgh: University of Pittsburgh Press, 1988); and, most recently, Mark J. Gasiorowski, *U.S. Foreign Policy and the Shah: Building a Client State in Iran* (Ithaca, N.Y.: Cornell University Press, 1991).

39. Quoted in Ahmad Ashraf and Ali Banuazizi, "The State, Classes and Modes of Mobilization in the Iranian Revolution," *State, Culture and Society* 1, no. 3 (1985): 4. This paragraph and the next draw heavily on Bill, *The Eagle and the Lion,* and on State Department documents held by the National Security Archive in Washington, D.C., especially a January 29, 1980, White Paper on Iran.

40. Quoted in Bill, *The Eagle and the Lion,* 233. Some observers say this made the shah overconfident of U.S. support, emboldening him to take the offensive with the slanderous letter against Khumaini that touched off the first protests in Qum. See Dariush Humayun, *Diruz va Farda: Seh Guftar darbareh-yi Iran-i Inqilabi* (Yesterday and tomorrow: Three talks on revolutionary Iran) (Washington, D.C.: Foundation for Iranian Studies, 1981), 62.

41. Graham, *Iran,* 86–87. Data in this paragraph are drawn from Graham, *Iran,* 98–103; "Iran: The New Crisis of American Hegemony," *Monthly Review* 30 (February 1979): 1–24; Dadkhah, "The Inflationary Process," 389 table 1; and Halliday, *Iran,* 165–66.

42. The shah, in *Kayhan International,* October 26, 1976, quoted in Graham, *Iran,* 103. In August 1974 he had promised: "We do not expect Iranians to tighten their belts, eat less and labour away for the promised heaven which is put off by a year every day. We try to offer the nation the welfare and care we have promised—today." In *Kayhan International,* August 2–3, 1974, quoted in Graham, *Iran,* 103.

43. Halliday, "The Iranian Revolution," 194. Data and analyses on 1977 are found in Halliday, *Iran,* 145; Fred Halliday, "The Genesis of the Iranian Revolution," *Third World Quarterly* 1 (October 1979): 9; Pesaran, "Economic Development," 286; Saikal, *The Rise and Fall,* 183, 191; Katouzian, *The Political Economy,* 259–60; Keddie, "Iranian Revolutions," 588; National Security Archive document 1745, telegram from the American Embassy, Tehran, to secretary of state, November 16, 1978, 1–5.

44. Khumaini, from a collection of speeches and letters published in 1973, quoted in Bashiriyeh, *The State and Revolution,* 60–61. On Khumaini's ideas and social base, see Keddie, *Roots of Revolution,* 207, 242; Khomeini, *Islam and Revolution*; Abrahamian, *Iran between Two Revolutions,* 445, 475, 477–79, 532–33; Ervand Abrahamian, "Khomeini: Fundamentalist or Populist?" *New Left Review* 186 (March-April 1991): 102–19. An important new study of many aspects of the emergent political culture is Hamid Dabashi, *Theology of Discontent: The Ideological Foundation of the Islamic Republic in Iran* (New York: New York University Press, 1993).

45. 'Ali Shari'ati, *From Where Shall We Begin?* and *The Machine in the Captivity of Machinism,* trans. Fatollah Marjani (Houston: Free Islamic Literatures, 1980), 30. See also Shari'ati, *Marxism and Other Western Fallacies* (significantly, the title is not his); Abrahamian, *Iran between Two Revolutions,* 464–70; Keddie, *Roots of Revolution,* 215–19, 221, 224; Brad Hanson, "The 'Westoxication' of Iran: Depictions and Reactions of Behrangi, Al-e Ahmad, and Shari'ati," *International Journal of Middle East Studies* 15 (February 1983): 1–23.

46. On Bazargan and the LMI, see Shahrough Akhavi, *Religion and Politics in Contemporary Iran: Clergy-State Relations in the Pahlavi Period* (Albany: State University of New York Press, 1980), 112–15; Keddie, *Roots of Revolution,* 210–15; Abrahamian, *Iran between Two Revolutions,* 458–59; H. E. Chehabi, *Iranian Politics and Religious Modernism:*

The Liberation Movement of Iran under the Shah and Khomeini (Ithaca, N.Y.: Cornell University Press, 1990).

47. On the National Front, see Sussan Siavoshi, *Liberal Nationalism in Iran: The Failure of a Movement* (Boulder, Colo.: Westview, 1988); Parsa, *The Social Origins,* 169–77. On the Tudeh, see Halliday, *Iran,* 231, 233–37, 262, 289, 297; Abrahamian, *Iran between Two Revolutions,* 451–57.

48. On the Mujahidin, see Abrahamian, *Iran between Two Revolutions,* 480–81, 489–95; Halliday, *Iran,* 240, 242; Keddie, *Roots of Revolution,* 238–39; Bashiriyeh, *The State and Revolution,* 74; Ervand Abrahamian, *The Iranian Mojehedin* (New Haven, Conn.: Yale University Press, 1989). On the Fada'ian, see Halliday, *Iran,* 241–42, 246–47; Keddie, *Roots of Revolution,* 237, 239; Abrahamian, *Iran between Two Revolutions,* 480–85.

49. For the events of 1977, I have drawn on Keddie, *Roots of Revolution,* 231–33; Abrahamian, *Iran between Two Revolutions,* 500–505; Katouzian, *The Political Economy,* 342; Muslim Students Following the Line of the Imam, *Asnad-i Laneh-i Jasusi-yi Amrika* (Documents from the spy nest of America), vol. 24 (Tehran: Muslim Students Following the Line of the Imam, [1980?]), 7; Fischer, *Iran,* 189–93; Zavareei, "Dependent Capitalist Development," 175–78; Farhad Kazemi, *Poverty and Revolution in Iran: The Migrant Poor, Urban Marginality and Politics* (New York: New York University Press, 1981), 86–89; Bashiriyeh, *The State and Revolution,* 112; Ashraf and Banuazizi, "The State," 6, 27; Amjad, *Iran,* 119; National Security Archive, document 01399, State Department, memorandum of conversation, John Stempel, May 25, 1978; *Kayhan,* February 2, 20, 22, 1978; March 25, 30, 1978; April 10, 1978; Bill, *The Eagle and the Lion,* 225; Nasser Mu'azzin, ed., *Dah Shab* (Ten nights) (Tehran: Amir Kabir, 1357/1978); Haj Sayyid Javadi, *Nameha* (Letters) (Tehran: Mudarres, 1357/1978). I would like to thank my research assistant, Javad Rassaf, for his study of the Iranian press.

50. Good sources for blow-by-blow accounts of 1978 include Parsa, *The Social Origins*; Paul Balta and Claudine Rulleau, *L'Iran insurgé* (Paris: Sindbad, 1979); Abrahamian, *Iran between Two Revolutions;* Keddie, *Roots of Revolution*; Fischer, *Iran.* I have also drawn on *Kayhan,* January-May 1978; Ashraf and Banuazizi, "The State," 9–10; Iranian Students Association in the U.S., *Shah's Inferno: Abadan August 19, 1978* (Berkeley, Calif.: Iranian Students Association in the U.S., 1978), 2ff.

51. In addition to works cited in note 50, I have drawn on the *Manchester Guardian,* September 5 and 6, 1978; *Le Monde,* September 6, 1978; Davani, *Nahzat-i Ruhaniyun*; Amjad, *Iran,* 126; Terisa Turner, "Iranian Oilworkers in the 1978–79 Revolution," in *Oil and Class Struggle,* ed. Petter Nore and Terisa Turner (London: Zed, 1981), 279–92; "How We Organized Strike That Paralyzed Shah's Regime: Firsthand Account by Iranian Oil Worker," in *Oil and Class Struggle,* ed. Petter Nore and Terisa Turner (London: Zed, 1981), 292–301; William H. Sullivan, "Dateline Iran: The Road Not Taken," *Foreign Policy* 40 (Fall 1980): 180. For evidence on the shah's shaky state of mind, see Hussain Fardust, *Zuhur va Suqut-i Saltanat-i Pahlavi: Khatarat-i Artishbud-i Sabiq Hussain Fardust* (The rise and fall of the Pahlavi dynasty: Memoirs of former Field Marshal Hussain Fardust), 2 vols. (Tehran: Ittila'at, 1991); Marvin Zonis, *Majestic Failure: The Fall of the Shah* (Chicago: University of Chicago Press, 1991).

52. This is a composite quote based on Abrahamian, *Iran between Two Revolutions,* 529, and Graham, *Iran,* 237. In addition to the sources already cited, on these events see A. B. Reznikov, "The Downfall of the Iranian Monarchy (January-February 1979)," in *The Revolutionary Process in the East: Past and Present,* ed. R. Ulyanovsky (Moscow: Progress, 1985), 254–312.

53. Mehdi Bazargan, *Inqilab-i Iran dar Dau Harakat* (The Iranian Revolution in Two

Moves) (Tehran: Daftar-i Nahzat-i Azadi-yi Iran, 1363/1984), 39, as translated in Ali Rahnema and Farhad Nomani, *The Secular Miracle: Religion, Politics and Economic Policy in Iran* (London: Zed, 1990). See also Abrahamian, *Iran between Two Revolutions,* 532–35; Keddie, *Roots of Revolution,* 250–51; Ashraf and Banuazizi, "The State."

54. See Kazemi, *Poverty and Revolution,* 2, 86–89, 95–96; Abrahamian, *Iran between Two Revolutions,* 522, 527, 535; Hooglund, *Land and Revolution,* 143, 146, 148–50; Valentine Moghadam [Sharhzad Azad, pseud.], "Workers' and Peasants' Councils in Iran," *Monthly Review* 32 (October 1980): 15–16; Garthwaite, *Khans and Shahs,* 141; Lois Beck, "Revolutionary Iran and Its Tribal Peoples," *MERIP (Middle East Research and Information Project) Reports* 87 (May 1980): 16–17, 19–20.

55. On the ulama, see Ashraf and Banuazizi, "The State," 16, 26, 34; Keddie, *Roots of Revolution,* 257–58; Abrahamian, *Iran between Two Revolutions,* 526–27. On the bazaar classes, see Bayat, *Workers and Revolution,* 95; Shaul Bakhash, *The Reign of the Ayatollahs: Iran and the Islamic Revolution* (New York: Basic Books, 1984), 191.

56. See Muslim Students, *Asnad,* 26:31; Ashraf and Banuazizi, "The State," 26; Bill, *The Eagle and the Lion,* 225; Abrahamian, *Iran between Two Revolutions,* 451, 522, 526; Katouzian, *The Political Economy,* 330 n. 9, 347, 353 n. 15; Zabih, *Iran's Revolutionary Upheaval,* 44, 84 n. 9; Fischer, *Iran,* 211; Keddie, *Roots of Revolution,* 251–52; *Kayhan,* February 21, 29, 1978; April 3, 1978, for a few of many reports on the youth and educational status of the demonstrators.

57. On the working class, see Ervand Abrahamian, "Iran's Turbaned Revolution," in *The Middle East Annual: Issues and Events,* vol. 1, ed. David H. Partington (Boston: G. K. Hall, 1982), 89; Fischer, *Iran,* 200–201; Abrahamian, *Iran between Two Revolutions,* 512, 517–18, 522–23, 525; Graham, *Iran,* 233; Bayat, *Workers and Revolution,* 6, 85–88, 92–94; "How We Organized Strike," 293–94, 299–300; Parsa, *The Social Origins,* 144, 147; Valentine M. Moghadam, "Accumulation Strategy and Class Formation: The Making of the Industrial Labor Force in Iran, 1962–1977" (Ph.D. diss., American University, Department of Sociology, 1985), 4, 10, 306, 308–11, 316, 318, 321–28.

58. Quoted by Kazemi, *Poverty and Revolution,* 95; see also 2, 86–89, 95–96; Abrahamian, *Iran between Two Revolutions,* 535; Hooglund, *Land and Revolution,* 143, 146, 148; Zavareei, "Dependent Capitalist Development," 175–76; *Kayhan,* February 28, 1978, which reports that most of the 628 individuals arrested in the Tabriz disturbances lived in the city's slum areas.

59. Annabelle Sreberny-Mohammadi, "The Power of Tradition: Communication and the Iranian Revolution" (Ph.D. diss., Columbia University, Department of Communications, 1985), 208. On women, see Keddie, *Roots of Revolution,* 248; Balta and Rulleau, *L'Iran insurgé,* 89; *Kayhan,* February 1, 1978, among many other references in the newspapers; Valentine Moghadam, "Industrial Development, Culture, and Working-Class Politics: A Case Study of Tabriz Industrial Workers in the Iranian Revolution," *International Sociology* 2 (June 1987): 168.

60. Abrahamian, "Structural Causes," quoting the *New York Times,* December 17, 1978. On the shah, see Halliday, "The Iranian Revolution," 196; Keddie, *Roots of Revolution,* 255–56. On pro-shah forces, see Alidoost-Khaybari, "Religious Revolutionaries," 498–505; Bashiriyeh, *The State and Revolution,* 115, 119; Abrahamian, *Iran between Two Revolutions,* 508; Ashraf and Banuazizi, "The State," 15, 34; Parsa, *The Social Origins,* 226ff.; *Kayhan,* January 3, 11, 14, 15, 16, 18, 19, 22; April 4, 6, 8, 13, 15, 18, 20, 1978.

61. Arjomand, "The Causes and Significance," 45; Bill, *The Eagle and the Lion,* 256; Halliday, "The Iranian Revolution," 195–96; Katouzian, *The Political Economy,* 347–48.

62. I have begun to explore these comparisons in "A Theory of Third World Social Revolutions." A larger project involving Mexico, Cuba, Chile, and Grenada is under way as well.

Chapter 8

Islamic Populism, Class, and Gender in Postrevolutionary Iran

Val Moghadam

What kind of revolution took place in Iran? What was its immediate outcome? And how has the revolution evolved? The immediate outcome of the 1977–79 Iranian revolution was the formal establishment of the Islamic Republic of Iran, overwhelmingly approved in a referendum on April 1, 1979. Yet the multiclass alliance that was so effective in resisting the military and toppling the Pahlavi state soon broke down into its constituent elements, and in an extremely contentious manner. This chapter examines the outcome of the Iranian revolution in terms of its most salient features: the trajectory of the Islamic-populist state and ideology, class conflicts, and the regulation of gender. Class and gender struggles predominated in the period from 1979 through 1981; these pitted peasants and workers against the centralizing state, non-Islamist women against the revolutionary Islamic state, and the secular left and liberals against the Islamic Republican Party (IRP). With the political triumph of the IRP in 1981, the cultural project of Islamization was intensified. In the 1990s, however, the Rafsanjani government appears more interested in economic issues, such as stimulating economic growth by supporting the private sector. This is suggestive of the process of *embourgeoisement* of the "Islamic revolution."

It may be useful to delineate the postrevolutionary situation in terms of a number of stages. (1) February to November 1979 began with the victory of the revolutionary forces and establishment of the Islamic Republic, and ended with the takeover of the American embassy and the resignation of Prime Minister Mehdi Bazargan. During this period tensions developed between some of the secular left and the new leadership. (2) November 1979 to September 1980 is another period, when the embassy issue was at center stage; Abulhassan Bani Sadr was elected Iran's first president; the Iraqis invaded Iran. (3) The period from September 1980 to June 1981 was dominated by the increasing conflict between the Islamists and Bani Sadr and his associates; it ended with Bani Sadr's impeachment. (4) From June 1981 to September 1982 a mini-civil war took place between the Mujahidin and the regime; the latter unleashed its terror also on the communist organizations; Iranian forces made major gains on the war front. (5) From about 1983 onward, state power rested firmly with the Islamists, who intensified the program of Islamization, especially in the areas of culture, ideology, education, law, morality, and lifestyle. The war with Iraq continued until 1988, and the state of the economy gradually worsened. (6) In the post-Khumaini and postwar situation, the state's attention is now focused on planning, development, and reconstruction, including economic liberalization and a self-administered stabilization program.

Throughout most of the 1980s, the war with Iraq and the project of Islamization served to attenuate the deep divisions within the regime itself over economic strategy and property rights. Populist economic measures substituted for a concerted development plan. Islamic populism enabled the regime to maintain the support of some social groups, and it functioned to keep the regime cohesive. The postrevolutionary state focused less on the accumulation process in the immediate interest of capital than on the legitimation and consolidation of political power and cultural hegemony. Once the latter was accomplished, and following the death of Ayatullah Khumaini and the end of the war with Iraq, the revolutionary process came to an end. National development, planning, and reconstruction now occupy center stage, and a policy of economic liberalization fully in line with the new international orthodoxy has been adopted.

The main text of this chapter consists of four sections. I begin with a discussion of the debate surrounding the nature of the Iranian revolution, and review some of the relevant works on the revolution and its aftermath. I then propose an alternative analysis of the revolution and its outcome based on the central organizing concept of populism. This section also includes a review of the literature on populism to underscore its relevance to the Iranian case. To a very great extent, populism helps to explain the fate of the social conflicts that figured so prominently, and often violently, in postrevolutionary Iran. The second section provides an account of these conflicts and of the regime's moves to consolidate its position. This section also analyzes the redefinitions of gender in terms of the political-cultural project of the Islamist leadership. It will be recalled that in the early 1980s legislation was adopted that effectively reduced the status of women to second-class citizens, and that throughout the 1980s compulsory veiling was strictly enforced. The strict regulation of women's appearance and comportment has been the subject of numerous commentaries. However, the gender dynamics of postrevolutionary Iran have not been properly integrated into the mainstream scholarship on the Iranian revolution and the Islamic Republic.

In the third section of this chapter I examine the trajectory of the populist movement and ideology. I explain the disintegration and ultimate dissolution of the original, broad populist movement in 1981, and discuss the function and efficacy of Islamic-populist ideology. In the fourth section I attempt to show that the Iranian revolution did not entail a shift from one mode of production to another.

This is because its leadership was rooted in a petty bourgeoisie incapable of reaching consensus on an economic program, because of the extent of state and national resources expended toward the war with Iraq, and because of the constraints of the world-system, which offer populist revolutions limited transformative potential. Whereas the global conjuncture in 1977–79 was favorable to a successful revolution, the world-system provided little scope for the transformation of developing countries, especially during the 1980s. As a result, though cultural and political changes have been profound in Iran, and populist economic measures were taken after the revolution, economic transformation has not occurred. In this chapter I shall also endeavor to show that the ad hoc populist economic measures resulted from the transitional and exceptional nature of the postrevolutionary state. Now that the revolution has run its course, social-property relations of a capitalistic type are being restored under the guidance of the new state managers.

The Iranian Revolution: Islamic or Populist?

There are some similarities, and some differences, between the analysis presented here and that of other theorists of the Iranian revolution and commentators on postrevolutionary developments. Dorraj has made a case for the populist nature of the revolution in a manner more systematic and theoretical than others who have applied the term *populist* to the Iranian case.[1] His focus, however, is on political culture as the key to understanding the revolution. More specifically, he argues that the secular and religious "neopopulist" political culture that emerged during the 1960s and 1970s found expression in the 1979 revolution.[2] Indeed, Dorraj traces the origins of this political culture not only back to early Shi'ism, but to the "primordial significance" of pre-Islamic Iranian religiopolitical traditions, in particular those of Zoroastrianism.[3] Thus, although Dorraj and I agree on the populist nature of the revolution, his focus on political culture diverges from my multicausal analysis; moreover, Dorraj's study does not consider postrevolutionary developments.

Similarly, Parsa examines in great detail the social and economic origins of the revolution, as well as the mobilization and collective actions of various groups and classes prior to and during the overthrow of the Pahlavi state.[4] In the last part of his book, Parsa explains that although broad segments of the population opposed the new state, they failed to consolidate their resources and act against a single target at the same time. The conflicts of the groups and classes that he reviews are the autonomy movements in Kurdistan and the Turkaman region, the peasantry, the universities, the workers' councils, and the bazaaris. He also examines the political conflicts pitting Islamists against communists and liberals. Parsa is quite correct in his assessment that schisms within the opposition groups, along with the clergy's enhanced ability to control the population through the establishment of a large revolutionary guard, ensured the survival of the new regime.[5] I share his focus on social and political conflict and agree that effective resource mobilization is crucial to successful opposition and to the seizure and maintenance of state power.

A number of authors have designated the revolution "Islamic" and argue further that it is completely *sui generis.* They also evince an antipathy to the revolution because of its violent and repressive outcomes.[6] My analysis and approach differ considerably in that I believe that an analytic (and political) distinction between the Iranian revolution and the Islamic Republic is warranted.[7] Indeed, analysis of the Iranian revolution—the complex causes and origins, the self-understanding of the participants of the revolution, the *esprit* of the revolutionary situation—is distorted when the outcome is retroactively read back. Perhaps more than any other revolution, the Iranian revolution is significant for the jarring disjuncture between the mood and aspirations of February 1979 and the situation in 1981 and afterward. The outcome of the 1977–79 revolution was by no means predetermined.

Arjomand's study of "the Islamic revolution in Iran" is sophisticated and scholarly, yet evinces a rather huge political bias: his barely disguised contempt for the Iranian revolution (and perhaps any revolution) and for the middle class, which, he claims, ludicrously preferred Khumaini to the shah.[8] He also argues that the outcome of the Iranian revolution was theocratic absolutism.[9] My view is that developments in postrevolutionary Iran went through distinct stages and were contradictory and eclectic in nature. The constitution, political structure, economic policies, and discourse of the Islamic Republic, I argue, were an amalgam of traditional and modern, republican and theocratic features; the term *Islamic populist* best captures these apparently contradictory features. Arjomand ends his book by proposing that the revolution be considered as an *integrative* social movement. This concept, he feels, is appropriate to what he sees as a religiously oriented reaction to social dislocation and anomie caused by rapid modernization, which was then followed by social integration through moral rigorism and the search for cultural authenticity.[10] Although I would not discount anomie as a factor in the causes of the revolution, and I would agree that the Islamic leadership was preoccupied with questions of identity and culture during the 1980s, the concept of integrative revolution does not capture the deep conflicts and divisions among the Iranian populace that followed Islamization.[11] However, Islamic populism as both ideology and movement did function to legitimate authority and enlist the support of the urban poor, lower middle class, and sections of the working class. Thus, the postrevolutionary regime deployed both force and concession to maintain power.

In none of the works discussed above have the gender dynamics of the revolution and its aftermath been systematically studied—even though "the woman question" figured so prominently in the discourse and the laws of the new regime.

Even those works that focus on culture, morality, religion, and identity as central features of the revolution do not devote attention to gender. It has been within the discipline of women's studies, including Iranian women's studies, that perceptive research has uncovered the salience of "the woman question," documenting its relevance to the Iranian revolution and the Islamic regime.[12] Let us now consider populism as both movement and ideology.

Perspectives on Populism

Populism is commonly understood to be a petty-bourgeois movement or ideology that posits the existence of an undifferentiated "people" and is led by a charismatic leader. But there is no general consensus among scholars on a single definition of populism. A body of literature has developed out of the Latin American experience, but scholars offer different perspectives on the sources and component parts of contemporary Third World populism. According to Worsley, the appeal of populism is not to any particular class, but to the "small man" in all classes: at times the smallholders and at other times the city poor.[13] Its most skillful proponents turn its vagueness into an asset, its open-endedness into a generalized ideology. Wiles has argued that the populist movement is based on the premise that "virtue resides in the simple people, who are the overwhelming majority, and in their collective tradition."[14] For Wiles, populists stress a moral outlook rather than a definite program, and tend to represent the fears and vision of "the little man," or the small proprietor. Drake contends that in Latin America, "the failures and dislocations of tardy and dependent capitalist development, rather than its absence, tended to produce populism.... When raw material-producing economies were jolted by market forces beyond local control, openings appeared for mass mobilization against traditional upper class, laissez-faire policies." Drake warns that "because these movements arose out of reactions against capitalist dislocations and abuses, however, does not mean that they were coherently anticapitalist ... , populism only promised modifications to cushion the shocks of capitalist growth."[15]

Raby notes that a revolutionary populist leadership may substitute for a nonexistent or ineffective proletarian party:

> Through bold action and direct appeal to the masses, disdaining political mechanisms and party structures, the revolutionary populist leadership is often able to "overtake" or outflank established parties and forces of the left, mobilizing broad popular support, exhibiting remarkable tactical and ideological flexibility and adapting with exemplary rapidity to sudden changes and challenges in a revolutionary conjuncture.[16]

Other scholars point out that, unlike nineteenth-century populism—whether in Russia, the United States, or Canada—contemporary Third World populism, and especially Latin American populist movements, are a by-product of urbanization. Rural-urban migration and the expansion of education create expectations of political participation and material benefits. But the existence of social disparities, the concentration of power, limited access to urban amenities and services, and the absence of sufficient employment opportunities create feelings of powerlessness, resentment, and frustration. These are among the propositions of the Latin American literature on marginality and on populism.[17] Although the concept of the informal sector has come to supplant that of marginality,[18] both concepts refer to groups of people who are excluded from the development process or are exploited beyond the purview of the state and social services. These are the vulnerable social groups to whom populist movements and discourses appeal and whose situation they promise to remedy.

Latin America has a rich populist tradition, with movements especially strong in the period between the two world wars. Among the most renowned populist leaders are Argentina's Perón, Brazil's Vargas, Mexico's Cárdenas, Peru's Haya de la Torre, Ecuador's Ibarra, and Bolivia's Paz Estenssoro. Populist leaders elsewhere include Egypt's Gamal Abdul Nasser, Ghana's Kwame Nkrumah, Guinea-Bissau's Amilcar Cabral, Indonesia's Ahmed Sukarno, Pakistan's Zulfikar Ali Bhutto, Tanzania's Julius Nyerere, Turkey's Bulent Ecevit, Algeria's Houari Boumedienne, Libya's Muammar Qaddafi, Syria's Hafez al-Asad, and the Baathists of Iraq. Modernizers all, they were (or are) active in the nonaligned movement and sought a "third way" between capitalism and communism, even though they tended toward left-wing positions and sometimes used the label "socialist." Their targets were foreign domination, economic underdevelopment, and exploitation. They were for social justice and national independence. According to Isaiah Berlin, populist ideas lay at the base of much of the "socialist" economic policy pursued by developing countries.[19] David Apter, whose 1965 study embraces under populism "almost all" the ideological and political trends in the developing world, defines them mainly as "predemocratic."[20] C. B. MacPherson, on the other hand, notes that ideologists in developing countries "have rejected almost wholly the liberal individualist utilitarianism of the West, but have drawn heavily on its earlier democratic tradition, the tradition of Rousseau and Populism."[21] Mouzelis also notes the "plebiscitary" character of populist movements and ideologies.[22]

The Soviet theorist V. Khoros defines a populist movement as one

> aimed at power for the benefit of the people as a whole which result[s] from the reaction of those, usually intellectuals, alienated from the existing power structure, to the stresses of rapid economic, social, cultural or political change. These movements are characterized by a belief in a return to, or adaptation of, more simple and traditional forms and values emanating from the people, particularly the more archaic sections of the people who are taken to be the repositories of virtue.[23]

To resolve the identity crisis generated by the domination of "alien" culture and values, populists tend to extol the virtues of "the common people as the essence of national identity while denouncing the 'anti-national' cultural and economic elites as well as foreign imperialists."[24] In this way, populist discourses tend to be grounded in nationalist and class rhetoric as well as traditional political symbols and cultural myths and imaginaries to mobilize the masses. Frequently, cultural revival of the past becomes a political weapon to mobilize the people under a common banner. Thus, Conniff has observed: "Populism everywhere forged a new cultural awareness among the masses, which has been one of its enduring legacies. It encouraged study of folkways and popular art forms, rescuing them from the disdain of elite European taste." The cultural revival of the past and glorification of national traditions, norms, and values is an integral part of the populist movement. Indeed, "the search for a popular culture answered an existential need to define the 'people' whose role in national life was expanding, and in whose name the populist campaigned."[25]

Vagueness and imprecision are hallmarks of populist ideologies. But what of the social composition of the populist movement, and its class content? Although the leaders of populist movements tend to come from the petty bourgeoisie and the rhetoric is directed to the "small man," the movement's composition is multiclass. Dorraj points out that populist movements are multiclass in two senses: first, insofar as their appeal cuts across class lines and they recruit from different social strata; second, in that there is no clear single class hegemony after the seizure of power.[26] This does not mean that populism is a classless movement, but rather that it is multiclass. Germani contends that where rapid social change has produced a working class that has not had sufficient time to acquire a working-class consciousness, this class is likely to adopt populism rather than socialism. Germani also notes that newly uprooted migrant peasants are particularly prominent in populist movements.[27] Dorraj argues that populism's primary supporters come from the lower and lower-middle classes; in turn, populist movements and leaders tend to implement reforms to benefit these classes.[28] Drake argues that the populist appeal among the masses is "associated with the desire for a charitable state to replicate the authoritarian, condescending relations historically prevailing between the upper and lower social orders."[29]

The role of charisma and the charismatic leader in populist movements has also been noted. Dorraj maintains that insofar as populist leaders substitute controlled mobilization from above for genuine democratic participation from below, they tend to be authoritarian, but gifted with personal charisma. To the extent that their charisma is dependent on a renewal of a mandate from the masses, they must allow formal public participation, even if it is devoid of democratic content. In times of deep social crisis, the personal charisma of the leader or leaders assumes a significant role. Although populism tends to be ideologically eclectic and programmatically contradictory, populist movements and discourses led by a charismatic leader have tremendous mobilizing effects.[30]

Writing from a Marxist perspective, Raby observes that the apparent lack of a clear class basis inevitably raises the question of Bonapartism.[31] Many populist movements appear to have a classless or déclassé leadership "suspended above" the major classes in conflict, in a manner that recalls Marx's discussion of Bonapartism.[32] But Raby concludes that populism cannot be understood as simply a variant of Bonapartism, because some populist movements have evinced a clearer class base than in the historical French case. Another reason contemporary Third World populism should be distinguished from Bonapartism is that the phenomenon should be situated within a specific historical conjuncture, that is, with reference to the specific national development context. Raby quotes a Brazilian theorist who states that "populist phenomena are directly linked to transformations in the relations of production, whether economic or social or political."[33] Contemporary Third World populism arises in the context of capitalist development of a dependent type, and is thus strongly anti-imperialist and directed against the industrial bourgeoisie, at least in its initial phases.

Laclau's concept of populism differs in important ways from the conceptualization above; for example, he does not treat populism sociologically, but only in terms of ideas. However, his discussion of the articulation of diverse discourses into a single and unifying one is relevant to the argument here. According to Laclau, in any struggle for hegemony the contending forces attempt to absorb national-popular (or populist) elements in their discourses and to articulate their objectives as the consummation of the popular struggle.[34] Often they articulate their interests in terms that other social forces accept as their own, and present their interests as the interests of the people. In the struggle for hegemony the contested terrain is not limited to the field of political power or economic strategy, for it also involves definitions of culture, identity, and authenticity. At such times language assumes paramount importance, and new significations of signs, events, and symbols emerge. Words are given new meanings and connotations, "social imaginaries" are reconstructed, new systems of historical narration are articulated, and culture is established as a field of struggle.[35]

Populism, therefore, is here understood as both ideology and movement. In their earlier manifestations, populist movements and ideologies emerged in the context of traditional and rural society disintegrating under the forces of modern capitalism introduced from without and generally perceived as alien, the absence of a viable indigenous bourgeoisie, and the emergence of an intelligentsia alienated from traditional values and existing society.[36] In the more recent experience of Third World countries, populism arises in the context of dependency, uneven development, and the absence of a viable national bourgeoisie; it is constituted by the convergence of diverse interests and social groups into a unifying discourse and coalition. Populist movements may be left-wing or right-wing; they may be reactionary, reformist, or revolutionary. For example, besides the Iranian case, examples of revolutionary populism are the armed forces movement of Portugal, 1974–75; the Peruvian revolution and officers in power, 1968–75; and the Sandinistas in Nicaragua, 1979–90. Some versions of populism are more statist, or more anti-imperialist, or more culturalist than others, but in nearly all cases, notions of "the people," "nation," and "unity" are substituted for class and class conflict, and are counterposed to foreign domination. This constitutes the strength of populist movements and the mobilizing power of populist rhetoric.

As I have argued elsewhere, and as Foran shows in chapter 7 of this volume, the various facets of populism described above were present in the Iranian revolution: a multiclass protest movement in the context of dependent capitalist development; a unifying, cross-class discourse; the absence of an effective socialist or working-class party; a petty-bourgeois leadership that appears above class interests; a charismatic leader; the special place of the urban poor; a search for a "third way." The concept of populism is useful in that it permits an understanding of the sources and character of the Iranian revolution and of the Islamic regime in the broadest sociological terms, while also situating the Iranian experience within the world system of states and markets and linking it to contemporary Third World politics, including developments in the region of the Middle East.[37]

World-System Limitations to Revolutionary Transformation

If populism allows us to understand the cross-class appeal of contemporary Third World radical movements, world-system theory offers a complementary explanation for the inability of revolutionary states to effect full social transformation. A revolution's capacity for social transformation is rooted in both domestic features and developments (social structure, class struggles, political conflicts, ideological formation) and international structures and conjunctures. Here the world-system perspective is especially helpful for suggesting the possibilities for and obstacles to revolutionary change at the global level. According to this perspective, the transformative potential of revolution within the existing capitalist world-system is limited, and the impact of revolution is variable. This follows from the very nature of the capitalist world-system, with its single division of labor across three economic zones: core, periphery, and semiperiphery. The three zones coexist in interdependence, but the core, which consists of the most developed economic systems and strongest states, dominates the other two. A significant contribution of this perspective is its emphasis on what Wallerstein has called "the limited possibilities of transformation within the capitalist world economy."[38] This is not to suggest that transformation is impossible; rather, the present unequal global system of states and the vagaries of the world market present obstacles to both development and revolution. Conceivably, a strong developmentalist state with the political will, considerable social backing, and sufficient resources could effect transformation. But a postrevolutionary populist state may be too fractious, and its program too vague, to be capable of more than limited social transformation. Furthermore, hostility on the part of superpowers, especially the United

States, or subversion by regional rivals, creates intractable obstacles to revolutionary transformation.[39] Nor are national economies immune from larger economic crises. As Chase-Dunn notes, "The way in which the pressures of a stagnating world economy impact upon national policies certainly varies from country to country, but the ability of any single national society to construct collective rationality is limited by its interaction within the larger system."[40]

There is now a growing scholarship on the problems of economic and political transformation in postrevolutionary societies.[41] Amirahmadi states that "a revolution in either the semi-periphery or the periphery will not lead to an automatic liberation from the constraining forces of the core as such forces are essentially economic in nature." However, they could make a difference in lessening the extent and impact of such core-imposed constraints, if the leadership were to follow a more prudent and planned strategy. Amirahmadi points out that although active support from "progressive states and other noncore capitalist nations" can also be expected to mitigate certain limitations faced by the postrevolutionary societies, they are not guarantees for a successful social transformation.[42] In addition to world-systemic constraints, there are internal conflicts engendered by class, ethnic, and regional identifications. These test the legitimacy and strength of the new regime, which may or may not survive the battles.

The constraints posed by the world-system and the contradictions of populist movements raise the interesting theoretical question of whether a Third World postrevolutionary regime can be an *exceptional* or a *transitional* state, the embodiment of unresolved issues of political power and economic strategy. Fagen has argued, following from the cases he has studied, that a fully articulated transitional state cannot be identified.[43] I propose, however, that the postrevolutionary Iranian state was just such a transitional state, and that the 1979 constitution was its exemplar. Indeed, the Iranian case may exemplify an important point made by Mouzelis:

> the possibility that, under certain conditions, the mode of domination may be more important than the dominant mode of production, either in terms of causal relations between political and economic agents, and/or in terms of functional relations between political and economic imperatives of reproduction.[44]

The populist revolution in Iran resulted in a "state" over which no one class had control and that was for ten years incapable of presenting and implementing a project for economic development.

Postrevolutionary Conflicts and Regime Consolidation

The revolutionary coalition of 1978–79 comprised the clerics, the traditional petty bourgeoisie of the bazaar, the leftist guerrillas, and the Westernized middle class as represented by, inter alia, the National Front, the Bar Association, and the Writers Association. The street demonstrations themselves were huge, more than two million strong in Tehran, and were made up of Iranians of all classes, save the small modern bourgeoisie tied to the shah. That the revolutionary alliance was multiclass and the discourse populist does not signify the absence of class conflict or class consciousness; these were clearly present in the workers' strikes and demands.[45] However, Pahlavi rule had resulted in a diminished role for liberals and the left and the absence of autonomous working-class organizations,[46] whereas the traditional petty bourgeoisie enjoyed independent organizations in the bazaar and the mosque.

During most of the revolution, the popular positive demand was condensed in the major slogan: *Istiqlal, Azadi, Jumhuri* (Independence, Freedom, Republic). In the last stage of the revolution the call for a republic changed to *Islamic government,* encouraged by the clerical leaders and their lay associates. Yet, despite its efficacy as a mobilizing ideology in the later stages of the revolution, the Islamic discourse was not a single, monolithic, and politically coherent ideology. Iran scholars have identified at least four versions of Islamic discourse: the "radical Islam" of the young intelligentsia, Khumaini's "militant Islam," the "liberal Islam" of people like Bazargan, and the "traditional Islam" of the ulama.[47] During the revolutionary conjuncture, these different strands of Shi'a Islam came together to form a compelling mobilizing discourse. In turn, the Shi'i discourse fused with the left-wing and liberal discourses to form a radical-populist revolutionary discourse. This discourse continued for some time after the revolution, but it became explicitly exclusionary of non-Islamists.

Nevertheless, after the revolution, the left organizations, principally the Fada'i, Mujahidin, Tudeh, and Paykar, became major political forces on the campuses, especially after the new government quickly reasserted control in the oil fields and some major factories. These organizations included substantial groups of people who had gained valuable political experience and insights in exile, while underground, or in prison. Their ranks were swollen by the many dissident students who returned to Iran en masse in the spring of 1979, as well as by daily recruits to the left cause. The left presence was keenly felt all that year, and very quickly a serious tension arose between the Islamists and the array of Marxist, socialist, and communist organizations and parties.

The postrevolutionary regime quickly sought to institutionalize itself, even while in the process the clerical and liberal wings of the new regime clashed over the meaning of "Islamic Republic." A series of steps were taken to obtain legitimation and power. First came the referendum on changing the political system of the country. The question on the ballot read, "Should Iran be an Islamic Republic?" There was considerable protest over the wording, and the Fada'i, National Democratic Front (led by a grandson of the late Premier Musaddiq), and several regional parties boycotted the referendum. On April 1, 1979, however, an over-whelming majority of voters answered in the affirmative. But the question of what the Islamic Republic should look like was still open.

Second, the Islamic Republican Party was formed by leading clerics. It was to become the official Islamist party, and increasingly intolerant of other parties in and around the political elite, notably the Azarbaijan-based Muslim People's Republican Party, led by Ayatullah Shari'atmadari, a liberal Muslim cleric opposed to direct rule by the clergy, Prime Minister Mehdi Bazargan's Movement for Liberation, and the National Front, the party of several cabinet members. The IRP was also violently opposed to the Marxist parties and organizations, although it tolerated the Tudeh Party (which had become totally supportive of Khumaini's "anti-imperialist" positions and contemptuous of the "bourgeois liberals") until 1982.

Third, revolutionary courts were set up that functioned outside the jurisdiction of the Justice Ministry. At first they concentrated on trying royalists and members of SAVAK. Later, they evolved into religious courts guided by the Shari'a (Islamic/Koranic law) that coexisted uneasily with civil law and courts of appeal until the latter were abolished in early 1983.

Fourth, a draft constitution was written in April and elections were held in August to select a small Assembly of Experts to study it. The original idea had been that a large, representative, and elected constituent assembly would draft the constitution. As a result of the change, and because of the clerical bias of the screening of candidates for the assembly, there was, again, much left-wing protest. But by now, each time such a protest took place, armed *hizbullahi* (young male progovernment vigilantes) or members of the Pasdaran (Islamic Guards) would harass and break up the gatherings. In the course of their deliberations, the Assembly of Experts, now dominated by the IRP, introduced and adopted the controversial concept of *vilayat-i faqih,* or rule by the supreme interpreter of the law—in this case, Khumaini. This met with the opposition of the left, of Shari'at-madari, and of the National Democratic Party (but not of the liberals in government). Nonetheless, the constitution, much of which was a quintessential radical-populist document on economic issues and matters of foreign policy, while also establishing Iran as an Islamic state, was overwhelmingly approved in another referendum in December. The constitution (of which more below) adopted the system of parliamentary elections, which were held on schedule with large voter turnouts even in the midst of crisis.

Fifth, the new regime undertook the transformation of the shah's military. By June 1979 the Pasdaran constituted a parallel force to that of the military and to the guerrillas. Soon controlled by the IRP, the Pasdaran monitored the activities of leftists and liberals, broke up demonstrations and strikes, kept a watch on army barracks and police stations, and suppressed ethnic revolts in Kurdistan and Turkaman Sahra. After the dissolution of Bazargan's original cabinet and his own resignation following the U.S. embassy takeover, the Islamists undertook a major purge of the military in the summer of 1980. Executions and purges continued until the Iraqi invasion in September. The Iraqis reckoned they would encounter an extremely weakened, demoralized, and ill-organized fighting force, as indeed the military was. They did not consider the Pasdaran, one of the major institutional supports of the new regime, and a formidable fighting force, as the Mujahidin were also to discover when they decided to take on the Islamists in June 1981. In time, the paramilitary Pasdaran became a full-fledged fighting force, complete with its own government agency. And the military, in the course of the war with Iraq, was revived and relegitimated.[48]

From the start, the new regime faced challenges to its authority and objectives. The first challenge came in early March 1979, when thousands of women protested against the new sexual politics and in particular Khumaini's decree that women appear in public in *hijab,* or Islamic dress. There had been a week of meetings, rallies, and demonstrations, during which non-Islamist women expressed their outrage and anxiety over the issue of *hijab.* Prime Minister Bazargan announced that Khumaini's statement had been misunderstood by some genuine women militants and consciously manipulated by left-wing troublemakers. As Tabari relates it, Bazargan said that there would be no compulsory veiling in government offices and, in any case, it was the view of the Imam that women should be guided, and not forced, to accept the veil.[49] *Hijab* was legislated the following year, when the Islamists' position strengthened. In the meantime, other steps were taken to regulate gender. The Ministry of Education banned coeducation, and the Ministry of Justice declared it would not recognize women judges. Childcare centers began to be closed down. Several Caspian Sea resort towns instituted sex-segregated beaches. The Family Protection Law of 1967 (amended in 1973) was abrogated in 1979 and replaced by Shari'a laws; this effectively denied women the right to initiate divorce.

Another conflict developed between the new regime and the left. The provisional government and the IRP sought to eliminate the many communist and socialist groups that had formed. In September 1979 the Pasdaran were dispatched to close down the offices and headquarters of the left parties and organizations. The left continued its activities, even with diminishing resources, but seemed incapable of uniting to form a broad oppositional front to the new regime. In part, this was because they were confused, and disarmed, by the regime's radical populism.

A third challenge to the new center came from Iran's periphery, in particular the national and ethnic minorities of Kurdistan and Turkaman Sahra, who were demanding autonomy. There and elsewhere, peasants were expropriating large landlords, and in the cities the left was agitating for land reform based on the concept of land to the tiller. In many areas, peasants and landlords clashed violently. The reactions of the authorities to these developments varied from locality to locality. In some areas, the revolutionary guards and local clerics took the side of the peasants; in others they sided with the landowners. The liberal government and the radical-populist Islamists in the IRP differed in their respective approaches. The government was against the land seizures, sometimes arguing that they would cause a decline in agricultural production, other times denying the existence of "feudal landowners" or downplaying inequalities in landownership. But government efforts to halt land seizures were stymied by the pro-poor rhetoric of Khumaini and the IRP. For example, Ayatullah Khumaini was repeatedly proclaiming that "the country belongs to the slum dwellers. The poor are the resources of this country." Ayatullah Bihishti stated that "the line of the revolution is anti-imperialism, anti-capitalism, and anti-feudalism." Ayatullah Bahonar, a member of the Revolutionary Council, announced that "regarding large landownership, the aim of the Revolutionary Council is to be able gradually to give these lands to those who work on them." Finally, Ayatullah Dastghaib, imam jum'eh of Shiraz, in his defense of the peasants, went so far as to encourage "the youth and farmers not to wait for the state to give them land. They, themselves, should act, seize lands from the feudals [feudal lords] and landowners, and cultivate these lands behind the banner of Islam."[50]

A fourth challenge came from labor. Workers' councils were proliferating, in part owing to left organizing efforts. These councils had emerged from the strike committees of fall 1978 to assume the management of factories. In Tabriz, Ahvaz, Isfahan, Tehran, and elsewhere, factories run by councils instituted various forms of workers' control. In many cases, workers were able to reduce working hours, obtain more favorable job evaluations and classifications, fire corrupt managers, hire additional workers, obtain pay raises, lower managers' salaries, and receive regular health examinations.[51] Throughout 1979 the workers' movement grew, and serious attempts were made to institutionalize workers' control and coordinate the activities of the councils. But the authorities were not in favor of worker control over the production process, or of independent labor organizations. This despite the fact that the populist regime had nationalized many private industries, the banking system, and the insurance companies. As Moaddel explains, the Law for the Protection and Expansion of Iranian Industry provided for the nationalization of industry in three broad categories: (1) heavy industry, including metals, automobile assembly, chemicals, shipbuilding, aircraft manufacture, and mining; (2) industries owned by fifty specific individuals and one family who allegedly had acquired their wealth illicitly through influence with the outgoing regime; and (3) industries in economic difficulty whose liabilities exceeded their net assets. By 1982, the properties of more than 230 of the richest capitalists had been nationalized, which altogether constituted over 80 percent of all private industry.[52] And yet the expropriation of Pahlavi-era capitalists did not mean that the regime favored workers' control—or any other power center. Thus the councils began to encounter harassment from the IRP-controlled Pasdaran, the government began to appoint its own managers (after all, the factories had been nationalized), and the IRP began to set up parallel "Islamic councils."

The rise of class and ethnic struggles, competition among various political parties, and the challenge of the left during that first year were dealt with by the Islamists in a novel fashion. Through the takeover of the American embassy in November 1979, the Islamists managed to undermine their rivals, discover (or fabricate) incriminating evidence against them, and impress the populace with their own anti-imperialist credentials. The seizure of the embassy and of hostages was a drama staged by the Islamists with the intention of creating a situation of permanent revolution and mass mobilization controlled by the IRP. Its architects must have studied Mao Zedong's ideological mobilizations, and especially the Cultural Revolution. (The "students" who occupied the embassy may be likened to the Red Guard.) This action allowed the Islamists to practice considerable ideological manipulation as well as violence—in the name of their supreme anti-imperialism. Conspiracies against the revolution were seen everywhere, and the "students" who had seized shredded embassy records diligently put them together to discover an array of information that could be used against the opponents of the IRP and of Islamization. Ayatullah Shari'atmadari, President Bani Sadr (elected in January 1980), members of the National Front, and a number of secular government officials were tarnished by this evidence.

In April 1980 the increasingly powerful IRP initiated an "Islamic cultural revolution" aimed at the universities, which had a pronounced left presence and were governed by councils. As Khumaini said in 1981: "Our universities have changed into propaganda battlefields. Many university teachers are at the service of the West. What frightens us is cultural dependence. We fear ... universities which train our youth to serve the West or serve communism."[53] Bani Sadr endorsed the scheme—which entailed pitched battles with students and closing down the universities for two years—so he could stay on the bandwagon. But his days were numbered, for in the absence of a liberal-left alliance the Islamists steadily increased their influence and power.

The left camp, too, was by now rather badly divided. The Fada'i organization split in early 1980 into a "Majority" wing that endorsed the regime as anti-imperialist and progressive and a "Minority" wing that regarded it as reactionary and as having fundamentally altered the character and direction of the revolution. The Tudeh Party was for all practical purposes the party of Khumaini, endorsing his every move and statement, and taking the side of the Islamists (on the basis of their presumed anti-imperialism and nonalignment) in the intensifying battle with Bani Sadr in 1981. The Mujahidin were not willing to unite on an equal basis with the secular left in an anti-IRP front.

The ideological manipulation and mass mobilization afforded by the U.S. embassy takeover heightened following the Iraqi invasion of Iran in September 1980. Far from undermining the new regime (the reason behind the Iraqi invasion), the war increased patriotic sentiment, rallied the population around the regime, and allowed the regime, and especially the IRP, to bolster and strengthen its political position and increase its institutional supports. Bani Sadr's position meanwhile weakened. When the Mujahidin decided to support the beleaguered president and organized street demonstrations against the IRP, an angry Khumaini repudiated Bani Sadr and the government moved to impeach him. What followed for roughly a year after Bani Sadr and Mujahidin leader Massud Rajavi fled to Paris in June 1981 (assisted by supporters within the air force) was a cycle of violence marked by spectacular Mujahidin assassinations and bombings and exceedingly brutal regime reprisals. This implosion suggested that the Iranian revolution, like the French Revolution before it, had devoured its young. In the end the IRP would win its domestic war.

The Trajectory of Populism

As shown in the previous section, the populist coalition that succeeded in overthrowing the shah survived until June 1981. But between 1979 and 1981 an intense political and ideological struggle ensued, with Khumaini's Islamic populism surpassing the other brands of populism, such as that of Bani Sadr. All ideologies are systematically reproduced through ideological institutions (educational system, family, religion, Islamic councils, communications systems) and protected and guaranteed by the repressive apparatus (police and military). In times of social and political change, whoever dominates these institutions will dominate the state. And so, for the first two years of the Islamic Republic, liberals and clerics competed for control over the parliament, the ministries, agencies, and military inherited from the Pahlavi state, and the twelve revolutionary organizations: Pasdaran, Reconstruction Crusade, Revolutionary Courts, Revolutionary Committees, Imam Khumaini Relief Agency, Martyrs' Foundation, Housing Foundation, Mostazafin Foundation, War Veterans Foundation, Islamic Propaganda Organization, Literacy Movement, Guilds Affairs Committee. The postrevolutionary rivalry and contestation became increasingly violent, until a mini-civil war erupted in June 1981 that eventually eliminated the liberals, the Mujahidin, and the left from the political terrain.

The importance of controlling the flow of information was understood early on, when radio, television, cinema, and the press came under the authority of the regime. Over time, independent newspapers were suppressed, and criticism by leftists and liberals disallowed. The shah's censorship, so excoriated by the Islamic opposition, was reinstated by them. Control over the means of dissemination and the repressive apparatus facilitated the systematic indoctrination of the new ideology, or the creation of a new "power/knowledge" complex, following the dissolution of the revolutionary populist alliance in 1981.

The battle over the universities, which began immediately after the revolution, intensified in the spring of 1980, when the authorities decided to end the power of the left-wing student councils, led by supporters of the Fada'i, Paykar and Mujahidin, by declaring the councils null and void. When the students refused to acquiesce, the Revolutionary Guards were sent to the universities. In April, the Islamic Cultural Revolution was launched, which entailed the closing of the universities—and some activist high schools—for two years, while the curriculum was Islamized and ideological criteria devised for the staff and student body. The IRP was primarily responsible for this move, which had the blessings of Khumaini and the support of President Bani Sadr. The Islamic cultural revolution was an ideological attempt to rectify *gharbzadigi*: deculturation through Westernization. But it was also a political move, intended by its designers to eliminate rivals and bolster their own position.

Among the most profound changes to result from the cultural revolution lay in the area of women's rights and gender relations. Although Khumaini praised women for their massive participation in the revolution, and the constitution mentions their important role, women were regarded as having been most vulnerable to *gharbzadigi,* to deculturation and imperialist culture. The stereotypical "Westoxicated" woman was a middle-class and Westernized woman without productive contributions or reproductive responsibilities. If she worked at all, it was as a secretary, and her work was largely decorative and dispensable. Her access to money was considered a waste, because it was used to cover the cost of her own clothing, cosmetics, and imported consumer goods. She was preoccupied with her physical appearance and wore miniskirts and excessive makeup. She would mingle freely with men, smoke, drink, and laugh in public. If she read at all, she read romantic novels; she picked her role models from among Hollywood stars, American soap operas, and pop singers. Her light-headedness and lack of interest in politics and national issues had made her easy prey for commercialization and contamination by the West.[54] The solution to this vulnerability to the slings and arrows of the imperialists was compulsory veiling.

In the summer of 1980 veiling was made compulsory, and throughout the decade it was strictly enforced. Women were also not allowed to wear cosmetics or perfume in public. Women's voices were banned from radio and female singers barred from television. Only those foreign films were imported that had women actresses with hair coverings (an unintended consequence of which was to spur a national film industry). An ideological campaign was waged to tie women to home and family. Women were restricted from certain professions, such as law, and women university students were not allowed into programs such as agricultural engineering and veterinary sciences.[55] The regime assumed a pronatalist stance, banning abortions and distribution of contraceptives, extolling the Muslim family, and lowering the age of consent. Women's responses to new gender codes varied by class and political/ideological orientation, and ranged from enthusiastic support to acquiescence to outright hostility. Some Islamist women criticized the imposition of some of the changes, in particular compulsory veiling, which they felt would alienate many supporters of the "Islamic revolution." Fereshteh Hashemi pointed out that veiling is meant to be undertaken voluntarily by believers, whereas

> not only have we made the religious dress a job requirement for believing women and even for non-believers (of the religious minorities, the Christians and Jews), we are even specifying form and colour of dresses—something that is not obligatory in Islam.... And if the Islamic system wants to establish Islamic norms in society in order to combat Westoxication, why is this done only to women?[56]

Another critical view of compulsory veiling from Islamist women was expressed at a July 1980 seminar by Azam Taleghani, Zahra Rahnevard, Shahin Etezad Tabatabai, and Ansieh Mofidi. They suggested that "instead of imposition of *hejab* on women, public decency—meaning modest dressing and not using make-up—should be considered all over the country and lack of its observance punished (though only by those in charge)," an allusion to vigilante attacks on women. As an example of punishment they offered the case of Algeria, where "this was done by painting the legs of women in short skirts."[57]

A rather apposite view of compulsory veiling was expressed by the Fada'i Khalq (Majority) organization:

> The Islamic Republic of Iran claims that the imposition on women of the Islamic veil is a step towards the "moral cleansing" of society and eradication of the degenerate culture of the monarchical order. Without smashing the social and economic foundations of contemporary capitalism upon which the monarchical order was based, however, cultural degeneration cannot be uprooted. Furthermore, the veil is totally irrelevant to the uplifting or degeneration of culture.[58]

In fact, the veil was far from irrelevant to the regime. The model of Islamic womanhood that it sought to impose on the population was an integral part of the political-cultural project of Islamization. The transformation of Iran was seen as incumbent upon the transformation of women. (Re)definitions of gender are frequently central to political and cultural change.

After the fall of Bani Sadr and the ascendancy of the IRP, a project for Islamization was instituted that was based on the notion of an undifferentiated "Muslim people" distinguished from all others. The new "national identity" or "cultural identity" was largely an ideological construct, as it was not based on the complexity of the social structure, the array of cultural groups, and the diversity of aspirations. At any rate, this new identity entailed a violent assertion of the new "true representatives of the people" versus "the enemies of the people"—the articulation of radical difference in matters of culture, and construction of an "Other-

ness": the West and its domestic mimics. An Islamic populist ideology was articulated that was based on a specific reading of Islam (messianic, revolutionary,
scriptural) and a definition of "the authentic" that privileged the *mustazafin* (the
downtrodden) and those who professed to follow the "Imam's line," but was
biased against all others. Middle-class women, secular intellectuals, Kurds, leftists, religious minorities, and others were excluded from the category of "the
Muslim people." The Islamic cultural revolution was based on the hegemony of
the Imam's line (Khumainism) and opposed to any notion of pluralism.

   And yet, even in the making of this "Islamic ideology," elements from popular
culture and the worldviews of other classes were articulated. National independence, a more equitable distribution of wealth and resources, and the special
place of the poor were important elements of Islamic populism, as they tend to
be in other forms of populism. Under Khumaini, the Islamic populism of Iran
was also strongly Third Worldist and intractably opposed to the superpowers.
And although the cultures of capitalism and communism were excoriated, economic features of both systems were rather liberally borrowed and applied to the
Iranian economy. What distinguished Iran's populism from that of other Third
World populist movements was its grounding in Shi'a Islam, the dominant political role of clerics (although they operate within a parliamentary republican system) and cultural practices such as *hijab* and the ban on alcohol. But Islamic populism was an effective mobilizing ideology that could appeal to various strata of
the population, including members of the educated middle class, which responded
positively to the nationalist and anti-imperialist discourse. Thus, although the
regime relied on, and deployed, force to retain power, there was an attempt to elicit
consent through the populist ideology and the new revolutionary institutions.

   The Constitution of the Islamic Republic is an amalgam of theocratic, modern,
and Third Worldist elements.[59] Its radical populism is expressed in its assertion
that "the Iranian Revolution ... has been a movement aimed at the triumph of
all oppressed and deprived persons over the oppressor." It then goes on to reject
both capitalism and socialism — "Government does not derive from the interests
of a certain class" — and asserts that "the economy is a means, not an end. This
principle contrasts with other economic systems where the aim is concentration
and accumulation of wealth and maximization of profit. In materialist schools of
thought, the economy represents an end in itself." The constitution also declares
"economic independence" from foreign domination and elimination of "poverty
and deprivation" to be among the basic goals of the Islamic Republic. This is in
keeping with the typical populist objective of a "third way," in Iran's case crys-
tallized in the slogan "Neither East nor West." The two most important and controversial aspects of the constitution are the principle of *vilayat-i faqih* (the government of the jurist) and the prescribed economic model. It is worth noting, as
Behdad has pointed out, that whereas the former generated heated debates in

the Assembly of Experts, the latter was passed in the early days of the Islamic Republic without much discussion or disagreement but became controversial in the years that followed.[60]

It is worth pondering the eclectic philosophical content of the constitution, as well as its inconsistencies and contradictions. On the one hand, the constitution establishes theocratic structures, such as the rule of the *faqih*; a twelve-member Council of Guardians overseeing the Majlis (parliament) to ensure that legislation is in accordance with both the constitution and Islamic law; and the Supreme Judicial Council, which must be dominated by *mujtahids* (Islamic jurists). The constitution also establishes Twelver Shi'a Islam as the official religion, describes the Islamic Republic as "a system based on the belief in religious leadership and continuous guidance," maintains that sovereignty derives from God, and mandates efforts toward "unifying the world of Islam." On the other hand, the constitution describes Iran as an independent state with a foreign policy predicated upon nonalignment. It also firmly establishes Iran as a *republic*; after the *faqih*, the president is the most powerful figure, and his role is described as "implementing the constitution and organizing the relationship between the three powers." Elected directly for a four-year term by an absolute majority of the votes cast, the president is the chief executive who signs and executes the laws passed by the Majlis.

Despite the renunciation of democracy as a Western import, the constitution is in part democratic in the adoption of such procedures as popular representation, majority vote, parliament, and separation of powers. According to the constitution, Iran has both a "popular system" and a "divine government." Islamic rhetoric notwithstanding, the parliamentary structure is based on Western models: the deputies of the Majlis (a unicameral parliament) are elected by the direct vote of the people (Article 62), as is the president; the prime minister and the cabinet are chosen on the president's suggestion and with the Majlis's vote of approval; representatives of councils of provinces, towns, cities, districts, villages, and productive and industrial units are elected by direct vote of the people (Article 100).[61]

The constitution also provides for "the rights of the people," all of which have been circumscribed by the explicit qualification that they accord with the laws of Islam, and are thus open to interpretation rather than regarded as inalienable. For example, the rights of women are guaranteed, but "in all areas according to Islamic standards." And: "Publications and the press are free to present all matters except those that are detrimental to fundamental principles of Islam or the rights of the public."

Political Economy of the Outcome

During most of the 1980s, the discourses, goals, and policies of the Islamic Republic were strikingly similar to those of populist Third World leaders and regimes mentioned previously—with the exception that the discourse and policies of the Iranian leadership also contain a Shi'a Islam dimension. In the early 1980s, the series of radical economic measures, in addition to a radical foreign policy, led some observers to speculate that Iran had "delinked" from the world-system, or that its economy had ceased to be part of the world capitalist system.[62] In fact, populist ideologies do not constitute a "third way," a permanent and coherent alternative to capitalism and socialism. Rather, they combine elements of both political philosophies and economic systems. Hence the inconsistencies and contradictions of Islamic populism in Iran. In this section I will endeavor to show that the populist economic measures of the regime were an extension of the populist revolution, that they followed from the regime's inability to unite around a common political and economic program, and that they were a function of the transitional and exceptional character of the postrevolutionary Islamic-populist regime in the early 1980s.

The Khumainist State

Developments during the 1980s give credence to Skocpol's observation that revolutions result in strong centralized states.[63] The revolution ushered in an expanded role for the state in the economy, which was facilitated by the nationalization of large business concerns, insurance companies, and the entire banking sector; the constitution of the Islamic Republic granted the government power over foreign trade. The war with Iraq also played a role in the evolution of the state and of the ruling group. The war required national mobilization that involved all Iranians in the war in much the same way as, in the French Revolution, the Committee of Public Safety's 1793 *levée en masse* rendered "all Frenchmen in permanent requisition for army service." State building was achieved in part through the incorporation and bureaucratization of previously autonomous revolutionary institutions (e.g., neighborhood committees, the Pasdaran, the Rural Reconstruction Crusade), the formation of a large number of new, war-related agencies and institutions, and the strengthening of the new fighting forces, the Pasdaran and Basij, in addition to the military inherited from the shah. All this contributed to the expansion of the state apparatus, though as yet in the absence of a dominant class controlling the means of production.

The Islamic Republic has been variously described as capitalist, an intermediate regime, fascist, and totalitarian.[64] Another perspective, found mostly in Persian-language writings of the left, but also argued by former Prime Minister Bazargan, regards the Islamic Republic to be Khumainist, an Iranian variant of Bonapartism. The idea of a Bonapartist regime had some resonance in left circles in the early days of the Islamic Republic. Certainly the power sharing by and political participation of secularists from the National Front (Karim Sanjabi, Dariush Furuhar), liberal Islamists (Mehdi Bazargan), conservative ulama (in the Council of Guardians), radical clergy (Ayatullah Taliqani), and Third Worldists such as Ghotbzadeh and Yazdi—all loyal to Khumaini, the charismatic leader of the revolution—suggested this. During 1979 there was not yet a consolidated state; in Iran, as in Bonapartist France, a ruling elite had not yet monopolized the organization of force and power. The writings of Nicos Poulantzas on the state, social classes, and political power were also used by left-wing writers after the revolution to come to grips with the character of the new regime.[65] The composition of the new regime, and the relative weight and hierarchy of the social groups represented, was a matter of much debate. But all the left analyses recognized the heterogeneity of the "power bloc" or the "organ of compromise," as the new political authority was variously called.[66] Just as Marx described Bonapartist France as an "exceptional state," the new regime was regarded as transitional and exceptional. In France's case, the exceptional character of the state derived from continuing class and political struggles, and was thus a transitional phenomenon of a period in which the bourgeoisie was incapable of putting its own house in order and presenting a common front to the peasantry and proletariat. In Iran's case, it reflected a period in which the question of class power, relations of domination and subordination, and property rights were not yet defined. Inasmuch as there was not one ruling class, there was not a cohesive, unified state representing any one set of interests. This is what gave the revolutionary state its high degree of autonomy. This also contributed to the new regime's popularity and legitimation, for it was seen by the masses to be above the class struggle.

Thus, it may be useful to call the postrevolutionary state *Khumainist,* and understand it as a transitional state arising from exceptional circumstances in which diverse interests contended and no one class held sway within the state apparatus or over the means of production. This would help to explain both the ability of the regime to carry out a series of ad hoc radical and populist economic measures with a redistributive orientation and its inability to establish a coherent economic plan. Let us briefly consider the redistributive economic measures.

The new regime had a mandate from the revolution to alter, if not transform, the shah's economic strategy (the system of production and accumulation) and the stratification system (the system of appropriation and distribution). Guidelines existed in the radical economic theories of Bani Sadr and Taliqani[67]—both of whom agreed that the state should have vast powers to organize economic life in order to ensure social justice and equality—and the left-wing groups (Fada'i, Mujahidin, Tudeh), who were greatly inspired by Latin American dependency theory. Moreover, workplace councils and workers' control had emerged during the revolution, and were rapidly proliferating in 1979. Peasants and national minorities were engaging in land seizures and attempting their own forms of councils, cooperatives, and autonomy. Workers and intelligentsia alike were in favor of nationalization, particularly of large firms, banks, insurance companies, and foreign trade. All this resulted in economic measures, during Bazargan's tenure and Bani Sadr's presidency, that were opposed to big capital, foreign cap- ital, and "dependent relations" with Western countries and the superpowers. As noted by Mazarei, the main developments were (1) the redistribution of wealth and income toward the lower-income echelons of society, (2) an increased role for the state in the provision of social welfare, (3) policies favorable to the agri- cultural sector, and (4) political and economic independence from the West and increased economic self-reliance.[68]

According to the 1979 constitution, the economy comprises three sectors: state, cooperative, and private. The state sector includes "all the large-scale and major industries, foreign trade, major mineral resources, banking, insurance, energy, dams and large irrigation networks, radio and television, post, telegraphic and telephone services, aviation, shipping, roads, railroads, and the like." In 1979, all banks were put under government ownership; contracts with multinational corporations were nullified and all major industries taken over by the state; for- eign trade was under de facto if not de jure control of the government. The lack of de jure state control reflected rejection by the Council of Guardians of parlia- mentary bills to establish formal state ownership as contrary to Islamic respect for private property and entrepreneurship. (The Council of Guardians was a body created to ensure that bills accorded with Islamic law and with the constitution, and was highly conservative in economic matters.) Economic sovereignty was to be achieved by means of a self-reliant strategy (*khudmukhtari*). Attempts focused on reviving agriculture and promoting small-scale productive units by means of various credit and price-support policies. A parallel policy of import-substitution industrialization and protectionism was also followed in the hope of stimulating domestic production of certain durable and nondurable consumer products. Most new industrial investment went to production units that used more local inputs. The nationalization of banks was meant to support the new changes. The mass media were used to convince the people that national independence could not be achieved without accepting hardship in the short run and making sacrifices in both levels and quality of living standards. The "Western pattern of consumption" was also denounced as non-Islamic and harmful to the goal of self-sufficiency.

Two crucial institutions were created to alter economic relations and to effect social justice: the Housing Foundation (which provided housing for the poor, particularly in urban areas) and the Reconstruction Crusade (which provided rural areas with electricity, water, feeder roads, schools, health clinics, housing, and other social and infrastructural services). Legislation was passed to reduce the gap among wage rates, and as a result workers' wages were raised by 60 percent. A policy of price support in the form of subsidies for basic needs items was instituted to protect the poorer groups from the rampant inflation that had fol- lowed the economic decline during the revolution. Modifications were proposed in the tax system to make it more progressive and to prevent excessive concen- tration of wealth. Nationalization of major industries, banks, insurance companies, and foreign trade was meant to weaken further possibilities of emerging large-scale private accumulation.

In the period immediately following the revolution, and as demonstrated by Behdad and Mazarei, redistribution was the principal policy goal, attained through the expropriation and reallocation of property, reorientation of government expenditures toward the lower-income and rural sectors, increased minimum wages and the rise of new parastatal institutions for the subsidization of the living standard of the lower-income segments of the population. These parastatal organizations included the Bunyad-i Mustazafin (Foundation for the Oppressed), which took over the assets of the Pahlavi family, the Jihad-i Sazandigi (Rural Reconstruction Crusade), and the Housing Foundation. These organizations were financed with confiscated property along with public and private funds. The proliferation of cooperatives and special attention to agriculture and the rural sector reflected the populist economic strategy. According to official figures, by June 1981 the Rural Reconstruction Crusade had built 15,000 kilometers of rural roads and distributed 15 billion rials in loans to peasants.[69] A concerted electrification program was also instituted. Ultimately, the economic model that was adopted in the Islamic Republic was what Worsley has identified as the typical populist economic strategy: the mixed economy, in which large-scale private ownership would be under the firm control of the state.[70]

These measures substituted for a concerted national development plan. In the Islamic Republic populist and redistributive economic measures (widespread distribution of food and allocation of some housing, cheap utilities, and oil, which favored the urban poor and war veterans and families of war "martyrs") substituted for rational planning and production investment. The latter proved impossible to develop because of deep divisions within the political elite. In 1980, the new parliament passed bills for further land reform and for the nationalization of foreign trade, but both were vetoed by the Council of Guardians. These vetoes of measures backed by the populists but opposed by the Council of Guardians went back and forth for several years. The major disagreement within the political elite was over the question of state control and nationalization versus the prerogatives of capitalists and the private sector. Among the controversial issues were land reform, labor law, urban tenants' rights, industry-first or agriculture-first economic development, heavy industrialization or appropriate technology, private ownership rights, and the direction and composition of trade. A five-year national development plan (1983–87, with a twenty-year horizon) was drafted in 1981 but was aborted in 1983 because of disagreements within the regime over the direction of development and investment.[71] Subsequent attempts to formulate a coherent and consistent development strategy ran into many ideological obstacles, political conflicts, and practical difficulties.[72] The main opposing factions were the "technocrats," who preferred a growth-oriented strategy with attention to specific sectors and expansion of the private realm, and the "radicals," who favored continued redistribution, regional development, and a strong state sector. In large part because of the cleavages within the ruling elite, and also because of the distortions caused by the war with Iraq (1980–88), the regime had uneven and limited success in redirecting the course of economic development in various sectors of the economy.[73]

Thus, we conclude that during most of the 1980s, whatever else the postrevolutionary Islamic regime was, it was not properly speaking a capitalist state: capital accumulation was not its raison d'être or defining feature. Nor can it be said that the bourgeoisie was the dominant political and economic class, and that its ideas held sway. During the 1980s, certainly until the death of Khumaini and the end of the Iran-Iraq war, the Iranian state was a transitional state that could institute only ad hoc populist economic measures. One may hypothesize that the Islamic Republic is following a Third Worldist pattern in which a fraction of the petty bourgeoisie (military or civilian) comes to power and evolves into a state or bureaucratic bourgeoisie.[74] Nowhere has a clerical caste played as dominant a role in politics and in state power as in Iran. However, Iran's clerics do appear to be part of the petty bourgeoisie. The regime's statist and nationalist ideological orientation also follows a Third World populist pattern.

Limited Social Transformation

Unlike other revolutions and revolutionary states—especially Russia, China, and Cuba—the Iranian revolution and the Islamic Republic are notable for their inability to transform socioproductive relations.[75] Changes have certainly occurred, especially in the "superstructure"—political system, cultural realm, official ideology—but the "economic base" has not been transformed.

What social structural changes have occurred? In the first instance, the dominant class under Pahlavi rule was dispossessed of its industrial, financial, and commercial holdings. The leaders of the Islamic Republic were not from the dominant economic (landed, commercial, or industrial) classes. Political and economic power shifted from the Pahlavi family and the big bourgeoisie (industrialists, financiers, large capitalist landowners) to the petty bourgeoisie: its traditional stratum is favored economically, whereas the new/modern wing occupies the bureaucracy and military. In the economy, the state sector became the largest sector, spanning industry and services (education, health, welfare, public utilities, rail and air transportation, communications, major media). The government implemented a series of populist economic measures intended to favor lower-income groups and the rural sector. The mosque became a powerful institution with a role to play in social welfare.

In the early years, the economic independence of the bazaar was checked by state controls (especially over prices and foreign trade) and the existence of a large public sector. Constitutional limitations on private property ("private ownership, legitimately acquired, is to be respected; the relevant criteria are determined by law") were a consistent source of tension between the state and the private sector, and between the pro- and anticapitalist factions within the regime. But by all accounts the bazaar has thrived, especially from the black market. According to Mazarei, the decline in oil revenues in the face of a high demand for foreign exchange caused by military imports and capital flight led to the intensification of capital controls, the introduction of a system of multiple exchange rates, and the rise of a very active black market for foreign exchange. The principal beneficiaries of this situation have been the bazaaris, who have become the nouveau riche of the Islamic Republic.[76] Moreover, as Behdad has shown, in spite of initial improvements in income distribution immediately after the revolution, distributional inequality has increased steadily since.[77] It is entirely conceivable that if the workers' councils had survived as strong and independent bodies, with the role in decision making and management they had initially sought, income distribution would not have deteriorated.

Most of the radical populist economic policies that were attempted at different points in the postrevolutionary period up to the end of 1982 had to be subsequently suspended, reversed, or modified under enormous domestic and international pressures, and owing to the exigencies of a war economy. As mentioned above, the first social, economic, and cultural development plan of the Islamic Republic was scrapped because of factional politics within the state. Support for agriculture, rural and regional development, small-scale productive units, labor-intensive techniques, major economic reforms, and social services was reduced. Wages and employment were frozen in the state sector, but price subsidies for basic consumption items continued. Taxes were increased in an attempt to reduce dependency on oil but also to boost the public budget. Under the new policy, deficit spending became acceptable to the government and a more active role was given to the private sector and market mechanisms. A number of nationalized industries were sold to the public or returned to their original owners, and the cooperative sector was left to its ambiguous and weak position in the economy. Modern technology again became acceptable to planners and policy makers. The money saved was not, however, put into building new industrial capacities. Rather, much of it went to the war effort.[78]

The war economy and declining oil revenues made state control over foreign trade imperative; the government reduced imports of luxury items and concentrated on importing foodstuffs, spare parts, raw materials, and other basic goods, in addition to weapons supplied principally by China and North Korea. Revolutionary ideology—and the constitution—required that Iran reduce its dependence on oil exports, diversify the economy, engage in balanced growth, and favor Third World and Islamic countries in its trade policy. But by 1982 the Islamic Republic was trading mainly with Western countries and capitalist Third World countries (West Germany, Italy, Japan, Turkey, Brazil), while also increasing economic ties with Eastern Europe (but not the USSR). Moreover, its foreign exchange receipts were still derived almost exclusively from oil exports—which the government increasingly sold for cash on the spot market at discounted prices.

The policy of diversifying the sources of dependency for exports and imports was only marginally successful. The price of oil continues to be determined within the capitalist world market.[79] Trade with socialist and Third World countries, except for Turkey and Pakistan, did not expand to any significant degree, despite frequent policy pronouncements to the contrary. With the failure of the new policy and worsening economic problems, the state turned to an emergency plan in 1986.[80] By the end of the decade, the Iranian government had overturned many of the early populist measures. The Islamic Republic's first five-year plan, which went into effect on March 21, 1990, will decrease the size of the public sector and encourage the growth of the private sector. Karshenas and Mazarei report that the government has adopted a policy of privatizing a notable proportion of the state-owned enterprises. The latter are to be gradually returned either to their previous owners or to the public. There will also be a shift from the earlier reliance on the agricultural sector to the expansion of manufacturing for export. Karshenas and Mazarei explain that as the scarcity of managerial and skilled resources is an impediment to realization of the plan, the government is actively encouraging expatriate entrepreneurs, technicians, and engineers to return to the country. Finally, they note that the government "has also recognized the necessity of reintegration in the world economy." Since 1990 the government has extended invitations to foreign investors, along with generous taxation and operations incentives. Joint ventures are encouraged in numerous areas, particularly in the fields of petroleum and petrochemicals.[81]

It should also be noted that the 1979 constitution was amended in 1989. One change was that the function of prime minister was dropped in favor of a strong presidential system. The current president of the Islamic Republic, Hujjatalislam Hashimi Rafsanjani, is a strong supporter of the stabilization and adjustment program, which is quite orthodox in nature. In one Friday sermon, President Rafsanjani expressed support for the government's elimination of subsidies and dual pricing, and defended the government's appeal to Iranian businessmen abroad to invest in Iran. This latter development has been widely disparaged by the economic radicals as constituting "the return of the capitalists."[82]

In a paper written in 1987, I suggested that two roads were open to Iran:

> One is to continue and strengthen the statist strategy currently in place. The alternative is to follow a now familiar Third World pattern, where restrictions on domestic private sector activities could be relaxed, especially if private entrepreneurs can be coaxed into becoming more export oriented. Further, the leadership might re-examine previous restrictions on transnational corporations and

other sources of private direct investment. In a word, they could effect a re-linking, albeit on different terms, with the world market or world capital.... In such a situation, TNCs can be particularly seductive; they can bring in capital that does not add to the foreign debt burden, they provide employment, and they can plug the developing country into an already existing international marketing network, boosting exports. This may yet be tried out in the Islamic Republic of Iran.[83]

It is clear that the second road has been taken by the authorities in the Islamic Republic. It would thus appear that Iran's populist revolution, and its exceptional and transitional state, has evolved into a capitalist social and political order.

Summary and Conclusions

Some authors have noted that the Iranian revolution appears enigmatic, not easily classified as either a bourgeois or socialist revolution.[84] Many authors have settled for "Islamic revolution" (also the definition of the Islamists themselves), which I find unsatisfactory in its emphasis on ideology reduced to religion. A related debate concerns the normative dimension: Can the Iranian revolution be regarded as emancipatory and historically progressive, as were previous revolutions? Or do the retrograde aspects of the revolutionary outcome undermine the romantic myth of revolution?[85]

The key concept I have adopted to understand and explain the contradictory processes and apparent anomalies of the Iranian revolution is *populism.* I have argued elsewhere that the Iranian revolution's populist nature derives from the contemporary international context of a world-system dominated by the United States, a regional context of the turn to Islamism as a solution to crisis, a national context of distorted development of a capitalistic type, and a broad-based revolutionary alliance with a unifying cross-class discourse.[86] The *differentia specifica* of the Iranian revolution were the increasing use of religious symbols of Shi'a Islam in the course of the revolution, the dominant role of a charismatic religious figure, and the assumption of state power by a clerical caste. The success of the anti-shah revolution lies in a propitious international context, as Skocpol has noted;[87] a populist alliance that included an unprecedented general strike; and the clergy's use of their traditional institutional base, the mosque, as well as seminaries and theological lecture halls, and their alliance with the bazaar, the traditional market.

The Iranian revolution ought not to be called an Islamic revolution because Islamization and clerical rule were consolidated *after* the revolution, following two years of intense political and social conflicts. And although the revolution certainly had a strong ideological dimension, this should not be reduced to its religious element (Shi'ism), for it was far more complex in its component parts.

After the February 1979 victory, the populist discourse of the revolutionary movement was transformed into the ideology of Islamic populism, which I have defined as the ideology of the transitional postrevolutionary Iranian state, led by the traditional petty bourgeoisie. This ideology and class stratum focused on politics and culture, such as changes in the legal system and regulation of gender, and was incapable of effecting complete social transformation, particularly in the realm of economic relations.

In the latter half of the 1980s, many of the radical-populist initiatives of the Islamist state undertaken in the early years were overturned. The objective of eliminating dependency is now regarded as infeasible, and state managers are actively pursuing the reincorporation of Iran into the capitalist world-system. This has coincided with a relaxation of earlier restrictions on women's mobility, including access to fields of study and occupations previously barred to them. The Islamist state has renounced its earlier pronatalist policy in favor of family planning; in 1991, newspapers were replete with articles and editorials on the need to curtail the high population growth rate. Although periodic crackdowns on women's dress continue, there are now more open criticisms of such actions, especially by outspoken Islamist women in professional and government positions. These women, as well as male "moderates" and liberalizers within the government, are keen to improve the legal status and social positions of women in the Islamic Republic.[88]

The trajectory from radical Islamic populism to what appears to be its endpoint, the institutionalization of a market economy, suggests that the ostensibly *sui generis* "Islamic revolution" is a variant of the classic bourgeois revolution.

Notes

My thanks to John Foran and Reza Afshari for critical comments on the first draft of this chapter.

1. Manocher Dorraj, *From Zarathustra to Khomeini: Populism and Dissent in Iran* (Boulder, Colo.: Lynne Rienner, 1990).

2. Ibid., 165.

3. Ibid., chaps. 3–6.

4. Misagh Parsa, *The Social Origins of the Iranian Revolution* (New Brunswick, N.J.: Rutgers University Press, 1989).

5. Ibid., 251.

6. Representative of these approaches are Said Amir Arjomand, *The Turban for the Crown: The Islamic Revolution in Iran* (New York: Oxford University Press, 1988); Mohsen M. Milani, *The Making of Iran's Islamic Revolution: From Monarchy to Islamic Republic* (Boulder, Colo.: Westview, 1988); M. M. Salehi, *Insurgency through Culture and Religion* (Boulder, Colo.: Lynne Rienner, 1988).

7. This has been my argument in "One Revolution or Two? The Iranian Revolution and the Islamic Republic," in *Socialist Register 1989,* ed. Ralph Miliband, Leo Panitch, and John Saville (London: Merlin, 1989), 74–101; and "Populist Revolution and the Islamic State in Iran," in *Revolution in the World-System,* ed. Terry Boswell (Westport, Conn.: Greenwood, 1989), 147–63.

8. Arjomand, *The Turban for the Crown,* 108–14.

9. Ibid., pt. II, especially chap. 8.

10. Ibid., 197–209.

11. Arjomand also seems to be using "integrative revolution" somewhat differently from the way Clifford Geertz applied the term, extending Edward Shils's work on primordial ties and civil society. Both Geertz and Shils emphasize primordial, personal, and sacred ties, and the search for identity, especially in modernizing contexts. For an elaboration of this early debate and a reformulation, see Allan Hoben and Robert Hefner, "The Integrative Revolution Revisited," *World Development* 19, no. 1 (1991): 17–30.

12. Among the outstanding treatments of gender in postrevolutionary Iran are the following: Azar Tabari and Nahid Yeganeh, eds., *In the Shadow of Islam: The Women's Movement in Iran* (London: Zed, 1982); Guity Nashat, ed., *Women and Revolution in Iran* (Boulder, Colo.: Westview, 1983); Haleh Afshar, "Women, State and Ideology in Iran," *Third World Quarterly* 7 (April 1985): 256–78; Valentine Moghadam, "Women, Work and Ideology in the Islamic Republic," *International Journal of Middle East Studies* 20 (May 1988): 221–43; Afsaneh Najmabadi, "Power, Morality and the New Muslim Womanhood," in *State and Culture in Afghanistan, Iran, and Pakistan,* ed. Ali Banuazizi and Myron Wiener (Albany: State University of New York Press, 1993); Nayereh Tohidi, "Modernity, Islamization, and the Woman Question in Iran," in *Gender and National Identity: Women and Politics in Muslim Societies,* ed. Valentine M. Moghadam (London: Zed, in press).

13. Peter Worsley, *The Three Worlds: Culture and World Development* (Chicago: University of Chicago Press, 1984), 293.

14. Peter Wiles, "A Syndrome, Not a Doctrine: Some Elementary Theses on Populism," in *Populism: Its Meanings and National Characteristics,* ed. Ghita Ionescu and Ernest Gellner (London: Weidenfeld & Nicolson, 1969), 166.

15. Paul Drake, "Requiem for Populism," in *Latin American Populism in Comparative Perspective,* ed. Michael L. Conniff (Albuquerque: University of New Mexico Press, 1982), 237.

16. David Raby, "Populism: A Marxist Analysis," *McGill Studies in International Development* 32 (1983): 3.

17. Gino Germani, *Authoritarianism, Fascism and National Populism* (New Brunswick, N.J.: Transaction, 1978); Gino Germani, *Marginality* (New Brunswick, N.J.: Transaction, 1980). This perspective was adopted by Farhad Kazemi in *Poverty and Revolution in Iran: The Migrant Poor, Urban Marginality and Politics* (New York: New York University Press, 1980).

18. On the informal sector, see Alejandro Portes and John Walton, *Labor, Class and the International System* (New York: Academic Press, 1981); Alejandro Portes, Manuel Castells and Lauren Benton, eds., *The Informal Economy: Studies in Advanced and Less Developed Countries* (Baltimore: Johns Hopkins University Press, 1989).

19. Cited in V. Khoros, *Populism: Its Past, Present and Future* (Moscow: Progress, 1984), 7.

20. David Apter, *The Politics of Modernization* (Chicago: University of Chicago Press, 1965), 2.

21. C. B. MacPherson, "Revolution and Ideology," in *Ideology, Politics and Political Theory* (Belmont, Calif.: Wadsworth, 1969), 304.

22. Nicos Mouzelis, *Post-Marxist Alternatives* (London: Macmillan, 1990), 190.

23. Khoros, *Populism,* 10.

24. Drake, "Requiem for Populism," 232.

25. Michael L. Conniff, "Introduction: Toward a Comparative Definition of Populism," in *Latin American Populism in Comparative Perspective,* ed. Michael L. Conniff (Albuquerque: University of New Mexico Press, 1982), 20.

26. Dorraj, *From Zarathustra to Khomeini,* 17.

27. Germani, *Authoritarianism,* 88.

28. Dorraj, *From Zarathustra to Khomeini,* 17.

29. Drake, "Requiem for Populism," 221.

30. Dorraj, *From Zarathustra to Khomeini,* 17. See also Mouzelis, *Post-Marxist Alternatives,* 189–90.

31. Raby, "Populism."

32. Karl Marx, *The Eighteenth Brumaire of Louis Bonaparte* (New York: International, 1967).

33. Octavio Ianni, quoted in Raby, "Populism," 21. This point has also been made by Mouzelis in his critical remarks on Germani's work and on Laclau's approach to populism. *Post-Marxist Alternatives,* 178–96.

34. Ernesto Laclau, *Politics and Ideology in Marxist Theory* (London: Verso, 1977), 100–111.

35. See John Thompson, *Studies in the Theory of Ideology* (Berkeley: University of California Press, 1984), 16–41; Mohammad Tavakoli-Targhi, "Revolutionary Discourses in Modern Iran" (mimeo, University of Chicago, Department of History and Center for Middle Eastern Studies, November 1987), 4.

36. Maurice Meisner, *Marxism, Maoism and Utopianism* (Madison: University of Wisconsin Press, 1982), 112.

37. The concept of populism is also useful for understanding Islamic revival in the Middle East, avoiding the tendency to explain events in the Middle East in terms of intrinsic properties of Islam. That is, the Islamist movements in the Middle East may be regarded as a type of populist movement.

38. Immanuel Wallerstein, "Dependence in an Interdependent World: The Limited Possibilities of Transformation within the Capitalist World Economy," in *From Dependency to Development: Strategies to Overcome Underdevelopment and Inequality,* ed. Heraldo Muñoz (Boulder, Colo.: Westview, 1981), 267–93.

39. The role of the United States as obstacle to revolutionary transformation would be pertinent to the case of Nicaragua. For a thorough discussion of the Third World's encounter with the United States, see Gabriel Kolko, *Confronting the Third World* (New York: Pantheon, 1988).

40. Christopher Chase-Dunn, "Marxism and the Global Political Economy" (paper presented at the annual meetings of the American Sociological Association, Washington, D.C., August 1990), 5.

41. Hooshang Amirahmadi, *Revolution and Economic Transition: The Iranian Experience* (Albany: State University of New York Press, 1990); Richard Fagen, Carmen Diana Deere, and Jose Luis Coraggio, eds., *Transition and Development: Problems of Third World Socialism* (New York: Monthly Review Press, 1986); Carlos Vilas, *The Sandinista Revolution: National Liberation and Social Transformation in Central America* (New York: Monthly Review Press, 1986); Terry Boswell, ed., *Revolution in the World-System* (Westport, Conn.: Greenwood, 1989).

42. Amirahmadi, *Revolution and Economic Transition,* 10.

43. Richard Fagen, "The Politics of Transition," in *Transition and Development,* ed. Fagen et al., 249–63.

44. Mouzelis, *Post-Marxist Alternatives,* 140. Here Mouzelis elaborates on the concept of relative autonomy of the state and of political practices, and argues that not all forms of state power can be explained in terms of the accumulation interests of a class. I find his argument quite apposite in the case of the Iranian postrevolutionary regime.

45. For details on the role of industrial workers in the Iranian revolution, see Valentine

Moghadam [Shahrzad Azâd, pseud.], "Workers' and Peasants' Councils in Iran," *Monthly Review* 32 (October 1980): 14–29; Valentine Moghadam, "Industrial Development, Culture, and Working-Class Politics: A Case Study of Tabriz Industrial Workers in the Iranian Revolution," *International Sociology* 2 (June 1987): 151–75; Valentine Moghadam, "Industrialization Strategy and Labor's Response: The Case of the Workers' Councils in Iran," in *Trade Unions and the New Industrialization of the Third World,* ed. Roger Southall (London: Zed, 1988), 182–209. See also Assef Bayat, *Workers and Revolution in Iran: A Third World Experience of Workers' Control* (London: Zed, 1987); Parsa, *The Social Origins,* 141–67, 267–75.

46. This is shown in Habib Ladjevardi, *Labor Unions and Autocracy in Iran* (Syracuse, N.Y.: Syracuse University Press, 1985).

47. Ahmad Ashraf and Ali Banuazizi, "The State, Classes and Modes of Mobilization in the Iranian Revolution," *State, Culture and Society* 1, no. 3 (1985): 3–40; William Shephard, "Islam and Ideology: Toward a Typology," *International Journal of Middle East Studies* 19 (August 1987): 307–36.

48. Dilip Hiro, *Iran under the Ayatollahs* (London: Routledge & Kegan Paul, 1985), provides a detailed narrative. See also Shaul Bakhash, *The Reign of the Ayatollahs: Iran and the Islamic Revolution* (New York: Basic Books, 1984).

49. Azar Tabari, "Islam and the Struggle for Emancipation of Iranian Women," in *In the Shadow of Islam,* ed. Tabari and Yeganeh, 14.

50. All quotes are from Mansoor Moaddel, "Class Struggle in Post-Revolutionary Iran," *International Journal of Middle East Studies* 23 (August 1991): 321. See also Azad, "Workers' and Pesants' Councils"; Bakhash, *The Reign of the Ayatollahs.*

51. Moaddel, "Class Struggle," 324; Azad, "Workers' and Peasants' Councils"; Moghadam, "Industrialization and Labor's Response"; Bayat, *Workers and Revolution.*

52. Moaddel, "Class Struggle," 324.

53. Imam Khomeini, "The Meaning of the Cultural Revolution," in *Islam and Revolution: Writings and Declarations of Imam Khomeini,* trans. and anno. Hamid Algar (Berkeley, Calif.: Mizan, 1981).

54. Tohidi, "Modernity, Islamization."

55. For further details, see the works cited in note 12 above. See also Valentine M. Moghadam, *Modernizing Women: Gender and Social Change in the Middle East* (Boulder, Colo.: Lynne Rienner, 1993), chap. 6.

56. Fereshteh Hashemi, "Discrimination and the Imposition of the Veil," in *In the Shadow of Islam,* ed. Tabari and Yeganeh, 193.

57. Azam Taleghani, Shahin Tabatabai, et al., quoted in ibid., 194.

58. Fedayeen-Khalq (*sic*), quoted in ibid., 136.

59. *Constitution of the Islamic Republic of Iran,* trans. Hamid Algar (Berkeley, Calif.: Mizan, 1980).

60. Sohrab Behdad, "The Political Economy of Islamic Planning in Iran," in *Post-Revolutionary Iran,* ed. Hooshang Amirahmadi and Manoucher Parvin (Boulder, Colo.: Westview, 1988), 107–25.

61. A booklet listing the amendments to the constitution (thirty-four of them) and the two additional chapters and articles (chapters 13 and 14, and articles 176 and 177) is available in Persian, as is the constitution, which includes the amendments.

62. Nodari Simonya, *The Destiny of Capitalism in the Orient* (Moscow: Progress, 1985), 130; James Petras and Morris Morley, "Development and Revolution: Contradictions in the Advanced Third World Countries—Brazil, South Africa and Iran," *Studies in Comparative International Development* 16 (Spring 1981): 514–35.

63. Theda Skocpol, *States and Social Revolutions: A Comparative Analysis of France,*

Russia, and China (Cambridge: Cambridge University Press, 1979).

64. On the regime as capitalist, see Fada'i-Minority, *Nabard-i Khalq* (The people's struggle) (Tehran: OIPFG, 1981). On the application of Kalecki's "intermediate regime," see Djavad Salehi-Isphahani, "Economic Consequences of the Iranian Revolution" (paper presented at the fifteenth annual meeting of the Middle East Studies Association, Philadelphia, November 1981). On the regime as fascist, see Said Amir Arjomand, "The Causes and Significance of the Iranian Revolution," *State, Culture and Society* 1, no. 3 (1985): 41–66; see also Fergus Bordewich, "Fascism without Swastikas," *Harper's,* July 1980, 65–71. On the regime as totalitarian, see Cheryl Benard and Zalmay Khalilzad, *The Government of God: Iran's Islamic Republic* (New York: Columbia University Press, 1984).

65. Especially cited was Nicos Poulantzas, *Political Power and Social Classes* (London: Verso, 1974).

66. The term *organ of compromise* was coined by the Fada'i group; *power bloc* was suggested by individuals associated with Rahai. The group Rah-i Kargar published a series of articles on fascism that considered the possibility that clerical fascism was taking root in Iran.

67. See Abulhassan Bani Sadr, *Iqtisad-i Tauhidi* (Economics of divine unity) (Tehran, n.p.: 1978); see also Seyed Mahmoud Taleghani, *Islam and Ownership,* trans. Ahmad Jabbari and Farhang Rajaee (Lexington, Ky.: Mazda, 1983).

68. Adnan Mazarei, Jr., "The Iranian Economy under the Islamic Republic: Institutional Change and Macroeconomic Performance (1979–90)" (Working Paper No. 6165, University of California, Los Angeles, Department of Economics, March 1990); Behdad, "The Political Economy"; Amirahmadi, *Revolution and Economic Transition.*

69. Hossein Bashiriyeh, *The State and Revolution in Iran, 1962–1982* (New York: St. Martin's, 1984), 177.

70. Worsley, *The Three Worlds,* 306.

71. Amirahmadi, *Revolution and Economic Transition,* 101–13.

72. Ibid., 115.

73. Mazarei, "The Iranian Economy."

74. For a somewhat similar approach applied to Algeria, see Rachid Tlemcani, *State and Revolution in Algeria* (Boulder, Colo.: Westview, 1986).

75. Nicaragua is another example of limited social transformation, although in its case the active hostility of the United States was much more determinant.

76. Mazarei, "The Iranian Economy."

77. Sohrab Behdad, "Winners and Losers of the Iranian Revolution: A Study of Income Distribution," *International Journal of Middle East Studies* 21 (August 1989): 327–58.

78. Amirahmadi, *Revolution and Economic Transition,* chap. 3.

79. Michael Renner, "Determinants of the Islamic Republic's Oil Policies: Iranian Revenue Needs, the Gulf War, and the Transformation of the World Oil Market," in *Post-Revolutionary Iran,* ed. Hooshang Amirahmadi and Manoucher Parvin (Boulder, Colo.: Westview, 1988), 183–209.

80. Amirahmadi, *Revolution and Economic Transition,* 164.

81. Massoud Karshenas and Adnan Mazarei, Jr., "Medium-Term Prospects of the Iranian Economy," in *Iran and the Arabian Peninsula: Economic Structure and Analysis* (London: Economist Intelligence Unit, 1991), 19–24.

82. See "Sowing Discord among the Nation—Strategy of Revolution's Enemies," *Kayhan International,* July 20, 1991, 3.

83. Valentine Moghadam, "Oil, the State, and Limits to Autonomy: The Iranian Case," *Arab Studies Quarterly* 10 (Spring 1988): 236.

84. Farideh Farhi, "Class Struggles, the State, and Revolution in Iran," in *Power and Sta-*

bility in the Middle East, ed. Berch Berberoglu (London: Zed, 1989), 90–113; Valentine Moghadam, "Iran: Development, Revolution and the Problem of Analysis," *Review of Radical Political Economics* 16 (Summer-Fall 1984): 227–40.

85. See Moghadam, "One Revolution or Two?" for a political reading of the Iranian revolution from a socialist perspective. See also Arjomand's works for a view on the other side of the debate.

86. Valentine Moghadam, "Socialism or Anti-Imperialism? The Left and Revolution in Iran," *New Left Review* 166 (November–December 1987): 5–28; Moghadam, "One Revolution or Two?"; Moghadam, "Populist Revolution."

87. Theda Skocpol, "Rentier State and Shi'a Islam in the Iranian Revolution," *Theory and Society* 11 (May 1982): 265–84.

88. The evolution of the various dimensions of Iranian women's status is explored in Moghadam, *Modernizing Women,* chap. 6.

Chapter 9

A Century of Revolution: Comparative, Historical, and Theoretical Perspectives on Social Movements in Iran

John Foran

It is time to draw up a provisional balance sheet of our reflections on social movements across Iranian history. The present volume represents a collective effort to reflect on the meanings of Iran's long century of revolutions since 1891. The fact that rebellions, revolutions, ethnic nationalist movements, and coups and countercoups have occurred so frequently and *for so long* bids us to think this through with the use of comparison and the application of theory. The fact that this has been a century of *revolution* means that we have to go beyond the social scientific literature on social movements (although much has been taken from this body of work, directly and indirectly) to conceptual frameworks where national-level struggles for power occupy center stage. But the *persistence* of revolutionary movements in Iran calls for creative rethinking of the standard writing on revolutions as well. My goal in this concluding chapter is to draw out the theoretical and comparative lessons of this volume, indicating briefly how Iran forces some rethinking of theories of social change, what comparative insights emerge from reflection on Iranian history, and where the frontiers of research on social movements in Iran currently lie.

Iran and Theory

The relationship of the studies contained in this volume to the social science literatures on social movements and revolutions bears explicit examination. "Social movement theory," of course, covers a vast territory that cannot be fully, or even adequately, explored here. A major recent review of the corpus by Doug McAdam, John D. McCarthy, and Mayer N. Zald argues that since the 1970s (and before the current emphasis on the "new social movements" and their theorizations) two major perspectives have come to dominate the field. These are resource mobilization theory (associated with McCarthy, Zald, and Anthony Oberschall) and the political process model (associated with McAdam and Charles Tilly, although the latter is often linked to resource mobilization as well, suggesting that these are in fact variants of a single paradigm). Resource mobilization theory tends "to emphasize the constancy of discontent and the variability of resources in accounting for the emergence and development of insurgency" and therefore seeks to understand how emerging social movements capture and utilize the resources needed to survive—communications networks, income flows, public spaces, and the like. The political process model, for its part, lays more emphasis on "(a) the importance of indigenous organizations, and (b) a favorable 'structure of political opportunities.'"[1] Some of the studies in this volume fit squarely within these frameworks, notably Misagh Parsa's resource mobilization treatment of the 1960–63 events and Sussan Siavoshi's look at the organizations active in the oil nationalization movement, implicitly rather close to the political process view of the world. Most of our studies, indeed, attend to aspects of social change identified as crucial by each of these perspectives.

By the late 1980s, important critiques and challenges to resource mobilization (RM) were being articulated, refocusing theoretical attention on such neglected topics as culture, identity, and the social psychology of participants. As Aldon Morris and Carol McClurg Mueller put this in their recent influential edited volume:

> From the very beginning, critics of the RM approach were quick to point out that social movements could not be reduced to business organizations or industries or to conventional political behavior. They argued that grievances, ideologies, manipulations of symbols through oratory and the written word, media portrayals, consciousness raising, and identities all had to be taken into account in studying a social movement. In short, the critics charged that RM was without a social psychology that could explain what real human beings do either inside movements or in reaction to them.[2]

In large part, this "turn" in social movement theory was a response to the conceptual challenges posed by what became known as the new social movements, for peace, for the environment, for gender (and, to a lesser degree, racial) equality, in Western Europe and North America. But just as some critics have questioned the intrinsic newness of the "new" social movements,[3] so the present studies suggest that the Third World setting and the historical sweep of Iran's social movements definitively rule out the rubric of the new social movements. Nevertheless, a concern for culture, ideology, power, and class is a constant feature of our analyses.

The varied insights of social movement theory, then, in its many forms, have provided us with useful leads for our work on Iran. Yet the First World origins of most of this literature, and the corresponding emphasis on organized political movements aimed more at reforming existing states and civil societies (however revolutionary some of these reforms would be), inevitably suggest that its applicability to Iran must come only at a relatively high level of abstraction. The social movements chronicled in this volume have for the most part been tremendous upsurges from below carried out in highly repressive contexts by loose alliances—

in one or another respect rather different from the professional social movement organizations and locally rooted affinity groups that populate the Euro-American debates. Thus, the stakes in Iran, more so than in the West, have been national in level, contestations over *state power*. This has implications for the nature of alliances and organizations, ideology and culture, and the impact of the world-system. Indeed, Third World realities have meant that the Iranian state, however much a despised target of these movements, has not always been the ultimate center of power in these struggles, which tend to spill across national boundaries into a world-systemic setting whenever the state has seemed in jeopardy.

As I suggested in chapter 7, the case of the Iranian revolution of 1977–79 has brought into question another theoretical discourse, that of the sociology of revolutions. And though the latter's own historical trajectory has mirrored the social movement literature's swing from social psychology in the 1960s to structuralisms in the 1970s and then partway back to culture more recently, the literature on revolutions, with a few notable exceptions such as Charles Tilly's oeuvre, has been kept strangely segregated from that on social movements. As I tried to argue earlier, this literature can tell us more about the Iranian case because its emphasis on national contests for power and its international and historical frames of reference make its fit with events in Iran since the tobacco rebellion rather closer than the social movements literature on the whole. Its limitations, however, are also quite telling, as they bring us to the frontiers of theory: *how* culture should be brought into relationship with political economy, where structure and agency intersect, and how micro- and macro-level contexts and processes interpenetrate remain unresolved questions with which the contributors to this volume have had to grapple empirically. While we may not have formulated general prescriptions for going about this, we have clearly seen, I think, that concrete historical analysis requires interdisciplinary consideration of culture, politics, and economy; the interplay of domestic and international actors and structures; and the daunting complexities and ultimate fragility of coalition formation. In all of these respects, Iran provides rich ground for theoretical refinements and further explorations.

Thinking across a Century of Revolution in Iran

In surveying the patterns of Iran's social movements of the past hundred years, we find six rebellions or revolutionary attempts—the tobacco rebellion in 1891, the Constitutional Revolution from 1905 to 1911, the autonomy movements in Kurdistan and Azerbaijan after World War II, the oil nationalization movement under Musaddiq from 1951 to 1953, the generalized effervescence of the 1960–63 period, and the Iranian revolution proper after 1977 (the Jangali guerrillas of 1916–21 might also be included, and are mentioned briefly below). Of these, only 1891 and 1979 can be counted as "successes" in any sense of the word. We also have two coup d'états, in 1925 and 1953, both successful. As noted in the introduction, this is a record with few parallels anywhere: China, Mexico, and Bolivia may come closest. Iran thus presents a case of what Jeff Goodwin has called "persistent insurgency,"[4] although by this he means intractable revolutionary wars such as Guatemala's from the 1960s to the 1990s, whereas Iran involves a series of discrete social movements over a much longer period of time. Let us reflect comparatively on the causes, processes, and outcomes of this pattern across Iran's several cases.

Causes

I have presented a theory of the causes of the 1977–79 revolution in chapter 7, with reference to the consequences of dependent development, the vulnerabilities of the exclusionary personalist state, the elaboration of effective political cultures of resistance and opposition, the grievances sharpened by an economic downturn, and the opportunities opened up by a favorable world-systemic conjuncture. Can these factors shed light on the outbreaks of other cases, in Iran and elsewhere?

In 1891, the impact of the first sustained Western penetration of Iran's markets, polity, and social structure, and the haplessness of the Qajar dynasty in the face of this, underpinned the country's first mass social movement of the modern era. The concrete expression of these structural trends was contained in the very issue at stake: the granting of a monopoly concession for Iran's entire tobacco crop by the monarchy to an English company. This galvanized a public that had been growing disquieted by the gradual European encroachment upon the country's sovereignty. As Mansoor Moaddel indicates in chapter 1 of this volume, embryonic discourses of nationalism and Islam under attack began to circulate, from the avowal of the Shiraz merchant who burned his entire tobacco stock rather than sell it to the English, saying, "I have sold this tobacco to God!" to the placard that appeared at Tehran embassies, inns, and mosques, asking: "The tobacco is Iranian, the consumers are Iranian, why is a foreigner the exclusive buyer and seller?"[5] An economic downturn was more *implied* by the general alarm about the concession than experienced by the population, an effective functional substitute for the real thing, it seems. And the international context was favorable in that England's rivals for hegemony in Iran, the Russians, were vehemently opposed to the concession.

The Constitutional Revolution saw an intensification of most of these factors. Economic penetration of Iran accelerated between 1890 and 1905, led by a huge rise in Russian trade, such that Marvin Entner has concluded: "To a remarkable extent, Persia had been drawn into Russia's economic orbit and was a functioning part of her economy."[6] The Qajar state was as recalcitrant to granting a measure of power to its subjects as ever. The political cultures of opposition had, in the interim, matured considerably, now including articulate demands, both religious and secular, for a constitution and national assembly, along with the first stirring of socialist ideologies in Iran, as Janet Afary has so well documented. Between 1900 and 1905 a marked economic downturn occurred, with high rates of inflation, unemployment, and urban hunger for bread. The defeat of Russia by Japan in their war in the Pacific in 1904–5 and the outbreak of a revolution at home stayed the tsar's hand when the Constitutional Revolution began; and British officials on the spot made the grounds of their embassy available to the strikers who shut down the Tehran bazaar and its mosques until the shah granted a Majlis and constitution in the revolution's moment of triumph in July-August 1906.

The international comparative context of these events is quite striking. Between 1905 and 1911, similar revolutions broke out in Russia, the Ottoman Empire, Mexico, and China, suggesting at least a prima facie case for a favorable world-systemic conjuncture. The similarities go deeper, however: all four of these states were autocratic (three were imperial monarchies); Mexico and Russia had undergone textbook spurts of growth in the previous generation; all witnessed an explosion of oppositional cultures involving ideas of democracy and republicanism, nationalism, and egalitarian ideals, with national variations, to be sure; and finally, worldwide economic uncertainty since 1900 and recession in 1907–8 found an echo in at least the Ottoman Empire and Mexico, if not elsewhere as well. These sketchy observations provide some suggestive leads for further, detailed comparative investigations.[7]

The events in Kurdistan and Azarbaijan in 1945–46 have their own specific characteristics, as Amir Hassanpour has shown in chapter 4. They differed from all the other national-level movements discussed in this volume in that they were struggles of oppressed national minorities ("nations," from their own point of view) within Iran. Yet if Kurdistan was relatively less industrialized than the rest of Iran, Azarbaijan and its capital Tabriz were poles of wealth and development; thus, in an odd sense, the two taken together can perhaps be viewed as an instance of the effects of dependent development. Their relations with the Iranian state were certainly marked by exclusion, underrepresentation, and denial of their aspirations. And the political cultures articulated by the KDP and DPA naturally drew on their respective linguistic, ethnic, and national identities in appeals powerful enough to paper over the real class differences present in and between the two movements. It is hard to say whether 1945 marked an economic downturn, but the war had certainly meant a decline in economic activity and increased hardships for most Iranians (and indeed, labor, liberal democratic, and tribal movements flourished elsewhere in the country at the same time). In the two rebellious provinces, the crucial difference was perhaps their location in the Soviet zone of occupation at a time of incipient Cold War definition, which facilitated the establishment of the two republics in the very beginning, at least.

Our factors recur in Muhammad Musaddiq's bold undertaking to nationalize

Iranian oil in 1951. Backed by an increasingly large and politically sophisticated urban middle- and working-class population (one of the effects of dependent development under Reza Shah in the 1930s), he directly confronted Muhammad Reza Shah's last-ditch efforts to rebuild an exclusionary state after the relative liberalization of Iran's polity during the World War II Allied occupation. This movement stands out for its predominantly secular political culture, based on Musaddiq's twin visions of a more democratic and an independent Iran. The conjuncture proved favorable in that the British, Musaddiq's initial adversaries in this affair, were taken unawares by the speed of the nationalization process and their lack of a foothold once they had been expelled from the country. The economic climate in 1949–51, like the political, was one of uncertainty and disorder heightened by a bout of inflation.[8]

In 1960–63, most of the factors come together, though, as always, in historically specific fashion. Iran was just beginning to experience the effects of the shah's industrialization and modernization plans as the oil economy resumed its growth after the British-led international embargo of the Musaddiq era came to an end in 1953. The shah was also reasserting his control politically, laying the foundations for the national security state of later in his reign with the establishment of SAVAK, increased policing of dissidents, and expansion of control over the army. As Misagh Parsa has shown, the wings of the movement — students, National Front, and clerical radical — were diverse, and their political cultures reflected this, with first one, then another, coming to the fore by itself. Parsa has also documented the difficult economic conjuncture of debt and inflation in the early 1960s, and the significant pressure from the United States for the shah to liberalize his regime, an opening that the opposition tried to broaden into a thoroughgoing change in the system, which in the end proved only a dress rehearsal for revolution a short generation later.

I have covered the relevant aspects of the 1977–79 events in considerable detail in chapter 7. Here, I would like to suggest the ways in which these events find parallels elsewhere in the Third World. At precisely the same time, as is well known, Nicaragua underwent a social revolution and El Salvador witnessed a major revolutionary attempt (the parallels of the late 1970s and the earlier worldwide conjuncture of 1905–11 would likewise make an interesting cross-national historical comparison). Nicaragua, despite its small size and lack of economic weight, did experience a relatively vibrant period of growth in the 1960s, led by agricultural modernization and some light industry. Somoza and the shah ran repressive, personalistic dictatorships of the same stripe. In Nicaragua, too, religion, nationalism, and socialism permuted into a powerful homespun ideology under the leadership of the Sandinistas. The 1972 earthquake that leveled Managua touched off a long period of economic stagnation in which Somoza enriched himself at all others' expense, and the same Carter human rights-oriented foreign policy that put the shah inadvertently off balance meant that Somoza, who had no illusions about liberalization, did not enjoy significant American support in the crisis. The Cuban revolution of 1953–59 shows the same pattern, occurring in "one of the four or five most developed nations in Latin America, and the most developed tropical nation in the entire world."[9] Batista as dictatorial analogue; Fidel's blend of national, democratic, and social justice themes; U.S. aversion to the regime after the repression of the 1957 Cienfuegos naval revolt; and an economic downturn created by the rebels themselves as they disrupted sugar production in the latter part of 1958 fill in the conceptual boxes in the model.[10]

Although these remarks are necessarily brief and compressed, it is my hope that they can at least suggest the broad comparability of the outbreaks of a number of Third World social movements, both across Iranian history and in other regional contexts. Comparative reflection on social revolutions—attempted and successful, in Iran and elsewhere—suggests some common causal patterns among Third World social movements aimed at taking state power that researchers may wish to pursue futher.

The Process of Rebellion

In an important forthcoming new work that dovetails with many of the concerns raised in this volume, historian Nikki Keddie meditates on the question, "Why has Iran been revolutionary?" In doing so, she draws attention to another interesting aspect of Iran's social movements that would seem to have few parallels. In each of the movements of the past hundred years, revolts have been urban, but not, as one might expect, confined to a single city, such as the capital. Keddie advances a number of possible explanations, ranging from the cultural unity of the central plateau to the historical fact that Tabriz, Qazvin, Isfahan, Shiraz, and Tehran have all served as capitals in the past five hundred years, to a well-developed argument that social movements in modern Iran have witnessed an unusually strong alliance between two prominent classes, the merchants of the bazaar and the ulama.[11]

Keddie's theses, provocative as they are, do not of course fully exhaust the subject of who, exactly, has made revolutions in Iran, and what form their processes have taken. Keddie's arguments, as well as those of the authors in this volume, point in the direction of the salience of broad urban coalitions of actors, what I have called in my own work Iran's multiclass, urban, populist coalition.[12] The classes involved in this alliance have included merchants and the ulama, but also more secular intellectuals among the leaderships. They could never have been mass movements without the participation of many groups lower in status, including artisans, industrial and service workers, and urban marginal classes. Historically in Iran, since at least the time of the tobacco rebellion (and, in fact, from earlier times as well), women have marched literally in the forefront of the crowds that confronted the state in demonstration after demonstration. Ethnicity, too, although a factor of division in the Iranian social structure along both tribal and confessional lines, has often been overcome up to a point in the movements discussed in these pages: Azeri-speaking Tabrizis played a leading role in the Constitutional Revolution, and Kurds rebelled on their own after 1979, to name just two instances, not to mention the independent role of ethnicity in the events in postwar Azarbaijan and Kurdistan chronicled by Amir Hassanpour.

The broadness of these coalitions has been one of the factors of their strength in touching off movements massive enough to force concessions from the state. This mass character has roots in the complexities of Iranian social structure, which go far beyond any simple two-class schema. It has drawn sustenance from the grievances created by integration into world markets on disadvantageous terms and the adamant refusal of the state to grant participation unless confronted with a unified population. And it has been expressed in diverse political cultural idioms given the different worlds inhabited by the actors who have made it up, a diversity that has often found common ground around basic shared concerns with national and popular sovereignty.

Equally remarkable in the process of these social movements have been the tactics employed, which have consistently been far more peaceful than their revolutionary counterparts outside Iran. This is not to say that violence has ever been far from the surface of these intense political clashes, but that it has tended to come overwhelmingly from the side of the government, directed against the movements, which have displayed remarkable restraint and resolve in its face. Sit-ins in the form of *basts* go far back in Iranian history, and have religious roots in the institution of the sanctuary that could be found from governments or private parties in mosques, shrines, and sometimes the homes of religious leaders. This form of gathering opened up opportunities for communication and respite from the violence in the streets, and was prominent in 1891, 1905–6, and 1977–78. Demonstrations were more confrontational forms of protest, but likewise unarmed and for the most part peaceful. Iran's social movements have produced countless large public demonstrations, sites of creative popular expression in the form of slogans, banners, and formally articulated political objectives. These have often been the tangible signals to the authorities that the movement opposing them would not bend, even in the face of massacres. When violence erupted, the deaths of activists meant the initiation of new rounds of protests, with bloodstained clothes paraded through the streets and funeral ceremonies providing the occasion for focused popular resentment to rekindle itself. Two final peaceful and effective tactics have been the boycott and the general strike, which were most successful in 1891 and 1978. The roots of these innovative tactics, it has been suggested, lie in Iranian political culture as well as creative appropriation of "Western" forms, and were to a degree forced on the population by the state's monopoly of the instruments of coercion (an intriguing parallel is suggested with the American civil rights movement). The results have been impressive in many ways, and bear more study by students of social movements and revolutions.

Outcomes

In turning to the outcomes of these movements, the issue at stake is how and why did their multiclass coalitions fragment? Why—with the exception of the movement to end the tobacco concession, and with the (only partial) exception of the recent revolution—is this a history of repeated defeats? How and why, on the other hand, did the two attempted coups of 1921–25 and 1953 succeed?

Initial successes gave way to ultimate fragmentation in every movement discussed in this book. Even in 1891–92, the movement contented itself with the cancellation of the concession; the radical intellectuals who wanted to make it a springboard for revolution or an end to all foreign concessions were unable to interest leading ulama in these wider aims. Part of an explanation for the fragility of these projects surely lies in the complex social and political cultural dynamics that shaped their visions. Every movement, as the essays in this volume document, tapped diverse political discourses to mobilize constituents. This was necessary because of the very diversity of the coalitions, by class, ethnicity, gender, and region. Often these differences were put aside and an admirable unity of action was displayed in order to attain the goal, whether it be the cancellation of an insulting concession, the grant of a constitution and national assembly, the establishment of regional autonomy vis-à-vis Tehran, control over Iran's oil, or the overthrow of the monarchy. Once a modicum of success had been won, however, the very heterogeneity that was necessary to achieve critical mass became a hindrance, as the different underlying groups and classes, each with its own vision of the future, came into conflict. This is most apparent in the fragmentation of the constitutionalist side after the 1909 restoration of the Majlis,[13] but it also shaped the limited outcome of the tobacco rebellion noted above, contributed to the decomposition of the Kurdish and Azarbaijani positions after World War II, fatally weakened the Musaddiq experiment in its final hours, and ensured that the various initiatives of the 1960–63 period would not coalesce, instead leaving them to be picked off one by one by the state. Even the recent revolution, the one most obvious "success" in this long record of upheaval, underwent this process, with dramatic and deadly consequences after 1979. As Val Moghadam explains in chapter 8, the ulama-dominated Islamic Republican Party skillfully outflanked all organized competitors among liberals, social democrats, and the left, and took control of the workers' councils, bazaar, countryside, educational system, mass media, the Majlis, and gender relations at the expense of the aspirations of many of the groups who had made the revolution in the first place.

Problems of underdevelopment, outside pressures, and the diversity of state institutions have also seriously hampered the efforts of these movements in power. Economic realities weakened the governments in Tabriz and Mahabad by 1946, undermined Musaddiq's short-lived "oil-less economy," and have kept the present government from delivering on many of the hopes of the population. These problems were not only the legacies of a long history of dependency and distorted development, but also sometimes the direct consequence of heavy outside pressures on the movements: English and Russian power held the line in 1892 to preserve their other concessions in the country; Russia sent troops in 1911 to close down the Majlis, with British acquiescence; Truman put enormous pressure on the Soviet Union in 1946 to withdraw from northern Iran in the opening shots of the Cold War; the United States, egged on by the British, used covert action to oust Musaddiq in the 1953 coup; and postrevolutionary Iran has had to contend with not only general U.S. hostility but a massive invasion and bloody war with Iraq. These pressures have rarely been withstood, especially when they have intersected with the fragmentation of the coalition internally; even when they have, as in the case of the Iran-Iraq war, they have irreparably damaged the prospects for real economic and political change.[14]

The two coups of 1921–25 and 1953 reveal some of the limits of social movements in Iran in terms of holding state power. The political situation in 1920–21, as Michael Zirinsky has shown, was one of crisis and weakness for the Qajar dynasty, faced by British proposals for a condominium in Iran (the notorious 1919 Agreement), the challenges of several regional movements, fiscal crisis, and lack of popular legitimacy. These created the vacuum into which strode the man of the hour, Reza Khan. The Qajars would prove no match for him once he was able to restore order as minister of war and skillfully neutralize external and internal forces. In 1953, the Pahlavi dynasty that he had created came within a hair's breadth of falling, but this time Prime Minister Muhammad Musaddiq fell victim to the difficulties of holding state power when only part of the state's institutions were under his control. Faced with slim majorities in the Majlis, a wavering army and police, and on thin constitutional ground himself after the shah's sudden departure at the height of the crisis, Musaddiq had little room to maneuver, given the coalitional, economic, and external problems documented by Sussan Siavoshi in chapter 5. A striking international comparison exists between these events and the fall of Allende in Chile in 1973. Both leaders had nationalized a key commodity "owned" by a foreign power; both faced international boycotts and blockades as a result; both were enormously popular among some segments of the population but had difficulty building the broad alliances needed to sustain themselves internally; and both ultimately fell to military coups designed in the United States by the CIA.[15]

One final international comparison to note is the contrast between the success of the 1979 events in Iran and the failure of the Salvadoran revolutionaries to come to power in the 1980s. Despite the broad structural similarities of dependent development and military rule, and the elaboration of vibrant opposition cultures, the Salvadoran revolutionaries faced three crucial differences. Military rule was collective, not personalized, and in the 1980s elections were offered that opened up the political system to a degree. Although there was a powerful current of liberation theology in El Salvador, embodied in the beloved archbishop Oscar Arnulfo Romero, the ideology of the Farabundo Martí National Liberation Front was resolutely Marxist-Leninist (far more so than the Sandinistas in Nicaragua). These factors pulled and pushed much of the middle class away from the populist alliance. Nor did the Salvadoran revolutionaries enjoy a world-systemic opportunity, as the regime received a massive U.S. infusion of weapons, advisers, and money under the Reagan administration, rather than lessons in human rights. El Salvador thus represents a case of attempted, but failed, revolution in circumstances where we might otherwise have expected a revolutionary movement to come to power.[16]

I have argued, then, that serious obstacles have faced all social movements in Iran, even when they have managed to attain a measure of state power. These findings suggest the daunting challenge that revolutionary social movements face in general, and call for further reflection on ostensibly successful outcomes. The fragmentation of revolutionary multiclass alliances is not unique to Iran: Further work must be done on the question of whether and how revolutionary social movements have avoided it. The future of Iran itself in the 1990s and beyond, of course, will also tell us much about how these processes are played out.

Frontiers of Social Movement Research on Iran

It remains to complete our account of where things stand in the study of social movements in Iran and in Iran itself. If much has been accomplished in the last decade, much remains to be done. For example, one of the least studied, yet most important, social movements in twentieth-century Iran, the Jangali (forest) movement that flourished in the Caspian province of Gilan during World War I and after, still needs a full-length treatment in English.[17] With roots in the socialist movement whose origins have been chronicled in this volume by Janet Afary, and with its defeat as one of the steps in Reza Khan's rise to the throne as told here by Michael Zirinsky, it calls out for careful investigation as a missing link in the chain leading from the upsurge of the Constitutional Revolution to the coup establishing the Pahlavi dynasty. It represents a fascinating mixture of nationalist, socialist, and militant Islamic discourses, as played out in the turbulent histories of its two most famous leaders: Mirza Kuchik Khan, a radical preacher, died on the frozen slopes of the Elburz mountains in December 1921, just months after he arranged the murder of his one-time collaborator, Haydar Khan, leader of the fledgling Communist Party of Iran. Behind them stood a vigorous mass movement interested in radical transformation of the Iranian countryside, something that has not come about to this day. In the context of the time, their fortuitous self-defeat played a crucial role in the rise of the Pahlavis to power in Iran, with fateful consequences for Iranian history. Their story deserves a full telling by a future student of social movements in Iran.

A glaring conceptual gap that runs through the whole literature on Iran is the intersection of ethnicity, class, and gender in the social structure and in movements for social change. This is perhaps understandable, as these are relatively recent concerns raised by feminist and ethnic studies scholars in the American academy. Just as there has been a vast increase in scholarship in English on Iran generally since the revolution by a new generation of Iranians working abroad, so these new concerns are starting to generate good new studies of gender in Iran, but there is a huge amount of work to do before the three principles of stratification receive adequate attention taken together, taken across time, and applied to social movements. Once a better, more sophisticated "map" of social structure has been drawn up for Iran and elsewhere, the next questions can be asked: Who makes revolutions, and why? And what difference does attention to mobilization by race and gender as well as class make for understanding the origins of social revolutions?[18] We have gone only a very small part of the way—and no doubt not far enough—in the present volume.

A third under-studied and difficult-to-study new area of inquiry on Iranian social movements lies in the field of social history. We need to know more—much more—about the everyday lives of the many classes and groups that have made up the social movements discussed here. Their daily concerns, ways of thinking and feeling, and the many small actions that have added up to bring each of these movements to our attention remain largely opaque to us. In part, no doubt, this is inevitable: knowledge of such subjects is difficult to obtain even in the present, let alone at such a distance, historically and spatially. For Iranian history, the sources are buried rather deep, if they were ever created in the first place, because of the difficult material and political circumstances of both the actors and their recorders throughout most of it. We have scattered studies of a few groups and classes at specific points in time, but there remain huge gaps in our knowledge: Iran still awaits its E. P. Thompson to draw these pieces together into a compelling treatment of its social history, which would be of immense value to scholars interested in its social movements.

If these are some of the conceptual frontiers of Iranian social movements, where do matters stand today, in late 1994? The Iran-Iraq war now thankfully over and the towering figure of the shah's overthrow, Khumaini, now dead, the clerical state faces an urgent need to deal with the unmet aspirations of the people who brought it to power by their actions in 1979. These needs remain pressing:

economically, although oil production and revenues are up, so are arms spending, foreign borrowing, and inflation.[19] All, including increased oil production, are problematic trends from the viewpoint of improving material living standards (if oil revenues are not invested with great foresight and wisdom, it is better to leave them in the ground, as Musaddiq once observed). Politically, the government of President Hashemi Rafsanjani seems solidly entrenched after his reelection for a four-year term in 1993. Yet Rafsanjani is under siege from both his "left" and his "right" (if such labels have any meaning in contemporary Iran): Islamists seek the export of the revolution throughout the Muslim world and the revival of a cultural (Islamic) revolution internally, whereas other factions, usually labeled "moderates" or "pragmatists," want to open the economy to the West and relax the state's intrusion into private life in order to attract professionals back to rebuild the country. The result is a continuing stalemate in terms of blueprints for the revolutionary reconstruction of society and economy, one that the U.S. hostage crisis and war with Iraq merely postponed.

What, then, does the future hold? Our reflections on Iran's century of revolution suggest that movements for change are persistently periodic across Iran's history. In the social sciences, however, prediction is impossible, if not illegitimate. The lessons of the past, if they are of any use here, betoken further upheavals until and unless the fundamental economic, political, cultural, and ultimately human issues faced by the people of Iran are tackled by the extraordinary coalition of forces it would take to make some progress with them, if not to resolve them. The memories of the activists who people these pages, as well as the dignity of the generations to come, deserve no less.

Notes

1. See Doug McAdam, John D. McCarthy, and Mayer N. Zald, "Social Movements," in *Handbook of Sociology*, ed. Neil J. Smelser (Newbury Park, Calif.: Sage, 1988), 697, and the sources cited therein. The classic works of the resource mobilization and political process perspectives, respectively, may well be John D. McCarthy and Mayer N. Zald, "Resource Mobilization and Social Movements: A Partial Theory," *American Journal of Sociology* 82 (1977): 1212–41; Doug McAdam, *Political Process and the Development of Black Insurgency, 1930–1970* (Chicago: University of Chicago Press, 1982). Charles Tilly straddles the line in *From Mobilization to Revolution* (Reading, Mass.: Addison-Wesley, 1978).

2. Aldon D. Morris and Carol McClurg Mueller, "Preface," in *Frontiers in Social Movement Theory*, ed. Aldon D. Morris and Carol McClurg Mueller (New Haven, Conn.: Yale University Press, 1992), ix.

3. Kenneth H. Tucker, "How New Are the New Social Movements?" *Theory, Culture and Society* 8, no. 2 (1990): 75–98. The classic new social movement text is Alberto Melucci, *Nomads of the Present: New Social Movements and Individual Needs in Contemporary Society* (Philadelphia: Temple University Press, 1989), although the term and its texts go back to the beginning of the decade.

4. Jeff Goodwin, "Why Insurgencies Persist, or the Perversity of Indiscriminate State

Violence" (paper presented at the annual meeting of the American Sociological Association, Miami, Fla., August 1993).

5. Both are quoted in Faridun Adamiyyat, *Shurish bar Imtiaznameh-i Rizhi* (The struggle against the tobacco concession) (Tehran: Intisharat-i Payam, 1360/1981), 25, 17. I discuss these events in "Dangerous Populations? Concepts for the Comparative Study of Social Movements in Qajar Iran," in *City and Society in Qajar Iran,* ed. Michael Bonine (in press).

6. Marvin Entner, *Russo-Persian Commercial Relations, 1828–1914* (Gainesville: University of Florida Press, 1965), 77.

7. I have made this comparison in a bit more detail in "Dangerous Populations?" and the Middle Eastern part of it in "Dependency and Resistance in the Middle East: 1800–1925," in *Political Power and Social Theory,* vol. 8, ed. Diane E. Davis and Howard Kimeldorf (Greenwich, Conn.: JAI, 1993). A broad comparative sketch has also been undertaken by John Mason Hart, *Revolutionary Mexico: The Coming and Process of the Mexican Revolution* (Berkeley: University of California Press, 1987), chap. 7.

8. More research should be done with respect to this claim. On the international plane, the argument is on surer ground; there had been little change in British attitudes since Winston Churchill had told the British Parliament in June 1914 that Iran was a particularly reliable source for Britain's oil needs because "neither the native government nor the native inhabitants are capable of pursuing a prolonged and formidable policy of hostility toward us." Quoted in D. C. M. Platt, *Finance, Trade, and Politics in British Foreign Policy, 1815–1914* (Oxford: Clarendon, 1968), 242.

9. Timothy P. Wickham-Crowley, *Guerrillas and Revolution in Latin America: A Comparative Study of Insurgencies and Regimes since 1956* (Princeton, N.J.: Princeton University Press, 1992), 166.

10. For more detailed analytic comparison, see my articles, "A Theory of Third World Social Revolutions: Iran, Nicaragua, and El Salvador Compared," *Critical Sociology* 19, no. 2 (1992): 3–27; "The Causes of Latin American Social Revolutions: Searching for Patterns in Mexico, Cuba, and Nicaragua," in *World Society Studies,* vol. 3, *Conflicts and New Departures in World Society,* ed. Peter Lengyel and Volker Bornschier (New Brunswick, N.J.: Transaction, 1994).

11. Nikkie R. Keddie, *Iran and the Middle East* (London: Macmillan, in press), especially chap. 5, "Multi-urbanism in Iran's Revolts and Rebellions."

12. John Foran, *Fragile Resistance: Social Transformation in Iran from 1500 to the Revolution* (Boulder, Colo.: Westview, 1993). See also the work of Valentine Moghadam on the populist aspects of Iranian social movements, in particular, "Populist Revolution and the Islamic State in Iran," in *Revolution in the World-System,* ed. Terry Boswell (Westport, Conn.: Greenwood, 1989), 147–63.

13. See John Foran, "The Strengths and Weaknesses of Iran's Populist Alliance: A Class Analysis of the Constitutional Revolution of 1905–1911," *Theory and Society* 20 (December 1991): 795–823 and the sources cited therein on this process.

14. For more on the reasons for the limits of the 1978–79 revolution, and for a comparison with Nicaragua, see John Foran and Jeff Goodwin, "Revolutionary Outcomes in Iran and Nicaragua: Coalition Fragmentation, War, and the Limits of Social Transformation," *Theory and Society* 22 (April 1993): 209–47.

15. I briefly discuss this comparison in *Fragile Resistance,* noting that it extends even to the similarities between their last words to the public. At his trial, after the coup, Musaddiq said: "Since it is evident, from the way that this tribunal is being run, that I will end my days in the corner of some prison, and since this may be the last time that I am able to address myself to my beloved nation, I beseech every man and woman to continue in the

glorious path which they have begun, and not to fear anything." Quoted in Farhad Diba, *Mohammad Mossadegh: A Political Biography* (London: Croom Helm, 1986), 189. While the coup was going on, Salvador Allende addressed Chile on September 11, 1973: "Probably Radio Magallanes will be silenced and the calm metal of my voice will not reach you. It does not matter.... I have faith in Chile and in her destiny. Others will surmount this gray, bitter moment in which treason seeks to impose itself. You must go on, knowing that sooner rather than later the grand avenues will open along which free people will pass to build a better society." This speech is found in Laurence Birns, ed., *The End of Chilean Democracy* (New York: Seabury, 1974). I have changed the translation slightly.

16. I develop this comparison in "A Theory of Third World Social Revolutions." It could be argued, of course, that the FMLN was not defeated militarily either, and that the negotiated solution to the conflict represents a victory, in some sense, depending on the future trajectory of events in El Salvador. On El Salvador's stalemate, see Goodwin, "Why Insurgencies Persist."

17. The main works on the subject include Ibrahim Fakhra'i, *Sardar-i Jangal* (Jangal commander) (Tehran: Intisharat-i Javidan, 1362/1983); Shapur Ravasani, *Nahzat-i Mirza Kuchik Khan Jangali va Avvalin Jumhuri-yi Shura'i dar Iran* (Mirza Kuchik Khan's movement and the first Soviet Republic in Iran) (Tehran: Chapaksh, 1363/1984); Mustafa Shu'a'iyan, *Nigahi beh Ravabit-i Shuravi va Nahzat-i Inqilabi-i Jangal* (A look at the relationship between the Soviet Union and the revolutionary Jangal movement) (Florence: Mazdak, 1970). In English, interested readers should consult Ervand Abrahamian, *Iran between Two Revolutions* (Princeton, N.J.: Princeton University Press, 1982), 112–16; M. Reza Ghods, *Iran in the Twentieth Century: A Political History* (Boulder, Colo.: Lynne Rienner, 1989), 78–88; Houshang Sabahi, *British Policy in Persia, 1918–1925* (London: Frank Cass, 1990), 108–38. See also chapter 3 of this volume, by Michael Zirinsky; and Foran, *Fragile Resistance,* 196–97, 200–201.

18. I have begun to explore questions like these in another context; see "Ethnicity, Class, and Gender in the Making of the Mexican Revolution" (paper presented at the meeting of the Society for the Study of Social Problems, Miami, Fla., August 1993).

19. Reported in *New York Times,* November 7, 1992; August 17, 1993.

Select Bibliography

Abrahamian, Ervand. "Communism and Communalism in Iran: The *Tudah* and the *Firqah-i Dimukrat.*" *International Journal of Middle East Studies* 1 (1970): 291–316.
——. "Structural Causes of the Iranian Revolution." *MERIP (Middle East Research and Information Project) Reports* 87 (May 1980): 21–26.
——. *Iran between Two Revolutions.* Princeton, N.J.: Princeton University Press, 1982.
——. "Iran's Turbaned Revolution." In *The Middle East Annual: Issues and Events,* vol. 1, ed. David H. Partington, 83–106. Boston: G. K. Hall, 1982.
——. *The Iranian Mojehedin.* New Haven, Conn.: Yale University Press, 1989.
——. "Khomeini: Fundamentalist or Populist?" *New Left Review* 186 (March–April 1991): 102–19.
Adamiyyat, Faridun. *Fikr-i Dimukrasi dar Nihzat-i Mashrutiyyat-i Iran* (The idea of social democracy in the Iranian Constitutional Revolution). Tehran: Payam, 1975.
——. *Idi'uluzhi-yi Nahzat-i Mashrutiyat-i Iran* (The ideology of the constitutional movement in Iran). Tehran: Intisharat-i Payam, 1355/1976.
——. *Shurish bar Imtiaznameh-i Rizhi* (The struggle against the tobacco concession). Tehran: Intisharat-i Payam, 1360/1981.
Adamiyyat, Faridun, and Homa Natiq. *Afkar-i Ijtima'i va Siyasi va Iqtisadi dar Asar-i Muntashir-Nashudeh-i Dauran-i Qajar* (Sociopolitical and economic thought in unpublished documents of the Qajar period). Tehran: Agah, 1356/1977.
Afary, Janet. "On the Origins of Feminism in Early 20th Century Iran." *Journal of Women's History* 1, no. 2 (1989): 65–87.
——. "Peasant Rebellions of the Caspian Region in the Iranian Constitutional Revolution." *International Journal of Middle East Studies* 23 (May 1991): 137–61.
——. "Grassroots Democracy and Social Democracy in the Iranian Constitutional Revolution, 1906–11." Ph. D. diss., University of Michigan, Ann Arbor, Departments of History and Near East Studies, 1991.
Afrachteh, Kambiz. "The Predominance and Dilemmas of Theocratic Populism in Contemporary Iran." *Iranian Studies* 14 (Summer–Autumn 1981): 189–213.
Afshar, Haleh. "Women, State and Ideology in Iran." *Third World Quarterly* 7 (April 1985): 256–78.
Afshar, Iraj, ed. *Awraq-i Tazahyab-i Mashrutiyat va Naqsh-i Taqizadeh* (Newly found papers of the constitutional era and the role of Taqizadeh). Tehran: Javidan, 1980.
Akhavi, Shahrough. *Religion and Politics in Contemporary Iran: Clergy-State Relations in the Pahlavi Period.* Albany: State University of New York Press, 1980.

Al-Ahmad, Jalal. *Dar Khidmat va Khianat-i Rushanfikran* (On the intellectuals' service and betrayal). Tehran: Ravaq, n.d.

Alexander, Yonah, and Allen Nanes, eds. *The United States and Iran: A Documentary History*. Frederick, Md.: University Publications of America, 1980.

Algar, Hamid. *Religion and State in Modern Iran, 1785–1906: The Role of the Ulama in the Qajar Period*. Berkeley: University of California Press, 1969.

Altstadt, Audrey. *The Azerbaijani Turks: Power and Identity under Russian Rule*. Stanford, Calif.: Hoover Institution Press, 1992.

Amirahmadi, Hooshang. *Revolution and Economic Transition: The Iranian Experience*. Albany: State University of New York Press, 1990.

Amirkhizi, Isma'il. *Qiyam-i Azarbaijan va Sattar Khan* (The uprising of Azarbaijan and Sattar Khan). Tehran: Tehran, 1960.

Amjad, Mohammed. *Iran: From Royal Dictatorship to Theocracy*. New York: Greenwood, 1989.

Amuriyan, Andre. *Hamasah-yi Yiprim* (The epic of Yephrem). Tehran: Javidan, 1976.

Andrews, William. "The Azarbaijan Incident: The Soviet Union in Iran, 1941–46." *Military Review* (August 1974): 74–85.

Arfa, Hassan. *Under Five Shahs*. London: John Murray, 1964.

Arjomand, Said Amir. "The Ulama's Traditionalist Opposition to Parliamentarianism: 1907–1909." *Middle Eastern Studies* 17 (April 1981): 174–90.

———. *The Shadow of God and the Hidden Imam*. Chicago: University of Chicago Press, 1984.

———. "The Causes and Significance of the Iranian Revolution." *State, Culture and Society* 1, no. 3 (1985): 41–66.

———. *The Turban for the Crown: The Islamic Revolution in Iran*. New York: Oxford University Press, 1988.

Ashraf, Ahmad, and Ali Banuazizi. "The State, Classes and Modes of Mobilization in the Iranian Revolution." *State, Culture and Society* 1, no. 3 (1985): 3–40.

Atabaki, Turaj. "Afsaneh-yi yik Ultimatum" (The myth of an ultimatum). *Chashmandaz* 3 (Autumn 1987): 54–68.

———. *Azerbaijan: Ethnicity and Autonomy in Twentieth-Century Iran*. London: British Academic Press, 1993.

Avanisian, Ardashir. *Khatirat-i Ardashir Avanisian* (Memoirs of Ardashir Avanisian). Köln, Germany: Hizb-i Dimukratik-i Mardum-i Iran, 1990.

Avery, Peter. *Modern Iran*. London: Ernest Benn, 1964. (New York: Praeger, 1965).

Aya, Rod. "Theories of Revolution Reconsidered: Contrasting Models of Collective Violence." *Theory and Society* 8 (July 1979): 39–99.

Azari, 'Ali. *Qiyam-i Shaikh Muhammad Khiabani dar Tabriz* (The revolt of Shaikh Muhammad Khiabani in Tabriz). Tehran: Safi 'Ali Shah, 1983.

Azimi, Fakhreddin. *Iran: The Crisis of Democracy*. New York: St. Martin's, 1989.

Bahar, Malik al-Shua'ra. *Tarikh-i Mukhtasar-i Ahzab-i Siyasi-yi Iran* (A brief history of the political parties of Iran). Tehran: Sipah, 1984.

Bakhash, Shaul. *The Reign of the Ayatollahs: Iran and the Islamic Revolution*. New York: Basic Books, 1984.

Balfour, J. M. *Recent Happenings in Persia*. Edinburgh: William Blackwood & Sons, 1922.

Balta, Paul, and Claudine Rulleau. *L'Iran insurgé*. Paris: Sindbad, 1979.

Banani, Amin. *The Modernization of Iran, 1921–1941*. Stanford, Calif.: Stanford University Press, 1961.

Bani Sadr, Abulhassan. *Iqtisad-i Tauhidi* (Economics of divine unity). Tehran: n.p., 1978.

Baqa'i, Muzafar. *Shinakht-i Haqiqat* (Understanding the Truth). Kirman: Toilers' Party, 1979.

———. *Ankeh Guft Na* (The one who said no). Franklin Lakes, N.J.: Mansur Rafizadeh, 1984.

Baraheni, Reza. *The Crowned Cannibals: Writings on Repression in Iran.* New York: Vintage, 1977.

Bashiriyeh, Hossein. *The State and Revolution in Iran, 1962-1982.* New York: St. Martin's, 1984.

Bayat, Assef. *Workers and Revolution in Iran: A Third World Experience of Workers' Control.* London: Zed, 1987.

Bayat, Mangol Philipp. "Women and Revolution in Iran, 1905-1911." In *Women in the Muslim World,* ed. Nikki Keddie and Lois Beck, 295-308. Cambridge, Mass.: Harvard University Press, 1978.

———. "Anjoman." In *Encyclopaedia Iranica,* vol. 2, ed. Ehsan Yarshater, 77-88. London: Routledge & Kegan Paul, 1983.

———. *Iran's First Revolution: Shi'ism and the Constitutional Revolution of 1905-1909.* Oxford: Oxford University Press, 1991.

Bazargan, Mehdi. *Inqilab-i Iran dar Dau Harakat* (The Iranian revolution in two moves). Tehran: Daftar-i Nahzat-i Azadi-yi Iran, 1363/1984.

Beck, Lois. "Revolutionary Iran and Its Tribal Peoples." *MERIP (Middle East Research and Information Project) Reports* 87 (May 1980): 14-20.

———. *The Qashqa'i of Iran.* New Haven, Conn.: Yale University Press, 1986.

Behdad, Sohrab. "The Political Economy of Islamic Planning in Iran." In *Post-Revolutionary Iran,* ed. Hooshang Amirahmadi and Manoucher Parvin, 107-25. Boulder, Colo.: Westview, 1988.

———. "Winners and Losers of the Iranian Revolution: A Study of Income Distribution." *International Journal of Middle East Studies* 21 (August 1989): 327-58.

Bharier, Julian. *Economic Development in Iran, 1900-1970.* London: Oxford University Press, 1971.

Bill, James. *The Eagle and the Lion: The Tragedy of American-Iranian Relations.* New Haven, Conn.: Yale University Press, 1988.

Bill, James, and Roger Louis, eds. *Musaddiq, Iranian Nationalism, and Oil.* Austin: University of Texas Press, 1988.

Bois, Thomas. [Lucien Rambout, pseud.]. *Les Kurdes et le Droit.* Paris: Les Editions du Cerf, 1947.

———. "Mahabad: Une éphémère république kurde independante." *Orient* 29 (1964): 173-201.

Brinton, Crane. *The Anatomy of Revolution.* New York: Vintage, 1965 [1938].

Browne, E. G. *The Persian Revolution of 1905-1909.* Cambridge: Cambridge University Press, 1910.

———. *Material for the Study of the Babi Religion.* London: Cambridge University Press, 1918.

Burke, Edmund, III, and Paul Lubeck. "Explaining Social Movements in Two Oil-Exporting States: Divergent Outcomes in Nigeria and Iran." *Comparative Studies in Society and History* 29 (October 1987): 643-65.

Cardoso, Fernando Henrique, and Enzo Faletto. *Dependency and Development in Latin America.* Berkeley: University of California Press, 1979.

Chaqueri, Cosroe, ed. *La Social-démocracie en Iran.* Florence: Mazdak, 1979.

———. "Sultanzade: The Forgotten Revolutionary Theoretician of Iran: A Biographical Sketch." *Iranian Studies* 17 (1984): 215-36.

————, ed. *Asnad-i Tarikhi-yi Junbish-i Kargari, Susial Dimukrasi va Kumunisti-yi Iran* (Historical documents of the workers, social democracy, and communist movement in Iran), vol. 19. Tehran: Padzahr, 1985.

————. "The Role and Impact of Armenian Intellectuals in Iranian Politics, 1905–11." *Armenian Review* 41 (Summer 1988): 1–51.

Chehabi, H. E. *Iranian Politics and Religious Modernism: The Liberation Movement of Iran under the Shah and Khomeini.* Ithaca, N.Y.: Cornell University Press, 1990.

A Collection of Musaddiq's Historical Speeches. Europe: Iran-i Azad, Organ of Organizations of the Iranian National Front in Europe, 1967.

Constitution of the Islamic Republic of Iran. Trans. Hamid Algar. Berkeley, Calif.: Mizan, 1980.

Cottam, Richard. *Nationalism in Iran.* Pittsburgh: University of Pittsburgh Press, 1979.

————. *Iran and the United States: A Cold War Case Study.* Pittsburgh: University of Pittsburgh Press, 1988.

Dabashi, Hamid. *Theology of Discontent: The Ideological Foundation of the Islamic Republic in Iran.* New York: New York University Press, 1993.

Davani, 'Ali. *Nahzat-i Ruhaniyun-i Iran* (Movement of the clergy of Iran). Tehran: Bunyad-i Farhangi-yi Imam Reza, 1981.

Davies, James C. "Toward a Theory of Revolution." *American Sociological Review* 27 (1962): 5–19.

Debbaxî, 'Ebdul Qadir. *Raperînî "Komeřey" Jê - Kaf: Welamêk be Namêlkey: "Jê Kaf Çi bû?"* (The uprising of "Komeřey" J. K.: A response to the pamphlet: "What was J - K?"). N.p.: Kurdish Democratic Party of Iran: n.d.; written in March 1982.

Diba, Farhad. *Mohammad Mosaddegh: A Political Biography.* London: Croom Helm, 1986.

Dihnavi, M., ed. *Majmu'a-yi az Mukatibat va Payamha-yi Ayatullah Kashani* (A collection of Ayatullah Kashani's correspondence and messages). Tehran: Pakhsh, 1982.

Dix, Robert H. "Why Revolutions Succeed and Fail." *Polity* 16 (Summer 1984): 423–46.

Dorman, William A., and Mansour Farhang. *The U.S. Press and Iran: Foreign Policy and the Journalism of Deference.* Berkeley: University of California Press, 1987.

Dorraj, Manocher. *From Zarathustra to Khomeini: Populism and Dissent in Iran.* Boulder, Colo.: Lynne Rienner, 1990.

Douglas, William O. *Strange Lands and Friendly People.* New York: Harper & Brothers, 1951.

Eagleton, William. *The Kurdish Republic of 1946.* London: Oxford University Press, 1963.

Edwards, Lyford P. *The Natural History of Revolutions.* Chicago: University of Chicago Press, 1927.

Elwell-Sutton, L. P. *Persian Oil.* Westport, Conn.: Hyperion, 1976.

————. "Reza Shah the Great: Founder of the Pahlavi Dynasty." In *Iran under the Pahlavis*, ed. George Lenczowski, 1–50. Stanford, Calif.: Hoover Institution Press, 1978.

Emîn, Newçîrwan Mistefa. *Hikûmetî Kurdistan, Rêbendanî 1324-Sermawezî 1325[:] Kurd le Gemey Sovêtî da* (back cover: Noshirwan Emin, The Government of Kurdistan, 22 January–17 December 1946: The Kurds in the Soviet Game). Utrecht, The Netherlands: KIB, 1993.

Entner, Marvin. *Russo-Persian Commercial Relations, 1828–1914.* Gainesville: University of Florida Press, 1965.

Fada'i-Minority. *Nabard-i Khalq* (The people's struggle). Tehran: OIPFG, 1981.

Faghfoory, Mohammad H. "The Ulama-State Relations in Iran: 1921–1941." *International Journal of Middle East Studies* 19 (1987): 413–32.

Fakhra'i, Ibrahim. *Sardar-i Jangal* (Jangal commander). Tehran: Intisharat-i Javidan, 1362/1983.

Fardust, Hussain. *Zuhur va Suqut-i Saltanat-i Pahlavi: Khatarat-i Artishbud-i Sabiq Hussain Fardust* (The rise and fall of the Pahlavi dynasty: Memoirs of former Field Marshal Hussain Fardust), 2 vols. Tehran: Ittila'at, 1991.

Farhi, Farideh. "State Disintegration and Urban-Based Revolutionary Crisis: A Comparative Analysis of Iran and Nicaragua." *Comparative Political Studies* 21 (July 1988): 231–56.

———. "Class Struggles, the State, and Revolution in Iran." In *Power and Stability in the Middle East,* ed. Berch Berberoglu, 90–113. London: Zed, 1989.

———. *States and Urban-Based Revolutions: Iran and Nicaragua.* Urbana: University of Illinois Press, 1990.

Fatemi, Faramarz. *The U.S.S.R. in Iran.* New York: A. S. Barnes, 1980.

Fatemi, Nasrollah Saifpour. *Diplomatic History of Persia, 1917–1923: Anglo-Russian Power Politics in Iran.* New York: R. F. Moore, 1952.

———. *Oil Diplomacy: Powderkeg in Iran.* New York: Whittier, 1954.

Fischer, Michael M. J. *Iran: From Religious Dispute to Revolution.* Cambridge: Harvard University Press, 1980.

Floor, Willem M. "The Guilds in Iran: An Overview from the Earliest Beginnings till 1972." *Zeitschrift der Deutschen Morgenländischen Gesellschaft* 125, no. 1 (1975): 99–116.

———. "The Merchants (*tujjār*) in Qājār Iran." *Zeitschrift der Deutschen Morgenländischen Gesellschaft* 126, no. 1 (1976): 101–35.

Foran, John. "The Modes of Production Approach to Seventeenth-Century Iran." *International Journal of Middle East Studies* 20 (August 1988): 345–63.

———. "Social Structure and Social Change in Iran from 1500 to 1979." Ph.D. diss., University of California, Berkeley, Department of Sociology, 1988.

———. "The Concept of Dependent Development as a Key to the Political Economy of Qajar Iran (1800–1925)." *Iranian Studies* 22, nos. 2–3 (1989): 5–56.

———. "The Making of an External Arena: Iran's Place in the World-System, 1500–1722." *Review* (Journal of the Fernand Braudel Center) 12 (Winter 1989): 71–119.

———. "The Strengths and Weaknesses of Iran's Populist Alliance: A Class Analysis of the Constitutional Revolution of 1905–1911." *Theory and Society* 20 (December 1991): 795–823.

———. "A Theory of Third World Social Revolutions: Iran, Nicaragua, and El Salvador Compared." *Critical Sociology* 19, no. 2 (1992): 3–27.

———. "Dependency and Resistance in the Middle East: 1800–1925." In *Political Power and Social Theory,* vol. 8, ed. Diane E. Davis and Howard Kimeldorf, 141–72. Greenwich, Conn.: JAI, 1993.

———. *Fragile Resistance: Social Transformation in Iran from 1500 to the Revolution.* Boulder, Colo.: Westview, 1993.

———. "Theories of Revolution Revisited: Toward a Fourth Generation?" *Sociological Theory* 11 (March 1993): 1–20.

———. "The Causes of Latin American Social Revolutions: Searching for Patterns in Mexico, Cuba, and Nicaragua." In *World Society Studies,* vol. 3, *Conflicts and New Departures in World Society,* ed. Peter Lengyel and Volker Bornschier, 209–44. New Brunswick, N.J.: Transaction, 1994.

———. "Dangerous Populations? Concepts for the Comparative Study of Social Movements in Qajar Iran." In *City and Society in Qajar Iran,* ed. Michael Bonine. In press.

Foran, John, and Jeff Goodwin. "Revolutionary Outcomes in Iran and Nicaragua. Coalition Fragmentation, War, and the Limits of Social Transformation." *Theory and Society* 22, no. 2 (April 1993): 209–47.

Garthwaite, Gene R. *Khans and Shahs: A Documentary Analysis of the Bakhtiyari in Iran.* Cambridge: Cambridge University Press, 1983.

Gasiorowski, Mark J. "The 1953 Coup d'Etat in Iran." *International Journal of Middle East Studies* 19 (August 1987): 261–86.

———. *U.S. Foreign Policy and the Shah: Building a Client State in Iran.* Ithaca, N.Y.: Cornell University Press, 1991.

Ghods, M. Reza. *Iran in the Twentieth Century: A Political History.* Boulder, Colo.: Lynne Rienner, 1989.

Gilbar, Gad G. "The Big Merchants (tujjar) and the Persian Constitutional Revolution of 1906." *Asian and African Studies* 11, no. 3 (1977): 275–303.

———. "Persian Agriculture in the Late Qajar Period, 1860–1906: Some Economic and Social Aspects." *Asian and African Studies* 12, no. 3 (1978): 313–65.

Goldfrank, Walter L. "Theories of Revolution and Revolution without Theory: The Case of Mexico." *Theory and Society* 7, no. 1 (1979): 135–65.

Goldstone, Jack A. "Theories of Revolution: The Third Generation." *World Politics* 32 (April 1980): 425–53.

———. "The Comparative and Historical Study of Revolutions." *Annual Review of Sociology* 8 (1982): 187–207.

Goode, James. "Reforming Iran during the Kennedy Years." *Diplomatic History* 15 (Winter 1991): 13–29.

Goodell, Grace. *The Elementary Structures of Political Life: Rural Development in Pahlavi Iran.* New York: Oxford University Press, 1986.

Goodwin, Jeff. "Why Insurgencies Persist, or the Perversity of Indiscriminate State Violence." Paper presented at the annual meeting of the American Sociological Association, Miami, Fla., August 1993.

Goodwin, Jeff, and Theda Skocpol. "Explaining Revolutions in the Contemporary Third World." *Politics and Society* 17 (December 1989): 489–509.

Graham, Robert. *Iran: The Illusion of Power.* New York: St. Martin's, 1979.

Green, Jerrold D. *Revolution in Iran: The Politics of Countermobilization.* New York: Praeger, 1982.

Grey, W. G. "Recent Persian History." *Journal of the Royal Central Asian Society* 13, pt. 1 (1926): 29–42.

Gurr, Ted Robert. *Why Men Rebel.* Princeton, N.J.: Princeton University Press, 1970.

Hakimian, Hasan. "Wage Labor and Migration: Persian Workers in Southern Russia, 1880–1914." *International Journal of Middle East Studies* 17, no. 4 (1985): 443–62.

Halliday, Fred. "The Genesis of the Iranian Revolution." *Third World Quarterly* 1 (October 1979): 1–16.

———. "The Iranian Revolution: Uneven Development and Religious Populism." *Journal of International Affairs* 36 (Fall–Winter 1982–83): 187–207.

Hanson, Brad. "The 'Westoxication' of Iran: Depictions and Reactions of Behrangi, Al-e Ahmad, and Shari'ati." *International Journal of Middle East Studies* 15 (February 1983): 1–23.

Hassanpour, Amir. *Nationalism and Language in Kurdistan, 1918–1985.* San Francisco: Mellen Research University Press, 1992.

Hiro, Dilip. *Iran under the Ayatollahs.* London: Routledge & Kegan Paul, 1985.

Homayounpour, Parviz. *L'Affaire d'Azarbaidjan.* Lausanne, Switzerland: n.p., 1967.

Hooglund, Eric J. *Land and Revolution in Iran, 1960–1980.* Austin: University of Texas Press, 1982.

"How We Organized Strike That Paralyzed Shah's Regime: Firsthand Account by Iranian Oil Worker." In *Oil and Class Struggle,* ed. Petter Nore and Terisa Turner, 292–301. London: Zed, 1981.

Huntington, Samuel. *Political Order in Changing Societies.* New Haven, Conn.: Yale University Press, 1968.

Hussami, Kerim. *Komarî Demokratî Kurdistan yan Xudmuxtarî?* (The Kurdish Democratic Republic or Autonomy?). Sweden: Binkey Çapemenî Azad, 1986.

Ironside, Lord, ed. *High Road to Command: The Diaries of Major-General Sir Edmund Ironside 1920–1922.* London: Leo Cooper, 1972.

Iskandari, Iraj. *Khatirat-i Siyasi* (Political reminiscences). Tehran: Intisharat-i 'Ilmi, 1989.

Issawi, Charles, ed. *The Economic History of Iran, 1800–1914.* Chicago: University of Chicago Press, 1971.

Ivanov, M. S. *Tarikh-i Nuvin-i Iran* (Modern history of Iran). Trans. (from Russian) Hushang Tizabi and Hasan Qa'im Panah. Stockholm: Tudeh, 1356/1977.

'Izzet, Mahmoud Mela. *Komarî Millî Mehabad* (The National Republic of Mahabad). Iraqi Kurdistan: Ebrahim Ezo, 1984; reprinted in Sweden in 1986.

———. *Dewletî Cimhûrî Kurdistan: Name u Dokûmênt* (back cover: Mahmud Mulla Izzat, *The Democratic Republic of Kurdistan [Correspondence and Documents]*, vol. 1. Sweden: Binkey Çapemenî Azad, 1992.

JAMI (Jibhi-yi Azadi-yi Mardum-i Iran). *Guzashteh Chiragh-i Rah-i Ayandeh ast* (The past is the light on the path to the future). Tehran: Ququnus, 1983.

Javadi, H., and K. Burrill. "Azerbaijan. X. Azeri literature in Iran." In *Encyclopaedia Iranica,* vol. 3, ed. Ehsan Yarshater, 251–55. Costa Mesa, Calif.: Mazda, 1989.

Javanshir, F. M. *Tajrubi-yi Bist-u Hasht-i Murdad* (The experience of the 28th of Murdad/August 19). Tehran: Tudeh, 1980.

Javid, M. A. *Dimukrasi-yi Naqis: Barrasi-yi Salha-yi 1320–32, Daftar-i 2–3: Azarbaijan* (Incomplete Democracy: A Survey of the Years 1941–53: Azarbaijan). [Europe]: Union of Iranian Communists, [1977?].

Jazani, Bizhan. *Tarh-i Jama'eh Shinasi va Mabani-yi Stratijy-i Junbish-i Inqilabi-yi Khalq-i Iran* (Sociological sketch and fundamentals of the strategy of the revolutionary movement in Iran). Tehran: Maziar, 1979.

———. *Capitalism and Revolution in Iran.* London: Zed, 1980.

Johnson, Chalmers. *Revolutionary Change.* Boston: Little, Brown, 1966.

Jwaideh, Wadie. "The Kurdish Nationalist Movement: Its Origins and Development." Ph.D. diss., Syracuse University, 1960.

Kambakhsh, Abdul Samad. *Nazari beh Junbish-i Kargari va Kummunisti dar Iran* (A look at the workers' and communist movement in Iran). Stockholm: Tudeh Party, 1975.

Kamrava, Mehran. *Revolution in Iran: The Roots of Turmoil.* London: Routledge, 1990.

Karbala'i, Shaykh Hasan. *Qarardad-i Rizhi-yi 1890 M* (The Régie contract of 1890). Tehran: Mubarizan, 1361/1982.

Karimi-Hakkak, Ahmad. "Revolutionary Posturing: Iranian Writers and the Iranian Revolution of 1979." *International Journal of Middle East Studies* 23 (November 1991): 507–31.

Karshenas, Massoud. *Oil, State and Industrialization in Iran.* Cambridge: Cambridge University Press, 1990.

Kasravi, Ahmad. *Tarikh-i Hijdahsaleh-yi Azarbaijan* (Eighteen-year history of Azarbaijan), vol. 1. Tehran: Amir Kabir, 1978.

———. *Tarikh-i Mashruteh-yi Iran* (History of constitutionalism in Iran). Tehran: Amir Kabir, 1984 [1951].

Katouzian, Homa, ed. *Khatirat-i Siyasi-yi Khalil Maliki* (Khalil Maliki's political memoirs). Hannover, Germany: Kushish Bara-yi Pishburd-i Nahzat-i Milli-yi Iran, 1981.

———. *The Political Economy of Modern Iran: Despotism and Pseudo-Modernism, 1926–1979.* New York: New York University Press, 1981.

———. *Musaddiq and the Struggle for Power in Iran.* London: I. B. Tauris, 1990.

Kazemi, Farhad. *Poverty and Revolution in Iran: The Migrant Poor, Urban Marginality and Politics.* New York: New York University Press, 1980.

Kazemi, Farhad, and Ervand Abrahamian. "The Nonrevolutionary Peasantry of Modern Iran." *Iranian Studies* 11 (1978): 259–304.

Kazemzadeh, Firuz. *Russia and Britain in Persia, 1864–1914.* New Haven, Conn.: Yale University Press, 1968.

Keddie, Nikki R. "Religion and Irreligion in Early Iranian Nationalism." *Comparative Studies in Society and History* 4 (1962): 266–95.

———. *Religion and Rebellion in Iran: The Tobacco Protest of 1891–1892.* London: Frank Cass, 1966.

———. "The Economic History of Iran 1800–1914 and Its Political Impact." In *Iran: Religion, Politics, and Society, Collected Essays,* 119–36. London: Frank Cass, 1980.

———. "The Origins of the Religious-Radical Alliance in Iran." In *Iran: Religion, Politics, and Society, Collected Essays,* 53–65. London: Frank Cass, 1980.

———. *Roots of Revolution: An Interpretive History of Modern Iran.* New Haven, Conn.: Yale University Press, 1981.

———. "Iranian Revolutions in Comparative Perspective." *American Historical Review* 88 (June 1983): 579–98.

———. *An Islamic Response to Imperialism: Political and Religious Writings of Sayyid Jamal ad-Din "Al-Afghani."* Berkeley: University of California Press, 1983 [1968].

Khami'i, Anvar. *Fursat-i Buzurg-i az Dast Rafteh* (The great lost opportunity), vol. 2. Tehran: Hafteh, 1983.

———. *Az Inshi'ab ta Kudeta* (From the split to coup d'état). Tehran: Hafteh, 1984.

Khomeini, Imam. *Islam and Revolution: Writings and Declarations of the Imam Khomeini.* Trans. and anno. Hamid Algar. Berkeley, Calif.: Mizan, 1981.

Khoros, V. *Populism: Its Past, Present and Future.* Moscow: Progress, 1984.

Khumaini, Ayatullah Ruhullah. *Sahifeh-i Nur,* 16 vols. Tehran: Ministry of Guidance, 1983.

———. *Dar Justuju-yi Rah az Kalam-i Imam: Daftar-i Yazdahum: Milligara'i* (In search of the path from the word of the imam: Book eleven: Nationalism). Tehran: Amir Kabir, 1984.

Kianouri, Noureddin. "The National Bourgeoisie, Their Nature and Policy." *World Marxist Review* 2 (August 1959): 61–65.

Kimmel, Michael S. *Revolution: A Sociological Interpretation.* Philadelphia: Temple University Press, 1990.

Kishavarz, Faridun. *Man Mutaham Mikunam: Kumiti-yi Markazi-yi Hizb-i Tudeh ra* (I accuse the Central Committee of the Tudeh Party). London: Jibhi Newspaper Publications, n.d.

Kuniholm, Bruce. "Azerbaijan. V. History from 1941 to 1947." In *Encyclopaedia Iranica,* vol. 3, ed. Ehsan Yarshater, 231–34. London: Routledge & Kegan Paul, 1989.

Kutschera, Chris. *Le movement nationale kurde.* Paris: Flammarion, 1979.

Laclau, Ernesto. *Politics and Ideology in Marxist Theory.* London: Verso, 1977.

Ladjevardi, Habib. *Labor Unions and Autocracy in Iran.* Syracuse, N.Y.: Syracuse University Press, 1985.

Lambton, Ann K. S. *Landlord and Peasant in Persia: A Study of Land Tenure and Land Revenue Administration.* London: Oxford University Press, 1953.

———. "The Tobacco Régie: Prelude to Revolution." *Studia Islamica* 22 (1965): 119–57.

———. *The Persian Land Reform.* Oxford: Clarendon, 1969.

Lenczowski, George. *Russia and the West in Iran, 1918–1948: A Study in Big-Power Rivalry.* Ithaca, N.Y.: Cornell University Press, 1949.

———. "United States' Support for Iran's Independence and Integrity, 1945–1959." *Annals of the American Academy of Political and Social Science* (May 1972): 45–55.

L'Estrange Fawcett, Louise. *Iran and the Cold War: The Azarbaijan Crisis of 1946.* Cambridge: Cambridge University Press, 1992.

Madani, Sayyid Jalal al-Din. *Tarikh-i Siyasi-yi Mu'asir-i Iran* (Contemporary political history of Iran), vol. 1. Qum: Daftar-i Intisharat-i Islami, Jami'i-yi Mudarrisin-i Hauzi-yi 'Ilmi-yi Qum, 1982.

Makki, Husayn. *Tarikh-i Bist Saleh-i Iran* (Twenty years' history of Iran). Tehran: Nashr, 1983.

———. *Kitab-i Siyah* (The black book). Tehran: n.p., n. d.

Malikzada, M. *Tarikh-i Inqilab-i Mashruteh-yi Iran* (History of the Iranian Constitutional Revolution), vol. 6. Tehran: Ilmi, 1979.

Martin, Vanessa. *Islam and Modernism: The Iranian Revolution of 1906*. London: I. B. Tauris, 1989.

Mazarei, Adnan, Jr. "The Iranian Economy under the Islamic Republic: Institutional Change and Macroeconomic Performance (1979–90)." Working Paper No. 6165, University of California, Los Angeles, Department of Economics, March 1990.

McAdam, Doug. *Political Process and the Development of Black Insurgency, 1930–1970*. Chicago: University of Chicago Press, 1982.

McAdam, Doug, John D. McCarthy, and Mayer N. Zald. "Social Movements." In *Handbook of Sociology*, ed. Neil J. Smelser, 695–737. Newbury Park, Calif.: Sage, 1988.

McCarthy, John D., and Mayer N. Zald. "Resource Mobilization and Social Movements: A Partial Theory." *American Journal of Sociology* 82 (1977): 1212–41.

McDaniel, Tim. *Autocracy, Modernization, and Revolution in Russia and Iran*. Princeton, N.J.: Princeton University Press, 1991.

McLachlan, K. S. "Land Reform in Iran." In *The Cambridge History of Iran*, vol. 1, *The Land of Iran*, ed. W. B. Fisher. Cambridge: Cambridge University Press, 1968.

Melucci, Alberto. *Nomads of the Present: New Social Movements and Individual Needs in Contemporary Society*. Philadelphia: Temple University Press, 1989.

Milani, Mohsen M. *The Making of Iran's Islamic Revolution: From Monarchy to Islamic Republic*. Boulder, Colo.: Westview, 1988.

Millspaugh, Arthur C. *The American Task in Persia*. New York: Century, 1925.

Moaddel, Mansoor. "The Shi'i Ulama and the State in Iran." *Theory and Society* 15 (1986): 519–66.

———. "Class Struggle in Post-Revolutionary Iran." *International Journal of Middle East Studies* 23 (August 1991): 317–43.

———. "Ideology as Episodic Discourse: The Case of the Iranian Revolution." *American Sociological Review* 57 (June 1992): 353–79.

———. *Class, Politics, and Ideology in the Iranian Revolution*. New York: Columbia University Press, 1993.

Moghadam, Valentine [Sharhzad Azad, pseud.]. "Workers' and Peasants' Councils in Iran." *Monthly Review* 32 (October 1980): 14–29.

Moghadam, Valentine. "Iran: Development, Revolution and the Problem of Analysis." *Review of Radical Political Economics* 16 (Summer–Fall 1984): 227–40.

———. "Industrial Development, Culture, and Working-Class Politics: A Case Study of Tabriz Industrial Workers in the Iranian Revolution." *International Sociology* 2 (June 1987): 151–75.

———. "Socialism or Anti-Imperialism? The Left and Revolution in Iran." *New Left Review* 166 (November–December 1987): 5–28.

———. "Industrialization Strategy and Labor's Response: The Case of the Workers' Councils in Iran." In *Trade Unions and the New Industrialization of the Third World*, ed. Roger Southall, 182–209. London/Ottawa: Zed/University of Ottawa Press, 1988.

———. "Oil, the State, and Limits to Autonomy: The Iranian Case." *Arab Studies Quarterly* 10 (Spring 1988): 225–38.

————. "Women, Work and Ideology in the Islamic Republic." *International Journal of Middle East Studies* 20 (May 1988): 221–43.

————. "One Revolution or Two? The Iranian Revolution and the Islamic Republic." In *Socialist Register 1989,* ed. Ralph Miliband, Leo Panitch and John Saville, 74–101. London: Merlin, 1989.

————. "Populist Revolution and the Islamic State in Iran." In *Revolution in the World-System,* ed. Terry Boswell, 147–63. Westport, Conn.: Greenwood, 1989.

————. *Modernizing Women: Gender and Social Change in the Middle East.* Boulder, Colo.: Lynne Rienner, 1993.

Moore, Barrington, Jr. *Social Origins of Dictatorship and Democracy: Lord and Peasant in the Making of the Modern World.* Boston: Beacon, 1966.

Morris, Aldon D., and Carol McClurg Mueller, eds. *Frontiers in Social Movement Theory.* New Haven, Conn.: Yale University Press, 1992.

Mouzelis, Nicos. *Post-Marxist Alternatives.* London: Macmillan, 1990.

Musaddiq, Muhammad. *Nutqha va Maktubat-i Dr. Musaddiq* (Dr. Musaddiq's speeches and correspondence). N.p.: Musaddiq Publications, 1969.

————. *Khatirat va Ta'alumat-i Duktur Musaddiq* (Dr. Musaddiq's memoirs and sorrows). N.p.: National Front Sympathizers Outside the Country, 1986.

Muslim Students Following the Line of the Imam. *Asnad-i Laneh-i Jasusi-yi Amrika* (Documents from the spy nest of America). Tehran: Muslim Students Following the Line of the Imam, n.d.

Nabdil, Ali Riza. *Azarbaijan va Mas'ali-yi Milli* (Azarbaijan and the national question). N.p., 1352/1973.

Najmabadi, Afsaneh. *Land Reform and Social Change in Iran.* Salt Lake City: University of Utah Press, 1987.

————. "Power, Morality and the New Muslim Womanhood." In *State and Culture in Afghanistan, Iran, and Pakistan,* ed. Ali Banuazizi and Myron Wiener. Albany: State University of New York Press, 1993.

Nashat, Guity, ed. *Women and Revolution in Iran.* Boulder, Colo.: Westview, 1983.

Nissman, David. *The Soviet Union and Iranian Azarbaijan: The Use of Nationalism for Political Penetration.* Boulder, Colo.: Westview, 1987.

Nizam Mafi, Mansureh Ittihadiyah. *Paydayish va Tahavvul-i Ahzab-i Siyasi-yi Mashrutiyyat: Daureh-yi Avval va Duvvum* (The formation and development of political parties in Iran: The first and second constitutional periods). Tehran: Gustareh, 1982.

Pahlavi, Muhammad Reza. *Answer to History.* New York: Stein & Day, 1980.

Paige, Jeffery M. *Agrarian Revolution: Social Movements and Export Agriculture in the Underdeveloped World.* New York: Free Press, 1975.

Parsa, Misagh. *The Social Origins of the Iranian Revolution.* New Brunswick, N.J.: Rutgers University Press, 1989.

Pesaran, M. H. [Thomas Walton, pseud.]. "Economic Development and Revolutionary Upheavals in Iran." *Cambridge Journal of Economics* 4 (September 1980): 271–92.

Pesaran, M. H. "The System of Dependent Capitalism in Pre- and Post-Revolutionary Iran." *International Journal of Middle East Studies* 14 (November 1982): 501–22.

Petras, James, and Morris Morley. "Development and Revolution: Contradictions in the Advanced Third World Countries—Brazil, South Africa and Iran." *Studies in Comparative International Development* 16 (Spring 1981): 514–35.

Pettee, George S. *The Process of Revolution.* New York: Harper & Row, 1937.

Pisyan, Najafquli. *Az Mahabad-i Khunin ta Karaniha-yi Aras* (From bloody Mahabad to the banks of the Aras). Tehran: Bungah-i Matbu'ati-yi Imruz, 1949.

———. *Marg bud, Bazgasht ham bud* (There was both death and return). Tehran: Bungah-i Matbu'ati-yi Imruz, 1949.

Qashqa'i, Muhammad Nasir Saulat. *The Years of Crisis in Iran: 1950–1953.* Houston: Book Distribution Center, n.d.

Rafi'i, Mansurah. *Anjuman.* Tehran: Nashr-i Tarikh-i Iran, 1983.

Rahnema, Ali, and Farhad Nomani. *The Secular Miracle: Religion, Politics and Economic Policy in Iran.* London: Zed, 1990.

Ramazani, Rouhollah K. *The Foreign Policy of Iran: A Developing Nation in World Affairs, 1500–1941.* Charlottesville: University Press of Virginia, 1966.

———. "The Autonomous Republic of Azarbaijan and the Kurdish People's Republic: Their Rise and Fall." In *The Anatomy of Communist Takeovers,* ed. Thomas Hammond, 401–27. New Haven, Conn.: Yale University Press, 1975.

Ravasani, Shapur. *Nahzat-i Mirza Kuchik Khan Jangali va Avvalin Jumhuri-yi Shura'i dar Iran* (Mirza Kuchik Khan's movement and the first soviet republic in Iran). Tehran: Chapaksh, 1363/1984.

Reznikov, A. B. "The Downfall of the Iranian Monarchy (January–February 1979)." In *The Revolutionary Process in the East: Past and Present,* ed. R. Ulyanovsky, 254–312. Moscow: Progress, 1985.

Ricks, Thomas. "U.S. Military Missions in Iran, 1943–1978: The Political Economy of Military Assistance." In *U.S. Strategy in the Gulf: Intervention against Liberation,* ed. Leila Meo, 28–68. Belmont, Mass.: Association of Arab-American University Graduates, 1981.

Rodinson, Maxime. *Islam and Capitalism.* London: Penguin, 1974.

Roosevelt, Archie. "The Kurdish Republic of Mahabad." *Middle East Journal* 1, no. 3 (1947): 247–69.

Roosevelt, Kermit. *Countercoup: The Struggle for the Control of Iran.* New York: McGraw-Hill, 1979.

Rosenberg, J. Philipp. "The Cheshire Ultimatum: Truman's Message to Stalin in the 1946 Azerbaijan Crisis." *Journal of Politics* 41 (1979): 933–40.

Sabahi, Houshang. *British Policy in Persia, 1918–1925.* London: Frank Cass, 1990.

Sadiq, Javad. *Milliyat va Inqilab dar Iran* (Nationality and revolution in Iran). New York: Intisharat-i Fanus, 1973.

Saikal, Amin. *The Rise and Fall of the Shah.* Princeton, N.J.: Princeton University Press, 1980.

Salehi, M. M. *Insurgency through Culture and Religion.* Boulder, Colo.: Lynne Rienner, 1988.

Samii, Kuross A. "Truman against Stalin in Iran: A Tale of Three Messages." *Middle Eastern Studies* 23 (January 1987): 95–107.

Sanjabi, Karim. *Umidha va Na-Umidiha* (Hopes and disappointments). London: Nashr-i Kitab, 1973.

Shaji'i, Z. *Namayandigan-i Majlis-i Shura-yi Milli dar Bist-u yik Daureh-i Qanun guzari* (Members of parliament in twenty-one legislative sessions). Tehran: Tehran University Press, 1965.

Shari'ati, Ali. *Marxism and Other Western Fallacies. An Islamic Critique.* Trans. R. Campbell. Berkeley, Calif.: Mizan, 1980.

Sheean, Vincent. *The New Persia.* New York: Century, 1927.

Shephard, William. "Islam and Ideology: Toward a Typology." *International Journal of Middle East Studies* 19 (August 1987): 307–36.

Shu'a'iyan, Mustafa. *Nigahi beh Ravabit-i Shuravi va Nahzat-i Inqilabi-i Jangal* (A look at the relationship between the Soviet Union and the revolutionary Jangal movement). Florence: Mazdak, 1970.

Siavoshi, Sussan. *Liberal Nationalism in Iran: The Failure of a Movement.* Boulder, Colo.: Westview, 1990.

Sicker, Martin. *The Bear and the Lion: Soviet Imperialism and Iran.* New York: Praeger, 1988.

Sivanandan, A. "Imperialism in the Silicon Age." *Monthly Review* 32 (July–August 1980): 24–42.

Skocpol, Theda. *States and Social Revolutions: A Comparative Analysis of France, Russia, and China.* Cambridge: Cambridge University Press, 1979.

———. "Rentier State and Shi'a Islam in the Iranian Revolution." *Theory and Society* 11 (May 1982): 265–84.

Smelser, Neil J. *Theory of Collective Behavior.* New York: Free Press, 1963.

Snyder, Richard. "Explaining Transitions from Neopatrimonial Dictatorships." *Comparative Politics* 24 (1992): 370–99.

Tabari, Azar. *Bibin Tafavat-i Rah az Kuja ast ta beh Kuja!* (See how far the difference is!). N.p., 1974.

Tabari, Azar, and Nahid Yeganeh, eds. *In the Shadow of Islam: The Women's Movement in Iran.* London: Zed, 1982.

Tafrishian, Abul-Hasan. *Qiyam-i Afsaran-i Khurasan 1324* (The uprising of the Khurasan officers, 1925/26). Tehran: Intisharat-i 'Ilmi, 1980.

Taleghani, Ayatullah Sayyid Mahmud. *Society and Economics in Islam: Writings and Declarations of Ayatullah Sayyid Mahmud Taleghani.* Trans. R. Campbell. Berkeley, Calif.: Mizan, 1982.

Taleghani, Seyed Mahmoud. *Islam and Ownership.* Trans. Ahmad Jabbari and Farhang Rajaee. Lexington, Ky.: Mazda, 1983.

Thorpe, James A. "Truman's Ultimatum to Stalin on the 1946 Azerbaijan Crisis: The Making of a Myth." *Journal of Politics* 40 (February 1978): 188–95.

Tilly, Charles. *From Mobilization to Revolution.* Reading, Mass.: Addison-Wesley, 1978.

Tohidi, Nayereh. "Modernity, Islamization, and the Woman Question in Iran." In *Gender and National Identity: Women and Politics in Muslim Societies,* ed. Valentine M. Moghadam. London: Zed, in press.

Tucker, Kenneth H. "How New Are the New Social Movements?" *Theory, Culture and Society* 8, no. 2 (1990): 75–98.

Turkaman, Muhammad. *Asnad Piramun-i Tuti'-yi Rubudan va Qatl-i Shahid Afshartus* (Some documents concerning the plot for the kidnap and murder of martyr Afshartus). Tehran: Organization of the Cultural Services of Rasa, 1984.

Turner, Terisa. "Iranian Oilworkers in the 1978–79 Revolution." In *Oil and Class Struggle,* ed. Petter Nore and Terisa Turner, 279–92. London: Zed, 1981.

Ullman, Richard. *Anglo-Soviet Relations, 1917–1923,* vol. 3, *The Anglo-Soviet Accord.* Princeton, N.J.: Princeton University Press, 1972.

Union of Islamic Students Associations. *Musaddiq va Nahzat-i Milli-yi Iran* (Musaddiq and the national movement of Iran). Europe: Union of Islamic Students Associations, 1978.

Upton, Joseph M. *The History of Modern Iran: An Interpretation.* Cambridge: Harvard University Press, 1960.

Vahdat, Manoucher. "The Soviet Union and the Movement to Establish Autonomy in Iranian Azarbaijan." Ph.D. diss., Indiana University, 1958.

van Wagenen, Richard. *The Iranian Case 1946.* New York: Carnegie Endowment for International Peace, 1952.

Walton, John. *Reluctant Rebels: Comparative Studies of Revolution and Underdevelopment.* New York: Columbia University Press, 1984.

Waterfield, Gordon. *Professional Diplomat: Sir Percy Loraine of Kirkharle Bt. 1880–1961.* London: John Murray, 1973.

Wickham-Crowley, Timothy P. "Understanding Failed Revolution in El Salvador: A Comparative Analysis of Regime Types and Social Structures." *Politics and Society* 17 (December 1989): 511–37.

———. *Guerrillas and Revolution in Latin America: A Comparative Study of Insurgencies and Regimes since 1956.* Princeton, N.J.: Princeton University Press, 1992.

Wilber, Donald N. *Riza Shah Pahlavi: The Resurrection and Reconstruction of Iran.* Hicksville, N.Y.: Exposition, 1975.

Wimbush, S. Enders. "Divided Azerbaijan: Nation Building, Assimilation, and Mobilization between Three States." In *Soviet Asian Ethnic Frontiers,* ed. W. O. McCagg and B. D. Silver, 61–81. New York: Pergamon, 1979.

Wolf, Eric R. *Peasant Wars of the Twentieth Century.* New York: Harper Colophon, 1969.

Wright, Denis. *The English amongst the Persians during the Qajar Period 1787–1921.* London: Heinemann, 1977.

———. *The Persians amongst the English: Episodes in Anglo-Persian History.* London: I. B. Tauris, 1985.

Yamgani, Parsa. *Karnameh-i Musaddiq va Hizb-i Tudeh* (The record of Musaddiq and the Tudeh Party). Tehran: Ravaq, 1979.

Young, Cuyler. "The Social Support of Current Iranian Policy." *Middle East Journal* 6, no. 2 (1952): 125–43.

Zabih, Sepehr. *The Communist Movement in Iran.* Berkeley: University of California Press, 1966.

———. *Iran's Revolutionary Upheaval: An Interpretive Essay.* San Francisco: Alchemy, 1979.

Zangani, Sarlashkar Ahmad. *Khatirat-i az Ma'muriyyatha-yi Man dar Azarbaijan* (Memoirs of my assignments in Azarbaijan). Tehran: n.p., 1974.

Zavareei, Manizheh. "Dependent Capitalist Development in Iran and the Mass Uprising of 1979." In *Research in Political Economy: A Research Annual,* ed. Paul Zarembka, 139–88. Greenwich, Conn.: JAI, 1982.

Zirinsky, Michael P. "Blood, Power, and Hypocrisy: The Murder of Robert Imbrie and American Relations with Pahlavi Iran, 1924." *International Journal of Middle East Studies* 18 (August 1986): 275–92.

———. "Harbingers of Change: Presbyterian Women in Iran, 1883–1949." *American Presbyterians: Journal of Presbyterian History* 70 (1992): 173–86.

———. "Imperial Power and Dictatorship: Britain and the Rise of Reza Shah, 1921–1926." *International Journal of Middle East Studies* 24 (November 1992): 639–63.

———. "A Panacea for the Ills of the Country: American Presbyterian Education in Inter-War Iran." *Iranian Studies* 26, nos. 1–2 (1993): 119–37.

Zonis, Marvin. *Majestic Failure: The Fall of the Shah.* Chicago: University of Chicago Press, 1991.

Contributors

Janet Afary is assistant professor of history and women's studies at Purdue University. She has published articles on various aspects of the Iranian Constitutional Revolution in the *International Journal of Middle East Studies* and the *Journal of Women's History*.

John Foran is associate professor of sociology at the University of California, Santa Barbara. He is the author of *Fragile Resistance: Social Transformation in Iran from 1500 to the Revolution* (1993) and numerous articles on development and social change in Iran and Latin America. He is currently writing a book on the origins of Third World social revolutions.

Amir Hassanpour was born in Mahabad (Kurdistan, Iran) and studied at Tehran University and University of Illinois at Urbana-Champaign. He has taught at Tehran University and University of Windsor (Canada) and has been a guest scholar at Uppsala University (1993–94). He is author of *Nationalism and Language in Kurdistan, 1918–1985* (1992) and has contributed articles on Kurdish history and culture to *Encyclopaedia Iranica*. His research interests include folklore, media, and economic, social, and cultural history.

Mansoor Moaddel is associate professor of sociology at Eastern Michigan University. His recent works include "Political Conflict in the World-Economy: A Cross-National Analysis of Modernization and World-System Theory" (*American Sociological Review*, December 1993); "The Egyptian and Iranian Ulama at the Threshold of Modern Social Change: What Does and What Does Not Account for the Difference" (*Arab Studies Quarterly*, summer 1993); *Class, Politics, and Ideology in the Iranian Revolution* (1993); and "Ideology as Episodic Discourse: The Case of the Iranian Revolution" (*American Sociological Review*, June 1992). Supported by a grant from the National Science Foundation, he is working on a project titled "Episode and Discourse: Islamic Modernism, Liberal-Nationalism, and Fundamentalism in the Middle East."

Val Moghadam is senior research fellow at the United Nations University's World Institute for Development Economics Research in Helsinki, Finland. Born in Iran and trained as a sociologist, she has published widely on Iran, Afghanistan, the Middle East, and gender and development issues. She is currently working on a book titled *Populism, Class, and Gender in the Iranian Revolution*. She is the author of *Modernizing Women: Gender and Social Change in the Middle East* (1993).

Misagh Parsa is a sociologist and teaches at Dartmouth College. He has also taught sociology at the University of Michigan. He is the author of *The Social Origins of the Iranian Revolution* (1989). His current research is a comparative analysis of the Russian, Iranian, and Nicaraguan revolutions as well as the conflicts in the Philippines.

Sussan Siavoshi was born in Tehran, Iran, and received her Ph.D. from Ohio State University. She is currently associate professor at Trinity University in San Antonio, Texas. She is the author of *Liberal Nationalism in Iran: The Failure of a Movement* (1990).

Michael P. Zirinsky took his undergraduate degree in government at Oberlin College, his M.A. in international relations at the American University, and his Ph.D. in modern history at the University of North Carolina at Chapel Hill. He teaches history at Boise State University, Boise, Idaho. His research and teaching interests focus on Western relations with the Middle East, especially Iran. He has published articles on American and British diplomacy in Iran and about Western missionaries in Iran in *International Journal of Middle East Studies, American Presbyterians, Nimeye-Digar, Iranian Studies,* and other journals. He currently is at work researching Western relations with Iran during the early twentieth century, focusing especially on the history of American Presbyterian missionaries in Iran.

Index